MW01633110

DEMOCRACY AND PUBLIC MANAGEMENT REFORM

Democracy and Public Management Reform

Building the Republican State

Luiz Carlos Bresser-Pereira

OXFORD

UNIVERSITY PRESS

PREFACE

This book is about the new democratic state that is emerging and about the reform that leads in that direction: public management reform. My central concerns will be, first, to understand how the modern state has transformed itself from the absolute state of early capitalism into the social-democratic state of today, and possibly into the social-liberal and republican state of the twenty-first century; second, to discuss the importance of the strong, legitimate, and democratic state in the global system; and third, to propose a model of public management reform—a tool for building this republican state.

The book takes an eclectic and 'reasonable' approach to the state and to the institutional reforms that are required which proceeds from the assumption that the Western world-political experience has been one of steady progress. Thus, despite the intense conflicts that have accompanied this progress, the best aspects of republicanism, liberalism, democracy, and socialism are in one way or another present in the modern democracies.[1] They are present in 'reasonable' terms. Unlike Aristotle in antiquity and John Rawls in the twentieth century, to whom ideas and institutions should be primarily reasonable, most political theorists of the past have treated ideologies or political doctrines in pure or radical terms. Such an unreasonable approach makes argumentation inoperative and compromise impossible, even though argumentation and compromise are the two major tools with which democracy achieves quasi-consensus and improves its institutions. The deliberately eclectic and reasonable approach in this book is coupled with a distinctly republican view of politics, since I believe that our political and social system is the outcome of the endeavour of self-interested citizens who are nevertheless able to perceive and promote the public interest. I do not share the dominant view in the social sciences that the social world is regulated by natural laws. I agree that structural constraints have to be taken into consideration, provided that this approach does not lead to moral cynicism or to generalized pessimism. A republican approach is neither cynical nor voluntarist. It assumes that institutional reform is possible, but that this process is the collective and often conflicting outcome of many minds, of all kinds of interests, and of different technical and emotional competencies in formulating and implementing public policies. Reforms will often be second-hand and biased towards the rich, leaving the poor unhappy and protesting. Republicanism has traditionally

---

[1] Habermas (1992) and Rawls (1993) see modern democracy as profiting from the liberal and republican political traditions.

been elitist or aristocratic; modern republicanism is democratic. Often reformers speak as if they are the only holders of reason or justice, yet no one may legitimately claim such a monopoly. The history of mankind was written by the elites, but we increasingly discover that the common citizens have a say, and that it is through democratic participation and deliberation that it will be possible to build a polity that makes sense.

Political science and political theory have been deeply involved in studying the constitutional and institutional changes that allowed the transition from the liberal state to the democratic state. Concepts like civil society, state, and government, political parties and voters' behaviour, parliamentary politics and lawmaking, the roles of the executive and the judicial branches, democratic transition and democratic consolidation—all these themes have been the object of extensive treatment in political science because they involved change, the new; because they originated in the novel and revolutionary character of democracy. Meanwhile, studies of the state apparatus and of public management have been retarded by a bureaucratic approach to public administration. Since the 1980s, however, public management reform has appeared in almost all advanced democracies and in a few new ones. This book discusses this historical change and the new theories that seek to explain it.

More significance is assigned here to the state than is usual in Anglo-American political science, to which the government process used to make more sense than the organizational and institutional structure of the state. The republican and liberal traditions that formed the American nation and shaped the modern United Kingdom clearly distinguish the state from the people, but they do not clearly separate the state from civil society. In fact, they use 'society', 'state' and 'nation-state' practically as synonyms: they refer to 'American society' when they mean the American political system or the American state. This practice, along with the fact that the state played a smaller role in the economic development of United Kingdom and United States than in other countries, probably explains why the concept of state is not much used in Anglo-American political science and why government is often identified with the state organization if not with the state in the broader sense. Yet the concept of state that I use is consistent with the new institutionalism which has recently become so influential in Anglo-American political science. In some ways, the attribution of a major role to institutions in shaping political behaviour and administrative action has been a characteristic tradition in American political thought since Woodrow Wilson.[2]

My emphasis in this book is historical and sociological rather than aprioristic or rational-choice. I believe that the latter approach, and particularly the idea that social mechanisms explain behaviour, is relevant to the study of

---

[2] Guy Peters (1999: 4) observes in American political thought the existence of an important institutionalist tradition of German origin starting with Woodrow Wilson (1889) and arriving at Evans, Rueschmeyer and Sckocpol (1985).

politicians and senior civil servants' action and accountability, but I see politics as an essentially historical and social phenomenon which requires for its understanding the systematic search for new technological and institutional facts that shape social and political change and define new social and institutional arrangements.[3] It is only by undertaking such historical analysis and discovering new historical facts that it is possible to identify the social mechanisms behind individual and collective behaviour.

To be scientific one does not have to be pessimistic. I acknowledge the classic collective action problem involved in public management reform: the beneficiaries of reform are dispersed and unorganized, while the individual beneficiary has little incentive to reform. Yet I also see the progress achieved by many countries in managing the state organization, and I do not accept the pessimistic conclusion that administrative reforms are unachievable. The combination of self-interest and republicanism is behind such progress.

This book is in four parts. Part I discusses the rise of the modern state, the gradual affirmation of democracy, the emergence of republican rights, and the challenges to the state represented by globalization and by the fiscal crisis of the social-democratic state. Since this is not a historical book, each phase is examined in summary form. My interest is in understanding the historical background to the new state or polity that is emerging in the twenty-first century. In Part II, I discuss the crisis of the welfare state in developed countries and of the developmental state in developing ones; and, as a response, the experience of public management reform in OECD countries and in a few developing countries. I conclude this part with an analysis of the range of accountability mechanisms used by democracies to control government officials, among which the NGOs, or public non-state advocacy organizations exerting social accountability, play a strategic role. In Part III, I define public management reform and present the basic reform model I have being working with in recent years since I was Minister of Reform of the State of Brazil (1995–8). This model includes a matrix based on a distinction between the exclusive and non-exclusive activities of state, on the relevant forms of ownership in modern democracies, and on three forms of administration of the state organization: patrimonial, bureaucratic, and public management. I discuss the main new organizational institutions required by the reform, particularly agencies and 'social organizations'. Finally, in Part IV I discuss some theoretical and political aspects of the reform, particularly the relations between public management reform and democracy.

This is not a book on management practices, but on political theory and on public management reform. I was able to write it because, first of all, as Minister of Federal Administration and Reform of the State in the first Fernando Henrique Cardoso administration, I led the Brazilian 1995–8 Public

---

[3] Methodology in the social sciences is examined in my paper 'Economics' Two Methods' (Bresser-Pereira 2003*h*).

Management Reform, and developed a theoretical model on the subject that I thought suitable to share more broadly. My job in the Brazilian government was to draw up and to introduce a 'reform of the state'. Yet, since reforming the state would involve reforming all major institutions, which was obviously beyond the terms of my mandate, the scope of my action was limited to public management reform, developing a special model of state organization, and founding the whole enterprise on a new concept of republican rights. In this job, I benefited from the experience of participating in a national public debate. Second, I benefited from what I learned from other countries' experience, particularly that of the United Kingdom, since I could count on the technical support of a highly qualified British team of consultants. Third, I could also count on the support of an excellent team of senior civil servants and consultants. Fourth, my varied academic background, combined with my studies of the professional or technobureaucratic middle class and of political theory, allowed me to maintain a broad and stimulating dialogue with the Brazilian professionals running state agencies and with academics in Brazil and abroad.

I write very little about Brazil in this book, but I never forget that I live in an intermediate developing country while writing about a reform that is taking place mostly in the advanced democracies. I well know that these countries face major problems, but they are not as serious as those faced by my country. Probably for that reason, and because I am firmly persuaded that economic and political progress is taking place despite all the miseries that modern societies still present, the reader in the developed country will probably be more critical of his own country than I am.

I owe thanks to many. In this preface, I mention just the ones involved in the development of the ideas presented here. In my Brazilian team, I owe thanks particularly to Angela Santana, Caio Marini, Ciro Cristo, Claudia Costin, Evelyn Levy, Leticia Schwarz, Paulo Modesto, Regina Pacheco, Marianne Nassuno, and Nelson Marconi. The latter two were also helpful in discussing the manuscript. Among my English consultants, I am indebted to Kate Jenkins, Caren and Eric Caines, and William Plowden. Among academics, conversations with Adam Przeworski, Ben Ross Schneider, Cícero Araujo, Edson de Oliveira Nunes, Fernando Luiz Abrucio, Gilda P. Gouvêa, Guillermo O'Donnell, Laurence Whitehead, Leslie Bethel, Livia Barbosa, Lazlo Bruszt, Marcus Melo, Maria da Conceição Tavares, Nuria Cunill Grau, Peter Spink, Philippe Faucher, Yoshiaki Nakano, and Yehezkel Dror were relevant in different ways. Finally, I want to thank my assistants: Cecilia Heise, who took charge of revising the book, and Carmen A. Varela. My main debt is, naturally, to my wife, Vera. I must also mention the support I received from the Getulio Vargas Foundation's Research and Publications Centre in São Paulo, and the opportunity that Oxford University offered me in 1999 and 2001 to study the British reform while visiting Nuffield College, St Anthony's College, and the Centre for Brazilian Studies.

CONTENTS

PART III   A DISCUSSION OF THE REFORM

Introduction

In a world of fast technological change and increasingly complex economic and social relations, political institutions also change fast. The two major political institutions acting in modern democracies—civil society and the state—assume new forms, new roles, and new ways of relating among themselves, thereby producing new democratic governance. In this book, I discuss two aspects of this global change: the republican democracy that is emerging in the twenty-first century and public management reform. The objective of this reform is to increase state capacity, to create a 'strong state': able to produce representative and accountable democratic governments; able to protect civil rights and assure markets, and so liberal; able to promote social justice, and so social; able to resist corruption and rent-seeking, and thus republican. The assumption from which I start is that, just as only a strong civil society may guarantee democracy, only a strong state may assure competitive markets.

A new social-liberal and republican state is emerging as a response to the challenges posed by globalization and by the endogenous crisis of the social-democratic state (or, in developing countries, of the developmental state). It is emerging also because voters are demanding more effective protection of the public patrimony, the improvement of public services, and better government officials, be they elected politicians or civil servants. A new state organization is emerging in order to respond to such demands—an organization that is more decentralized, with more autonomous and more accountable agencies. A new public management is coming into being because senior civil servants are able to acknowledge the political character of their job instead of adhering to the semi-fiction that they remain a neutral bureaucratic body just responding to elected politicians. As long as the political scientists and journalists analyse and criticize the forms through which bureaucrats protect their own interests in the policymaking process, while organizations of civil society strive to make them and the elected politicians more accountable, bureaucrats have no alternative but to recognize their political role.[1] In this process, they will eventually be more

---

[1] By the 'bureaucratic politics approach' I mean the approach adopted by Kozak and Keagle (1988). It criticizes the 'bureaucratic dogma' that 'depicted politics (or policy making) and administration as two separate realms' (Kozak 1988: 4). The rational choice approach is widely known: its achievements and shortcomings will be discussed throughout the book.

capable of distinguishing their corporate political interests from the public interest. In this book I use the expression 'government officials' to refer to both elected politicians and senior civil servants, in order to underline the political character of the two groups of actors operating in the strategic core of the state.

I argue in this book that these changes, taken together, will lead developed countries from twentieth-century social democracy to the republican democracy that will characterize the twenty-first century. As for the intermediate developing countries, they will also change in the same direction, although with an inevitable economic and political lag that each country will try to reduce on its own behalf.

Demands for change come from within and outside the nation-state. Change originates from within as economic growth and democracy advance, as citizens in civil society or in the public sphere become more active and demanding; as crises induce transformation and make policymakers learn from mistakes. Change comes from outside as successful experiences in one country may be adapted and copied by others, as globalization forces business enterprises to compete and requires national governments to support this competition. Globalization makes countries interdependent, but the nation-state remains the source of political power required to organize the interests of each given society. On the microeconomic or supply side, these changes are empowered by increasing labour productivity, which originates in technological and scientific progress, in universal access to education and to health care, in the gains coming from free trade, and in improved management. At the macroeconomic level, despite financial crises that continue to plague global capitalism, reform is being reinforced by economic stability and growth.

In the past, tribes, city-states, feuds, and empires defined the political organization. In modern times, nation-states or countries are the basic political unit. The word 'nation-state' (or 'country') is used in this book to identify the politically encompassing entity endowed with sovereign powers. Within each nation-state, we find a society and a state. Within the society, civil society is society organized politically outside the state organization; it is the collection of citizens acting in political life, equipped with the power they derive from organization, knowledge, and wealth. Civil society is formed by all members of society acting politically, and by the corporate and social accountability organizations of civil society. While in the concept of 'people' all citizens are equal, the concept of civil society takes into account the weight that each citizen has deriving from his or her organizational capacity, wealth, or knowledge.

The expression 'state' may have several meanings, despite its long usage. According to Quentin Skinner, 'by the end of the fourteenth century, the term *status* had also come to be regularly used to refer to the state or condition of a realm or commonwealth' (Skinner 1989: 93). Often this expression is equivalent to the nation-state. In this book, 'state' is used with a narrow and a broad meaning, both distinct from the nation-state, which is the encompassing political unity. The state is an abstract entity—Hobbes's 'artificial person'—meaning, in narrow terms, the organization or apparatus formed by politicians and civil servants endowed with monopolistic powers to define and enforce the law over individuals and organizations within a given national territory. In broad terms, the state, besides being this bureaucratic organization uniquely endowed with 'extroverse' power,[2] is the sum of the institutions, starting with the national constitution, defining the legal system, the system of rights and obligations or the rules of the social game. To each form of state in this broad sense corresponds a political system or a political regime.

The concept of state owes more to the German structural and institutional tradition, originating with Marx and Weber, than to the Anglo-American individualist tradition. Within the nation-state, the state is understood as an institutional power system through which conflicts are channelled and resolved, and institutions defined and enforced. Yet, as Theda Skopol remarks, 'the state properly conceived is not [a] mere arena in which socioeconomic struggles are fought out. It is, rather, a set of administrative, policing, and military organizations headed, and more or less coordinated by, an executive authority'. I use 'government' not as a synonym of state (as it is usually done in common parlance), but to refer to (a) the group of people, in the executive, legislative, and judicial branches of the state, who head the state organization, and (b) the governing process, the process of deciding on public policies and institutions. I use the expression 'governance' only rarely, but, when I do use it, I mean the complex governing process in modern democracies, in which not only government officials but also civil society and a legion of different and conflicting political actors interact in the context of an economic and institutional reality.[3]

In a simple political model characterizing liberal democracies, politicians in the higher echelons would constitute the government, while civil servants would just take care of public administration. Such a model has never been representative of twentieth-century liberal as well as social democracies, and it is still less representative in the new republican democracy that is emerging, in which elected politicians and senior civil servants are involved in government and public management—that is, in taking major political decisions—and in implementing efficiently the decisions taken. In advanced democracies the state is not autonomous from society, nor is it over society, but it is an expression of civil society—it is an expression of the relative powers that individuals hold as a consequence of their control of organizations of civil society, of capital or economic resources, and of knowledge. The state is permanently involved in reforming institutions, changing the law at the legislative branch, interpreting it, at the judicial branch, and in policymaking at the executive branch. Senior state bureaucrats or civil servants are a central and

---

[2] 'Extroverse' because its power goes beyond the members of the state organization to include all individuals living within the national territory.

[3] I refrain from using this expression 'governance' because, despite the increasing importance of the other political actors operating in civil society, state decisions continue to be taken essentially by elected and non-elected government officials.

well identifiable piece of the governing process. As Bert Rockman (1992: 165) observed, "The organizational continuities of bureaucracy across diverse environments are impressive. . . Administrative elites sit atop important and continuously powerful instruments of policy".

Thus, I centre my attention on senior civil servants that structure and manage the state organization, but this does not mean that I underestimate the role of the street-level bureaucracy, of that civil servants that have direct contact with citizens at schools, hospitals, police and welfare departments, lower courts, legal services. These people, working usually at local or municipal level, have a major responsibility for the quality of public services. And in many ways, they were practical pioneers of public management reform. If we read, for instance, the book that for the first time called attention to new public management, Osborne's and Gaebler's *Reinventing Government* (1992), we will verify that most examples of the reinvention of government break down old bureaucratic rules and innovation in public service are local examples. On the other hand, Michael Lipsky (1980: 71), in a pioneering work on this kind of bureaucracy, argued that street-level bureaucrats are not just by the rule bureaucrats, but they take decisions, they establish routines, they invent devices to cope with uncertainties and work pressures, in this way defining public policies. Their work involves an inner contradiction, which is probably the source of their institutional inventiveness: 'On the one hand, services are delivered by people to people, invoking a model of human interaction, caring and responsibility. On the other, services are delivered through a bureaucracy, invoking a model of detachment'. To explain why street-level bureaucrats eventually pioneered public management reform we should add to this contradiction two related facts: in the twentieth century they became numerous and the number of their contacts the public—their clients —, was increased exponentially. Facing everyday new problems, they exercised discretion and were innovative.

In this book, instead of speaking of 'public administration' that is an expression associated to bureaucratic reform, and, historically, is mostly concerned with the effectiveness of state power, today, in the realm of modern democracies, I speak of 'public management', which assumes state effectiveness and searches for state efficiency and political accountability. I will be critical of bureaucratic public administration, but I will emphasize the crucial role that a competent professional bureaucracy has in public management reform. Second, instead of acknowledging only civil, political, and social rights, I am concerned with republican rights and obligations. Third, despite globalization, which makes nation-states more interdependent but not necessarily less strong and relevant, it will be within the nation-state, under the state organization and institutions, that citizens' rights and interests will continue to be best protected. The nation-state also asserts political rights in so far as political institutions make governments more representative, more participatory, and more accountable. And the nation-state protects social rights in so far as the state organization is able to collect taxes and guarantee health care, education, and a minimum income for all. Finally, the nation-state holds republican rights, the rights related to the protection of the public patrimony, as long as competent state institutions are combined with the required republican virtues of government officials.

To continue defining the terms used in this book, we have at least four central forms of ownership in contemporary capitalism: private, state, public non-state, and corporate. The state organizations and the public non-state ones are in principle public since they are oriented to the public interest, although, from a legal point of view, the public non-state organizations are private. We have two types of public non-state organizations (or non-governmental organizations, NGOs): public non-state service organizations or just service NGOs, such as non-profit universities or hospitals, and public non-state social accountability organizations or just social accountability NGOs. Instead of 'social accountability' I may refer to 'political advocacy' organizations to designate the same type of organization. I prefer 'public non-state organizations' to 'NGOs' because, although unusual, this designation does not confuse 'state' with 'government', and because it stresses that the organization is public but not part of the state apparatus. I call 'social organizations' those public non-state service organizations that are subsidized by the state. Corporate organizations, such as unions are private since they represent particular interests. Public non-state organizations and corporate organizations form the 'third sector'. I refrain from using this expression, as well as the expression 'non-profit', because it refers to two quite different forms of non-profit organization: public and corporate. Yet I will often use the expression 'civil society organizations' to designate the sum of the corporate organizations and the public non-state social accountability organizations, as long as both are active politically outside the state apparatus. I use 'civil society' in a broader sense, to include also individuals outside the state who exercise political power because of their wealth or their knowledge; but, in modern civil society, political power not held by public officials (elected politicians and senior civil servants) derives essentially from the organizations of civil society that they run.[4] These definitions, particularly the distinction between 'service' and 'social accountability' public non-state organizations, are important in this book, because the former will have a central role in providing social and scientific services, while the latter will be strategic in making government officials more accountable and in making democracy more representative.

---

[4] Until the eighteenth century, 'civil society' was practically a synonym of political society, as opposed to the 'natural state'. After the consolidation of the capitalist state, Hegel starts using the term 'civil society' as distinct from 'state' or 'political society'. It is thus that I use the term, especially in my works on the democratic transition in Brazil. Not only associations and NGOs but also individuals and their interests are part of civil society in so far as they are involved in some political action. 'Civil society' as consisting only of non-profit entities is a normative definition, which changes the meaning of an expression that has been in use for almost two centuries.

In this book, I discuss the reform of the state organization and the introduction of new public management tools. Together, these changes comprise public management reform—a broad change that has been taking place since the mid-1980s in most developed countries, and since mid-1990s in some intermediate developing countries like Brazil. My approach to the study of this reform does not necessarily conform with that of other authors or practitioners. My discussion adopts the perspective of the republican as well as the liberal values that are proving necessary to guide the modern social-democratic state. The objective is not to downsize the state according to the ultra-liberal ideal of the minimal state, but to increase government capacity so that state institutions and markets advance jointly towards the four major political objectives that contemporary democratic societies have set for themselves: political stability, freedom, social justice, and economic development.

Public management reform is part of the institutional reform that has gained momentum since the 1980s. Some of these reforms were market-oriented, as with trade liberalization and privatization; others state-enabling, like fiscal adjustment and public management reforms. As such institutional reforms have always involved some degree of liberalization, they have often been called 'neo-liberal'. Yet, I prefer to use the expression 'neo-liberal' in a more strict sense to characterize the reforms aiming to the minimum state. Liberalizing reforms were necessary not only because state organization grew excessively since the 1930s and led to an endogenous crisis of the state organization (fiscal crisis and a crisis in the bureaucratic way of managing it); globalization challenged the state organization exogenously as it represented real, although often overstated, constraints on the nation-state's autonomy in adopting policies. Thus, institutional reforms were not intended just to enhance the market coordination of economic systems. Since crisis and globalization debilitated the state organization, reforms, particularly fiscal adjustment and public management reform, are enabling the state to organize markets and social life more effectively.

In this book I discuss institutional reforms, particularly public management reforms, at a time when countries are finally overcoming the fiscal crisis that has afflicted them, to different degrees, since the 1970s, but also at a time when globalization continues to challenge national states and societies. I discuss the cyclical character of state intervention and state crisis, and relate them, on one hand, to the economic slow-down that took place in the 1980s and, on the other, to the ultra-liberal ideological wave that began at that time. The two basic arguments in this book are, first, that after the classic citizens' rights have been basically assured, the state organization and, more broadly, the public patrimony, including the public environment, must be protected. To build a republican state is to build a state that is able to protect itself against powerful individuals while asserting individual rights against its own power. Building the republican state requires good institutions, politicians, and senior civil servants endowed with a combination of self-interest and civic virtues, and an active and participatory civil society. Second, my claim is that the necessarily social character of the modern state must be tempered by its liberal vocation. The social-democratic state represented an advance on the liberal-democratic state, but at the cost of excessive state intervention: the emerging social-liberal state will achieve a new equilibrium. Public management reform is not the only required reform, but I believe that it is an essential one to advance democratic governance in the world.

Reforming institutions and the state apparatus in contemporary democracies is a challenge that involves technical competence and republican virtue. Modern democracies are liberal because they are based on individual freedom and market competition, social because they try to assure social rights or offer social protection, and republican because, on the one hand, they are supposed to protect the public patrimony and, on the other, because its citizens have obligations to promote the public interest. In this sense, republic is not the alternative to monarchy, as it was originally, but to a regime captured by private interests. Citizens in democracies are supposed to have some degree of commitment to the common good or public interest. In saying that, I am making not just a normative affirmation but also a positive one. It is impossible to understand modern democracies as made up of individuals who are exclusively looking out for their own interests. Since individuals do that, rational choice theory is able to explain many aspects of political behaviour, but as they also cooperate and assume responsibilities for the public patrimony or, more broadly, for the public interest, we need a broader explanation.

Following the capitalist revolution and the emergence of the modern state, we may distinguish three ideal types of state administration and two major reforms of the state structure organizations. By 'reforms' I mean profound institutional changes, and not just the usual changes in the organization chart that each new government usually undertakes. The ideal types of state organization are, successively, patrimonial administration, bureaucratic administration, and public management; the two reforms, civil service reform and public management reform. As we learned from Max Weber, patrimonial administration is bureaucratic but traditional. It has a long history, having originated in the Chinese imperial system and reaching its greatest extent in modern absolutist states. Patrimonial administration was not 'public' in the sense that it was not oriented to the public interest. It was based on the direct interest of the prince and of the patrimonial aristocratic and bureaucratic elite, and on the indirect interest of the landed aristocracy and the bourgeoisie. In modern times, this type of administration is associated with the absolute monarchies that emerged just before industrial capitalism and democracy. It confuses the private patrimony of the prince with the public patrimony.[5] It survives in imperfect democratic systems in the form of clientelism or the pork barrel.

The first historic reform of the state organization was civil service reform, representing the transition from patrimonial administration to bureaucratic public administration. Max Weber classically describes civil service reform as involving a professional civil service, universal procedures, and legal legitimacy. As it is extensively discussed in the first part of the book, civil service reform took place at different periods: in Europe in the nineteenth century; in the United States at the beginning of the twentieth century; and in Brazil in the 1930s. Most developing countries never experienced civil service reform, although they have modern bureaucracies.[6] Bureaucratic reform signalled a major advance in public administration and in the protection of public patrimony. Public management reform is the transition from bureaucratic administration to public management. The civil service remains professional and rational, but rationality depends on managerial decision-making rather than on the strict observation of bureaucratic procedures. Rather than locating control in legal procedures, public management calls for contracted objectives, managed competition, and several schemes of social accountability.

Public management reform began in the 1980s. It borrowed many ideas and strategies from private business management, and represented a response to new demands originating in the enormous growth and increasing complexity of society and government. As Ash Amin and Jerzy Hausner observe, there is an interactive process within governance: 'the history of modernity has been that of an increasing complexity in the patterns of social and economic organization'.[7] New public management as well as a larger and reformed role for the state are some of the consequences of this growing complexity and of the speed of technological change in the global system. From the beginning of the twentieth century, the state took on new activities in society and economy that were inconsistent with the bureaucratic way it was run. By adopting either partial reforms or policies that disregarded bureaucratic principles, government officials tried to fit public administration into the new realities. In the 1980s, some OECD member countries, mainly the United Kingdom, New Zealand, Australia, and the Scandinavian countries, finally engaged in public management reform. In the 1990s, this reform was extended to the United States, Canada, Chile, Brazil, and Italy. A new theoretical framework emerged, concerned mainly with more efficient public services oriented to the client-citizen, and more accountable civil servants. It was not by accident that public management reform took place in democratic

---

[5] According to Weber's (1922: 236) classic definition, 'in the pure type, patrimonial domination, specially of the state-type, regards all governing powers and the corresponding economic rights as privately appropriated economic advantages . . . In particular, the appropriation of judicial and military powers tends to be treated as a legal basis for a privileged status position of those appropriating them'.   [6] This is, for instance, the case of Mexico.
[7] Amin and Hausner (1997: 1). See also Edgar Morin (1990) and Robert Delorme (1995).

countries. As shown in this book, it is consistent only with democratic regimes.

Ben Ross Schneider distinguishes three rather than two historical administrative reforms: 'Weberian, managerial, and accountability or democratic reform.'[8] I see no reason for distinguishing the second reform from the third. Public management reform is a broad institutional change, which is being undertaken by social democratic or conservative democratic political coalitions, but never by authoritarian regimes. It presupposes the existence of a democratic system, and it should be viewed as a tool for making not only the state apparatus more efficient but also government officials more accountable and so more democratic. Alasdair MacIntyre's communitarian and moral critique of 'managerialism' (1981) mixes up bureaucratic and managerial power. Yet it is an interesting critique in so far as it reminds us that efficiency does not replace political and moral criteria and, thus, cannot be the only standard by which to judge public policies. The assumption that bureaucrats may be inefficient but managers are always efficient is just a 'moral fiction', an ideology. The political objectives that contemporary democracies pursue—social order, freedom, social justice, and well-being—cannot be reduced to efficiency, nor can some agents, bureaucrats or managers, be assumed to have a monopoly of the required knowledge to achieve it.

My interest in this book is in the forms that the state or the political system adopted historically. The reforms observed social and economic constraints, but involved some degree of freedom for the policymakers. My assumption is that the political prevails over the economic realm, that politics has precedence over production and distribution. Notwithstanding the triumph of capitalism, which led either to materialistic and deterministic explanations of history following, often disguisedly, Marx's original formulation,[9] or to rational choice explanations of political behaviour that reflect in a different way the same economic bias, I am persuaded that we will understand the enormously complex world in which we live only if we recognize that the construction of freer, wealthier, and more just societies depends on the collective action of men, and on their capacity to build good and enforceable institutions, rather than on powerful market forces. Alain Touraine, in the tradition of the major sociologists of the past, sees today's modernity on one side reduced to individualism and materialism, on the other denied by postmodernism, but sees a way out in the dialogue of Reason and the Subject. Modernity involves the separation of politics from religion, the advance of science and technology, and an increasing role for markets, but it also requires the affirmation of the individual as a Subject, a social actor able to change the

---

[8] Schneider (2000); Heredia and Schneider (2003).

[9] Journalists writing on globalization are keen to this kind of naïve historical materialism. Take, for example, this quotation from William Greider (1997: 18): 'The global economy . . . mocks the assumption of shared political values that supposedly unite people in the nation-state.'

social relations in which he is embedded. He does not speak of republicanism, which is a central theme of this book, but he reasons in the same vein when he says: 'modernity will not exist without rationalization, but will not either without the configuration of subject-inside-the-world who judges himself and society responsible' (Touraine 1992: 238). The prevalence of politics over production, of the state over markets, of the collective and free will of citizens over the economic system does not escape from economic constraints, but is the condition for a democratic polity. A central concern in this book is with the efficient management of the state organization, but I will not forget the priority of the political realm, and I will bear in mind that ideas and values are eventually the determinant criteria for action, independently of the weight represented by the economic constraints. In other words, I will discard an economic determinism that today is implicit in most economic, administrative, and even political considerations.

I

The Rise of the Modern State

1

Historical Forms of State

Concepts like nation-state, civil society, public sphere, state organization, institutions, government, and public management belong to the political realm of society, while markets, business enterprises, and consumers are in the economic realm. The two spheres are interrelated, but it is important to distinguish them when one tries to define the core characteristics of the new state and of the new public management that is emerging. These characteristics will be essentially political, because they are the outcome of the conflicts, arguments, and compromises in which people are daily engaged. They embody decisions taken by citizens in the realm of civil society and, eventually, by politicians and senior civil servants in the realm of the state itself, in order to create and reform institutions, to organize the state apparatus, and to shape its public administration. Such decisions are building a new state which, besides being democratic, liberal, and social, is republican because it asserts republican rights and involves the political participation of republican citizens.

Politics is the art of achieving legitimacy and running the state through either negotiation and argument or compromise and persuasion rather than sheer force. Whereas in markets producers and consumers try to promote their interests to the greatest possible degree, in politics, besides interests, it is necessary also to consider values. In markets there is a quasi-automatic and relatively efficient competitive mechanism allocating resources and distributing benefits, while in the political sphere nothing is automatic or given. Everything happens through decisions which face constraints—economic and institutional—, but which are not 'necessary' since they involve choice, respond to interests, and refer to moral principles. In a democratic regime, the formation of citizens' wills and representatives' decisions are preceded and clarified by public debate. Citizens cannot be concerned only with their self-interest. Given that societies can exist only when conflict and cooperation are combined dialectically, a reasonable percentage of citizens is also supposed to nurture feelings of solidarity towards others or to possess some republican virtues. On the other hand, the growth of the state apparatus involved the rise of a powerful group of bureaucrats and politicians, whose role, in a democracy, is to protect citizens' rights, and to develop lasting institutions and temporary public policies aiming at social order, freedom, social justice, and welfare.

A Long Historical Process

The new state that is emerging at the beginning of the twenty-first century is the outcome of a long historical process in which state institutions evolved in each nation-state. It is the result of the cross-fertilizing process through which, since the Greeks and Romans established their republics, other countries imported and adapted institutions. It is the outcome of wars and revolutions that advanced or hindered economic and political development, of technological progress and economic transformations, which, coupled with political development, made possible the rise of capitalism and, later on, of democracy—and, thus, sustained self-improving economic and political development.

In pre-capitalist times, government decisions seemed less relevant. Tribes became transformed into empires or city-states, which were, later, replaced by the modern nation-states. Civilizations rose and fell in accordance with a vast cyclical process. Within each society, political regimes changed, often in a sort of cyclical way, from more to less authoritarian forms of government, but always remained authoritarian. With the emergence of capitalism and modern nation-states, political change ceased to be essentially cyclical, history ceased to repeat itself, and assumed a direction—the direction of progress, according to Enlightenment philosophers, or of rationalization, according to Weber, or to economic abundance, according to twentieth-century economists. In any case, capitalism and, in a second moment, democracy have been proving capable of generating their own continuous improvement, that is, of promoting self-sustained economic and political development.

In order to situate historically the discussion developed in this book about the state, about how its governance progressed towards democracy, and about how the strategy for its organization and management advanced, I will limit myself to the 'modern state'. When, out of the old empires and the feudal system, the modern nation-state emerged, it was the fruit of both an increasing division of labour and the rise of capitalism. The emergence of the modern state implied an increasing separation, upwards, of the state from the monarch and, downwards, of the state organization from civil society.

The state subsequently underwent a long historical political transition from authoritarian rule to democracy. In this process, first of all, citizens' rights were asserted in four major steps. In the eighteenth century, the liberal revolution defined civil rights; in the early twentieth century, a democratic revolution affirmed political rights; in the first part of the twentieth century, a social revolution included social rights among citizenship rights; and, in the last quarter of the century, a republican revolution started defining and enforcing republican rights,[1] while political participation by citizens, whether individually

---

[1] In relation to the first three affirmations of rights, this historical sequence follows T. H. Marshall's classical contribution on the subject (1950), and, in relation to republican rights, my own analysis (Bresser-Pereira 2002*a*).

or organized in civil society, gave substance to a new republicanism.[2] In this process, the state began as authoritarian, later became liberal, and finally became democratic. In its turn, civil society, while undergoing an internal process of democratization, increasingly gained political power over governments, politicians, and senior civil servants.

Second, from the economic and technological standpoints, in this long historical period first came the commercial revolution, with the advance of navigation techniques and the great discoveries; second, the industrial revolution, with steam power; third, the second industrial revolution, with the internal combustion engine and electricity; and fourth, the communications revolution, with information technology and the Internet. In this historical process, the state's relationship to the market was transformed with each revolution, giving rise, correspondingly, to the absolute, the liberal, the social-democratic, and the social-liberal state.

Third, corresponding changes were taking place at the societal level. Together, the first industrial revolution and the liberal revolution produced the capitalist revolution, giving rise to a new and large ruling class—the bourgeoisie or the capitalist class. The second industrial and the communications revolutions generated an enormous professional or techno-bureaucratic middle class. While the bourgeoisie was associated with capital and innovation permitting the realization of profits, the professional class was related to the command of technical and organizational knowledge, allowing the realization of high salaries. Again, from this societal perspective, the state received several names: the capitalist state, the bureaucratic state, and the post-capitalist state.[3]

In the political realm—the realm of the state—political elites, civil society, and citizens occupy centre stage; in the economic and technological sphere—the sphere of markets—the corresponding role is performed by individuals and social classes (capitalists, workers, and professionals). The historical process is the outcome of the continuous interaction between the two major institutional mechanisms that coordinate modern nation-states—the state and the market—so that all advanced economies are essentially mixed economies: they are not pure market economies, much less state polities. The state, while a set of institutions, establishes the legal conditions under which markets operate; while an apparatus endowed with special powers reforms institutions, enforces the law, and, through economic transfers, compensates for or moderates the social and economic disequilibria inherent in markets.

Michael Mann distinguishes two forms of state power: 'despotic power'— 'the range of state actions that the state (elite) is empowered to undertake

---

[2] The word 'revolution' is here used to mean simply a major political change. The only one of the revolutions referred to that was so in a strict sense was the liberal revolution, which expressed itself in the American and the French Revolutions.

[3] Karl Marx was obviously the founding analyst of the capitalist revolution. For a more recent analysis, see, among others, Peter Berger's *The Capitalist Revolution* (1986).

without routine, institutionalized negotiation with civil society groups . . . '
and 'infrastructural power'—'the capacity of the state actually to penetrate
civil society, and to implement logistically political decisions throughout the
realm' (Mann 1986: 113). The power of the state would be as effective as these
two powers. This view has the merit of suggesting that power may come from
the top or from the bottom of society, from the 'state elite', or from religious
movements, economic classes, and military elites that form civil society. Yet
to include military elites in civil society involves an undue broadening of the
concept of civil society. The state elite in each historical model of the state is
formed by an endogenous bureaucracy (administrative, military, and religious)
and by members of the social class holding economic power within civil society.
In the pre-capitalist state and in the modern absolute state, this class is the
landed aristocracy, which shares power with the patrimonial bureaucracy. In
the liberal state, to the aristocracy is added the bourgeoisie or capitalist class.
In the liberal-democratic state, the aristocracy loses decisive influence, and
the bourgeoisie is the only significant social class participating in the state
elite from civil society; from within the state, besides the state bureaucracy
we have now elected politicians participating from the state elite. Finally, in
the social-democratic state, private bureaucracy, now transformed into a professional middle class, starts to participate in the state elite, sharing power
with government officials (professional politicians and state bureaucrats or
civil servants). In this process, the state elite not only changes and broadens
its scope; with democracy it becomes also more representative and more
accountable. Despotic power gradually loses strength, and infrastructural
power becomes democratic.

State intervention follows a cyclical pattern, as I will argue below. Responding
to market failures, as in the 1920s and 1930s, it increased its scope. Yet the
growth of the state involved necessarily distortions that, in the 1970s, led to
fiscal crisis and, more broadly, to a crisis of the state. This crisis and the acceleration of globalization cleared the way for privatization and market deregulation,
which, however, soon reached their own limits. Thus, when reforming the state
became a major item on the agenda of all countries in the 1990s, I was not
surprised. This book sums up my views about these reforms, with a special
emphasis on public management reform. Two assumptions—the cyclical crisis
of the state and the need to protect republican rights—indicated the general
orientation: to redefine the role of the state, to rebuild state capacity, to manage
the state apparatus more efficiently and more democratically.

The Stages of the State

In Table 1.1, I summarize the stages through which the modern state has passed
historically, taking for reference the more developed nation-states. It began as

TABLE 1.1. *Historical types of state and of state management*

State according to the political regime	State according to the managing form	Corresponding type of democracy
Absolutist state	Patrimonial administration	—
Liberal state	Bureaucratic public administration	—
Liberal-democratic state	Bureaucratic public administration	Liberal or elitist democracy
Social-democratic (welfare) state	Bureaucratic public administration	Social or plural democracy
Social-liberal and republican state	Public management	Republican or participatory democracy

authoritarian and patrimonial in the sixteenth and seventeenth centuries: it was the absolutist state organizing patrimonial monarchies. In the nineteenth century, it turned liberal and bureaucratic: the liberal state imposed the rule of law and assured civil rights, that is, the rights to life, freedom, and private property, but remained authoritarian, as the poor and women did not vote.[4] In the first part of the twentieth century, the transition to democracy was completed: it was the time of the liberal state, of elitist or liberal democracy, and, still, of bureaucratic administration. In the second part of that century, the state becomes social-democratic, protecting social rights and promoting economic development; the administration remains bureaucratic, but assumes a developmental character; democracy now is social or plural rather than just liberal. At the beginning of the twenty-first century, the state is aiming to become social-liberal and republican; democracy is aiming to become partici-patory or republican; and administration is aiming to become managerial, or inspired by the principles of new public management.

When I talk of the absolutist, liberal, liberal-democratic, social-democratic, social-liberal, and republican states, the adjective refers to the basic nature of state organizations and institutions; when I say patrimonial, bureaucratic, and managerial states, I am referring to the way the state organization is managed. The third column of Table 1 shows the corresponding types or forms of democracy. Given the definition of democracy used in this book, according to which, besides the rule of law and the constitutional system, the guaran-tee of basic liberties and competitive elections defining government requires universal suffrage, we cannot speak of democracy in the liberal state. With the rise of the absolutist state, the separation of the public realm from the private

---

[4] Note that I use the word 'liberal' in the European rather than the American sense, where 'liberal' came to mean 'progressive', almost social-democratic.

became inevitable. The liberal state 'resolved' the question through the constitutional and liberal revolutions (the Glorious Revolution, the American Revolution, and the French Revolution), and, in a second instance, through civil service reform. With the former, the rule of law was established; with the latter, bureaucratic public administration replaced patrimonial administration. Yet the political regime remained authoritarian. The liberal-democratic state, in its turn, overcame authoritarianism, but raised the question of social justice. The social-democratic state attempted a response to the social rights question and the problem of equality of opportunity, but proved inefficient in a world in which economic efficiency becomes increasingly imperative. The social-liberal state remains committed to social justice, while the republican state is a response to the misuse of public funds as well as to the inefficient supply of social and scientific services. The republican state is not the ideal political regime of virtuous citizens, but it is a state that counts on good institutions and a reasonable number of committed citizens, able to guarantee classical citizenship rights, but also to protect the *res publica* from being captured by private interests.

These historical forms of state, as well as the corresponding forms of democracies, involve cumulative additions of human rights. The liberal state adds the rule of law and respect for civil rights; the liberal-democratic state establishes liberal democracy as long as it assures political rights—the rights to vote and to be elected—for all citizens; yet democracy remains elitist, as long as politicians are accountable only at the moment of their election. The social-democratic state adds the protection of social rights, expressed in the welfare state. The corresponding democracy ceases to be purely elitist and becomes social-democratic or plural, as the new political weight of corporate organizations has to be accommodated, and a free media gives rise to public opinion. Finally, the republican state adds the protection of republican rights—rights that every citizen has guaranteeing that the public patrimony be used for public means—while participatory or republican democracy implies that politicians and senior civil servants are becoming additionally accountable through societal accountability organizations. In so far as, first, a plural democracy emerges out of corporate organizations and, second, republican democracy arises from social accountability organizations, civil society is becoming increasingly cohesive and active.

Such historical forms of state, or of political regime, do not involve inevitable and well-defined stages of political development in all democratic countries. And we should not suppose that each form of state resolves the problems posed by its predecessor. They are just a simple way of understanding how governance evolved through time, taking as paradigm cases Western European countries like France and England, and the United States—so different from one another, but with so many common features, starting with the fact they were the first nations to complete the industrial and capitalist revolutions. If the transition to a new stage, or to a new form of state, did not require that the problems posed by the previous historical form were resolved, they were somehow faced and tackled. The following chapters will focus on the political process through which the state or the political system changed when men and women, having become citizens, started searching for social order or political stability, freedom, social justice, well-being, and the protection of the public patrimony. Following T. H. Marshall's basic scheme of the successive historical affirmation of human rights, and Barrington Moore's approach to democracy as the outcome of the struggle and progressive extension of citizens' rights,[5] I will investigate the development of historical forms of state and corresponding forms of democracy from the point of view of the extension of citizens' rights—from the assertion and enforcement of civil rights; second, of political rights; third, of social rights; and, finally, of republican rights. Such rights have been reasonably well-defined and incorporated in the constitutions and laws of civilized countries, so that their affirmation will guide my short historical analysis, although I am well aware that they have not been fully guaranteed even in the more advanced countries.

---

[5] Marshall (1950); Barrington Moore (1966). On this aspect of Barrington Moore's work, see Charles Tilly (1998).

2

Absolute State and Patrimonial Administration

How can we analyse, using nothing more than stylized facts, first, the rise of the modern absolutist state and, second, the transition of the absolutist state into the liberal one? Chapter 1 related the evolution of the historical forms of state to the affirmation of human rights. In this chapter I assume state formation to be an essential part of the capitalist revolution and of the modernization process that begins with the Renaissance and the commercial revolution. The first modern national states emerged in France, England, Portugal, and Spain during the fifteenth and sixteenth centuries, together with mercantilism and the interest in securing large and stable markets. They assumed the form of the absolutist state, which Hobbes was the first to describe as the outcome of a social contract between citizens and the monarch to overcome the state of nature. Historically, the absolute state is the outcome of a political agreement between the emerging bourgeoisie and the monarch. Another way of viewing this historical process—in this case beginning with the Greek republics—is as a process of transition from the city-state to the large modern state, and from a political regime where the *civitas* plays a major role to the one in which civil society gradually emerges and, in some way, replaces the classical *civitas*. In a first moment in the Greek republic, the city-state's small community of citizens—the *civitas*—constitute a government in themselves without the intermediation of a state apparatus. In a second phase, with capitalism, large nation-states emerge, but remain authoritarian, led by political and wealthy elites. In a third stage, after the Glorious Revolution in England and the French Revolution, the political regime turns liberal. Finally, in a fourth step, states become democratic, as a large and vigorous civil society or public sphere starts to play, in some way, the role played in the past by the *civitas*.[1]

---

[1] I regard 'public sphere' and 'civil society' practically as synonyms. Jürgen Habermas, in his classic analysis of the public sphere (1961), does not differentiate between the two. He would do that, in my view wrongly, 30 years later, in *Between Facts and Norms* (1992). In this book, he maintains the broad meaning of the public sphere, but gives civil society a normative and limited definition, along the lines of Cohen and Arato (1992).

In the Greek republic, citizens took direct charge of government. In the modern state, acting as private individuals, citizens take care of their private interests, while hiring professional politicians and bureaucrats to constitute the state organization and take care of government; but this does not mean that they relegate politics to a secondary role. On the contrary, as active citizens become organized and debate in civil society, they become increasingly influential.

The growth in the sheer number of participants in political entities involved a trade-off: to the extent that the number of individuals increased, classical republican values, expressed into full participation in political life, lost ground. Greek or Roman citizens were often also soldiers, deriving their income mostly from the control of the state. In contrast, in modern capitalist societies citizens derive their income from their private activities, and pay taxes that finance the hiring of armed forces and bureaucrats to work for the state organization. In the Italian city-states, where the modern state first surfaced historically, merchants hired bureaucrats to perform political and military roles. The separation of the public from the private was beginning. This evolution meant that the *civitas*—the community of citizens—had lost political significance, because politics was tending to become the monopoly of a class of public officials, initially composed of military and bureaucratic officials, and, later, also of elected politicians.

For centuries, the concept of citizenship had been losing meaning: under feudalism and also in the absolute or patrimonial state, individuals were reduced to subjects. Yet the emergence of a status group of professional government officials (military, civil servants, and politicians) was the distinctive mark indicating that the modern state was born. The Greek city-state could not properly be described as a 'state' in the modern sense of the word, since there was no state organization distinct from civil society. The same can be said of the ancient empires. There was government, but no state. The state is a modern political phenomenon that emerges in the northern Italian republics from the twelfth century, when the rising commercial bourgeoisie hires bureaucratic officials to manage and defend its cities (Araujo 2002). It emerges in the form of republics in merchant cities, but soon, in England, France, Portugal, and Spain, we will see the formation of much larger nation-states within the framework of monarchic regimes. While the republican city-states were mostly involved in long-distance, 'foreign' trade, the new nation-states allowed commercial activities to develop freely within a given national territory. While the city-state could indulge in being republican, the nation-states had no alternative but to be monarchic, if not despotic.

In hypothetical terms, the absolute state was the outcome of a Hobbesian social contract; in actual terms, the consequence of an historical agreement between the monarch and the new emerging merchant bourgeoisie at the expense of the power of the feudal lords. Its main objective was to avoid the customs charged by feudal lords, and the threat the feudal system posed to trade. Through this informal political pact the king was able to obtain the fiscal resources to strength his military power and impose his rule on the feudal aristocracy that levied local taxes. On their side, for the first time since the Roman Empire, the merchants had then a clearly defined territory in which to trade under institutions that secured property rights and contracts.

Political and economic considerations are important in understanding the rise of the modern state, but administrative considerations are no less relevant. The modern state begins in political terms absolute; in economic terms mercantilist; and in administrative terms patrimonial. The monarchy, which confounded itself with the state, was a major economic and political patrimony, receiving revenues from taxes and from participation in monopolist corporations. It used these fiscal resources to maintain a dependent patrimonial aristocracy, living at the court, to take care of war, and a patrimonial bureaucracy to collect taxes and administer justice. The patrimonial bureaucracy, like the previous ancient or classical bureaucracies, was already a professional group hired on the basis of its expertise. It was, however, permeated by all kinds of nepotism, lacking the relative independence from political power which would be acquired only in the nineteenth century, as a result of the European bureaucratic or civil service reforms. In the patrimonial state there was no clear distinction between the public patrimony and the private. But three of the five basic characteristics of the modern state were already present: a constitution or legal system, a civil service, and a government presiding over the population of a given territory. An independent parliament and political parties would appear only in the liberal state. In the absolute state, government officers were essentially bureaucratic. Only with the liberal state would the figure of the modern professional politician legitimized by elections appear.

The historical formation of modern nation-states, beginning with the absolute state and the definition of the national territories open to domestic trade, corresponds to the capitalist revolution—first mercantile, then industrial—and to the balance of powers system that characterized international relations following the Westphalia treaties of the seventeenth century. Among the absolute monarchs, Louis XIV was probably the most representative. Absolutism triumphed under him. The modern state was there, but remained marked by all kinds of medieval institutions. As Theda Skopol (1979: 52) observes, 'although the authority of the absolutist administration was supreme, its distinctive structures—royal councils and intendancies—did not actually supplant the decentralized medieval institutions as seigneurial domains and courts, municipal corporations, and the provincials states (representative assemblies) . . . '. In other words, the new absolutist and centralized institutions were superimposed on the established arrangements rather than replacing them.

Yet this historical continuity should not lead us to minimize the contribution that Louis XIV's rule made to the formation of the modern state. The patrimonial bureaucracy, whose income originated in the taxes collected by the central state, accumulated power and privileges. Reproducing what had already occurred in Portugal, part of the French aristocracy, which lived on rents and other income originating in land ownership, took positions in the royal administration, thus becoming dependent also on state revenues.[2] In other words, the French state changed into a patrimonial state. Now, prestige depended on position more than on blood. 'Under Louis XVI the court ceremonial changes, and the highest state function gains preference over the highest lineage', according to Henry Jacoby (1969: 31).

The absolute state would still have a long history after Louis XIV's long reign in France. It experienced a crucial moment in the Prussian absolute monarchy and the constitution of another powerful national bureaucracy. Yet, after the Glorious Revolution in England—almost a bourgeois revolution—the decline of the absolute state began. One of the partners of the absolute state, the bourgeoisie, soon learned that such an association would and should be transitory. For the new emerging class, the constitutional state, the rule of law, and the legal system that protected property rights and contracts were essential. Having once been party to a political agreement, although a loose one, the bourgeois class rightfully felt entitled to participate in the institutionalization of the new legal system. The times of politics were beginning for the new middle classes. Yet the absolute power of the monarch contradicted this demand—a contradiction that would be partially overcome only with the establishment of a constitutional political system.[3] The times of the liberal state, which would be dominant in the nineteenth century, were arriving. The Glorious Revolution—which may be viewed as the first modern revolution—opened the way for the transformation of the English state into a truly modern state. As John Brewer observes, after 1688 the 'British state underwent radical transformation, acquiring all the main features of a powerful fiscal-military state: high taxes, a growing and well organized civil administration, a standing army and the determination to act as a major European power' (1988: 137).

The absolute state and the patrimonial bureaucracy reach their peak in the eighteenth century. Brewer offers an excellent picture of this moment in Britain. Following but improving the French model, making it more flexible, the British administration expands and modernizes while retaining its patrimonial character. The parliament, which had hindered the growth of central government in the previous century, now shows more interest in developing a strong state able to compete with Britain's major rival, France. The numbers

---

[2] The classical analysis of patrimonial rule in Portugal and Brazil was done by Faoro (1975).

[3] This contradiction would only be solved with the democratic state, a century later.

in the bureaucracy increase steadily during this period. It is essentially a fiscal and judicial bureaucracy concerned with law implementation, customs, excise taxes, salt taxes, and wine taxes. The Treasury or the Exchequer, and the Post Office, are the other main state agencies offering positions for the growing bureaucracy. Now we have full-time employees rewarded with salaries rather than fees. Each has a prospective career with progressively higher remuneration culminating in a government pension. Yet we are not in the presence of the modern bureaucracy. England's state apparatus in the eighteenth century is a mixture of medieval and modern institutions. As Brewer observes:

Offices were held under a variety of tenures—for life, at pleasure, through treasury warrant or royal patent . . . Active officers, unlike absentee officials, were in a position to cultivate directly their financial interests at the expense of the state. They granted preferential treatment to taxpayers, litigants or government suppliers in return for extra fees, treats and bribes. (Brewer 1988: 70–2)

Yet it would be a mistake to see this patrimonial administration as merely corrupt and inefficient. Committed to the civil service reform which modernized the British state, nineteenth century critics exaggerated the faults of the previous system. The state apparatus advanced hugely in the eighteenth century. Brewer suggests that it was the outcome of a 'compromise by which private and political interests were accommodated within government administration . . . a compromise between political clientage and administrative efficiency' (Brewer 1988: 74–5).

3

The Liberal State and Civil Service Reform

In T. H. Marshall's classic analysis of citizenship rights, the Enlightenment philosophers and the English courts defined the civil rights that would serve as the foundation of the liberal state in the nineteenth century. Through civil rights, citizens won the right to freedom and property vis-à-vis a state that used to be oppressive and despotic (Marshall 1950). 'Nation-state' and 'citizen' (endowed with political rights) are political concepts that arose concurrently. It was not by accident that Hobbes, besides *Leviathan*, wrote a book centred on the citizen, *De Cive*. Hobbes was simultaneously theorizing about the absolutist state, whose main objective was to assure political security or stability within the borders of the new nation-state, and about the new citizen who, by 'signing' a social contract, made a trade-off between individual freedom and social security. Yet at the moment that Hobbes conceived the social contract as a new way of legitimizing the absolute power of the king, he was undermining radically this same power. By asserting that the king's authority was founded, not on religion, but on contract, he was establishing the basis for the idea of citizenship rights. He was planting the seed or establishing the foundations of the liberal state—foundations from which Locke, Montesquieu, Rousseau, and Tocqueville built the constitutional and liberal edifice. If the individual, by his own will, renounces freedom in the name of social order, this means that the original power is with him, not with God: the individual who is part of a nation-state is by definition a citizen. The citizen is a member of the nation-state endowed with rights and obligations, and so able to interfere in the making of the law. Law, in its turn, is the basic form that institutions assume; it is the normative system of citizens' rights and duties. Citizenship spreads and asserts itself at the same time as individuals acquire rights and participate in a republican way in the creation of law. Therefore, rights and civic obligations are at the core of the ideas of reason, law, state, and citizenship that emerge in the eighteenth century, with the great Enlightenment philosophers.

Citizenship rights are rights that have been won: they are always the outcome of a historical process in which individuals, groups, and nations strive to acquire and assert them. No one has ever been more emphatic and inspired in affirming such a view than Rudolf Von Ihering: 'all and any rights, whether they are people or individual rights, they only assert themselves by a continuous inclination for fight' (Von Ihering 1872: 15). Norberto Bobbio (1992: xvi) follows the same line. Adopting a firm position against the idea of natural rights, he argues that rights emerge when they can and must do so. They are historical rights that emanate from continuous political battles engaged in over time. They emerge in determined circumstances, related to the defence of new liberties. In the eighteenth century, political and legal philosophers needed a metaphysical concept like natural rights, since the legal definition of such rights was yet to be undertaken in national constitutions and in universal declarations of rights. Today, this job has been done, but we still may speak, like Ronald Dworkin (1977), of 'moral rights'—rights that are morally shared by the community—particularly in the case of countries like Britain, which still does not have a written constitution, or the United States, whose constitution is concise and was drafted more than 200 years ago. Moral rights, however, are not arbitrary rights, nor are they just deduced from reason. When society shares a citizenship right, this means that such a right is the product of historical political battles. Major philosophers like Kant or Rawls contributed to the formulation of a rational concept of justice. Philosophers, social scientists, moralists, politicians, and citizens generally are supposed to have rational ideas about rights and social justice, but none is entitled to a monopoly of rationality and truthfulness. As citizens' rights, the concepts of social justice and freedom are the outcome of historical social conflict and of increasing but always precarious consensus, rather than of an ahistoric public reason.

The struggle for citizenship rights is, in its first manifestation, a struggle of the bourgeoisie or the middle classes. It is a liberal defence of the rule of law and of civil liberties. The two major revolutions of the eighteenth century, the American and the French, which are often called the great democratic revolutions, are in fact liberal ones. They both preceded the industrial revolution and particularly the second one represented the transfer of political power from the old aristocracy to the emerging bourgeoisie. With these two revolutions, as well as with the previous Glorious Revolution, which ultimately was of the same character, the liberal state replaced the absolutist state. Parliaments and constitutions gained in importance, and, besides the rule of law, liberal or negative freedom—'la liberté des modernes', according to Benjamin Constant (1814)—was definitively established. While to the Greeks and Romans (the ancients) freedom was positive,—the freedom of the *civitas* participating in the political process—liberal freedom (modern freedom) was equated with civil liberties—the rights to freedom of movement and of thought, property rights, the right not to be prosecuted by retrospective law, and the right to individual respect. There was as yet no universal right to vote or to be elected: that would be the central political battle of the second part of the nineteenth century, when most liberals had finally become democrats.

The nineteenth century was the century of industrial capitalism, economic liberalism, and the liberal state. As Karl Polanyi acutely observes, the century's social history was the result of a double movement: the extension of market organization to 'real' commodities, and the restrictions imposed on 'fictitious' ones—labour, land, and money. In the liberal state was already embedded the seed of the social state: the protection of labour and of the environment, and, also, the control of money:

> While on one hand markets spread all over the face of the globe and the amount of goods grew to unbelievable proportions, on the other hand a network of measures and policies was integrated into powerful institutions designed to check the action of the market relative to labour, land, and money. (Polanyi 1944: 76)

The new institutions signalled the rise of the liberal state, *pari passu* with modern markets.[1] The rule of law was established, civil rights came to be protected, but democracy was distant, and social justice still further away. The seeds of democratization, however, were there, as capitalism affirmed itself as the dominant mode of production and as political power ceased to have divine origins. The *civitas* did not exist any more, but, as a kind of trade-off, a sizeable civil society or public sphere gradually emerged to replace it.

In the more advanced European countries the nineteenth century was not only the century of industrial capitalism and classical liberalism; it was also the century of bureaucratic reform, through which the state apparatus eventually gained a fully modern or capitalist character. Although administrative, the bureaucratic or civil service reform was essentially a political phenomenon directly related to the rise of the rule of law and of classical liberalism. Through it, patronage ceased being a central political strategy. Patronage had been adopted, first, by the monarch and his ministers and, second, by politicians in parliament, to obtain political support among their clienteles or constituencies. The latter became larger and larger as an increasing percentage of individuals obtained voting rights and became full citizens, while the number of bureaucratic positions did not increase proportionally. Thus, while the arguments for patronage, essentially related to loyalty, lost persuasiveness, the case for entrance examinations and for an autonomous and merit-based civil service that would be more effective and efficient for that reason gained strength. Bureaucratic reform became a central aspect of the state's modernization, and was politically inevitable.

---

[1] When I speak of the liberal state, I have in mind what I have previously defined as classical liberalism or the liberal tradition.

Civil Service Reform in Prussia

Max Weber, being a liberal, was concerned with the authoritarian aspects of bureaucracy. In his extraordinary analysis of the rise of bureaucracy and of the corresponding legal or bureaucratic type of authority, he was the first analyst to fully understand the intimate relationship between the rise of capitalism, the modern state, and modern bureaucracy. In his words,

On one hand, capitalism in the modern stages of development requires the bureaucracy, though both have risen from different historical sources. Conversely, capitalism is the most rational basis for bureaucratic administration and enables it to develop in the most rational form, specially because, from a fiscal point of view, it supplies the necessary money resources. (Weber 1922: 224)

Weber was eventually an enthusiast of the 'purely bureaucratic type of administrative organization', which, according to him, 'is, from the purely technical point of view, capable of attaining the highest degree of efficiency' (Weber 1922: 222). For him, the history of mankind was the history of modernization, and the bureaucratic model was, in some way, the quintessence of this development. Weber had no alternative but to acknowledge the superior rationality of bureaucratic domination. He lived in a Germany that had experienced enormous progress under Bismarck, who had been able to unify the country around Prussia and to complete bureaucratic reform. According to Hans Rosenberg, 'Bismarck was also, as almost all Prussian ministers and imperial chancellors, a sect bureaucrat promoted to high political office. From its inception until 1918, except for a few months in 1848, the Prussian state was governed by "impartial" career bureaucrats, "non-political" army officers, and landed Junkers' (Rosenberg 1958: 25). Weber was concerned about the authoritarian aspects of bureaucratic rule but, as long as he compared 'modern' bureaucracy with traditional forms of administration, he had no alternative but to see bureaucracy as the epitome of rationality.

From reading Weber on modern bureaucracy one may believe that the ideal type that he describes existed in reality. In fact, the Prussian bureaucracy was never as professional, as impersonal, and above all as efficient as he suggests. On the other hand, when I speak of a 'bureaucratic reform', one can infer that I am speaking of a neatly defined period in which patrimonial administration changed into modern bureaucracy. In the case of Germany, no such period existed. The bureaucratic reform began in the late eighteenth century, and was concluded only in the late nineteenth century. Reading Hans Rosenberg's *Bureaucracy, Aristocracy and Autocracy*, we learn that the whole process involved a political struggle between two aristocracies—a rising bureaucratic aristocracy and a declining noble and landed aristocracy. The struggle took place in the realm of an absolute monarchy where, contrary to what happened in England and France, the liberal state never became dominant. In the second half of the eighteenth century, the two Frederick William monarchs, I and II, promoted bureaucracy in the framework of a patrimonial state. At that time, neither special education nor special examinations were required for becoming established in the bureaucracy. The custom of purchasing positions was still in place. Thus, observes Rosenberg, 'until the military reforms of 1806, bureaucratic administration continued to be on a limited scale an object of private ownership and a source of personal gain within the "nationalized" domain of the Prussian state under the central direction of the king' (Rosenberg 1958: 79).

Change was inevitable. It began as early as 1770 with the introduction of compulsory entrance examinations. Yet, even after that, 'the higher administrative service formed more than ever a self-recruiting and increasingly 'streamlined' hierarchy which identified itself with aristocratic valuations and interests' (Rosenberg 1958: 181). The *Bildung* idea or ideology, calling for the complete education of the individual, technical as well as ethical, was part of this process. It was a social movement and an ideology that legitimized high bureaucracy, which, by the end of the eighteenth century, felt strong enough to ask to be called not 'royal servants' but rather 'servants of the state' or 'professional officials of the state', who 'claimed the dignity of an exclusive political intelligentsia'. Bureaucratic reform actually accelerated under Napoleon's occupation between 1807 and 1813. Not only were new ideas coming from France but, more important, Prussia felt challenged, and had to react to the challenge. These were times of intense reform—of the 'Reform Prussia' movement, in which a new alliance was forged between merit and politics, between the landed aristocracy and the rising bureaucratic aristocracy, at the expense of the patrimonial nobility.[2]

Thus, bureaucratic reform in Germany took a long time, and besides its specifically administrative aspect was the outcome of a major political conflict among the Prussian elites. On one side, there was the nobility—the patrimonial and the landed nobility; on the other, the rising bureaucracy, whose upper stratum was also comprised of an aristocracy. In this process, the other rising class—the bourgeoisie—played a minor direct political role: it remained restricted to the economic sphere. The two aristocracies ruling the state knew that their role was to assure the institutional conditions required for investment and innovation to take place, but, differently from what happened in Britain, in the US, and even in France, they did not share power with the business class. According to Rosenberg,

During the era of absolutism the bureaucracy acquired an *esprit de corps* and developed into a force formidable enough to recast the system of government in its own image. It restrained the autocratic authority of the monarch. It ceased to be responsible to the dynastic interest. It captured control of the central administration and of public policy. (Rosenberg 1958: vii–viii)

---

[2] Rosenberg (1958): 200, 213, 216.

Charles Tilly, writing about state formation in Europe, quotes this passage and adds: 'In similar ways, bureaucracies developed their own interests and power bases throughout Europe' (Tilly 1992: 117). Let us briefly check this affirmation in Britain, France, and United States.

Civil Service Reform in Britain

The Britain civil service reform starts with the 1853–4 Northcote-Trevelyan Reports, but it effectively moved ahead only with the Orders in Council of 1870. By the end of the century, the reform was completed, and from then until the 1980s—when public management reform begins—the major characteristics of the British civil service would remain intact. The 1853–4 reports are significant because their aim was to create a centralized administrative bureaucracy accountable primarily to the most senior leaders, and because they proposed the creation of a merit-based civil service. Yet their outcomes in terms of actual reform were limited. As Bernard Silberman (1993: 350) observes, 'close analysis suggests that the report's significance was overstated'. The central problem faced by the British public administration was patronage—more specifically, decentralized patronage, because since the beginning of the century the politicians had developed a patronage system according to which the decisions on who benefited, although controlled by a central office, were in fact taken by each individual Member of Parliament as long as the 'patronage rights' were local. Such patronage was viewed as a necessary feature of democratic politics—in fact, of the patrimonial state. Disraeli, for instance, declared in 1858: 'The spirit of the party in the country depends greatly on the distribution of patronage . . . . There is nothing more ruinous to political connection than the fear of justly rewarding your friends, and the promotion of ordinary men of opposite opinions in preference to qualified adherents' (quoted by Silberman 1993: 348). The Northcote-Trevelyan reports waged a war against such views, but it was defeated. The two authors were unable to demonstrate that a general examination system, or a merit-based professional bureaucracy, was superior—more efficient and more oriented to the public interest—than a patrimonial bureaucracy. Members of Parliament viewed it as necessary for the affirmation of their own political power, and rejected public examinations on these terms, mixing up the private and the public interest. On the contrary, they argued, 'the ability to pass an examination was no assurance that an individual adhere to the proper codes of behaviour which guaranteed the public spiritedness of action'. And this kind of argument prevailed for a while. During the 15 years after the reports, only 0.3 per cent of positions filled by new civil servants were awarded on the basis of open competition. Nevertheless, in 1859, by creating the 'established offices', the Superannuation Act defined the offices and granted to the office-holders the right to a pension, which would be a reward for satisfactory performance. With this, the idea of merit and career gained ground: 'the legislation, in effect, established the notion of career rather than just office-holding or employment' (Silberman 1993: 350, 369, 370).

In 1870, under a Liberal cabinet, the reports' seeds sprouted. George Trevelyan, commenting on the consequences of the Order in Council of this year, remarks:

Gladstone abolished patronage in all public offices and made competitive examination the normal entrance to the civil service. To select men for practical careers on the report of examiners had seemed an absurd proposal to Palmerston and the aristocratic politicians of the previous era . . . Trained intellect was henceforth to be a young's man best passport, instead of social patronage or fashionable friends. (Trevelyan 1942: 568)

Indeed, in 1870 competitive examination was finally made the normal method of entry into civil service. The universities, particularly Oxford and Cambridge, had their roles greatly enhanced. Before that the universities were prestigious but small organizations, which rejected the idea of providing professional or technical education. They were supposed just to teach and research the sciences and the humanities. After the institution of entrance examinations for the civil service, however, this view began to change fast. Special schools could provide technical and professional education, but were unable to transmit to future civil servants the ethos of civil service—and such an ethos, the idea that the civil servant is an agent of the public interest, was then generally accepted in Britain. In fact, together with the bureaucratic reform, an educational reform took place in Britain. The two were mutually supportive. The year 1870 was also a turning point in the country's educational history. Basic education was made universal by the creation of elementary schools supported by national grants. On the other hand, the universities, which remained the exclusive realm of the upper classes, were supposed to provide to the ablest an education that would transform them into an elite which shared common values and ethical principles—a political, bureaucratic, academic, and business elite. The bureaucratic elite— office-holders, politicians, or civil servants—derived their status directly from the professional competence that they were supposed to learn in the universities—a humanistic and ethical competence rather than a technical one, since such a competence was oriented to the protection of the public interest.

The Order in Council of 1870 broadly defined the reformed British civil service. After it, several initiatives completed the reform, which, by the end of the century, could be considered completed. Patronage became negligible in the appointment of civil servants, to either the lower or the upper civil service. While the state remained liberal, the state organization was growing and gradually assuming new roles. Bureaucratic reform responded to new demands. It made this apparatus more centralized and coherent—not necessarily more efficient, but certainly more effective.

Civil Service Reform in France

In France bureaucratic reform was completed at about the same time, although it began earlier, with the French Revolution. In their search for political equality, the first concern of the revolutionaries was to eliminate feudal rights to given positions, and the possibility of selling bureaucratic offices—two paramount characteristics of patrimonial administration. By 1790 both reforms had already been made effective; the 1791 Constitution confirmed them. This, however, does not mean that patronage had ended. On the contrary, it had increased. The old regime had its rules. Patronage was part of the game, but followed custom. After the revolution, the lack of clear rules and, as Silberman observes, 'the very uncertainty facing the political leaders of the various assemblies led them to make appointments largely on the basis of loyalties—both personal and revolutionary'. Soon there was an enormous increase in the number of bureaucratic rules, but these rules did not change 'the continuing reliance on patronage as the primary means of recruitment and appointment and on loyalty as the basic criterion' (Silberman 1993: 96). With the increase in the number of bureaucratic rules, however, a new branch of law was emerging—administrative law—whose role would be central in France in the long process of bureaucratic reform.

With Napoleon the political regime became more authoritarian, and the power of the bureaucracy was strengthened. The Constitution of the Year VIII (1799) was dictatorial and bureaucratic. The French state was bankrupt. According to André Maurois, 'the Directory did not have one franc in the treasury. In this moment Napoleon revealed his extraordinary capacity for administrative organization as well as his scorn for the more basic liberties'. The administration was fully centralized. Prefects, vice-prefects, mayors, all local authorities were now chosen by Paris. Yet this did not provoke protests 'as long as the nation wanted order, and the choice of the civil servants was competent' (Maurois 1947: 360–410). In order to assure the continuity of such administrative competence, and to define clearly, within a broad civil service, the upper-level civil service, the major careers or *grand* corps, Napoleon required that recruitment to this level be made through the law school in the university or, otherwise, through the *grandes écoles*, that is, the prestigious institutions responsible for the technical and liberal professions, which already existed but were now enhanced and granted more public recognition. The human basis for the great French state was in this way established. The state was then able to recruit, through the law schools and the *grandes écoles*, a substantial percentage of the more talented young people that the French educational system produced. In 1945, with the creation of the École National d'Administration (ENA) this system was further formalized and centralized, but its basic rationale remained the same. More than just a school of public administration, ENA is an institution for recruiting and selecting, through a complex examination system, some of the brightest young Frenchmen and French women to occupy the key positions in the French bureaucracy.[3] On the other hand, 'the Constitution of the Year VIII created the basis for the structural autonomy of the state organization'. It gave the administration the power to nominate and revoke civil servants, and to issue regulations. 'These prerogatives remained at the heart of the executive action and power over the next century' (Silberman, 1993: 106).

In the decades that followed the Napoleonic years, the French administrative system did not much change. With defeat in the Franco-Prussian war of 1871 and the rise of the Third Republic, liberals were finally in power, and reform regained pace. Twenty years later one could say that the French civil service reform had been completed, and France could now count on a competent, well-structured, and autonomous body of upper-level civil servants. The 1872 law on the organization and duties of the Conseil d'État was a landmark in the reform. A mixed judicial and administrative body, the Conseil d'État, created in 1799, was charged with protecting the public patrimony against rent-seeking but, at the same time, with protecting the citizen against state abuses. All administrative regulations became subject to final judicial review by the Conseil, which, in this way, acted as a supreme court in relation to administrative law.[4] This enhanced the rule of law, limiting severely the power of the minister in the cabinet. On the other hand, the Conseil d'État became the major administrative agent in regulating the entrance competition system—the public *concours*—and the civil servant's career and discipline system. Progress would continue, particularly with the reforms just after the Second World War, but it is reasonable to say that the French bureaucratic reform was complete by the end of the nineteenth century, by which time the civil service organization and mode of operation had become institutionalized.

Civil Service Reform in the United States

Of the four civil service reforms examined here, the American was the last to occur. It began with the 1883 Pendleton Act, and may be considered completed in 1923, when the Personal Classification Act defined the basic characteristics of American civil bureaucracy—characteristics that would remain stable for at least the next 50 years. Only in the 1990s, with public management

---

[3] As Pierre Bourdieu (1989: 101) observes, 'similarly to the English public schools, institutions like Science-Po and ENA recruit students according to procedures to assure them the more endowed ones . . . they limit themselves to 'teach the fish to swim'.

[4] As George Latour (2002: 46) observes, 'in France we have since Napoleon two fully distinct juridical systems: the judicial and the administrative. The first decides on the conflicts between private people—private law—as well as on the crimes penal law; the second decides on all conflicts with the administration. While the judicial system is dominated, in the final instance, by the Court de Cassation, administrative law is controlled by the Conseil d'État (in its contentious role)'.

reform—specifically President Bill Clinton's 'reinventing government reform'—would they start to change significantly.

As Tocqueville understood so well, the regime that emerges from the War of Independence in the United States is the first in the world to which the word 'democracy' can be applied. Yet, probably because this advance occurred so early, this political regime embodied a special kind of democracy—actually a mixture of classical or bourgeois liberalism with aristocratic democracy. As David Schultz and Robert Maranto (1998: 33) observe, 'the government by gentlemen that existed under the six first presidents produced a federal service more representative of their landed gentry background than of the general population'. The first American presidents ruled their country very much as constitutional monarchs did. In relation to the civil service, the recruitment system was clearly aristocratic and patrimonial—civil servants would be chosen according to birth and educational criteria. Dismissal was exclusively the president's prerogative.

With the election, in 1828, of Andrew Jackson, we have a first and major change. Paradoxically, he decided to deepen the patronage system in order to make it more democratic. Probably this was the price to be paid for the transition. Jackson was a Democrat, and the first president who did not represent the American aristocracy, but rather a larger constituency of businessmen and middle-class people. His election meant a major change in the American political system. The dual party system in force today originates from Jackson's reforms and political struggles. He attacked the old system in which the patrimonial bureaucracy occupied public offices as if they were private property, and inaugurated the 'spoils system', promoting patronage and limiting office tenure, in order to strengthen political parties and to make bureaucracy more responsive to the president's and the politicians' public policies. In his own words:

Offices were not established to give support to particular men at the public expense. No individual wrong is, therefore, done by removal, since neither appointment to nor continuance in office is a matter of right. The incumbent became an officer with a view to public benefits, and when these require his removal they are not to be sacrificed to private interests. (Quoted in Schultz and Maranto 1998: 38)

Office tenure did not exist in law, but did so in practice. Only the president could dismiss a civil servant—which he did, but sparingly. Jackson, with the spoils system, changed that. He wanted an appointment system based on a political rather than a social class criterion. 'Jackson sought, and accomplished, to a considerable degree, the rationalization and legitimation of patronage in the form of term appointments as the means for ensuring the "publicness" of the administrative system' (Silberman 1993: 241).

With the passage of the Pendleton Act in 1883, the American civil service reform finally began. The act re-established the Civil Service Commission and established tenure and entrance examinations. It signalled the demise of the spoils system and the formal introduction of the merit system. American society, particularly businessmen, was dissatisfied with the generalized corruption and inefficiency that the spoils system had produced, and pressed for reform. Intellectual groups, mostly liberal ones, also pressed for reform. The Democrats, out of government for years, saw in the reform a way of weakening the Republican Party's control of federal offices.[5]

Yet the Pendleton Act's effects were limited because its provisions did not apply to States and municipalities. In the following years, a major effort was made to approve similar Acts at these two levels, where corruption and nepotism were widespread. Yet these efforts soon lost momentum as reform candidates, including Pendleton, lost elections. A political and intellectual debate started among reformers and anti-reformers on how to reconcile the relatively autonomous operation of a merit-based bureaucracy with the political values of representative democracy. With the Populist movement, Jackson's argument was back. A competent and independent bureaucracy was required, but it could be seen as threat to democratic representation. The solution that was found was to define the civil servant as an apolitical official, neutral in relation to political interests. With time it became the obvious solution, but it was, nevertheless, a precarious one, since modern democracies did not solve their representation problem.

According to Schultz and Maranto, a second problem, in this case related to the Progressive rather than the Populist movement, preoccupied reformers: 'While early reformers stressed rooting out moral corruption as the impetus for reform, the Progressives became increasingly more concerned with efficiency and economy as a goal of bureaucratic reform' (Schultz and Maranto 1998: 74). In the 1880s Woodrow Wilson, who would later become President, published two essays on public administration, favouring an independent body of competent officers applying the laws that politicians would discuss and approve. These essays, particularly the second, 'A Study of Administration', from 1887, would become classic references in the public administration literature. Wilson tried to demonstrate in this essay a central point in the civil service reform that at that moment was taking place in the United States, Britain, France, and Germany: that public administration was a science, following principles and methods which were essentially different from those inspiring politics, and so reform was justified not only on moral grounds but also on scientific ones (Wilson 1887). It was scientific because it was rational, or efficient.

Schultz and Maranto claim that Wilson's essays did not have much influence at the time they were published, and that other works, such as Frank J. Goodnow's *Politics and Administration*, proposing essentially the same argument,

---

[5] The Pendleton Act was introduced by the Democratic Senator George Pendleton during the Garfield administration. James Garfield, a Republican, was often viewed as a weak president.

were more influential. Goodnow was particularly adamant in rejecting party control over the administration as a way of harmonizing the expression and execution of the popular will. On the contrary, he argued:

That popular government shall not be lost in our case, depends very largely on our ability to prevent politics from exercising too great influence over administration, and the parties in control of administration from using it to influence improperly the expression of the public will. (Quoted in Schultz and Maranto 1998: 77)

In fact, with contributions like those by Wilson and by Goodnow, the bureaucratic ideology, essential to the success of the civil service reform, was being competently built. As well, a new development was taking place at the political level that would promote bureaucratic reform. Starting in 1893, a series of Republican victories at national and particularly at State level brought to power 'progressive' liberal politicians, who, recognizing the alternation of power that characterized democracy, soon discovered a new and central argument for removing agencies at all levels from politics or patronage: if they did not profit from the opportunity to do that, the probability that in the next election patronage would turn against them was high. The reforms that were successfully introduced in the two decades between 1890 and 1910 'were clearly aimed at destroying the hold of the professional politician over the resources necessary to organize and mobilize voters' (Silberman 1993: 268).

The reform gained impulse at the beginning of the twentieth century with the election of Theodore Roosevelt to the presidency. In order to strength his position in relation to the Republican Party's political leaders, Roosevelt obtained the support of the liberal-progressive Republicans. Attacking party patronage became a basic way of controlling both the administration and the party. At the same time, he dedicated his attention to the creation of technical bureaux which would be insulated from politics. It is reasonable to say that the American civil service reform was completed by the end of the Roosevelt administration. Yet Silberman sees the Personnel Classification Act of 1923 as the reform's capstone. Through it the bureaucratic career became fully developed. The law created a system of classes, grades, and services. Positions requiring the same general training were grouped into classes. Classes were divided into positions requiring different levels of skills and experience. To the Personnel Classification Board, created by law, was given the role of defining the rules for classifying and allocating each position to the appropriate class, grade, and service. Additionally, the law was clear that external training in the universities would be an essential means for creating civil servants. This approach, concludes Silberman, assured to the American civil service a particular and outstanding characteristic: instead of motivating young people to prepare themselves for a government career, it suggested that 'individuals prepared themselves for careers as professionals and practiced *that* career wherever there were opportunity' (Silberman 1993: 281). With this, the bureaucratic reform of the American liberal state was completed: the country could now count on a state apparatus that would be strategic in supporting the enormous prosperity and increase in worldwide power that it would experience in the twentieth century.

4

The Transition to Liberal Democracy

Two related historical facts opened the door to liberal democracy or the liberal-democratic state. On the one hand, in the seventeenth and eighteenth centuries, social contract theory imposed a major setback to the divine legitimacy of political rulers. After Hobbes, Locke, Voltaire, and Rousseau, the ideology that derived monarchs' power from divine will lost credibility. The social contract, first understood as an alienation of the power to the monarch, was later viewed simply as a delegation of power to political rulers. Who delegated political power was a new political entity: the people—an initially amorphous entity, which slowly gained form, as subjects turned gradually into citizens and organized themselves as a civil society. On the other hand, the capitalist revolution—embracing the mercantile, the industrial, and the liberal revolutions—changed the basic way of appropriating the economic surplus. This no longer depended on the control of the state, but increasingly depended on the realization of profits in the market. For the first time in history, authoritarian regimes ceased to be a necessary condition for the survival of the ruling classes.

Throughout the nineteenth century, democracy gradually became equivalent to the good state as long as it proved to be the system that most reliably assured political stability or social order. More than that, democracy was recognized, despite all its drawbacks, as the political regime that best attends the interest of the poor as well as of the rich. After the liberal revolutions, capitalists feared that democracy would allow the workers to vote for socialism at elections. Yet this fear gradually diminished as workers did not demonstrate the will to do this. Thus, at the beginning of the twentieth century, we eventually see the first real democracies. As Robert Dahl asserts, 'although some of the institutions of polyarchy appeared in a number of English-speaking and European countries in the nineteenth century, in no country did the demos become inclusive until the twentieth century' (Dahl 1989: 234).

The struggle for universal suffrage, which would complete the transition from the liberal to the liberal-democratic state, was hard. Not only were conservatives against it, but so were liberals. Liberal democracy involved an equality of civil and political rights that bourgeois liberalism of the nineteenth century had difficulty in accepting.[1] A second round of democratic consolidation took place after the Second World War, when the defeated powers—Germany, Japan, and Italy—made their transitions to democracy. Given the level of economic development achieved by those countries, democratic transitions should have already happened there. The war was a consequence of this backwardness, and eventually resolved it. Finally, a third round of democratic transitions and consolidations took place in the 1980s in the more advanced Latin American countries, like Brazil and Mexico, followed by some successful Asian countries like South Korea.[2]

Two New Arguments for Democracy

Today there is a consensus for the democratic state. Even for developing countries, democracy has become the most desirable form of government. Until recently, elites in advanced and developing countries had their doubts about that. In Latin America, for instance, the advanced democracies and local elites supported authoritarian regimes, and even authoritarian coups, for fear of communism. Not any more. Developed countries may still support authoritarian regimes in Asia or Africa, but only for lack of a real democratic alternative. Today's basic classification of political regimes is not the ancient Greek one. The essential distinction is not between monarchy, aristocracy, and democracy, but between democratic and authoritarian regimes. The Greeks did not use the expression 'authoritarian', but it is obvious that monarchic and aristocratic regimes were authoritarian, as indeed were their corrupt forms: tyranny and oligarchy. Thus, the Greeks preferred authoritarian regimes provided that the ruler or the rulers were benevolent. They would rather count with this than risk democracy, whose prospects of stability were meagre. The same position was held by all politicians and philosophers since then until the last part of the nineteenth century. Today this view is unacceptable. We may discuss the relative advantages of a republic or a monarchy, but the assumption is that we are referring to a parliamentary and constitutional regime. What has changed? Why has democracy become the preferred political regime? Why does it assure social order more effectively than other regimes? What was the new historical fact that made modern democracies much more stable than before and, especially, more stable than authoritarian regimes? There are no simple answers to these questions. Nevertheless, I will try to offer one. I have

---

[1] The best account of this fight is probably in Goran Therborn's paper, 'The Rule of Capital and the Rise of Democracy' (1977).

[2] Note that I speak of democratic consolidations, not of democratic transitions, because often democratic transitions are artificial, granted formally by authoritarian local elites, or imposed by foreign countries, while consolidations—if they are to take place—are embodied in the economic and social tissue.

been questioning myself since the mid-1970s, when Brazil started its transition to democracy. In the late 1970s, seven years before the real democratic transition took place, I sketched an answer to the question, and published a book explaining why the transition to democracy had begun and why it would be successful.[3] I argued that Brazil would necessarily return to democracy because it had already completed its 'capitalist revolution' and that, in a fully capitalist system, democracy is the only political regime that makes sense in the long run. In the short run a threatened capitalist class may choose authoritarian rule, as was the case in Brazil in 1964. But in a market economy, as long as the direct control of the government ceases to be a survival condition for capitalists, they will become, first, less resistant and, finally, supportive of the people's demands for democracy.

With the advent of capitalism, for the first time in the history of mankind the appropriation of the economic surplus ceased to depend directly on the use of violence, as profits were now realized in the market. Thus, the direct control of the state by the ruling classes, which was a condition for the existence of those classes, ceased to prevail. This major change opened the way to democracy. The capitalist revolution was the new historical fact that made democracy viable and, eventually, desirable. After it, or due to it, the formation of the first nation-states was also completed. The three basic institutions that characterize the new national and international orders—the constitutional system, the modern state apparatus, and the market—were finally in place. We have now the political coordination of constitutional societies according to the legal system, as well as the economic coordination of these same societies through the market system, both regulated and enforced by a professional bureaucracy operating inside the state organization. For the first time the market economy has become dominant, and so the economic surplus has ceased to be mainly appropriated by dominant groups by means of violence or through control of the state, but takes the form of profits achieved in the market. People who had completed this revolution had for the first time the possibility of creating and consolidating democratic institutions.

The capitalist revolution—the transition from traditional to market economy—represents a landmark in the history of civilization. It turned profit into the economic motive, and made capital accumulation and technical progress the means to that end. It is the change from tradition to reason and interest. It was the outcome of modernity and its principal cause. It begins with the

---

[3] Bresser-Pereira (1978). A second book was published in the year when the democratic transition was completed (Bresser-Pereira 1985). In the previous year, in a book published in the United States (Bresser-Pereira 1984), one of the chapters, 'The Dialectics of Redemocratization and "Abertura"', summarized the argument. While in the well-known studies about democratic transitions edited by O'Donnell, Schmitter, and Whitehead (1986), the transition in Brazil is seen mainly as an internal question among the military—a victory of the soft-liners over the hard-liners—and as a response to international pressures, I present it as the outcome of the existence of a well-established business class in the country. When this is true, authoritarian regimes are short-lived.

commercial revolution, mercantilism, and religious reform, and is completed with the Enlightenment, the industrial revolution, and the scientific revolution. It is not necessary to repeat here what Marx and Weber describe and analyse better than anyone else, or to discuss how, after the transition to the market economy, a new and large professional middle class emerged alongside the working class and the bourgeoisie, and became a central factor in stabilizing politics.

With the capitalist revolution, the form of the appropriation and allocation of the economic surplus changes radically. In pre-capitalist times, the appropriation of the economic surplus depended directly on political power, because such appropriation was to a high degree the outcome of the threat and the use of violence. In pre-capitalist societies, the distribution of income was essentially a political question. Thus, the control of the state, or political power, became crucial. To obtain wealth and prestige one had first to be politically powerful. Economic surplus was originally appropriated through warfare. Through it, the dominant groups were able to collect war booty, to enslave the defeated, or to impose heavy taxes on the acquired colonies. As society changed from tribal to more complex forms of organizations, like city-states, empires, and finally nation-states, taxation became increasingly important. Throughout these historical processes, the military and landed aristocracy, with the support of a patrimonial bureaucracy and of a religious hierarchy, appropriated the economic surplus from peasants and merchants. Religious legitimacy was always an essential part of the process, but the very survival of empires and dominant oligarchies depended on their capacity to hold political power and wage war. In such a system, political power is so crucial that elites cannot indulge in democracy. To be economically rich means to be politically dominant. There is no separation between the public and the private as long as the control of the public patrimony is the privileged means to achieve property and wealth. The poor that Aristotle identified as the sponsors of democracy will often press for freedom, for civic and political rights, but elites will resist ferociously. They will resort to all forms of violence because violence is the only way of securing the economic surplus. Since markets exist only marginally, there is no other real condition for wealth and income appropriation but with the control of the state. Occasionally the people or the merchants may gain some power, and establish some form of democracy or republic, but the new regime will soon be wiped out, given the enormous interests involved in political power.

After the transition to market economy, this situation changed dramatically. Now we have a society coordinated by a constitutional system and a market system. Now economic theory emerges and is able to specify the economic laws determining the distribution of income in the form of rents, profits, and wages. When the capitalist revolution is completed, not only profits but also wages start to be regularly governed by the market. From that moment, the control of the state ceased to be crucial to wealth acquisition and distribution. It remained relevant, but no longer a necessary condition for the economic elite's existence. Thus, the new capitalist class could do what the previous dominant classes could not: indulge in democracy. It would no longer have the necessary strength and/or motivation to conserve authoritarian rule. Thus, this change in the manner of appropriating the surplus was a central factor that made democracy viable.

From the point of view of the bourgeoisie, this change could be viewed as a 'negative' argument in favour of democracy. It gave to the capitalist class a reason or an opportunity for not opposing democracy. Yet, from the capitalist revolution one can also derive a positive argument related to 'large numbers'. With the capitalist revolution, democracy became the rational option for the business class because for the first time we had a really large, numerous, dominant class—large enough to require institutions that formally regulated how its members would share political power. The aristocratic ruling class, however plagued by internal and murderous struggles, was always small. Their members settled their conflicts personally or in small groups. The emerging capitalist class, being much larger, required a more impersonal, secure, and legitimate method of distributing and sharing power. The institutions of liberal democracy offered exactly that to the substantial bourgeois and professional middle classes that were emerging to positions of wealth and power.

Other Rational Motives

Apart from these two historical factors— one that reduced the dominant class's resistance to democracy, the other that motivated it positively in its direction—a third basic historical factor promoting for democracy materialized: the demands of the poor or the working class. Goran Therborn's essay on this subject remains the basic reference. He shows persuasively that democracy was achieved in the developed countries as a result of a long and difficult battle waged by the working class (Therborn 1977). Long before, Aristotle adopted as the leading motive of his book *Politics* the conflict between the rich, who defended oligarchy, and the poor, who were in favour of democracy. Although often used against the poor by demagogues of all kinds, democracy's basic support always came from them. Elites before the capitalist revolution were necessarily aristocratic or oligarchic. Only in recent times, they tended also to accept democracy.

In the new capitalist context, the rich gradually began to realize that the poor did not, in fact, present a threat to their rule as long as they did not have a real alternative to the capitalist system. For long this was not self-evident, given, on the one hand, the fact that the Marxist radical critique made liberalism apparently inconsistent with the protection of the social rights demanded by the poor, and, on the other, the fact that the socialist challenge seemed real. In the twentieth century, however, socialist ideals proved not to be realistic, as the so-called socialist regimes eventually took the perverse form of a bureaucratic system. The poor were not ready to achieve political power, which was captured by a new techno-bureaucratic or professional middle class. In 1989, when the Soviet Union collapsed, the socialist ideal had long been dead, and the immense majority of the workers in advanced democracies felt no sympathy for it. The poor had understood that there is no real alternative to capitalism. Adam Przeworski has elaborated the classic analysis of the class compromise that characterizes modern capitalism. He starts from the assumption that, if workers are given the right to vote, they should, in principle, vote rationally for a socialist government. Yet they do not, because on the one hand, as long as capitalists control investments, 'they are thus in a unique position in the capitalist system: they represent the future universal interests while interests of all other groups appear as particularistic and hence inimical to future developments'. As well, workers do not have the assurance that 'moving to socialism would immediately and continuously improve workers' material conditions. On the contrary, they are not certain that socialism is more efficient than capitalism, and anyway, if it is, the transition to socialism may involve a deterioration of workers' welfare'. Since 'workers have the option of improving their material condition by cooperating with capitalists, the socialist orientation cannot be deduced from the material interests of workers'. The alternative of a class compromise was open to workers. Or, concludes Przeworski, 'a class compromise is possible only on the condition that workers have a reasonable certainty that future wages will increase as a function of current profits' (Przeworski, 1985: 139, 177, 180).

When Przeworski speaks of socialism, he is actually speaking of what I call statism, which, for some time in the twentieth century, was an existing economic and political alternative to capitalism. While he developed this extraordinary political analysis showing that it would not necessarily be rational on the part of workers to opt for statism, and that they could make a compromise with capitalists if their wages increased with profits, I was developing an economic analysis that led me to a similar conclusion. It is a classical (instead of Keynesian, or neoclassical) economic growth model in which I inverted the classical theory of income distribution: profits were the determinant variable, while wages were the residual or dependent variable. The rate of profit is supposed to be relatively constant in the long run because this is a necessary condition for capitalists to invest. Since there was no real economic alternative to capitalism, the economic system and its institutions had no choice but to adopt strategies—institutional, technical, and economic—to avoid the decline of the rate of profit. In this historical and economic model, I presented stylized facts that explain long-run capitalist development. The relatively exogenous variable in the model is technical progress, which changes historically from capital-using to neutral and, finally, to capital-saving, while the rate of profit remains in constant the long run, and the wage rate is the outcome. Since the wage rate increases approximately at the same rate as that of labour productivity, workers had good reason not to rebel and to keep participating in the capitalist system.[4] The fact that workers, eventually, have no better alternative than to make a compromise with capitalists was perceived not only by workers but also by capitalists. And, as long as the latter understood this, they saw less and less reason to fear democracy. On the contrary, they became increasingly confident in democracy. Democracy could mean the guarantee of social rights besides civil and political rights. It could require wage increases, but this would not hurt as long as these increases did not threaten the long-run profit rate. On the contrary, they could sustain the profit rate to the extent that they maintain effective demand, as Keynes demonstrates.

As it became rational for workers or the poor to support capitalism and to fight for democracy and for social rights, it also became rational for capitalists to support democracy while moderately resisting welfare initiatives. Workers increasingly understood that their wage demands faced limits, while capitalists increasingly became persuaded that democracy could facilitate workers' demands, but, as a trade-off, also provide a legitimate political system, more able to assure political stability than authoritarian rule.

In addition, capitalists realized that democracy makes the rule of law much more secure—and nothing is more important for business activity than a stable constitutional and legal environment. Democracy better assures social order, first, because it protects property rights and enforces contracts, two essential conditions for market economies to work and grow; second, because the emergence of social rights and the welfare state reduces extreme inequalities and limits exclusion, thus further contributing to order; and third, because the existence of political rights gives individuals and groups a reasonable opportunity to exercise some voice and even to participate in government. In the first instance, elite bourgeois groups alternate in power. Later, the workers and especially the professional middle class start to share power with capitalists, while public opinion becomes a political force.

The several transitions that led pre-capitalist societies to capitalism and to democracy are complex. There is no simple rule: pathways differ from country to country. In the twentieth century many developing countries that had not completed their capitalist revolutions became democratic, either because their elites decided to emulate advanced countries or because the latter pressed for such change. In contrast, we have the opposite situation in some countries, of which the most obvious example is Singapore. The existence of

---

[4] Bresser-Pereira (1986). Rigorously speaking, the wage rate increases at the same rate as the productivity increase when technical progress is neutral, or, in other words, when the product-capital relation is constant. When technical progress is capital-using, the wage rate will increase at a smaller rate than productivity, and when it is capital saving, it will increase at a higher rate than the rate of productivity increase. Note that in the three alternatives real wages are increasing.

an 'enlightened' ruler may explain this fact. Further advances in democratic governance will continue to vary. In any circumstance, the first historical form of modern democracy tends to be an elitist form of democracy—liberal democracy.

Liberal Democracy Becomes a Reality

Thus, gradually, all major political actors became persuaded that democracy is the regime that is most favourable to business as well as to workers. This transition process was slow. It took a whole century—the nineteenth century. This was the period of the liberal state, discussed in the previous chapter. The transition from the liberal state to the liberal-democratic state was finally completed with the extension of the right to vote to women and the poor. The times when democracy was dominated by greedy and turbulent factions, as depicted by the ancient Greek philosophers, were over. Workers, capitalists, and the new professional middles classes—the three social classes that characterize modern capitalism—eventually 'signed' an informal social and political contract.

The expression 'liberal democracy' is often used to refer to all advanced democracies. In this book, I do not give this expression such a broad meaning. In the second part of the twentieth century such democracies, especially the most advanced European countries but also the United States, were rather social democracies. In this historical overview of the emergence of the modern state, liberal democracy is just the first form of democracy emerging from the semi-authoritarian nineteenth-century liberal state. Gradually we saw the transition from the liberal to the liberal-democratic state, or from the semi-authoritarian form of liberalism that characterized the nineteenth century to liberal democracy characterized by universal suffrage, competitive political parties, regular elections, representation, and political accountability only at elections.[5] In his 1942 classic book *Capitalism, Socialism and Democracy*, Schumpeter defines liberal democracy as the institutional arrangement in which politicians acquire the power to decide competing for the people's vote. Yet, he adds:

Democracy does not mean and cannot mean that the people actually rule in any obvious sense of the terms 'people' and 'rule'. Democracy only means that the people have the opportunity of accepting or refusing the men who are to rule them . . . Democracy is the rule of the politician . . . The voters outside of parliament must respect the division of labour between themselves and the politicians they elect. They must not withdraw confidence too easily between elections and they must understand that, once they have elected an individual, political action is his business and not theirs. (Schumpeter 1942: 284, 285, and 295)

---

[5] Liberal democracy corresponds to the elitist concept of democracy developed by Schumpeter.

Schumpeter could not be clearer. Besides normatively defining democracy, he was empirically describing the type of democracy of his time. The first half of the twentieth century was the time of liberal-democracies or of the liberal-democratic state.

This historical analysis demonstrates that the definition of the good state is permanently changing. S. E. Finer (1997: 79, 87), in his monumental study of the history of governments, adopts five criteria to evaluate the good polity: defence ability, internal law and order, non-extortionate taxation, provision of public works and welfare, and rights and citizenship. Some of these criteria remain important, others do not. Defence, for instance, remains crucial to major countries, not to small ones. One can no longer say that 'the ability of the polity to defend its population against invasions, plunder, or enslavement by outside enemies is primordial and a polity that cannot do this has, *pro tanto*, failed', unless this ability presupposes military support coming from strong neighbours or from a supporting international community. On the other hand, it is significant that Finer, evaluating ancient governments, did not include social justice among his criteria. Maybe he did that because philosophers could write on justice, could ask for social justice, but real social justice was something to which they could not realistically aspire given well-established institutions like slavery and servitude. The same is true of democracy. Commenting on the 'rights and citizenship' criterion, he writes: 'Athens's democratic concept of such citizenship and participation was rejected in Europe till 200 years ago and never ever surfaced everywhere'.

Thus, it would not be reasonable to appraise a government and a state in antiquity, in the Middle Ages, or in the times of absolutism and of the building of the first nation-states, in terms of whether or not it was democratic. None was. Some states could respect the rule of law more than others. Some monarchs or princes could be more or less benevolent, but all their people were subjects, not citizens. Democracy was out of the question. Since the twentieth century, however, after new historical facts made democracy a real possibility, the democratic criterion became central to the definition of the good state. The general explanation for this is probably in Marx's proposition that men collectively pose problems only when they have some possibility of solving them. In other words, men are sufficiently realistic not to set themselves unattainable tasks.

In early twentieth century the more industrialized countries start to deserve the name of democracy as long as the five characteristics that I view as essential to this political regime were present. Democracy is the constitutional regime assuring the rule of law, freedom of association, speech and information, the universal right to vote and to be elected, and minorities' rights, whose government members are regularly chosen according to majority rule through free and competitive elections. In other words, I understand as democratic a political regime that broadly satisfies Dahl's criteria defining a polyarchy.[6] This is a minimal definition of democracy, which should not be confused with the minimalist or elitist concept of democracy that Schumpeter advanced a little later. In the twentieth century, democracy or polyarchy, defined by the five minimum characteristics cited above, became finally dominant in the more economically advanced countries. The first country to adopt universal suffrage was New Zealand, in 1893. The adoption of universal suffrage does not mean that a country has completed its transition to democracy, but in most advanced countries this was clearly the case. Such countries had long been constitutional or rule-of-law regimes. Freedom of thought and association and regular elections had existed also for some time. When the propertyless and women were finally entitled to vote, the minimum conditions for democracy materialized. As Wanderley Guilherme dos Santos observes, the number of voters doubles or more than doubles in most countries in the year that universal electoral suffrage is adopted (Santos 1998: Table II). The liberal-democratic state was finally a reality.

It is interesting to observe that some developing countries assured the universal right to vote, although they had not finished their capitalist revolution, and their political regimes probably could not be viewed as democracies. This is particularly the case with some Latin American countries. Yet the full transition to a market economy, which defines the capitalist revolutions, is not a condition for democracy; it is a condition only for a consolidated democracy. Given international pressure from developed countries, or the natural tendency of local elites in developing countries to import institutions from abroad, some or all characteristics of a polyarchy may appear in countries where the economic surplus continues to be appropriated and allocated mainly through the state organization, and so do not present the economic and social conditions required to be stable democracies. Conversely, there are countries that have already completed their capitalist revolutions, but lag in the transition to democracy. This is the case with some successful Asian countries. And there are also countries like Germany, which made the transition to democracy after completing its capitalist revolution but given some particular historical circumstances, later relapsed into authoritarian rule.

Dahl speaks of three periods of the growth of polyarchy: 1776–1930, 1950–59, and the 1980s. Samuel Huntington (1991), probably inspired by Dahl, proposes three waves of democratization. In each wave the countries that had become capitalist and liberal made their transition to democracy, while others were just following the wave. By the end of the twentieth century, besides most of the English-speaking and the European countries, all Latin American and an increasing number of countries in the other continents were

---

[6] Dahl (1971; 1989: 233). Yet note that, although I believe that Dahl's distinction between modern democracy and polyarchy is useful in certain circumstances to distinguish an ideal form of government from reality, and also from [ancient?] Greek democracy, in this chapter I use 'modern democracy' or just 'democracy' and 'polyarchy' as synonyms.

democratic. Democracy had become the dominant political regime. Once established, liberal democracy proved to be able to correct and improve itself. In the developed countries liberal democracy began when the universal right to vote was extended to all, including women. It began as an elitist democracy, of the type that Schumpeter assumes as being the only possible one. Yet democracy progressed in all rich countries, so that by the mid-twentieth century it had changed, as we will see in Chapter 5, into a civil society or a public opinion democracy—a political regime where the public space is a reality and where public debate forming opinion has a crucial role. Intermediate developing countries, which completed their capitalist revolutions later, in the mid-twentieth century, and completed their transition to democracy in the 1980s and the 1990s, are still elitist democracies. This is the case, for instance, with Brazil and Mexico.

5

The Social-Democratic State

The fight for socialist ideas and for social rights dated from the twentieth century, but only after the Great Depression of the 1930s signalled the crisis of the liberal democratic state, and political conditions emerged favouring greater state intervention in the economy, the upholding of social rights, or a welfare system. At that moment the social democratic state was emerging. With it, democracy ceased to be just liberal; it became also social or plural, not only because it started to effectively offer social protection but also because political power became less concentrated in an elite, and public opinion for the first time had political weight. Andrew Shonfield opens its 1960s classic book *Modern Capitalism* with the question: 'What was that converted capitalism from the cataclysmic failure which it appeared to be in the 1930s into the great engine of prosperity of the post-war Western World?' (Shonfield 1969: 3). The question was timely, although he could have also asked what converted democracy from the failure it appeared to be into the only legitimate political regime. Shonfield adds that one answer to the question could rest on the denial of the validity of the question itself. Capitalism—and, I would add, democracy—changed so much from the 1930s to the 1960s that it could be considered misleading to apply the word 'capitalism' to describe them. Yet the change was not so great. The central features of capitalism—capital accumulation, wage labour, market allocation of resources, separation of the public and the private realms—remained. As for democracy, it had advanced only as political equality had gained more substance than in the times of elitist democracy, and as public opinion gained political relevance. Thus, the question remains: what transformed capitalism and democracy in a success history? And how was it possible that 'prosperity has not depended . . . on a shift in the distribution of incomes in favour of profits and against wages'? (Shonfield 1969). Shonfield dedicates his whole book to answering these questions. The more general conclusion that he reaches is that these outcomes reflected the accelerated pace of technological progress and 'the conscious pursuit of full employment'. He goes on to conclude that the new era of capitalism that opened with the end of the Second World War was particularly related to this latter factor, which depended on the theories developed

by Keynes to achieve full employment. He lists the five outstanding features
of the new reality:

1. There is a vastly increased influence of the public authorities on the management of
the economic system . . . 2. The preoccupation with social welfare leads to the use of
public funds on a rising scale . . . 3. In the private sector the violence of the market has
been tamed . . . 4. It was now common to be taken for granted . . . that each year should
bring a noticeable increase in the real income per head of the population . . . 5. The
characteristic attitude in large scale management . . . is the pursuit of intellectual coherence. (Shonfield 1969: 63, 66–7).

Shonfield, as an economist, writes more about the economic and social
system—capitalism—than on the political one, but the increased role assumed
by the state is evident. The era of the liberal democratic state was over; the social-
democratic or welfare state was emerging. Now, the more appropriate designation of the political regime should be social democracy rather than liberal
democracy. The only explanation for the insistence on using the expression
'liberal democracy' to designate the modern political regime is the ambivalent
meaning of the term 'liberalism' in the United States, where 'liberals' are political liberals, not economic liberals, and the promoters instead of the critics of
the social-democratic state. Although the United States had been one of the
slowest among the advanced countries to assign a decisive role to the state, the
New Deal was a privileged moment in the rise of the social-democratic state.
As Alan Brinkley observes, 'the New Deal was not only an effort to deal with
the particular problems of the 1930s; it was also a process of building government institutions where none existed, of choosing among various prescrip-
tions for an expanded American state' (Brinkley, 1998: 38). The two forms of
state intervention that would characterize the social-democratic state—
increased regulatory power and increased capacity to tax in order to stimulate
economic growth and deal with social problems—were already present in
Roosevelt's New Deal. After the Second World War this new political and economic regime became dominant among developed countries. In Western
Europe and Canada, it was fully developed; it remained incomplete in the
United States in spite of the pioneering political changes of the 1930s and the
continuing dynamism of the American economy.

The social-democratic state is the outcome of the increasing political
capacity of the working class and, particularly, of the middles classes.
Organized in unions, and having a say in centre-left political parties, they
were able to demand the assurance of their social rights through social protection by the state. But, as Karl Polanyi (1944) stresses, the creation in modern capitalism of welfare systems, whose origins lie in Bismarck's Germany,
was a response to an intrinsic requirement of the market system. Capitalism
eliminated the organic forms of existence, reducing the labour force to the
condition of merchandise to be exchanged in the market. It destroyed the

traditional institutions that protected life and work, but it could not destroy work itself. On the contrary, it required the protection of man against the market. With nature, a similar process would take place some time later, after the United Nations' 1972 Stockholm Conference on the environment. In its own interests, the capitalist system had no alternative but also to protect the environment.

After the Second World War, deliberate state intervention in the market and the guarantee of the universal rights to health care, basic education, a minimum income, and fair employment conditions defined the emerging social-democratic state. Throughout this historical process, the number of social goods that were to be politically secured increased. Social goods are the goods most valued by a given society. Power, wealth, and divine grace were central in the absolute state. In the liberal state, civil liberties and security were viewed as the two main social goods. In the liberal-democratic state, political equality was added as a major social good. With the social-democratic state, social protection through health care, free basic education, minimum income mechanisms, and social security were added to the list, as equality of opportunity gained a central place among social values. Power and wealth have always been the demand of the rich; freedom and the rule of law the request of the middle classes; universal education, health care, and a minimum income the claim of the poor.

We should not view the rise of the social-democratic state just as a historical change towards social justice. For sure, it has this dimension domestically, within each developed country. Yet, Bill Jordan (1996: 122) developed a theory of social exclusion based on a rational choice approach, which asserts that individuals choose to join together associations of all kinds (from families and clubs to political parties and states) excluding outsiders from the goods that they supply to each other. According to this 'group theory', the welfare states are one of these groups. They are a form of collective action able to satisfy their own citizens' interests by creating 'institutions that overcome the inefficiencies, inequities and downright perversities of the interwar period. But from the point of view of the world economic system, they were rather successful distributional coalitions which captured the rents associated with advanced industrial production for their capitalists and workers, to the long-term disadvantage of their counterpart developing countries'.

This observation is crucial for the understanding of the durability of the social-democratic compact existing in the developed countries. Jordan is actually using, with a rational choice vocabulary, the classical 'Prebisch's thesis' that Latin American structuralist economists developed in the late 1940s to legitimate the developmental state that not only Latin American but also Eastern and South-Eastern countries were adopting as a counter strategy. According to this theory, the developed countries were able to capture the productivity gains (instead of reducing costs and prices, as economic theory predicted) due to the existence of a strong organization of workers into unions.[1] Thus, when, in the 1980s, the neo-liberal wave surfing in the wave of globalization attempts to dismantle the welfare state, it does not succeed. Capitalist and technocrat groups controlling the large multinational corporations believed that they could gain from this demarche. Yet, within each developed country, this attempt eventually failed because the social contract involved in the social-democratic state protected not only workers but also capitalists and the professional middle class.[2]

Even within the national frontiers of the developed countries, however, Jordan observes that the welfare state's success in avoiding social exclusion and poverty was partial. The rich, from capitalist or professional middle class origin, but controlling either large sums of capital or of technical and organizational knowledge, and also unionized labour were able to protect the rents (monopolist incomes) that they are able to capture from unprotected workers, deprived communities, and, increasingly, from immigrant groups.

Social or Plural Democracy

With the rise of the social-democratic state, liberal democracy transformed itself into social democracy or plural democracy—a political regime that conserved the central aspects of liberal democracy, such as regular elections, competitive political parties, representation, protection of civil and political rights. This also involved three key elements: first, reflecting the increased political power of unions and other corporate organizations representing interests, bargaining or compromise became a central political practice; second, public opinion started to make politicians somewhat accountable between elections; and third, the protection of social rights finally became reasonably effective.

David Held, referring to the model of democracy which emerges principally in the United States and whose principal interpreter is Robert Dahl, labels it 'plural democracy'. Given that the social aspects of the form of democracy that exists in both the European countries and the United States, the label 'social democracy' is equally appropriate. The two central or novel characteristics of plural democracy are bargaining among numerous interest groups and a new role for public opinion. These phenomena existed in liberal or elitist democracy, but in a much smaller degree. Yet Held adds another central

---

[1] The Prebisch thesis was first defined by Raul Prebisch (1950), with the participation of Celso Furtado. Hans Singer (1950) developed a similar theory independently. For a historical account, see Joseph Love (1996).

[2] The attempt of dismantling the developmental state failed in the East and South-East Asian countries, but it was successful in Latin America, which even adopted neo-liberal reforms and macroeconomic policies that the developed ones did not, and this is probably a basic reason why the region lagged behind since 1980.

feature: the relatively non-hierarchical character of pluralist democracy. Citing the work of Robert Dahl, David Truman, and Almond and Verba to substantiate his analysis, he argues:

In the pluralist account, power is non-hierarchically and competitively arranged. It is an inextricable part of an 'endless process of bargaining' between numerous groups representing different interests, including, for example, business organizations, trade unions, political parties, ethnic groups, students, prison officers, women's collectives, and religious groups.[3]

Held remarks that Dahl's position does not require that control over political decisions be equally distributed, nor that all individuals and groups have equal political 'weight'. Yet he observes that the pluralist emphasis on the 'empirical' nature of democracy presents two major problems. First, the pluralists did not compare their model of democracy with competing models. Second, their work tended to represent a justification of the post-Second World War 'Western' democracy. In his words:

The writings of the key pluralist authors tended to slide from a descriptive-explanatory account of democracy to a new normative theory. Their 'realism' entailed conceiving of democracy in terms of the actual features of the Western polities. (Held, 1996: 207)

The American pluralist writers probably had no alternative. Although trying to be as scientific or realistic as possible, they expressed enthusiasm for the American democratic system in the three decades after 1945. Despite the limitations of all political analysis, they offered a major contribution to the understanding of the advanced democracies of their time, and of how they differed from the earlier elitist version. Yet it is necessary to emphasize that they did not accord political relevance in their theory to the social accountability organizations or NGOs because at that time the role of those public organizations was still limited. They were concerned, rather, with corporate organizations, with interest groups. In political science, the problem of citizens' participation was limited to a debate on the decision to vote—something difficult to explain from a rational-choice or economic point of view, but real.[4]

Concern with the protection of social rights and, more broadly, of human rights marked the transition from the liberal to the social-democratic state, and from liberal to social democracy. Jürgen Habermas observes that Marshall's analysis of the concept of citizenship, with three successive citizens' rights, 'is part of a widespread tendency that sociologists call *inclusion*. In an increasingly differentiated society, an increasing number of people acquire inclusive rights of access to and participation in an escalating number

---

3 Held (1996: 202). Held refers to Truman's *The Governmental Process* (1951), Almond and Verba's *The Civic Culture* (1963), and Dahl's earlier works (1956, 1961, 1978).

4 For discussion between the economic concept of democracy, espoused by rational choice theorists, and a sociological approach like that adopted by pluralist political scientists centred on the decision to vote, the basic reference remains Brian Barry (1978).

of sub-systems . . . '[5] But he warns that Marshall's analysis tells a linear story that does not highlight the crucial role of political rights in citizenship by placing them on the same level as the others. In the second half of the twentieth century, civil, political, and social rights were subsumed under the name of 'human rights'. The 1948 Universal Declaration of Human Rights proclaimed the universal validity of these rights, which became positive and legal with the covenants of 1966 and other core treaties. In abstract terms, citizens' rights and human rights are synonymous: they encompass all rights. Yet, in historical terms, the idea of 'human rights' appears in the 1970s, identified especially with civil rights, as a reaction against the authoritarian regimes that became dominant in developing countries. Since the 1930s, the emphasis has shifted greatly to social rights. Civil and political rights were considered to be assured, or to be 'formal' rights, the product of a 'formal democracy' that would become 'substantive' only when social rights were also defended. This was the left's classic position until the 1960s. However, in the 1960s and 1970s, when authoritarian right-wing regimes took over in a great number of countries, especially in Latin America, and began to violate civil as well as political rights, the left was forced to consider its position. Given state violence against left-wing politicians, many of them belonging to the middle class, and given torture and murder, it became essential to take into account not only the political rights expressed in democracy, but also civil rights. Moreover, it became clear that the civil rights, that were assumed to have been won, were limited to the upper and middle classes: it was required to extend them to the poor.[6] After democracy's restoration, it became clear in many countries that not only the human rights of the political opponents of authoritarian regimes were at stake. It was necessary also to defend the civil rights of the poor, of the powerless and oppressed, of the victims of social exclusion.[7]

During the 1970s and 1980s, the Catholic Church played a decisive role in Latin America in defence of the civil rights or, in a wider sense, of the human rights, of both political opponents and the powerless and oppressed.[8] At the same time, organized civil society, and particularly the public non-state social accountability organizations, came to play an increasingly important role in

---

[5] Habermas (1992: 78). Wanderley Reis (1990: 168), on the other hand, sees social rights and the welfare state as a functional requirement of capitalism itself. Offe (1984) points out that this functional character does not take away the character of these rights as the outcomes of struggle. Yet he introduces a discussion on the relative loss of functionality of these rights – a loss that gave rise, in the 1980s, to the crisis of welfare state.

[6] According to Elisabeth Jelin and Eric Hershberg (1996: 3): 'Whereas it was once commonplace to differentiate among civil, political and social rights, and to conceptualize citizenship primarily in terms of social rights, in the 1980s basic human and civil rights could no longer be dismissed or taken for granted. Instead, they became the centre of political activism and intellectual preoccupation.'

[7] For example, according to the auditor of São Paulo's Police, Benedito Domingos Mariano, 'the victim of torture is generally man, black, poor and lives in the periphery' (*Folha de S. Paulo*, 1 January, 1997).

[8] Regarding Brazil, the main document about this matter comes from the Arquidiocese de São Paulo (1985). See also Paulo Sérgio Pinheiro and Eric Braun (1986).

the defence of human rights,[9] while the press assumed a more and more strategic role in this matter.[10] Thus, although in the developing countries authoritarian views are still held by a considerable part of the population, the transition to democracy opened the way for the defence of the human rights of the poor and the powerless, starting with the affirmation of the right to life and to respect.[11] Social rights remained important, but the almost exclusive emphasis on them lost legitimacy, since it rested on the mistaken presumption that civil rights were already secured for all (in fact, in the new democracies they were secure just for the elite) or on the biased point of view that civil rights would be guaranteed only when social rights were.[12]

In their struggle for citizenship rights, the poor have nowhere won a complete victory. The era of an elitist liberal democracy is over but the establishment of social democracy or plural democracy (often deprecatingly called by its opponents 'mass democracy') is far from complete. In the twentieth century, this struggle became wider, as long as democracy granted the poor formal citizenship. The change from formal to actual citizenship—from citizens who have rights legally to citizens who have them in reality—became the central political and institutional problem faced by the social-democratic state. This change involved increased political participation on the part of the poor, and their achievement of minimum social rights.[13] Education and a free press played a central role in this process of institutional change. On the other hand, citizenship is also the outcome of practice: it is something that one acquires in defending his or her own rights. That is why sociologists and anthropologists have stressed the growing importance of social movements in

[9] Public non-state institutions are improperly called either non-governmental or non-profit organizations. 'Non-governmental' would be appropriate if we treated 'government' and 'state' as synonyms instead of viewing the state as the basic political organization and government as the group of politicians and senior civil servants in the top of the three branches of power running the state organization, and also as the governing process. Non-profit or Third Sector organizations include unions, which are corporate bodies. Public non-state organizations are oriented towards the public interest. NGOs (non-governmental organizations) are a form of public non-state organization, but charities, foundations, and 'private' non-profit universities are also included in the concept of public non-state ownership.

[10] See specially the book-report by Gilberto Dimenstein, *Guerra dos Meninos* (1990). The contribution of the media in this direction were summarized in Dimenstein (1996). The foreword of this book, written by Paulo Sérgio Pinheiro (1996), is significantly titled 'The Past is not Dead: It is not Past Yet'.

[11] This authoritarian attitude is expressed in the lack of indignation towards violations of human rights in the socially excluded sectors, or even in support for those violations among considerable sections of society. Nancy Cardia (1994), reporting research on acquiescence in the violence against the socially excluded, sees the problem as a case of 'moral exclusion of groups regarded as being on the margins of society', in a context of a lack of power of the governed over the rulers, of alienation from the process of legislation, of ignorance about the meaning of civil and political rights, and of lack of channels of access to the mechanisms of legal protection.

[12] Debate on individual and social rights, however, continues, through discussion of the ideals of freedom and solidarity. See, for instance, Luís Cardoso de Oliveira (1996).

[13] I have called 'citizenship contradiction' the political problem resulting from the existence, in Brazil, of a large number of citizens who have the right to vote, but who are not conscious of their political and social rights and obligations (Bresser-Pereira 1996).

building citizenship through the assertion of social and civil rights.[14] The bourgeois middle class originally won civil or liberal rights. In the twentieth century, the advance of social rights may be explained only by the increasing capacity of the poor to defend their interests. The liberal-democratic state was still an elitist state, but it allowed for the inclusion of the poor in the political process, which made the transition to the social-democratic state inevitable.

Civil rights were oriented directly against the state: they assumed an oppressive state, but, paradoxically, they required state (legal) protection. The objective was to limit state interference in the private lives of citizens.[15] In contrast, once the poor achieved political rights, social democrats assumed that the state could and should provide protection for them: the affirmation of social rights implied extending the state's activity. In the case of civil rights, the assumption was that an oligarchy controlled the state. It was probably the same assumption that led Marx to call the state the 'instrument of the dominant class'. In the case of social rights, that assumption had to be dropped, since in social democracies the middles classes eventually acquired the major political influence over the framing of public policies and institutions, while the poor acquired a moderate but noticeable one.

Four Models of Capitalism

The social-democratic state was a major political advance on the liberal-democratic state. While the liberal-democratic state assured only civil rights, the social-democratic state warranted, in addition, social rights. That is why, when we compare the European countries, in which the transition to the social-democratic state has been completed, with the United States, which has been unable to complete it, we observe that income distribution is fairer and social rights are better assured in the former than in the latter countries. Countries like Britain, New Zealand, and Australia are in an intermediate situation. In spite of the immense wealth in the United States, almost 40 million Americans cannot count on health care; approximately 13 per cent of the American population live under the poverty line, against around 5 per cent in the social-democratic countries. If the quality of a political regime—or of a democratic governance—is to be measured by the extent to which it provides the four basic political

---

[14] As Ruth Cardoso (1994: 90) observes, 'Citizens' rights haven't arisen in a vacuum, they have a history, and refer to a precise concept. But this concept is no longer able to relate to what actually happens, because it is based on the idea of individual rights and, presently, through the struggle of social movements, there is a full recognition that there are also collective rights'. See also Eunice Durham (1984) and Vera Silva Telles (1994) on the subject.

[15] Formally, civil rights are not only rights against the state. They are also rights of each citizen against other citizens who steal from or attack him. The criminal law, as a public law, is designed to guarantee citizens' civil rights against criminals: more widely, to guarantee the rights of citizens, of enterprises, and of the state itself against criminal actions.

goods valued by modern societies—social order, freedom, social justice, and well-being—there is little doubt that the more advanced European social-democratic societies have today political regimes preferable to the American one. Yet it is often argued that, compensating for injustice, in the mainly liberal-democratic American state the economic system is more efficient than in the social-democratic system: that it produces more wealth. I have serious doubts about this. It should be noted that, since the Second World War, it is only in the last decade that the American economy has grown at a faster rate than, for instance, France or Germany. Yet, from this thin evidence, and from higher unemployment rates in Europe, some ultra-liberal ideologues have derived the confirmation of their ideological preconceptions: the economic superiority of the liberal-democratic state to the social-democratic state. It is true that, in some social-democratic states, excessive regulation of business and labour may reduce competition and represent a negative incentive to entrepreneurship. But, as a trade-off, in more equal societies like the social-democratic ones, cooperation stimulates efficient work, greater social security makes workers readier to accept innovation, and—what is more important—assures legitimacy to governments, which, consequently, are not constrained to adopt explicit or disguised populist policies to ensure popular support. Thus, once reformed, with the elimination of some forms of bureaucratic overprotection, the social-democratic state tends to be more efficient as well as more just. It is not necessary to erase the welfare system, to cut social benefits. What social-democratic countries need is public management reform and some greater labour-market flexibility, as the Netherlands, Sweden, and Denmark have achieved. In the early twenty-first century, unemployment in these countries was lower than in the United States, and still they maintained their welfare state, and, more generally, their commitment to social rights. Public spending continued to amount to around 50 per cent of GDP in these countries. Flexibility in labour markets meant chiefly some reduction in job tenure and increase in part-time work, while governments developed effective policies to retrain and help the jobless to find work quickly, and unions agreed to restrain wage demands. It was not necessary to copy the American system and dismantle the welfare state, as ultra-liberals supposed.

Gosta Esping-Andersen, in a book that is now required reading on the subject, identifies 'three worlds of welfare capitalism': liberal, corporate, and social-democratic welfare capitalism, with the United States, Germany, and Sweden as the representative regimes.[16] According to Esping-Andersen, the 'liberal welfare state' follows a 'residual' criterion: the state assumes responsibility

<hr>

[16] Esping-Andersen (1990). Goodin et al. (1999: 262) used this classification to conduct an investigation in three countries representing the three forms of welfare state: the United States, Germany, and the Netherlands. After an extensive analysis, they concluded that 'the social-democratic welfare strategy is strictly dominant over both the others. The social-democratic welfare regime is at least as good as (and usually better) either of the other welfare regimes in respect of all the *social* objectives we traditionally set for our welfare regimes'. The classic studies of the corporatist regime are those by Schmitter (1974) and Streeck and Schmitter (1985).

when the individual or the family fails.[17] It limits universalistic rights, adopting instead means-tested assistance; economic inequality remains high. In fact, such a system, which characterizes the American state, did not fully reach the social-democratic stage: it remains between the liberal state and the social-democratic state. While corporate welfare capitalism privileges social integration, the social-democratic welfare capitalism, equality. Yet for the sake of simplicity I will not distinguish between the two forms in a book where this is not the central question, and also because all corporatist systems include powerful social-democratic political parties.

The existence of the social-democratic state does not depend on a social-democratic party holding office. It requires only that the fight for social rights, principally championed by centre-left political coalitions, be one of the two options in the alternation of political parties in government that characterizes modern democracies. In the 1980s and 1990s, the ultra-liberal ideological wave attempted to eliminate these advances and to retreat from the social-democratic to the liberal-democratic state, but it did not succeed. It was more successful in implementing radical reforms, like the privatization of the basic social security system, in some developing countries, which were unable to protect themselves from ideological excesses.[18] Opposition between conservative and liberal political parties characterized liberal democracies; opposition between social-democratic and liberal (now turned conservative) political parties defined the social-democratic state. This is typical of Europe. In the United States, where the New Deal began to put into practice the social-democratic state but where the process was never completed, opposition between liberal (now turned political liberal or progressive liberal) and conservative remained. These parties continue to alternate in power, as is proper in democracies, but an electoral victory by a conservative political party in the United States does not mean a return to the liberal state, just as a victory by a liberal party in Europe does not signify a return to the liberal-democratic state. Such outcomes may mean no more than the imposition of some limits, not necessarily ill-conceived, to the advances in social protection achieved. There is no better evidence for this than the fact that tax burdens in the developed countries do not decrease. On the contrary, despite the 1980s and 1990s neo-liberal waves, and the effort of conservative politicians to reduce taxes, state expenditures and the tax burden have continued to grow moderately.

More extended social protection in the continental European countries than in the United States is just one of the differences that begin to appear between capitalist countries with the emergence of the social-democratic state. The central concern in this book is not to emphasize such distinctions—I am interested, rather, in the more general structural and long-term changes

---

[17] Esping-Andersen quotes R. Titmuss (1958) on this matter. Titmuss developed a distinction, today classical, between the residual and the institutional welfare states.

[18] In relation to social security reform, this is the case with Chile and Argentina.

that the state and the state organization are undergoing—although I note that capitalism may assume many forms. Since the mid-twentieth century, there have been four relevant forms of modern capitalism. All are capitalist societies and economies, since they all feature private ownership of the means of production, wage labour, and market coordination. All tend to be democratic, although the less developed ones in particular may not be. All have a modern state organization and an institutional or legal system that defines the market and the government system. They differ among themselves, however, according to two related criteria: the extent to which the state intervenes in the market, and the extent to which it protects social rights.

The two countries that were first industrialized—Great Britain and United States—head the first group, which could be called the 'Anglo-Saxon market model of capitalism'. Australia, New Zealand, and, to a certain extent, Canada also display this model of capitalism. In the second group we have Germany, France, and the Scandinavian countries, which define the 'European social model', to which the other European countries belong, including Russia. Third, we have the 'Asian developmental model', headed by Japan and followed by the fast-growing countries of East Asia. India is a special case in this group, as it shares many characteristics of the fourth and final group. This is the 'Latin American mixed model', which is not exclusive to Latin America, but is typical of Brazil, Mexico, and Argentina. In this classification, communist or statist countries are excluded, although some, like China, already display strong capitalist traits. The same is true of most African and some Asian countries which have not completed their respective capitalist revolutions.

The Anglo-Saxon market model of capitalism is the one in which the state has the smallest role in complementing the market in the coordination of the economy. Although it includes only countries with high per-capita incomes, social protection is limited. Individualism, technological innovation, and competition prevail. The European social model is characterized by a more active state complementing and regulating markets, and by an extensive guarantee of social rights, and may be subdivided into a Rhenish, or corporatist, model and a Scandinavian model. The Asian developmental model is defined by a still more active, 'developmental' state, in complementing market coordination of the economy, but offers limited social protection, which is supposed to be provided by families and business enterprises. Finally, the Latin American mixed model is mixed because it began as developmental but, unlike what happened to the Asian countries, substantially dismantled its developmental state during the neo-liberal wave of the 1980s and 1990s; it is committed to social rights, but cannot count on having the necessary means to provide effective social protection. As Whitehead observes, while Latin America adopts without much resistance the reforms aimed at dismantling its developmental state, East Asian 'policymakers were reluctant to dismantle economic models that, in addition to delivering sustained growth, had provided defences against excessive foreign intrusion in domestic economic matters' (Whitehead 2002: 3–4).

This classification has similarities with Michel Albert's distinction between the 'American' and the 'Rhenish' models; or with Gøsta Esping-Andersen's three types of welfare capitalism: 'liberal', 'corporate', and 'social-democratic'; or with Goodin et al.'s categories comprising a 'liberal', a 'corporatist', and a 'social-democratic model'; or with Peter Hall and David Soskice's recent classification of the OECD countries as 'liberal market economies' and 'coordinated market economies'; or even with John D. Stephens' distinction between 'liberal-democratic states', 'Christian-democratic welfare states', 'social-democratic welfare states', and 'wage-earner welfare states' (Australia and New Zealand).[19] However, these classifications give too little salience to the Asian model, and none includes intermediate developing countries like South Korea or Brazil. Although some countries are more 'social-democratic' than others, and the 'welfare state' is more real in some countries than in others, for the more aggregate level of analysis present in this book I will limit myself to including in the general category of 'social-democratic states' all advanced democracies and most intermediate ones in the second part of the twentieth century. To be sure, in each model of capitalism the state organization will be different, the institutions will be different, the social networks will be different, basic values will diverge. Yet, since all economies to which I am referring are capitalist, since all respective polities are democratic, and, thus, since in all these social and political systems the working classes and particularly the middle classes already have a reasonable political voice, all states, although differing from each one, will have social-democratic institutions protecting social rights. Besides, since no country can indulge in being wholly at the whim of market forces, in all countries, including the more market-coordinated, the state will take substantial regulatory action.

A Developmental Bureaucracy

Between the 1940s and the 1970s, the rise of the social-democratic state implied an enormous increase in the size of the state apparatus in all four models of capitalism, and required a new bureaucracy to run it. The classic upper-level bureaucracy—the one that was strengthened by civil service reform—was a bureaucracy of law school graduates or of generalists. Now, besides a larger number of officers with such a professional profile, it requires more 'technicians' or 'experts'. From the latter, more than just following bureaucratic regulations was required. In the new areas in which the state was

---

[19] Albert (1991); Esping-Andersen (1990); Goodin et al. (1999); Hall and Soskice (2001); Stephens (2002).

becoming involved, areas not directly regulated by law, these officials were supposed to take decisions, draft plans, and define policies. Among the technicians, engineers and the new profession of economists gained a special relevance. The latter, working in the finance ministries, in the planning ministries, in the central banks, in social security agencies, in regulatory agencies, and in development agencies, soon assumed a major role. Since, particularly from the 1940s to the 1970s, these technicians or experts and their governments were mainly committed to economic development, we may call these new civil servants the 'developmental bureaucracy'.

In the Anglo-Saxon countries, the rise of this new bureaucracy was not as visible as in the European, the Asian, and the Latin American countries, where the role of the state in promoting economic growth was more accentuated. In the United States this bureaucracy is still more noticeable in international organizations like the United Nations, the IMF, and the World Bank than in the American state organization itself, although the state does employ a large number of 'modern' bureaucrats. Actually, the classic bureaucrats were already modern; what distinguished the new bureaucracy or technobureaucracy was its technical competence in making viable the new role of the state—an economic role to provide for market stabilization and to complement and correct market allocation and the distribution of resources. Since the depression of the 1930s made clear that markets were unable to assure economic stability and full employment, Keynesian macroeconomic policy emerged along with the state institutions required to implement it. Since the experience of late industrialization, starting with Germany and Japan, demonstrated that the state could perform an active role in fostering economic growth, particularly in the first stages of development, developmental economic policy arose along with the respective institutions, particularly planning ministries and development banks. Finally, later, since markets were unable to regulate quasi-monopolist markets, regulatory policy was devised and regulatory agencies created. In the intermediate developing countries, like Brazil, India, Mexico, or Korea, the emergence of this new bureaucracy was so conspicuous that the corresponding type of state was called 'developmental' rather than 'social-democratic'. There is a large literature on this bureaucracy, which, however, it is not proposed to survey here.[20]

In developed as well as developing countries this mostly economists' bureaucracy played and continues to play a strategic role. The bureaucracy as a whole was transformed from a mere status group to a social class principally because, in the private, in the state, and in the non-profit organizations, an enormous number of new managers were required. But, within this larger bureaucracy, the leading role played by the state bureaucracy and particularly

---

[20] In relation to Brazil, I would like to cite works by Luciano Martins (1976); Edson de Oliveira Nunes (1984); Ben Ross Schneider (1991); and Gilda P. Gouvêa (1994).

the developmental bureaucracy of economists was key to assure it political power and a relative ideological consistency.

Yet the rise to power of the developmental bureaucracy within the social-democratic state did not involve a major administrative reform. While the transition from the liberal to the liberal-democratic state was marked by civil service reform, the transition from the liberal-democratic to the social-democratic state just required the creation of the new organizational institutions involved in welfare and in the economic administration of the new state. Real reform was not undertaken because the strategy was, rather, to add new and more autonomous state agencies, like 'public foundations' and state-owned enterprises. The second major administrative reform in the history of the modern state—public management reform—would begin when the crisis of the social-democratic state pointed towards the transition to a social-liberal and republican state. One of the reasons why the social-democratic state did not last long is the fact that it was not reformed, and turned suffocated by a large and dysfunctional state bureaucracy.

6

The Crisis of the Social-Democratic State

The size of the state is continuously increasing since the late nineteenth century. If we measure it by expenditures in relation to GDP, we verify that the average expenditure was 10.7 per cent around 1870, 18.7 per cent in 1920, 27.9 per cent in 1960, 43.1 per cent in 1980, and 45.6 per cent in 1996 (Tanzi and Schuknecht 2000: 6–7). The social-democratic state was successful in promoting economic growth and social justice in the developed countries between the 1930s and the 1970s. In this last decade, however, three different though related historical processes—the neo-liberal ideological wave, the fiscal crisis of the state, and globalization—gained momentum and led the social-democratic state into crisis, opening the way for the transition to the social-liberal state. As a kind of compensatory or counter-movement, at the same moment we see the emergence of republican rights and the first indications that the new state that was emerging, besides being social-liberal, would be characterized by republican or participatory democracy. My discussion in this chapter of the crisis of the social-democratic state assumes that state intervention or regulation takes place according to a cyclical pattern. I will also show that the market-oriented reforms that came out from the crisis, although aimed at giving a greater role to market coordination of the economy, were not necessarily intended to weaken the state. On the contrary, the concomitant emergence of republican rights indicates that successful reforms strengthen it. In the next two chapters, I discuss the emergence of republican rights and globalization—both processes pointing in the direction of a stronger, not a weaker, state. I will then be ready to discuss the present transition to the social-liberal and republican state.

The market-oriented reforms starting in the 1980s were a response to the excessive and distorted growth of the state since the Great Depression. Depending on their intensity and objectives, these reforms—fiscal adjustment, privatization, trade liberalization, and public management reform—may be labelled either neo-liberal or social-liberal and republican. They will be neo-liberal reforms if they imply a radical strategy of downsizing the state apparatus; social-liberal and republican if they liberalize markets from excessive regulation while rebuilding state capacity weakened by the crisis.

The Crisis of the 1980s

The 'golden age' of capitalism—the high rates of growth that prevailed in the 1950s and 1960s—came to an end with the suspension of the convertibility of the dollar in 1971 and with the first oil shock in 1973. These were the symptoms of the downturn of a long wave, or of the end of a long cycle of state expansion. In the 20 years of this golden age, the social-democratic state achieved its zenith. The golden age, embodying the social-democratic state, must, in the words of Stephen Marglin, 'be understood as a set of inter-locking institutions', which have as historical background a macroeconomic structure, and corresponded to a given international order.[1] In the 1980s, the crisis of the state was particularly serious in eastern Europe, where a fully statist regime broke down, and in Latin America, where the developmental state, which had successfully promoted industrialization in the region since the 1930s, ended in foreign debt and fiscal crises. High inflation (if not hyper-inflation) and radical reduced growth rates were the outcome of the crisis, indicating that fiscal and balance-of-payments adjustment policies, and market-oriented institutional reforms were urgently required. In the developed countries the crisis came earlier because it was not artificially financed by foreign indebtedness, was less destructive, and was sooner overcome, given the reforms and, principally, the macroeconomic stabilization policies that were promptly adopted. The economic slowdown in these countries reduced growth rates to half of what they had been in the 20 years following the Second World War, while in the highly indebted developing countries income per capita remained quasi-stagnant since 1980.[2] Only the East Asian countries, which were able to avoid the fiscal crisis of the state, continued to grow at high rates.

In the 1990s, the first economy to resume growth was America's. There are many explanations for this, but I would suggest only three. First, it was natural that the world's hegemonic nation was the first to show signs of a new long wave of growth. Second, macroeconomic management by the Federal Reserve Bank, led by Alan Greenspan, was particularly competent. Instead of using 'conservative' (fearful rather than prudent) monetary strategy adopted by most central banks, namely, a 'comfortable' interest rate consistent with price stability, the American Fed practised the 'lowest' interest rate consistent with such stability. In this way, it maintained aggregate demand in constant tension or balance with aggregate supply, fuelling full employment, while the Europeans, with higher interest rates, maintained a comfortable (because it surely avoids inflation) but costly distance between the two aggregates, aggregate demand lagging behind aggregate supply. The main costs were unemployment and

---

[1] Marglin (1990: 60). We owe to Stephen Marglin the classic discussion of the golden age.
[2] Between 1980 and 2003 the average growth per capita income of the highly indebted countries remained below 1 per cent a year.

lower than potential growth rates. Third, the United States was the first country to overcome the fiscal crisis. Instead of deficits, in the early 1990s the Treasury started to produce budget surpluses. Yet this ten-year-long expansive cycle ended in 2000, and American society will have to face new challenges, most of them related to institutional rigidities and economic inequalities— challenges that only a state endowed with a higher degree of political legitimacy and greater tax capacity than the American state has today, will be able to effectively face.

While the economic crisis of the 1930s was a crisis of the market, the 1980s economic slowdown was a crisis of the state. In developed countries, it was the social-democratic state that was in crisis, in the developing countries it was the developmental state. Its basic endogenous causes were a fiscal crisis of the state, a crisis in the mode of state intervention, and a crisis in the bureaucratic way of managing the state. The underlying assumption is that the state, apart from ensuring property rights and contracts, has an essential role in microeconomic coordination and macroeconomic stabilization. In all countries except Britain and the United States, the state played a major role in realizing forced savings and financing capital accumulation. In all countries, including Britain and the United States, the state was strategic in promoting technological development and international competitiveness. Thus, whenever there is a significant economic crisis, we must look for its origins either in the market or in the state. The Great Depression of the 1930s stemmed from a malfunction of the market, while the Great Crisis of the 1980s arose from the crisis of the welfare state or the developmental state.

The first signs of a fiscal crisis of the state appeared as early as the 1970s. James O'Connor's classic book, *The Fiscal Crisis of the State*, dates from 1973. Already at that time O'Connor viewed the crisis as the outcome of a conflict between the working classes and the middle classes on the one hand, who demanded more and better social services or social protection from the state, and capitalists and part of the same middle class on the other, who resisted paying the required taxes. Claus Offe, who participated with O'Connor in the Capitalist State Group, advanced the analysis of the welfare state's crisis throughout the 1980s with similar arguments, although giving more relevance to the political aspect of the crisis (O'Connor 1973; Offe 1973, 1984). I wrote my basic piece on the subject in the late 1980s, discussing the cyclical character of state intervention, which is summarized in this chapter. At that time the neo-liberal ideological wave was at its peak; and I showed that, although worrying, the state reducing reforms then initiated were less harmful to continued economic growth and social justice than most commentators thought because it was part of a cycle that, after some time, would swing back (Bresser-Pereira 1988). In 1992, Pierre Rosanvallon summarized the arguments on the crisis of the welfare state (Rosanvallon 1992). A little later, in 1993, I proposed that, instead of a neo-liberal approach, the countries hurt by the crisis and the international authorities in Washington should adopt a 'fiscal crisis of the state approach', concentrating efforts on reforms rebuilding state capacity (Bresser-Pereira 1993, 1996). They should change the mode of state intervention and give more room for market coordination of the economy while conserving the state's strategic role in economic growth and social protection. They should implement market-oriented reforms, but such reforms should aim at building a stronger state, not a weaker one. In 1994, I became aware that some developed countries were beginning public management reform. Realizing the potential of this reform in strengthening state capacity, I developed a general model of state reform, which materialized in the Brazilian 1995/97 public management reform, and is theoretically developed in his book.[3] It was clear at that time that the endogenous causes of the crisis of the social-democratic state included not only the fiscal crisis and excessive intervention by the state, but also the unreformed bureaucratic way of managing it.

Different Responses to the Crisis

Reforms intended to rebuild state capacity are a response to globalization, which reduces the autonomy of national states in formulating and implementing public policy, and, more directly, a reaction to the crisis of the social-democratic state in the advanced countries and to the collapse of the developmental state in the developing ones. The new dominance of financial international markets, which is in the core of the globalization process, was facilitated by the fiscal crisis of the state, which in turn, aggravated it, opening the way for a neo-liberal, conservative wave. In the advanced countries, the response to the crisis was fast and effective. Already in the 1970s, these countries engaged in fiscal adjustment policies and, in the 1980s, in privatization and trade liberalization, which culminated with the Uruguay Round and the creation of the World Trade Organization. On the other hand, at the same time or a little later most of the countries started public management reform, or to 'reinvent government'—making it economically more efficient and politically more effective.

In contrast, developing countries, particularly those of Latin America and eastern Europe, delayed adjustment and reform, and, in the early 1980s, became trapped in a huge debt crisis, which weakened their capacity to protect their interests in the world economic arena. Macroeconomic stability and institutional reforms became imperative. Fiscal adjustment and currency devaluation were the first macroeconomic policies adopted, privatization, and trade liberalization the first economic reforms. In the 1990s, some developing

---

[3] As I noted in the preface of this book, the opportunity that I had in the first Cardoso administration to head the Ministry of Federal Administration and Reform of the State (MARE) was central for this development.

countries, like Brazil and Chile, started public management reform. The fundamental reason behind the reforms was the crisis of the state. Yet their explicit goal, as it was formulated by neo-liberal ideologues, was not to rebuild the state, but to withdraw it from all economic and even social responsibilities. Such ideas were widely current in the advanced countries, but reforms were undertaken cautiously, even in the United Kingdom where most of them originated in the Thatcher administration. Only in New Zealand did state reform take a radical vein, but in 1999 the social-democratic party, which initiated the reforms, including public management reform, regained power, and a return to the middle ground followed.

Again in contrast, in the highly indebted developing countries, particularly in countries like Chile and Argentina, reforms were radical. Social security, for instance, was privatized—something that no developed country seriously considered. Overdue trade liberalization reforms were combined with the full acceptance of property rights demanded by the rich countries, and—what was more damaging—with full financial liberalization, which, by withdrawing each country's capacity to control its exchange rate, made their economies vulnerable to volatile international financial flows. In Chile, a return to the middle ground, in 1990, after the transition to democracy, and the imposition of controls to the entrance of volatile capitals (in this case, following the example of the East Asian countries) were major factors keeping the economy under control. Different was the fate of Argentina, where the radicalism of reforms coupled with an extended overvaluation of the peso—a mistaken policy that lost the support of the US Treasury and the international agencies only when it was too late   led to deep political and economic crisis.

The Argentinian crisis of 2001 was to neo-liberal reforms what the 1982 Mexican crisis was to the developmental growth strategy. In the early 2000s, when it became clear not only in Argentina that neo-liberal reforms failed to produce all the economic gains and the electoral support that were expected, they began to come under political scrutiny. Such reforms aggravated the income concentration process, which was already under way given the acceleration of technical progress increasing the demand for skilled people and reducing the demand for the non-skilled. Privatization, which was extremely successful when the privatized industries were competitive, delivered dubious results in the case of natural monopolies, like the distribution of energy. Politicians stopped talking of downsizing the state, and remembered that governments were supposed to guarantee basic social services and welfare. It was clear that the era of the state-led model of growth was over, but people started to realize that the era of the neo-liberal alternative was also over. Between the two, it became increasingly clear that there is a mixed alternative—a social-liberal alternative—which values markets in resource allocation but reaffirms the strategic role played by the state in the social, scientific, and economic realms.

The Crisis of the State Defined

Bureaucratic organizations have a long-term tendency to grow. Thus the state apparatus, as the largest and most important bureaucratic organization, will tend to grow in the long term. Yet this tendency should not be exaggerated or made linear. The state tends to grow absolutely as societies become richer and more complex, but it does not necessarily tend to grow relative to the society. The share of public expenditures or the share of the state-controlled production of goods and services in GDP may increase, but moderately and in a cyclical and changing way. This crisis, however, is no longer the result of the chronic shortage of demand cited by Keynes. Thus, it is not a market crisis, as was the case in the 1920s and 1930s. Nor can it be attributed to the acceleration of technological progress accompanying the rise of information technology, which might cause temporary unemployment but, in fact, is the source of growth, not of the lack of it. The main cause of the great crisis of the 1980s is rather the crisis of the social-democratic and the developmental states, which stopped being factor favouring development and came, partially, to hinder it as they grew too large and were captured by private interests. Only East and South-East Asia escaped the economic crisis, precisely because they managed to avoid the fiscal crisis of the state and the debt crisis. But even there, in the 1990s economies such as those of Japan and Korea already showed signs of the exhaustion of the state-led development strategy.

The crisis of the social-democratic state that I refer to is not a vague concept. On the contrary, it has a specific meaning. The state enters into a fiscal crisis as it loses public credit while its capacity to generate public savings diminishes or even disappears: public savings (the difference between public revenues and public consumption, including interest), which used to be positive, become negative.[4] Consequently, the state's legislative and regulatory capacity falls in proportion to the severity of the fiscal crisis.

The crisis of the 1930s was a crisis of the market—a market that was not able to assure employment and an even distribution of income. Hence, when Keynesian macroeconomic policies and ideas proposing indicative economic planning appeared in the 1930s, they were immediately adopted and led to a considerable improvement in the performance of the national economies. In the 1950s, the idea of a state with a strategic role in promoting technical progress and capital accumulation was commonplace, together with the idea that it was responsible for ensuring a reasonable income distribution. However, these successes led to an explosive growth of the state not only in the field of regulation but also in the social and productive spheres. In order

---

[4] The concept of public savings (public revenues less public consumption) is seldom utilized but is essential to understand the fiscal crisis of the state. Instead, conventional economics uses the concept of the budget deficit, which is also important but treats equally public consumption and public investment.

to finance this growth, the tax burden, which accounted for around 10 per cent of GDP at the beginning of the century, grew to 30–60 per cent; the number of civil servants whose tasks were unrelated to the exclusive activities of the state increased substantially; and the number and size of state-owned enterprises was multiplied many times. The state became not only social but substantially more bureaucratic than it was before, in so far as, with the purpose of promoting social welfare, technical and scientific growth, and economic development, it directly hired workers such as teachers, doctors, nurses, social workers, artists, engineers, scientists, and so on as if they were civil servants.

When a system or an organization grows, distortions soon emerge. State transfers were diverted from legitimate objectives to meet the special interests of businessmen, middle-class groups, and public bureaucrats. Rent-seeking became increasingly widespread as economic agents tried to capture the public patrimony—the *res publica*. State-owned enterprises, which at first had been a powerful mechanism for achieving forced savings to the extent that they made monopolistic profits and reinvested them, soon saw this role wane, and at the same time their performance proved often to be inefficient, as they were increasingly subject to bureaucratic control.

Bureaucratic public administration, which had proved effective in fighting corruption and nepotism in the small liberal state, was now revealed as highly inefficient in directly providing the major social and scientific services. Classic bureaucracy is suited to perform the exclusive activities of the state, but proved to be inefficient in providing the services that the citizen-customers started to demand in the twentieth century. The ensuing crisis led governments in advanced countries to engage in public management reform, while the developing countries, except those of Asia, adopted merely state-cutting reforms under the auspices of World Bank and IMF.

First, in the early 1980s, the crisis of the state took the form of a fiscal crisis. In most developing countries, it also assumed the form of a foreign debt crisis. As public savings (tax revenues less consumption expenditures) became negative, the state lost financial autonomy and became economically immobile, incapable of promoting capital accumulation. Consequently, its managerial limitations became more evident. The crisis of governance, which in extreme cases took on the form of hyperinflationary episodes, became all-embracing: the state was no longer an agent of development but an obstacle to it. Yet we should not view this crisis as 'definitive'. In the next section I will argue that this crisis does not indicate that the downsizing process, which begins in the 1980s, is a long and irreversible trend. On the contrary, it is a cyclical crisis, which already shows signs of swinging back. The institutional, market-oriented, reforms starting in the 1980s were and still are a response to this cyclical crisis, as long as they involved strengthening state capacity.

The crisis of the social democratic state is not only fiscal: it includes a crisis of the mode of state intervention—particularly the direct provision of social services by the state—and a crisis of the bureaucratic way of managing government. These three factors are endogenous, since they are related to the cyclical nature of state intervention. There is, however, an exogenous cause—the globalization process—that I will discuss in Chapter 7.

The Cycles of the State

The size of state apparatus and the degree of state regulation expand and contract cyclically; in each new cycle the mode of state intervention changes. For a while, state regulation increases, the state assumes an increasing role in coordinating the economic system, and the size of the state, as measured by the tax burden in relation to GDP, increases. We can distinguish three major areas of state regulation: micro-allocation of resources, macroeconomic policies defining the exchange rate and the interest rate that will influence the level of savings and investments, and micro-macro determination of income distribution among social classes and among sectors of the economy. In these three areas, the state apparatus increases and regulation advances because it is successful, because the state is performing roles that markets are either unable to perform or inefficient in doing so. It increases because it responds in an effective way to the demands of society. Yet as state intervention increases, be it in terms of its share in GDP or in terms of the degree of regulation of the economy, regulation tends to become excessive and dysfunctional. The basic symptoms indicating that the expansion of the state went too far are excess regulation hindering instead of stimulating economic activity, huge public deficits leading to a large public debt, and particularly negative public savings, which have as joint consequences macroeconomic instability, and diminished rates of growth. In this moment, the inefficiency of a self-centred bureaucratic civil service becomes apparent, while criticism of state intervention rises. This is the moment when the cycle of state expansion turns down, and privatization, deregulation, and other market oriented reforms surface become a must.

This hypothesis of the cyclical nature of state intervention conflicts both with static theories, which assume a given level of state intervention as ideal, and with historical theories, which claim a long-term tendency towards the nationalization of the large business enterprises. For neo-liberals, the ideal level of state intervention is very low; for statists, it is very high. Pragmatists hold an intermediate position. Although I am closer to the pragmatists, I would say that these three positions are misleading as long as they assume the existence of an 'ideal' or 'optimum' relation between market and state control. My hypothesis is that this ideal relation will necessarily vary historically and according to the cycles of state intervention.

Although a historical tendency can be traced showing increasing state intervention, I propose that this tendency is limited and not linear. It is implicit in Marx and explicitly developed by Adolph Wagner, according to whom, as per capita income increases, nations will spend a larger part of their national product through government. Wagner presents several reasons for that increase: the increasing complexity of legal relationships, a rise in social conflicts due to the increasing density of urban areas, the insufficiency of private savings for investments requiring large sums of capital, increasing need for investment in the production of goods whose benefits cannot be fully appropriated to the private investor (thus, whose production involves externalities, in modern terminology), and the need to regulate private monopolies (Wagner 1893; Wildavsky 1985). Marxist economists explain state growth as a counter-tendency to the law of the falling rate of profit. The state nationalizes the low-profit industries in order to assure a satisfactory average rate of profit for the private sector. Keynesians emphasize the need for state regulation to complement the market's coordinating role and to solve the chronic insufficiency of demand. Social democrats stress welfare protection and the income-distributing role of the state.

Public choice theory explains the growth of the state in terms of the demands of special interest groups. Mueller and Murrell (1985: 31) argue that the assumption behind Wagner's law is that the income elasticity of the demand for public goods exceeds the income elasticity of its demand for private goods. This leads to state growth because 'the formation of bargains between parties and interest groups lead to an increase in government size'. Denis Mueller (1987) enumerates five basic explanations for state growth: the demand of public goods, the distribution of income, the inducement of interest groups, the interests of the state bureaucracy, and fiscal illusion about the true size of the state. I would say that all these reasons or explanations are compelling. The statistical evidence supporting Wagner's thesis is overwhelming. Thomas Borcherding, for instance, verified that in the United States government expenditures (federal, State, and local) increased from 7.7 per cent to 21.4 per cent of GDP from 1902 to 1933, decreased to 20.4 per cent of GNP up to 1940, and then increased steadily, reaching 35 per cent of GNP in 1978. In Germany, total public expenditures as a proportion of GDP increased steadily from 15.7 per cent to 42.5 per cent of GDP from 1913 to 1969. In the OECD countries, general government expenditures as a percentage of GDP increased from 26.3 per cent (unweighted average) in 1960 to 47.0 per cent in 1982.[5] But neither the theoretical arguments nor the empirical evidence can be taken as definitive. Wagner wrote his work in Germany at the end of last century, when the state had assumed a decisive role in promoting Germany's late industrialization. However, after its industrial take-off, German state intervention followed a pattern similar to other latecomers in the industrialization process: it diminished in the productive and financial areas while increasing in the regulatory and welfare realm.

---

[5] Borcherding (1985: 361); Ernest Mandel (1972: 488); Saunders and Klau (1985).

There are economic and political limits to the growth of the state. The relations between state and society, as well as between state and market, are not arbitrary. These are the two mechanisms that respond for the coordination of an economic system. Although they are not parallel institutions, it is possible that they also have complementary roles in the coordination of the economy. State and market are supposed to perform such roles in a balanced way. A state that grows too much in relation to the market will sooner or later have to limit its expansion. The historical process of relative reduction of the economic role of the state, initiated in the mid-1970s, was just a phase in the cyclical pattern of state intervention. The slowdown of the capitalist economies which then took place is in part a consequence of the distortions and inefficiencies provoked by the previous growth of the state. As these distortions were perceived by society, at the same time as globalization implied increased competition among countries, a conservative and ultra-liberal ideological wave was in place. State failures were made responsible for all problems, market failures were dismissed. Social expenditures should be severely curtailed, institutions should be reformed: trade liberalization, privatization, and labour deregulation became central concerns. Such reforms would be a necessary condition for nation-states being able to compete internationally. The assumption was that individuals or families are able to protect themselves. The objective was to reduce the state to a minimum: to eliminate or substantially reduce the welfare state. Yet, despite the strength of the ultra-liberal wave and the fact that many market-oriented reforms were designed and implemented, particularly trade liberalization, no reduction in social expenditures occurred. On the contrary, they increased. This is particularly clear in the OECD countries. In the beginning of the 1980s social expenditures were around 20 per cent of GDP; in the early 2000s, 24 per cent. On the other hand, confirming the hypothesis that state intervention follows a cyclical pattern, after the mid-1990s the ultra-liberal wave lost momentum.[6] The expected 'increased flexibility' of social rights mostly failed, except with unions being more open to part-time jobs and wage reductions in times of crisis. One of the few tenets of the ultra-liberal wave related to social rights which proved durable was its critique of labour tenure. Yet it became increasingly clear that social-democratic countries, where a developed welfare system was in force, conferred on their business enterprises greater freedom in discharging employees, as long as lay-offs were less threatening because the unemployment insurance system and the retraining and reallocation system effectively assisted them. The ultra-liberal wave had been successful in trimming the state's excesses, not in replacing the state's social roles with the market. Instead of reducing the state to a minimum, voters demanded from

---

[6] I presented the hypothesis that the growth of the state follows a cyclical pattern to the symposium 'Democratizing the Economy', Wilson Center and University of São Paulo (Bresser-Pereira 1988). A definitive English version of the paper was published in *World Development* in 1993.

politicians that the state performed its classic role of maintaining public order and security, and delivered the social services that the social-democratic state used to deliver. The novelty was that the state should perform its functions efficiently. The era of fiscal adjustment, trade liberalization, and privatization was over. What had to be done in these areas had been done. Now, efficient delivery of public services was the challenge. Now, the era of public management reform had finally come of age. A new cycle of the state was beginning.

7

The Global System and the State

We saw in Chapter 6 that the crisis of the state was the outcome of an endogenous factor (the cyclical character of state intervention) and of an exogenous one (globalization). Globalization is a historical economic process through which capitalist markets, particularly financial markets, became global, and a political process which created a complex system of international institutions and a global civil society. Globalization is creating a new system of international relations based on competition among nations through their business enterprises. More than that, it is creating a global system, an economic and political system whose central institutions, besides the classic nation-states, are the United Nations and the legal system built around it. In this system, power and resources remain highly unevenly distributed among nations and individuals, conflict between interests remains the rule, but the era of the classical balance of power diplomacy is over: now we have what I propose to call 'globalization's politics'.[1] While in the balance of powers diplomacy, which existed following the formation of the modern state and particularly following the Westphalia treaties, major nation-states disputed territories and viewed each other as enemies to be threatened with wars, in the new global system countries are economic adversaries competing in world markets. These international markets and all other social and cultural international relations are regulated according to a complex political process, in which argumentation and compromise are complemented with threats, although the latter are acquiring an increasingly economic rather than military character.

Globalization imposed limits to the autonomy of the nation-states in framing social and economic policies, but these limits are not as extensive as the proponents of what I call 'globalist' ideology suggests. Arising from a dramatic reduction in the costs of international transportation and, principally, of communications, globalization led to a huge increase of world trade, international financing, and direct investments by multinational corporations. It also meant a rise in international competition to undreamed-of levels and

---

[1] Bresser-Pereira (2002c). Countries may still use military threats, the United States particularly, but they have power only over small countries, and even in this case outcomes may turn detrimental to the aggressor, as it was the case of the Iraq 2003 war.

a reorganization of production at a worldwide level sponsored by the multi-national corporations. The market gained much more space at a worldwide level and transformed international competitiveness into a necessary condition for the survival of the economic development in each country. The consequences were, as it is always the case when the market prevails, better resource allocation and increased productive efficiency. On the other hand, there was a relative loss of autonomy by the state: its ability to protect the economy from international competition and, what is worse, from international financial flows, was hampered. Since markets always act in favour of the strongest, income concentration was greater than before, both among countries and among citizens of a single country. Among countries, because the more capable are in a better position to impose its interests on the weaker. This became particularly clear when the financial opening promoted by the rich country in the early 1990s caused among the intermediate developing countries a succession of balance of payment crises. Income concentration was also greater among the citizens of each country because, with the surge of technical progress, the demand for the most efficient and better educated rose more rapidly than that for the less educated. In this case, however, the rich countries were in a weaker position: given trade liberalization that came with globalization, the workers in poor countries had one advantage: since their wages were considerably lower, developing countries' exports to developed countries soared, thus depressing the wages of less skilled workers in developed countries. Thus, globalization exerted a twofold pressure on the state. On the one hand, it weakened the state's ability to protect its own citizens. On the other hand, such new challenges made the role of the state more strategic: it indicated that the democratic state had to be more effective and more efficient in carrying out the tasks that citizens required from it.

Analysts often identify globalization with an increasing international integration of economic activity under multinational enterprises, but such integration, although real, has been exaggerated.[2] The new information technology was the central underlying change. It reduced the costs and increased the speed of communications, enabling financial markets to work internationally in real time, and an international civil society to mobilize people for political causes. Its proponents use globalization as an ideology, while its adversaries criticize it as such. Yet to see globalization as an ideology is just wrong. The issue is not to be for or against globalization, but to understand its consequences and to try to develop policies that profit from the opportunities that it offers, while guarding against the threats that unrestrained markets may imply. Globalization played its part in leading the social-democratic state into crisis. To be sure, it made nation-states more interdependent. In this

---

² Bob Sutcliffe and Andrew Glyn (1999: 120). They show, for instance, that foreign direct investment has been increasing, but that in 1995 it corresponded respectively to only 4.4% and 8.2% of the domestic investment in developed and developing countries.

chapter, I do not intend to review globalization, but to show that, if it initially propelled the neo-liberal wave and strengthened market allocation of resources, as a trade-off it ended in requiring a stronger and more strategic state rather than a weaker one.

The Global System and 'Globalism'

It is no mere coincidence that the word 'globalization' gained currency after the Soviet Union's collapse and China's overture to the world and to capitalism. These were the two major countries that remained relatively closed to global markets. As soon as they were opened, the global system became a new definitive historical fact, while wars among major capitalist countries aiming at defining national markets or opening international ones, such as had characterized balance-of-powers diplomacy, lost meaning. On the other hand, the collapse of the Soviet Union completed the Second World War's job of defining most national frontiers. For centuries, war was the major tool of national affirmation, but now we have to look for other instruments and different behaviours if we expect to understand the emerging new patterns of international relations among nation-states. As Rawls observes, 'the crucial fact for the problem of war is that constitutional democratic societies do not go to war with one another' (Rawls, 1999: 8). The era of balance-of-power diplomacy is over. Economic competition, rather than threats of war, will dominate international relations. The common assertion that modern democracies do not wage unjust wars is false; what is new is that when they get involved in this kind of war they rather incur losses than reap gains. Wars in the world that is emerging out of globalization will have a limited scope; they will make sense for the major nations only as police wars to stop local wars (Bresser-Pereira, 2002c).

The configuration of global capitalism, or of the new global system, took centuries. It was marked not only by technological change and economic growth but also by the affirmation of two basic and complementary institutions: the nation-state and free national markets. After the 1930s Great Depression, the social-democratic state was the new capitalist pattern. For some time, there was a dispute between economic planning and Keynesian economic policies, but the latter proved to be more sensible and durable. Economic growth, which gained full historical significance in the nineteenth century, after the first capitalist revolutions in England, the United States, and France, achieved momentum in the twentieth century. With the social-democratic state, cyclical crises continued to characterize capitalist development, but crises ceased to have devastating economic consequences. Yet a longer cycle—the cycle of state intervention—manifested itself in the mid-1970s, given a previously excessive and distorted growth of the state organization. Concurrently, the reduction in transportation and communication costs and the dramatic increase in the speed of communications led world markets to grow at a faster pace than nation-states' GDPs. This fact, coupled with the explosive rise of global financial markets and with the emergence of an increasingly strong net of international relations, not only among nations but also among individuals, firms, associations, and NGOs, led to globalization. Larger and even medium-sized business enterprises turned multinational. Today, 53,000 multinationals and their 400,000 suppliers and distributors employ around 200 million workers out of a total world workforce of around 2 billion. Yet they represent one-third of total production and two-thirds of total world trade. Multinationals' direct investments and intense intra-firm trade made production effectively global. Capital flows of around $US2 trillion dollars a day completed the dramatic change in economic relations among nation-states.

Today, we see the effective dominance of global markets. Trading with goods, services, technology, money and credit, and making direct investments abroad are not the only games in town but they are the ones that really count. All sorts of international rules protect markets, making them open and increasingly secure. Only labour markets have not yet turned global, although the strong immigration flows into rich countries point in this direction. Several new historical circumstances contributed to globalization. On the the one hand, there was the acceleration of technical progress, the information technology revolution, and the reduction in transportation costs; on the other hand, the end of the cold war, growing pressure for trade liberalization coming from the dominant American economy, and, finally, the increasing acceptance of the idea that international trade may be—although not necessarily—a win-win game. Combined, these six factors changed the world in the last quarter of the twentieth century.

Globalization involves the worldwide spread of capitalism; it comprehends a set of economic relations, institutions, and ideologies that have as a central characteristic the opening of commercial and financial markets all over the world. Boaventura de Souza Santos, discussing the problem, distinguishes two theories about globalization: one, based on the work of Immanuel Wallerstein, attributes to it a paradigmatic change; the other, based on the French regulation theory, views it as a crisis of the ongoing regime of accumulation and mode of regulation.[3] The distinction is interesting, especially because it gives the required relevance to the change that is taking place, shunning some interpretations that, based on the fact that international markets were already particularly open in late nineteenth century, try to downgrade the process. Referring to the first theory, Souza Santos observes that 'according to the issues and circumstances, the process of globalization may be seen either as

---

[3] Souza Santos (1995*b*). For the referred contributions, see Wallerstein (1979, 1991, 1995); Aglietta, (1979); Boyer (1990).

highly destructive of irreplaceable identities and equilibria, or as the propitious inauguration of a new era of global or even cosmic solidarity' (Souza Santos 1995*b*: 260). Both alternatives are radically opposite and unlikely to happen, but they underline the dimension of the change that is taking place.

The changes behind globalization lasted the entire twentieth century, but they became apparent only in the last three decades. Essentially, they involved the conclusion of the more decisive phenomenon of modern times: the capitalist revolution. This revolution brought a new form of surplus appropriation, and required open markets to make capital accumulation viable. For centuries, since it began, the capitalist world was fighting constantly for the definition of frontiers and the opening of markets. Globalization completed this historical process in the second half of the twentieth century. Its outcome was the global system, or the capitalist global system. This system is woven by economic, social, cultural, political, and legal relations. The United States is the hegemon in this system, but it is far from all-powerful. It is hegemonic in economic and military terms, but that is about all. All attempts to associate such relative hegemony with previous empires, including the British Empire, are preposterous. Other nation-states conserve sizeable power at regional and even international levels. The second major power-centre in today's world, the United Nations, does not have economic or military power, but has the legitimacy derived from multilateral law and the international policy system. It is a pure outcome of the global system.

Negri and Hardt analyse this new global system perspicaciously and innovatively, but give it a misleading denomination, 'Empire'. They say: 'Empire is the political subject that effectively regulates the global exchanges, the sovereign power that governs the world . . . Sovereignty has mistaken a new form, composed of a series of national and supranational organisms united under a single logic rule. This global form of sovereignty is what we call Empire'.[4] Thomas Friedman sees globalization similarly, as the new international system: 'globalization is not the only thing influencing events in the world today, but to the extent that there is a North Star and a world wide shaping force, it is this system. What is new is the system; what is old is power politics, chaos, clashing civilizations and liberalism' (Friedman, 2000: xxi). The authors quoted could not be further apart in ideological and methodological terms, but it is significant how they reach a similar general conclusion: a new global system governs the world.

My central disagreement with the majority of the analysts of globalization, from the left or the right, is related to the conventional idea that nation-states

---

[4] Negri and Hardt (2000). The expression is misleading because 'empire' does not mean what the dictionaries say about this word, but the global system to which I am referring. Although acknowledging the hegemonic role played by the United States in the world, they correctly do not identify it as a classic empire. The era of empires is over. It was the Bush administration that made this equivocal identification, and waged a war against Iraq with disastrous consequences for the country he governs.

have seriously lost autonomy in this global system. I accept the 'global governance approach', which posits that the principal units of analysis are 'global, regional or transnational systems of authoritative rule-making and implementation' (Held and McGrew 2002: 9), but just as a conception of world politics, not as the view that nation-states have lost relevance within their frontiers. Countries become more interdependent, but national governments retain considerable autonomy to take decisions regarding economic and the social life. And they remain the key actors in international life. In economic terms, the global system may be defined as generalized competition among nation-states through their business enterprises. If one believes that this definition is too strong, we offer another: the global system is generalized competition for world markets among business enterprises, supported by their respective nation-states. Once accepted, either of these two definitions, which everyday experience corroborates, has an obvious consequence: nation-states become more interdependent but more, not less, strategic.

Globalization should be clearly distinguished from 'globalism'. Globalization is an economic and technological fact with a major political consequence—it gave rises to the Global System—while 'globalism' is just one of its political consequences. Globalism is an ideology coming from the centre of the system that asserts, first, that there is today an international community that is independent of nation-states, and, second, that the nation-states have lost the autonomy to define their national policies, having no alternative but to follow the rules and constraints imposed 'naturally' by global markets. This kind of ideology has an origin in the multinational corporations. Economic globalization was originally the outcome of the rise in these corporations of a large and ever increasing group of international business executives. As Barnett and Müller observe in their classical book on the multinational corporations, 'the men who run the global corporations are the first in history with the organization, technology, money, and ideology to make a credible try at managing the world as an integrated unit'.[5] Barnett and Müller viewed the problem critically. Other authors, more directly related with the multinational corporations, like Kenich Ohmae, wrote important books where the titles already suggest their commitment with the globalist approach: *Triad Power—The Coming Shape of Global Competition*, and *The Borderless World*.[6] Although there is grain of truth in what is claimed, since nation-states are more interdependent than they were before, in fact this is an ideology that supports the interests of multinational corporations and of the major countries in which they have headquarters. The states existing in each national state, and

---

[5] Barnett and Müller, 1974: 13.

[6] Ohmae (1985, 1990). It is interesting to observe that Kenichi Ohmae is associated with McKinsey and Co., one of the few effectively multinational corporations in the world. It is multinational because, being a firm of consultants, it is not a 'capital's corporation' but a 'managers' corporation': a business enterprise that depends wholly on its human resources.

so, the nation-state itself remains powerful, conserving a sizable degree of independence for collecting taxes, granting citizenship rights, defining law and public policies.

In fact, globalization makes nation-states more strategic. Although large business enterprises operating in several countries came to be called 'multinationals', they are effectively transnationals. With rare exceptions, each one knows which government to ask for help when facing international problems, and each government knows its enterprises. Look, for instance, at the conflicts at the World Trade Organization. International business enterprises are often in conflict, but ambassadors in Geneva have no doubt which enterprise they are supposed to back. Take another example, China, and the enormous economic growth this country is experiencing. In a book edited by Peter Berger and Samuel Huntington, the Chinese author concludes his analysis of the Chinese way of facing globalization with the following words:

The Chinese case demonstrates a new type of cultural globalization: a managed process in which the state plays a leading role, and the elite and the populace work together to actively claim ownership of the emergent global culture. (Yan, 2002: 44)

Global Markets Require Strong States

The endogenous crisis of the social-democratic state and globalization led ultra-liberal analysts to predict and preach the reduction of the state to a minimum. Yet this proposition advanced only modestly, because strong markets and a healthy economy require a strong state, an effective regime in which political power is legitimized and property rights and contracts honoured. Globalization, to move forwards, demands stronger, not weaker, nation-states. The balance between state and market coordination may follow a cyclical pattern, as I have suggested before (Bresser-Pereira 1988), but it is not difficult to see that the countries with more free and active markets are also those with more effective state agencies and state institutions. Since the late 1990s, when the neo-liberal ideological wave lost momentum, this fact began to become evident. After September 11 2001, however, it gained full significance. It is in moments of crisis that the importance of state institutions and organizations becomes apparent.

In the United States, change was more evident. Confidence in politicians, which had been falling since the 1960s, returned powerfully. It is in times of crisis that people remember how important government is. According to public opinion surveys starting in 1958, confidence in politicians fell consistently until 1980, recovered partially in the early 1980s, to fall again until 1994 (Norris 1999: 6). After the events of September 11, however, it returned to 1960s levels.[7] Analysts have interpreted this fall in confidence as a crisis of

---

[7] *The Economist*, 12 January 2002, based on University of Michigan and Gallup data.

democracy. Yet Pipa Norris, surveying a large literature on the subject, came to a different conclusion in her edited book *Critical Citizens*. She and the research group use David Easton's analytic framework distinguishing between support for the political community, for the regime (which the research group subdivided into regime principles, performance, and institutions), and for the political actors (Easton 1965), and conclude that, while public support for the political community and for regime principles remained high, support for regime institutions, regime performance, and for politicians declined, suggesting the emergence of 'critical citizens'. In other words, support for the democratic state remained high, but it fell for government performance. In her words: 'There has been an erosion of public support for the core institutions of representative government, including parties and parliaments, in recent decades . . . but not for democratic values and principles' (Norris, 1999: 21, 27). I will return to the concept of critical citizen when discussing state building from a republican perspective. The essential point to consider here is that a strong state, a strong political regime is a central characteristic of the modern and more advanced democracies. Citizens may and should be highly critical of politicians and of the organizational institutions in which they act, but may respect the rule of law and basic democratic principles. In the rich countries there is no crisis in this respect, except probably in the United States, whose basic democratic institutions are not changing as fast as the economy and society, and have been suffering from the stress of being the hegemonic economic and military power.[8]

If we look carefully into the market-oriented reforms that have taken place since the 1980s, it appears that the more successful ones were able not only to liberalize markets but also to increase government capacity and to strengthen state institutions. This was the rule in the developed countries. In Britain, for instance, we may disagree with Thatcher's reforms, but we have to admit that they did not weaken the British state; on the contrary, they made it stronger, more able to direct collective action towards political objectives.

In developing countries, however, this was not always true, as the case of Argentina demonstrates. This country followed or tried to follow all the guidelines coming from Washington and New York, and yet in 2002 its efforts ended in disaster. Privatization was chaotic and ruinous, but we can say that this was a problem of implementation, not of conception. In the case of macroeconomic policy, however, this excuse cannot be applied. Given an obviously overvalued currency, badly needed fiscal adjustment proved unfeasible because expenditure cuts were not accompanied by GDP growth and

---

[8] An indication of such crisis in the US became apparent after the September 11 events. With the alleged aim of fighting terrorism, some civil rights were eliminated. *The Economist* (8 December 2001), reviewing the Bush administration's acts involving the secret detention of more than 600 foreigners, suspension of the attorney–client right to secrecy, racial profiling, extended powers of government surveillance, and trial by special military tribunal, admits that these were 'disturbing' executive decisions, although 'no, not quite a dictatorship'.

increased revenues, as long as business enterprises showed no confidence in investing or salaried workers in consuming. The IMF, heading what I called the Second Washington Consensus—a disastrous economic strategy based on capital-account liberalization and 'growth with foreign savings' that Washington authorities adopted in the 1990s in relation to developing countries—demanded severe fiscal adjustment from Argentina, but accepted gladly the peso's overvaluation (Bresser-Pereira and Nakano 2002). In doing so, it linked a hard budget constraint to a soft current account constraint. Thus poorly designed reforms and fiscal adjustment, coupled with incompetent macroeconomic policies, weakened the Argentinian state, leading the country into a severe economic and political crisis.

Argentina's crisis called attention to the need for stronger state institutions and organization. The political regime must be legitimized by citizens, the law must be respected, and the state apparatus must be competent, fiscally and administratively. Nation-states remain the basic political unit that warrants collective interests and citizenship. Globalization makes nation-states more interdependent, not weaker. An ordered or secure globalization requires technically competent state organizations and politically strong, legitimate, and effective nation-states. Citizens require a strong state to protect their rights, to assure their security: not only personal and political security but also the security arising from a good educational system, an effective health care system, a minimum income system, and a pension system. Markets assure relatively efficient resource allocation, but do not protect citizens. Global markets and generalized competition make insecurity still more manifest. To achieve the security required, citizens have no alternative but to organize collective action in the form of a strong democratic state—a state that in the twenty-first century will be social-liberal and republican.

8

The Emergence of Republican Rights

We saw in the preceding chapters that the excessive and distorted growth of the state organization has provoked, in the 1980s, the crisis of the social-democratic state and the onset of the neo-liberal wave. Soon, however, the successive financial crises of the 1990s, coupled with the historical recognition of republican rights and the need to protect the *res publica*, represented a check on this ideological process. More broadly, during the whole twentieth century, two major new historical facts—globalization and democracy—were shaping the world to come. We may define this century in many ways, but there is little doubt that the twentieth century was the century of democracy and of globalization. In the previous chapters, I discussed the rise of the democratic state, the endogenous and cyclical crisis state, and the challenge to the state represented by the emergence of a global system. In this chapter I return to the political discussion and discuss the emergence of republican rights within contemporary democracies.

The emergence of republican rights took place while we observed a renewal of republicanism, or of republican ideals, expressed in the ideas of political philosophers and theorists, and founded on an effective political practice of citizens organized in civil society. I understand republican rights as the right all citizens have to the public use of the *res publica*—of the public patrimony— including the flow of resources involved in the revenues of the state and of public non-state organizations.[1] When citizens in modern democracies defend the public patrimony against the attempts of powerful individuals to capture it, they are exercising their republican rights. In the twentieth century, when the *res publica* became large, representing between a third and a half of all nations' income, the greed of individuals and groups for it has increased, and its protection has become historically imperative. Concomitantly, the increasing abuse of the environment by the industrial societies required that this other basic form of public patrimony was protected. This same century, however, was also the century of democracy and citizenship affirmation all

---

[1] I first developed the concept of republican rights in 1997, in a paper published in Portuguese, which I wrote as a theoretical foundation for the 1995 Brazilian Public Management Reform. A revised version is now available in English (Bresser-Pereira 2002*a*).

over the world. The resistance to these forms of private capture of the public patrimony and the rise of the idea of the republican rights was facilitated by a democratic polity in which the tensions between the private and the public realms, and between republican, liberal, and socialist values, are resolved.

Liberal values stressed civil rights; democratic values enshrined political rights; socialism stressed social rights. Republican ideals preceded liberal ones, as they had their origin in the Roman republic and in the northern Italian city-republics of the fourteenth and fifteenth centuries. Originally, they gave priority to citizens' duties, to their civic virtues, not their rights. Now, in recent times, a new republicanism has emerged to show that the condition for the success of the entire citizens' rights enterprise is to combine the liberal and the socialist approach to the republican. Protecting the public patrimony is not a new historical fact. It became a major concern from the moment that the public patrimony became clearly distinguished from the monarch's figure. A major historical response to this concern in the nineteenth century was civil service reform and the emergence of a professional bureaucracy. In the late twentieth century, democracy became the dominant political regime, and new tools emerged for the defence of the *res publica*, among which I try to demonstrate that public management reform has a special role.

The emergence of republican rights and the consolidation of democracy as the dominant political regime are part of a same historical process. Democracy has changed into 'a universal value', demanding from citizens a growing concern over public matters.[2] While the struggle for human rights—civil, political and social rights—gained new prominence in the second half of the twentieth century, a profusion of new rights appeared. Jurists spoke about 'diffuse interests' and 'diffuse rights', United Nations' documents referred to 'third generation rights', which include rights to solidarity, peace, and economic development. Of these diffuse interests or third-generation rights, some became more specific as the social movements behind them gained strength and the possibility of drafting these rights into law became realistic.[3] However, as Bobbio observes, these rights 'constitute a category which is still too vague and heterogeneous' (Bobbio 1992: xiv). They are aspirations rather than rights. This is not the case with republican rights. They can be transformed into law, they may be enforced. Just as citizens have the right to liberty and property (civil rights), the right to vote and to be elected (political rights), and the right to work, education, health care, and a minimum income (social rights), they also have the right that the *res publica* remain at the service of everyone instead of being captured by private interests (republican rights).

---

[2] Carlos Nelson Coutinho (1980). The title of his classic 1980 book on democracy is *Democracia como um Valor Universal*.

[3] The first-generation rights would be civil and political rights, and those of the second generation, social rights.

The concern about protecting the *res publica* became dominant only in the last quarter of the twentieth century. During the 1970s, a progressive Brazilian political scientist, Luciano Martins, for the first time to my knowledge, used the expression 'privatization of the state' to convey its capture by private interests (Martins 1978). Concurrently, Anne Krueger, a distinguished conservative economist in the United States, defined 'rent-seeking' as the search for extra-market revenues through the control of the government (Krueger 1974). The two authors were referring to the same problem and manifested the same concern: the need to protect the *res publica* against the greed of powerful individuals and groups. As the protection of the republican rights became a dominant theme, the need to 're-found the republic' also became clearer. It was necessary to reform the state, making government officers more accountable and limiting the greed of rent-seeking groups. Reforming the state, protecting the public patrimony, making government officials more efficient and accountable became central problems in political science. Since the 1980s, globalization and the fiscal crisis of the state had made institutional reform a new priority. Checks and balances, bureaucratic public administration, and democracy itself—the main institutions that are supposed to protect public patrimony—had to change: checks and balances should be complemented by administrative competition to be more effective; bureaucratic public administration should be changed into public management to become more efficient; democracy should make politicians more accountable and citizens more participatory. In this re-foundation or rebuilding process, one thing seems to have become clear: the protection of republican rights is an essential task for policymakers and reformers. Yet the protection of the *res publica* requires a precise conceptualization of these new rights emerging in history.

Republican Rights

It is difficult to define republican rights in legal terms. Thus, jurists prudently speak of interests instead of rights, and qualify them as 'diffuse'. They also refer to them as 'collective rights', or to 'subjective public rights', an expression that designates all the rights of individuals in relation to the state: rights that spell out what the state must not do (especially curtailing freedom) or must do (especially guaranteeing the social rights). Republican rights could be included in this category, but defining them in this way would excessively enlarge the concept, and in the end invert their meaning. When I refer to republican rights, I do not mean the rights of the citizen against the state— such as civil rights—but the rights of the citizens of a given state against the individuals or groups who want to capture the public patrimony.

There are three fundamental republican rights: to the environmental patrimony, to the nation's cultural patrimony, and to the economic public patrimony that the state apparatus controls. The threats to the environment and to the nation's artistic and historical patrimony are well known. In the case of the economic public patrimony, we also have obvious threats, such as corruption and nepotism, but other threats like economic subsidies or the payment of salaries to certain civil servants inconsistent with their modest contribution, are subtler and often difficult to identify.

Although based on general, if not universal, moral principles, republican rights emerge in order to answer concrete problems of modern societies. The systematic defence of the historical-cultural patrimony of nations is an enterprise that dates from the first half of the twentieth century. Awareness of the existence of rights over the historical-cultural patrimony has gradually been gaining force, perhaps as a way to assert national identities in an era of globalization, but it has never assumed a dramatic or urgent character. The rights to the public environment emerged more recently. Such rights gained universal acknowledgement after the United Nations' 1992 Stockholm summit. Since then, the defence of the environment, originally promoted by left-wing groups, has become a general concern. The concern with such republican rights is historically a new phenomenon, but the defence of the *res publica* was always a central concern. Penal law provides for penalties for those who usurp the public patrimony in a corrupt or illegal manner. Administrative law emerges with civil service reform to defend the public patrimony against corruption and nepotism. Yet republican rights related to the economic patrimony gained their status as a separate and distinct set of rights only in the last quarter of the twentieth century. The most general reason for this new concern with public patrimony or the *res publica* is the huge growth of the state in that century, making the nation's economic patrimony strategic, and the great interest in the protecting environmental patrimony, threatened as it is by unrestrained industrialization.

The attacks on the public economic patrimony may take several forms. First, there are the classic forms of violence against the public thing: corruption, nepotism, and tax evasion. In the second place, there are resulting gains of unfounded (but victorious) lawsuits against the state.[4] Finally, there are the 'modern' and badly defined forms of violence exercised against the *res publica*: improper transfers or subsidies that assume several forms depending on the beneficiaries. Economic policies may provide certain companies or individuals with an undue and excessive range of state benefits—subsidies, fiscal waivers, and protection from competition—without economic justification. Social policies often provide benefits to, and protect the social status of, individuals and groups, mainly members of the middle class, who hold greater

---

[4] Obviously, it is not easy to distinguish the 'unfair lawsuits against the state'. They are often the result of their author's bad faith, and they succeed only if the lawyer, and also judge who is supposed to defend the state are corrupt. Law suits with some combination of these three elements are common in societies in which the *res publica* is poorly protected.

voting power.[5] Besides corruption, tax evasion is a form of violence that has been included in criminal law in civilized countries.[6] The law usually does not regard nepotism[7] or, more broadly, the use of public office for personal gain generally as a crime, but the state essayed to prevent such wrongdoing through civil service reform: the requirement for public exams in recruiting civil servants, detailed regulation, and the checks and balances system. Yet inefficient public services, personnel redundancies in the public sector, and salaries well above those attached to similar functions in the private sector remain usual in the modern state, and also represent violations of citizens' republican rights.

In some countries, unfair lawsuits against the state often involving huge damages to the state treasury are a new form of capturing the state patrimony. Today Mafias are organized to do that, speaking on behalf of individual rights. They reveal that the liberal judicial system has not yet succeeded in over-coming its anti-state bias. The Brazilian judicial branch often acts on these occasions as if it was facing the problem of defending civil rights against an oligarchic and absolutist state. There is no doubt that democratic progress in the last two centuries has meant guaranteeing such rights. Yet, since modern societies have succeeded reasonably well in protecting civil rights, the problem of protecting the *res publica* has assumed a fundamental relevance, which contemporary judicial systems have difficulty in managing. They often do not possess clear criteria for distinguishing between proper and improper economic transfers by the state, between vexatious and legitimate lawsuits against the state. The defeat of the state in such law suits derives, in certain cases, simply from corruption, but in most cases it is a consequence of the judicial system's failure to acknowledge republican rights, and of the fact that administrative law is unable to characterize and punish the new forms of damage against public interest. Only recently has it become clear that the first concern of administrative law must be the defence of the *res publica*, not only against corrupt government officers but also, if not especially, against rent-seekers.[8] Fiscal transfers and waivers are typical rent-seeking offences against republican rights. They assume the form of public policies oriented towards income distribution or the promotion of technological development; and they may be those things or just attempts to capture the state patrimony. Here we are in a grey area, intrinsically poorly defined. Contrary to ultra-liberal

---

[5] The conclusive analysis of the capture of social policies by the middle class was made by Robert Goodin and Julian Le Grand (1987) when discussing the welfare state. According to the authors, the welfare state's attempts at redistribution are always followed by benefits granted to the same middle class that manages them.

[6] In Brazil, a 1965 law defined the crime of tax evasion. Yet in 1990 Congress repealed this law.

[7] Although not regarded as a crime, nepotism is generally defined as an 'act of improbity', and so it may generate civil responsibility if it is proved.

[8] Actually, administrative law has fallen into a crisis, derived from its strictly bureaucratic origin, which is based on the Napoleonic Code of 1800. While the world was experiencing a technological and managerial revolution, the common body of administrative law remained untouched.

thought, some of these transfers are required, since they involve social solidarity. Distinguishing proper from improper transfers is a fundamental challenge of modern democracies.

Modern societies have made little progress in the legal protection of rights to the public economic patrimony. Historically, the legislative branch has made such rights positive, and the judicial branch conceptualized and interpreted them, only when offences against republican rights materialize in the social consciousness. Thus, better definitions of these rights, better characterizations of the forms and manners of their transgression, and embodying them in effective and enforceable rules are major challenges. In many of its aspects, however, administrative law is still attached to its origins: to nineteenth century liberalism. In that century, administrative law emerged as a discipline and was concerned with three fundamental problems that are at the heart of republican rights: (1) the assertion of state power or sovereignty and the supremacy of the public interest over the private; (2) the defence of the state against corruption and nepotism; and (3) the regulation of public administration and its bureaucracy. Yet, faithful to economic liberalism, in the nineteenth century administrative law paid less attention to republican rights than to civil rights: it was concerned with the guarantee of civil rights against an assumed despotic state; in the twentieth century, concerned with the emergence of the welfare or social-democratic state, it incorporated social rights in its agenda. In this process, administrative law found itself caught in a basic contradiction. It asserted the supremacy of the public interest, but ended up disregarding the new republican rights, notwithstanding the fact that the rise of the tax burden made them crucial. Instead, administrative jurists have concentrated on defending civil and social rights against the state.

Yet, liberal and social rights may easily come into conflict with the right to the *res publica*. While liberal democracy was dominant, the priority of civil rights was unavoidable. In the same way, while inequality and injustice marked social relations, the overriding importance of social rights was essential. In developed countries the first problem was adequately solved, and in the effectively social-democratic countries the second problem was also faced.[9] Once civil, political, and social rights have been tackled in a reasonable way, asserting republican rights has become essential in developed countries. Only when civil, political and social rights have been protected, and social rights have been dealt with, will republican rights enjoy the necessary definition and enforcement. In developing countries, the same problem is also fundamental. Principally in Latin America, some developing countries have reached a reasonably consolidated form of democracy only in the last quarter

---

[9] A developed country is not necessarily 'civilized', depending on the concept of civilization we adopt. A civilized country is not only a rich country but also a fair one. Przeworski (1995) has defined a civilized country as the one in which less than 10% of the population is under the poverty line. According to this definition, the United States would not be a civilized country.

of the twentieth century, and are still far from an equitable social system. Nevertheless, one knows that underdevelopment is characterized by the superimposition of historical phases. This is a source of conceptual confusion for the analysts, but it is also an opportunity that the most creative developing societies can seize.

In the twenty-first century, the great challenge to be faced by administrative law is to protect the state or, more precisely, the *res publica*, and in so doing to protect the citizen: citizen-taxpayer, who pays taxes and has the right to efficient and effective services rendered by the state; citizen-user, who is a beneficiary of services and has the right to demand good quality; citizen-citizen, who has the right to the *res publica*.

Threats, Overlapping Consensus, and the Public Interest

To sum up, corruption, bribery, tax evasion and nepotism are obvious offences against the *res publica*, as are inefficient administration, excess of personnel, and unjustified subsidies. Yet transgressions of this sort against the *res publica* present a major difficulty. What is the public interest? How can one tell whether a certain policy reflects the public interest or privileges special interest groups? It is not reasonable to identify the state with absolute rationality, with the public interest idea, as Hegel suggests, or to turn the state into an exclusive agent of dominant classes, as Marx and Engels suggest. Actually, in contemporary social-liberal democracies, marked by political representation of several groups of interests, by class coalitions of all kinds, nobody has a monopoly on the definition of public interest. Each group, each class seeks to represent the public interest corporately, in such a way that we have a permanent heterogeneity of conflicting 'public interests'. This does not mean, however, that the public interest does not exist, that the defence of the *res publica* in the name of the public interest is impracticable. Neither does it mean that it is possible to protect the public interest only indirectly by the action of self-interested individuals operating in the market, as contemporary ultra-liberalism claims. The very fact that interest groups dispute among themselves as to what represents the public interest, implies that it exists. Nobody argues about something that does not exist. The difficulty in defining the public interest or the common good indicates it cannot exist per se, independently of the values and beliefs shared by citizens. The common good exists through the quasi-consensus—or, in John Rawls' words, through 'overlapping consensus'—reached by civilized and democratic societies on what constitutes the public interest—and a common moral system. To reach a reasonable consensus in the form of public reason, Rawls posits, as one of the

three conditions that have the virtue of being reasonable, readiness to cooperate and to make compromises. In his words:

The basic political institutions . . . tend to encourage the cooperative virtues of political
life: the virtue of reasonableness and a sense of fairness, a spirit of compromise and
a readiness to meet others halfway, all of which connected with the willingness to
cooperate with others on political terms that everyone can accept. (Rawls, 1993: 163)

Thus, this consensus comes from the distinction between self interest and
civic values as determining factors of human motivation. If it is accepted that
individuals are motivated only by self-interest, as has become current among
neoclassical economists and rational-choice political scientists, the republican
idea of a consensus on the public interest becomes contradictory, as does the
idea of citizenship.[10] Yet the belief that such a view represents the classical
eighteenth and nineteenth century liberalism is false. Classical liberalism
assumed self-interest, but rejected explicitly, as John Stuart Mill emphasized,
the doctrine whereby human beings should not concern themselves about the
well-being of one another, unless their own interest were involved: 'Instead of
any diminution, there is need of a great increase of disinterested exertion to
promote the good of others.'[11] Civic values are concerned with the good of the
others, with the common good. They are not a republican's prerogative, since
classical liberals also classically shared them. If we view civic values—the values that permit the Greek *paidea*—as an integral part of the human being, we
can then think about the formation of consensus on the public interest.
Education and public debate lead to this consensus in civilized societies.
When, criticizing modern conservative thought, which supposes self-interest
as the unique human motivation, Paul Davidson and Greg Davidson tells:

Nations are built on the two motivating forces of both self-interest and civic
values . . . Civilized society requires public cooperation by appealing to national ideals
of fairness and justice in the pursuit of self-interest and efficiency. (Davidson and
Davidson, 1996: 20).

A civilized or a well-ordered society and the creation of consensus on the
meaning of the public interest are the result of substantive rationality oriented towards objectives. It is the outcome of 'reasonable' citizens making
trade-offs between self-interest and the public interest. Even when instrumental

---

[10] One should observe that, in the same way as the citizen defined by political philosophers is a
social and historical construction, the individual assumed by neoclassical economists, who performs
freely in the market, despite the radical abstraction involved in the concept, is also a historical construction, being both related to the state which shelters the economic individual and the political
citizen. About the socially constructed character of the individual, see Leda Paulani (1996).

[11] John Stuart Mill (1859: 92). When Boaventura de Souza Santos (1995*a*: 225) asserts that 'the
return to the principle of market in the last twenty years represents a social and political revalida-
tion of liberal thought, to the detriment of citizenship', he is referring to an ultra-liberalism,
adopted, for instance, by Bastiat, but not by its more authoritative formulators, like Adam Smith
and John Stuart Mill. Merquior (1991) makes a clear distinction between old and new, or modern,
liberalism.

rationality becomes dominant and renders the quest for efficiency or economic development a fundamental value, civic value, which allows for collective action and the definition of the public interest, is essential as well. Through these civic values, we achieve the consensus or quasi-consensus on the public interest, which becomes each citizen's expression of its republican rights.

The public interest is the foundation of republican rights. The public interest exists as a positive concept: it is the interest sanctioned by the parliament and the courts in the form of positive law. It exists sociologically or historically in the minds of every citizen concerned with politics. In order to move beyond a general concept of public interest and be able to protect the *res publica*, public debate and the consequent quasi-consensus and overlapping consensus are important. Together, they create the conditions for the identification of the public interest in each case being discussed, and for the collective manifestations of scorn or revolt when it is under threat.

Defenders and Offenders

Each historical form of state had traditionally a different main defender. In the eighteenth century, the champions of civil rights and of the liberal state were the English courts and the Enlightenment philosophers. In the nineteenth century, liberal and democratic politicians were key factors in the advance of the democratic state not only against conservative but also against radical liberals.[12] In this process, popular social movements played a major role.[13] In the twentieth century, European socialists, from Fabian and Catholic idealists, to social-democratic activists, revolutionary Marxists, and the corresponding social movements were in the centre of the affirmation of social rights. In modern democracies, public prosecutors, politicians from the opposition parties, social advocacy activists, and journalists play a decisive role in protecting republican rights. They enforce the demand for transparency in managing the public patrimony—a major tool against violation of republican rights.

In the case of republican rights and the republican state, each type of public patrimony will have its specific defender. Artists and art curators are among the major champions of the protection of the cultural and historical patrimony; biologists and environmentalists direct their attention to the environmental patrimony. According to this logic, economists and civil servants should be the main defenders of the economic public patrimony, although it falls to jurists and philosophers to define these rights, and to the judicial system to implement them. Theoretical economists have been important in drawing the limits between legitimate and illegitimate economic and social policies. On the other hand, economists and public managers working

<hr>

[12] Norberto Bobbio, 1988.   [13] Goran Therborn, 1977.

in the finance ministries of various countries are directly responsible for fiscal and foreign-accounts balance, and, therefore, for vetoing the misuse of public resources. Economists have the criteria to evaluate public policies that protect the public interest instead of just conveying special interests, and to distinguish legitimate forms of state intervention from those that are not.[14] The economic criteria that they adopt challenge the standard neoclassical model, which vetoes state intervention, ignoring or underestimating monopoly power, externalities, information costs, moral hazard, asymmetry of information, incomplete markets, and increasing returns to scale. Yet the application of these criteria in each case is a complex process. A broad evaluation of each problem, preferably preceded by public debate, is required. Eventually decisions will be taken, and their capacity for protecting the public patrimony will depend on the debate, on the incentive system conditioning decision-makers, on their technical competence, and on their republican virtues.

The republican and social-liberal state looks for efficiency, on which economists have much to say, but also for social justice. In this case, moral criteria are essential. When the state ensures universal health care, primary education, or a basic welfare system, its expenditures may have an economic explanation, but they are, rather, a response to moral imperatives. On the other hand, private appropriation of the *res publica* might be accompanied by economic, social, and even moral justifications, since the economic and ethical criteria that distinguish legitimate state intervention from the illegitimate private appropriation of the public thing through state intervention are always strongly influenced by ideology. Often, left- and right-wing views come into conflict and make the debate irrational. It is good for democracy and the public debate that people define themselves as right or left, since the former prioritize order while the latter are ready to risk order in name of social justice, but the public debate will arrive nowhere if the two groups adopt a radical stand.[15]

The decisive role of defining and enforcing republican rights will always fall to judges, public prosecutors, and state attorneys. The latter defend the state in the courts. Yet the defence of republican rights falls specifically to the state's prosecutors. In practice, this branch of government initiates the legal actions related to the protection of the environment and the public economic patrimony. In all democratic states, there are specific institutional organizations that are supposed to protect the public patrimony. In the Brazilian Constitution, the most innovative of them is probably the Public Prosecutors' Office (the Ministério Público).[16] Actually, the Constitution gave such extensive

---

[14] See Stiglitz (1989, 1993*b*, 1994); Przeworski (1990); Rapaczynski (1996).

[15] I developed further this distinction between left and right in Bresser-Pereira (2001*b*).

[16] Before the 1988 Constitution, the Prosecutors' Office was also responsible for the defence of the Union in the courts. Since then a new entity, the Union's General Advocacy, performs this role.

powers and autonomy to the Public Prosecutors' Office that it has practically become a fourth branch. Yet its actions often fail in the courts, for two reasons: first, because the Brazilian legal system is still more concerned to defend civil rights against a powerful state than republican rights against powerful individuals; and second, because, as new forms of violence against the *res publica* emerge every day, courts have difficulty in enforcing rights that lack accurate definition. An interesting institution for the defence of the *res publica* in the French State is the *Conseil d'Etat*. Its role is clearly that of defender of the *res publica*: besides advising the government, this state organization constitutes a court of last resort, though of an administrative character, when the state is involved. In judging actions against the state, the *Conseil d'Etat* approach is to protect the public interest; the principle of the supremacy of public interest is fully adopted. In countries where an institution of this kind does not exist, the protection of the public patrimony becomes more difficult.

In the liberal tradition of civil rights, citizens' interests are in opposition to those of the state, although, in a contradictory way, the state is supposed to represent the public interest. The contradiction may be resolved only if we adopt, besides a liberal perspective, a republican one that takes into consideration the public interest and establishes a clear distinction between the public interest to be represented by the state and the private interests of the state bureaucracy. When either civil or republican rights are endowed with legitimacy, their satisfaction promotes the public interest, the interest of the state, although it may not promote the bureaucracy's or the administration's interests.

The major and more obvious threat against the republican state is corruption. Next to it is tax evasion. Although extremely relevant, I will not treat such problems here. Corruption is older than the state, and tax evasion was born with it. Bureaucratic reform was unable to cope with this problem, and I don't suppose public management reform will solve it. The only thing that can work on this matter is democratic deepening, which means the combination of social control and media control with an effective police and an active and public prosecuting institution. Public management reform is fully consistent with all these requirements; it will be an auxiliary tool against corruption. The same may be said about nepotism, which was the main target of the emergence of the liberal state and of the bureaucratic model of public administration which characterized it in organizational terms. Thus, I will omit such vulgar offenders, and look for a more sophisticated type of rent-seeker: the patrimonial, corporative, and populist groups.

Patrimonial and corporative groups have in common the fact that both are free-riders, agents who, following Olson's law of collective action, expect that the majority will not do the same, and therefore do not hesitate in privatizing the state, in capturing it (Olson 1965). Unlike Olson, however, I do not believe that all individuals are free-riders, or that his pessimistic view of collective action is as general as he presumes. Bobbio is correct when he accepts

Weber's definition of the state as the holder of a monopoly of legitimate power 'because most citizens are not virtuous, but vicious' (Bobbio and Viroli 2001: 9). Yet, as responds Maurizio Viroli, 'if there are no citizens ready to be vigilant, to commit themselves, to be able to resist the arrogant and serve the public good, the republic dies, turns into a place where some dominate while others serve' (Bobbio and Viroli 2001: 10). Thus, it is impossible to explain modern democracies without counting on the cooperation of some citizens endowed with republican virtues and able to look after the public interest. The criminal, the rights violator, is always a free-rider: he knows the laws that organize social life, he knows that, if everybody transgresses the law, the legal system will lose its efficacy and disorder will spread; yet, as the majority obeys the law, he knows that there is room for free riding. Mancur Olson's law and the rational choice argument assume that free riding is the normal if not the only possible behaviour. Yet, paradoxically, the assumption has as a prerequisite the fact that the bulk of the people cooperate, and among those who cooperate many act according to republican values in order to design and implement the required institutions that will prevent free-riding and rent-seeking. Rational-choice emerged in the 1960s in political theory, challenging the sociological and legal approaches to politics. The underlying assumption was Olson's law. In the 1980s, when neo-institutionalism became fashionable, rational choice essayed to be consistent with it, but this would be possible only if such an approach discarded its radical self-interest approach and made way for republican attitudes, at least on the part of the politicians who define the required new institutions.

What distinguishes patrimonialists from corporativists is the way they are involved in rent-seeking. While the former confuse the public patrimony with their own in a direct way, corporativists do so by formally representing some interest group of businessmen, workers, or middle-class professionals. Thus, pork barrel and nepotism are classic expressions of patrimonialism, while the systematic identification of group or class interests with the public interest defines corporativism.[17] Also among the offenders against the public interest are the economic populists and neo-populists.[18] What characterizes economic populists is the scope they want to give to rights and their resistance to taxation. Conservatives also oppose taxes, but when they are not also

---

[17] I am expressly using the word 'corporativism' instead of the usual 'corporatism' because I want to reserve the latter to a political pattern of social class negotiation intermediated by the state, along the lines originally defined by Philippe Schmitter (1974), and identified with a perverse although highly widespread political behaviour.

[18] There are many kinds of populism. I am using the adjective 'economic' before populist and neo-populist to distinguish them from classical or political populism, which consists in the politician having a direct relation with voters without the intermediation of political parties. One can be a political populist without being an economic one. In Latin America, for instance, Getúlio Vargas and Domingos Perón were political populists, but only the latter was also an economic populist. On the concept of economic populism and the populist cycle, see Adolfo Canitrot (1975); Guillermo O'Donnell (1977); and Jeffrey Sachs (1989).

populists they limit rights accordingly. Populists, be they conservative or progressive, do not accept budget constraints, and offer to voters more than the state revenues permit. They do so by incurring budget deficits and by developing macroeconomic policies that overvalue local currencies—which will artificially increase wages and consumption. In any case, the outcome is deficits—budget, trade, and current account deficits. Neo-populists, for their part, keep a fiscal balance but overvalue the currency. Economic populism and neo-populism represent an attack to the republican state as they lead to state insolvency. Economic populism was widespread in developing countries before the 1980s debt crisis. After that, neo-populist practices tended to replace it. In the more advanced countries, we may see signs of both attitudes, but in a reduced form, since politicians and voters have learned their evil consequences. Such threats are not limited to the republican state, but apply to and are present in all kinds of democratic states. We could even say that in the republican state that is emerging in the advanced countries such threats are minor. They are indeed so when compared with what happens to less developed economies. In such economies, these threats are flagrant, while in the more advanced countries they are subtler. Rent-seeking or sheer corruption becomes more sophisticated, involving several forms of inefficient and abusive use of public resources. Yet the threat is there, and will have to be faced if the transition to a republican state is the objective. Republican citizens will count on many tools to achieve it, which, in the strictly political realm, falls under the title of participatory and deliberative democracy, and in the administrative realm comprises public management reform. Participatory and deliberative democracy involves an increased role for civil society and public debate, while public management reform aims at making the state apparatus more efficient and effective, and public managers more autonomous and accountable.

9

The Social-Liberal State

The account of the modern state formation that I have been sketching in this book is a history of economic and political progress. The absolute state represented progress in relation to the feudal past, as the liberal state represented a major advance in relation to absolutism, the liberal-democratic state a step ahead in relation to classical liberalism, and the social-democratic state an improvement in relation to the liberal-democratic. The political values involved in liberalism, democracy, socialism have historically been in conflict, but there is no reason why we cannot see them as complementary rather than just conflicting, provided that we do not radicalize liberalism, socialism, and even democracy. Socialism is here understood not as a type of society competing with capitalism (statism competed with capitalism and was defeated), but as a value or as an ideology. While liberalism is oriented to freedom, and republicanism to responsibility, socialism is centred in the idea of social justice. Or, in the words of Zygmunt Bauman,

Socialism is the sharp and permanent pang of conscience that pushes us to correct or remove the successive varieties of injustice. I don't believe in the possibility (and even in the desirability) of a 'perfect society', but I believe in a 'good society', defined as the society which incessantly recriminates itself for not being good enough, and not doing enough to make it better. (Bauman, 2003: 7)

A purely market, as well as a fully state-coordinated, economy never existed in history. Both a radically liberal and a fully statist economic system are nonsense. Markets have to be regulated and moderately adjusted by the state and the institutions of civil society. Capitalist societies are mixed economies in which the state, market, and society's informal mechanisms act as coordinating principles. As Elmar Altvater observes, 'the invisible hand of the market had to be supported by the visible hand of the state intervention, and both require the "third hand" of a network of social and economic institutions' (Altvater 1991: 328). Market, state, and civil society complement each other in coordinating the economy and, more broadly, society. Combining or aggregating the values of republicanism, liberalism, socialism, and democracy is what modern polities have been doing, in spite of the ideological conflict around ideas and labels. In the twentieth century, the modern state had been liberal, because the basic liberties were reassured and markets had a major role; democratic, because voting rights were extended to all; and socialist, because social rights were recognized and a welfare system created. The question, now, is to know which form the state will take in the twenty-first century. Is it legitimate to speak of a stage ahead, in which the state will be social-liberal and republican? In this chapter I discuss the social-liberal state, in the next, the republican. It is the same polity viewed from two different perspectives.

We may find many origins of the concept of social liberalism, or liberal socialism. John Stuart Mill, for instance, ended his years as a liberal and a socialist. The several forms of democratic socialism are also liberal. In the twentieth century, Norberto Bobbio studied and discussed the theme extensively, having as a basic reference the works of two Italian liberal socialists, Piero Gobetti and Carlo Rosselli.[1] After Rosselli, a liberal-socialist tradition developed in Italian political thought particularly through Guido Calogero.[2] While classical liberals and socialists were fighting each other, Calogero and Bobbio insisted in the possibility of a compromise.[3] Yet we should not limit social liberalism to this line of thought. The whole discussion about market socialism, in which Oscar Lange and Friedrich Hayek were engaged on opposite sides in the 1930s, and which is alive in works by Pranab Bardhan and John Roemer, is related to the social-liberal ideal.[4] Yet the basic reason why it makes sense to speak about the social-liberal state emerging in the twenty-first century is the general acknowledgement on the part of modern European socialists that political liberalism and market coordination of the economy are two prerequisites of democracy. On the other hand, we have to consider the commitment of American liberals to the welfare state and to social justice. Their liberal political ideals are consistent with their fight for social rights in the United States.

Since liberalism and democracy have become dominant, capitalist countries have been experiencing a true political development—a development that can be measured by the increasing number of citizenship rights being assured to an increasing number of people in an increasing number of countries. Democracy has become a universal value, an objective for everybody. Problems with representation and accountability may remain troublesome;[5] inequality

---

[1] Gobetti was the editor of the journal *Rivoluzione Liberale*, in which the first works on social-liberalism appeared, and was a social-liberal. Carlo Rosselli, a socialist and a liberal, was anti-Fascist anti-Marxist. He wrote the first significant works on the subject (1924, 1930).

[2] I became so interested in this alternative that, in 1993, I went to Turin specially to interview Bobbio on the subject (Bobbio 1993).

[3] Calogero (1968); Bobbio (1988, 1993). In the interview, Bobbio underlines the compromise character of social-liberalism. For surveys, see Bobbio (1990); Rego (2001).

[4] Hayek (1935, 1948); Lange (1936–37); Lange and Taylor (1938); Bardhan and Roemer (1992, 1993). Stiglitz's (1994) critique of the attempt of market socialists to adopt the standard neoclassical model represented by general equilibrium theory was aimed at such a model, not at market socialism.   [5] Przeworski (1997); Przeworski, Stokes, and Manin (2000).

and injustice may remain a reality everywhere; the world continues to face hunger, genocide, unreasonable wars, privileges of all sort, corruption. Yet, in spite of all the limitations that freedom and justice face, there is little doubt that the world today is better than it was a hundred or two hundred years ago.

The social-democratic state was a consequence of the First World War and of the Great Depression. Measured in terms of the tax burden, the state organization grew extraordinarily for 50 years, made countries considerably more prosperous and slightly more just, came to a crisis in the 1980s, and, at present, is beginning to be replaced, not by the minimal state as the ultra-liberals expected but by the social-liberal state. And, as we will see in Chapter 11, democracy in the twenty-first century will be neither neo-liberal nor social-democratic, but participatory and republican, consistent with the social-liberal state. Why call this state not just democratic, or social-democratic, but social-liberal? It is social because it is committed to social rights; it is liberal because it believes, more strongly than the social-democratic state, in individual freedom and in market coordination. Let me explore more fully these two ideas.

Social Liberalism as a Synthesis of Liberalism and Social Democracy

The concepts of liberalism and socialism are elusive ones, but they have one common origin: the capitalist revolution and modernity. First came liberalism, as a political alternative to the absolutist state, as an economic alternative to mercantilism and royal monopolies, and as an ideological justification of capitalism. Socialism followed, and soon assumed the utopian roles of an alternative to liberalism and a critique of capitalism. In realistic terms, it was merely a necessary critique of the excesses of social injustice involved in market capitalism. While democratic liberalism affirmed civil rights, democratic socialism asserted social rights. When bureaucratic socialists attempted to transform socialism into short-term reality in the Soviet Union, what they were able to achieve was authoritarian bureaucratism or statism, which proved effective in promoting primitive accumulation through the state, but inefficient in coordinating a modern and complex economy, and anti-democratic.

Liberalism was a revolutionary ideology in the eighteenth and nineteenth centuries, and opposed to conservatism. In countries like the United States, in which socialist ideals did not fall on fertile ground, probably due to the enormous economic success of capitalism, liberalism, specifically political liberalism, defines progressive or social-democratic ideology in opposition to conservatism.[6] In continental Europe and in Latin America, where socialist ideas advanced further, progressive politicians are socialists or social-democrats, and oppose themselves to conservative economic liberals, increasingly called neo-liberals or ultra-liberals. Michael Sandel underlines the two meanings of liberalism in the United States.

> In common parlance of American politics, liberalism is opposite of conservatism; it is the outlook of those who favour a more generous welfare state and a greater measure of social and economic equality. In the history of political theory, however, liberalism has a different, broader meaning. In this sense, liberalism describes a tradition of thought that emphasizes toleration and respect for individual rights. (Sandel 1996:4)

Except when specifically mentioning 'classical' or 'economic' liberalism, I use the word 'liberalism' with the second meaning. Depending on its interpreter, American political or modern liberalism comes close to what I call social liberalism. When I say that the state of the twenty-first century will be liberal, I am, first, saying that civil rights will be asserted, that individual freedom, property rights, and individual respect will continue to have a central role in the polity. I am also saying that market coordination of the economy will have a larger role than statists and even social democrats suppose. The liberalism I am speaking of will not please ultra-liberals like Robert Nozick or Milton Friedman, for whom government should be committed to just the protection of civil rights, nor even conservative liberals like John Gray, but it may please such liberals as John Rawls, Michael Walzer, or Ronald Dworkin.[7] When I claim that the state will be social, I am counting on agreement, not from utopian or bureaucratic socialists, but possibly from a substantial social-democratic tradition represented by, for instance, Norberto Bobbio, Jürgen Habermas, Alain Touraine, or Adam Przeworski.[8]

Bobbio (1993) believes that social-liberalism involves a compromise between liberals and socialists. In saying this he has in mind 'pure' concepts of liberalism and socialism. Yet if citizens adopt more reasonable concepts of these two political ideals, the compromise to be made is more 'internal' than a compromise between socialists and liberals. By an 'internal' compromise I mean a compromise that one makes with oneself. If you are a liberal concerned with social justice, you will have to compromise with radical liberal ideals and accept the protection of social rights; if you are a socialist, you have to compromise your socialist ideals and accept that political liberty comes

---

[6] In the United States, liberalism brings together academics of quite different theoretical allegiances, like John Rawls and Michael Walzer, Adam Przeworski and Joshua Cohen, Jon Elster and Stephen Holmes. They have, however, common adversaries: orthodox Marxists and the anti-liberal non-Marxists. Holmes criticizes some of the latter in *The Anatomy of Antiliberalism* (1993): Joseph de Maistre, Carl Schmidt, Leo Strauss, Alasdair MacIntyre, Christopher Lasch, and Roberto Mangabeira Unger.

[7] Nozick (1974); Friedman (1962); Gray (1993); Rawls (1993); Walzer (1983); Dworkin (1977, 1985).

[8] Bobbio (1984, 1985); Habermas (1981, 1992); Touraine (1992, 1999); Przeworski (1990, 1991).

first. In fact, more than a compromise between liberalism and socialism, social liberalism is a synthesis of the liberal-democratic and the social-democratic ideals.

The social-liberal state is social because it maintains socialist commitments to social rights. This is not a normative claim but one based on observation of electoral behaviour in developed countries. In spite of the ultra-liberal ideological wave that began in the 1980s, citizens continue to expect and require that the state guarantee social rights and deliver social and scientific services. Citizens may be individualistic, and certainly do not like to pay taxes, but they rely on the state to guarantee their rights to work, minimum income, health care, and basic education. They expect the protection of the state. They know that in a capitalist society each one is supposed to take care of its own interests, but they are not willing to count only on their individual abilities to guarantee such rights for their families.

Is it rational to behave in such terms? Would it not be preferable to pay fewer taxes and leave these matters to each individual, as the ultra-liberal and conservative preach? This is not the time for a normative discussion on this matter. I simply observe that ultra-liberal attempts to eliminate social rights did not win political support and eventually failed in the more advanced democratic countries. The failure of the 'Contract with America' in the United States in the 1990s is just one example of what I am saying. People may be individualist, but they probably are not so individualist as to accept that essential goods and services, such as basic education, health care, unemployment insurance, a minimum income, and a basic pension system, depend just on their own savings or on their own private insurance plan. The ideological debate between left and right, between progressives and ultra-liberals, will certainly continue, but the ultra-liberal wave that started in the late 1970s is over. The alternation of power between left and right political coalitions will continue to define democracies, but the return to the nineteenth or early twentieth century liberal democracy is out of the question.

On this line of thought Duane Swank recently argued that pressures from globalization and from the neo-liberal wave are real but were unable to eliminate the welfare state in the developed democracies. The author differentiates the larger welfare state from the (relatively small) liberal welfare state, and argues that the former count on institutions and programmatic structures which are able to resist the pressures of internationalization more effectively than the latter: 'As a result, we are not likely to see substantial convergence around a market-conforming model of minimal public protection' (Swank 2002: 5).

Bob Jessop recognizes that the social-democratic state, which he calls 'Keynesian welfare state', fell into a crisis in the 1970s, and asks himself whether the new state that is emerging will be able to maintain the dynamism of the accumulation process (Jessop 1993, 1994). In the 1970s and

1980s I studied the capitalist development process and wrote a book on the long-term classical model of economic growth, in which I concluded that this question makes little sense.[9] Capitalism has historically proved to be flexible enough to change and maintain a relatively stable long-term rate of profit and process of capital accumulation, in which technical progress is not only labour-saving but also capital-saving. Jessop calls the new emerging regulatory regime 'Schumpeterian workfare state'. Contrary to conventional Marxism, he correctly views this state as dynamic, that is, promoting innovation in open economies, but subordinating social policy to the needs of market flexibility or to international competition requirements. Thus, there is a relationship between my concept of a social-liberal, republican state and Jessop's Schumpeterian workfare state. The state remains actively promoting innovation and national economic growth, combining market mechanisms with strategic intervention. The difference in the two models lies in the fact that Jessop believes in a greater increase in work flexibility than I do. Such flexibility would damage the protection of social rights to a greater degree than I observe actually occurring, and would promote a concentration of income that could otherwise be avoided. The concentration that occurred in the last quarter of the twentieth century derived essentially from the dramatic acceleration of technical progress, which increased the demand for skilled middle-class labour—a new middle class endowed with a relative monopoly of technical and organizational knowledge, including that relating to finance and entertainment. However, when the university system increases the labour supply of technical, financial, organizational, and entertainment experts, reducing the present knowledge lag, labour markets will cease to press for more income concentration, while voters will have better political opportunities to demand compensatory social policies, and we will see the social-liberal and republican state reversing the trend of income concentration. In the more advanced societies, I believe that such a reversal is already beginning to take place. The income concentration that has taken place since the 1980s originated also in a reduction in the demand for labour in general stemming from lower economic growth rates worldwide, and, particularly in Europe. In the advanced European countries the existence of unemployment or under-employment of one-tenth of the workforce, who are also unskilled, created a 'social fracture' which in some ways replaced the 'fracture of the past between the bourgeoisie and the workers'.[10]

---

[9] Bresser-Pereira (1986). In this book, I used Marxist tools to come to 'non-Marxist' conclusions—conclusion that modern Marxists still have difficulty in accepting, in spite of the new historical facts that changed capitalism and required a new analysis.

[10] The concept of a 'social fracture' was used by Jacques Chirac to win the first round of the French 2002 presidential elections. Claude Lefort commented on it, and underlined its suitability for understanding contemporary France, in an interview to Alcino Leite, *Folha de S. Paulo*, 5 May 2002.

Contracting Out Social Services

In the social-liberal state, the fact that the state remains committed to social protection does not mean that the state will continue to grow, or that all social and scientific services that the society decides that should be provided by the state will be directly provided by civil servants located in the state apparatus, as was the standard policy in the social-democratic state. For the first time in history, one of society's major concerns is that the state organization delivers efficiently exclusive state services, which involve state power, as well as social and scientific services. In political terms, it is not enough that the state apparatus be effective: now social services must be evaluated according to their quality/cost ratio. Such a change, which on one side global markets and the competition among nations, on the other democracy have induced is already taking place in more advanced countries and in intermediate developing countries like Brazil. A bureaucratic public administration changes gradually into new public management, public managers become more autonomous, and, as a trade-off, more accountable, as politicians realize that efficient and high-quality social and security services matter in elections. In bureaucratic public administration, the major governance concerns were social order and administrative effectiveness. In the new state that is emerging, citizens or voters assume that the political regime achieved political stability and is reasonably effective in enforcing the law. Now, the major political concerns are democratic accountability and administrative efficiency. The challenge is to extend to social services the economic efficiency which business enterprises assure in the production of goods and services, while maintaining their public character.

We have seen that the social-democratic state hugely enlarged the concept and the scope of civil service. Yet this greater scope given to civil service proved inefficient in the provision of social and scientific services, as bureaucratic administration did not permit the use of more adequate means to achieve the desired outcomes. The modern state is supposed to offer law and order or security services, public utilities' services, and social and scientific services; and must do so efficiently and with high quality. Law and order services are part of what I call the exclusive activities of the state; public utilities' services guarantee society's infrastructure; and social and scientific services are an answer to citizens' social rights. To make available such services to the population is a legitimate role of the state, but with the exception of the security services, this does not mean that the state must provide them directly. Instead, in the case of public utilities, privatization is the adequate solution if the activity does not constitute a natural monopoly or involve large Ricardian rents. If they do, they should remain state-owned enterprises and be managed as private enterprises. When we study the experience of privatization, we realize that privatizations of firms tended to be successful in competitive industries, but problematic—to say the least—in monopolistic ones. To create a private monopoly out of a state-owned monopoly makes little economic sense.[11]

In the case of social and scientific services, the problem is more complex. In the modern social state the two basic social services—health care and basic education—should be, in principle, fully financed by the state. What is not so clear is who should provide such services. In the social-democratic state, civil servants directly provide them; in the social-liberal state, competitive non-profit organizations financed by the state already are or will be in charge. The tendency, following the principles of public management reform, is for the state to contract out the services to public non-state service organizations and to render them accountable through a mixture of management contracts, managed competition, and social accountability mechanisms.

This strategy of assuring social and scientific services is one of the central characteristics of the newly emerging social-liberal state. This state is large in terms of public expenditures but small in terms of personnel, as long as strictly speaking civil servants are supposed to perform only the exclusive activities of state, among which is included the contracting out of services. Thus, we are far from the minimal state which would guarantee just property rights and contracts. The state does not get smaller. If we measure the size of the state by the tax burden, that is, by state expenditures in relation to GDP, it remains about the same. Actually, it tends to augment moderately, as education, health care, and security costs are likely to increase in relation to the average costs of industrial products.

The emerging new state tends to contract out social and scientific services for three reasons. First, pressure for efficiency, or for cost reduction, becomes stronger as the size of such services increases. Second, the demand for political accountability increases proportionally. Third, while efficiency is extremely difficult to achieve when the state directly delivers the service, it becomes relatively easier when the service is contracted out to non-profit organizations that compete among themselves. For this last reason, in the new state that is coming into being only the activities that by their nature are exclusive to the state, and so monopolistic, will remain within the state apparatus. Even in these activities, public management reform attempts to achieve efficiency, but in full knowledge of the restrictions involved. The managerial strategy is to develop some form of management contract whereby a strategic plan and performance indicators are defined. But it is not easy to define these indicators clearly and precisely. If the activity does not involve state power, managed competition—through the creation of quasi-markets—is a much more efficient way of achieving efficiency and political accountability. It makes no sense to consider this activity as a state monopoly and to use civil servants to

---

[11] The Brazilian experience of privatization of the electrical power industry is clear. For the British one, see the papers in Bishop, Kan and Mayer (1995).

perform it. What makes sense—and is being increasingly adopted by advanced democracies—is the state contracting non-profit competitive organizations to provide social and scientific services. Services will be more efficient and citizens will have more choice. In the recent past, the state realized that it was more efficient to contract out certain services to business enterprises; it therefore opted to do the same with construction, transportation, catering, data processing, and communications. Since the 1990s, the state has increasingly contracted out social and scientific services to non-profit organizations instead of delivering them directly.

Why would the social-liberal state contract non-profit organizations to provide social and scientific services instead of regular business enterprises? In the case of health care and education, essentially because those organizations are better fitted to deal with such crucial and delicate matters, involving as they do basic human rights. Business enterprises are supposed to compete for profits, while public non-state service organizations are fitted to compete for excellence and recognition. This type of competition is best suited in social and scientific areas. Although regulated by private, not public, law, non-profit organizations are 'public' because they are directly oriented to the public interest. Also, they do not depend on the classical liberal principle that legitimizes business enterprises: 'if each one defends his own interests, competition in the market will automatically guarantee the public interest'. This principle is crucial to the understanding of the role of economic competition in capitalism, but inadequate when applied to markets that are imperfect, and still more inadequate when competitive criteria are not primarily economic. The legitimacy of organizations working in the social and scientific sectors arises from their commitment to human and public values.

Competition does not necessarily mean markets, and, to be sure, does not require profits. Schools, universities, hospitals, museums, symphony orchestras may compete not for profit but for recognition and for the positive evaluation of experts, peers, and citizens-clients. In the United States and more recently in Britain, universities, for instance, are essentially controlled in this way. When citizens become organized in the realm of civil society through NGOs or citizens' committees in order to control state agencies and contracted-out services, we are speaking of social accountability. When management contracts are established and performance indicators defined, we have managerial control *stricto sensu*. When evaluation and comparison are possible, we have managed competition. When evaluators are the customers themselves, we can speak of a quasi-market. Whenever some form of competition is possible, it results in higher-quality and more efficient services. Managed competition will usually involve contracting out. Contracts may take many forms. They may be explicit or implicit. They always require transparency and evaluation by customers, peers, or experts. The politicians and senior civil servants who are charged with the decision to allocate public money for these services have to be as accountable as the institutions that receive the money. But what is important to note is that contracting out and managed competition make it possible for the organizations that deliver the services to become more autonomous—that is, less controlled by classic bureaucratic procedures—and, therefore, more efficient. Additionally, they become more accountable to the society that finances them. More accountable because managed competition is a powerful control system: performance indicators and an incentive system emerge out of competition, from comparing the performance of competing organizations, instead of being arbitrarily decided. More accountable because, when services are provided by autonomous agencies, organizations and committees involved in social accountability become empowered.

More Market Allocation and More Regulation

The central difference between a social-democratic and a social-liberal state lies in the fact that the social-liberal state, although acknowledging the importance of the state, relies heavily on markets or on competition. The social-liberal state is a market-oriented state: it 'believes' in competition—which is not viewed as contrary to cooperation—while the social-democratic state counts more on cooperation and planning than on competition. This faith in markets and in competition is expressed in two ways: first, in rejecting the idea of the state being a producer of goods and services for the market and supporting the privatization of competitive state-owned enterprises; second, in affirming that non-exclusive activities of the state, like social and scientific services—which are not essentially monopolistic—are not supposed to be directly provided by the state. The state should finance the social and scientific services to a large extent (fully in the case of basic education and health care), but public non-state service organizations should provide them competitively. The social-liberal approach believes in markets for resource allocation, but it does not accept the existence of a self-regulating market, defined according to neoclassical general equilibrium theory and ideology: free markets alone do not guarantee either economic development or social justice. Market-oriented reforms were in fact needed, but not in the radical form demanded by the neo-conservatives; they were necessary to correct the distortions caused by the excessive growth of the state and to eliminate arbitrary interference in defining relative prices. Yet a return to the liberal state of the nineteenth century was definitely unfeasible. Instead of reducing the state to a minimum, the social-liberal centre-left proposed rebuilding government capacity, providing the state with governance and governability, so as to enable it—in a new cycle of limited but effective state intervention—to once again complement and correct market failures.

Building government capacity means recovering public savings; overcoming the fiscal crisis; redefining the ways by which it intervenes in the economic and social spheres; substituting managerial for bureaucratic public administration; contracting non-profit, public non-state service organizations to competitively provide education, health care, and cultural services. It means making a transition from a state that directly provides social services, and even produces goods and services through state-owned enterprises, to a state that acts as a regulator, facilitator, or provider of funds to foster economic and social development through non-profit organizations.[12]

If the new priority given to state reform was a political and administrative answer to the crisis of the state, we can understand why rebuilding rather than reducing it to the minimum became the central objective of successful reforms. Often this simple idea was not clear in the minds of politicians and civil servants involved in fiscal adjustment, privatization, trade liberalization, social security, and public management reform—which helps to explain the many policy mistakes in drafting and executing reforms (Bresser-Pereira 2002*b*). According to the neo-liberal or ultra-liberal ideology, reforming the state just means downsizing it. Yet, except for privatization, little has been achieved in this respect. The best way of measuring the size of the state is by its expenditures in relation to GDP. Between 1980 and 1996, a period when the conservative wave was strongest, this ratio increased from 41.9 to 45.0 per cent, rather than diminishing (Tanzi and Schukenechet 2000: 6).

State-owned enterprises are a typical characteristic of the social-democratic state. In the social-liberal state, only natural monopolies may remain state-owned. Whenever competition is possible, the state does not intervene. When competition is possible but imperfect, regulation will act as a partial substitute for competition. Thus, the privatization process that has been occurring worldwide since the 1980s is a clear manifestation of the rise of the social-liberal state. When we speak about regulatory reform, we are speaking about the regulatory agencies that the state is supposed to set up after the privatization of quasi-monopolies, particularly in the area of public utilities. Contrary to what some ultra-liberals hoped, however, regulatory reform does not mean less, but more, regulation. As Giandomenico Majone observes, 'what is rather observed is never a dismantling of all regulation—a return to a situation of *laissez faire* which in fact never existed in Europe—but a combination of deregulation *and* re-regulation' (Majone 1996: 2).

The tendency of capital to concentrate through mergers and acquisitions, and the capacity that large firms have to create monopolistic advantages, will require more regulation, not less. A common critique of the social-democratic

---

[12] A systematic presentation of this view can be found in Bresser-Pereira, Maravall and Przeworski (1993). In practical terms, the shift towards economic policies aimed at fiscal adjustment and state reform in social-democratic governments, which took place in France (1981), Spain (1983), and Brazil (1995), were manifestations of this new stand of the modern social-liberal centre-left.

state was that it over-regulated the economy, thereby opening the door to rent-seeking. Thus, it was time to reform and deregulate. In fact, this view is simplistic, and is not borne out by reality. It is true that, in some instances, regulation became excessive, requiring deregulation. Yet in the new social-liberal state the general tendency will continue to be in the direction of more regulation, because the main objectives of regulation are to defend competition and protect the consumer. As the sheer size of societies to be governed increases, as economic growth as well as scientific and technological progress makes them increasingly complex, markets alone are unable to offer adequate answers to the new challenges. Citizens require regulation to protect their health, the environment, the public patrimony, and competition itself. Good governance comes with better and more encompassing institutions, involving more rather than less regulation—but regulation that is liberal because it enhances competition instead of hindering it.

In summary, the social-liberal state will be the basic political organization of the twenty-first century. Certainly it will not be a social-democratic and bureaucratic state, since that was that form of state which fell into crisis. Nor will it be the neo-liberal state dreamt of by neo-conservatives, since there is no political support or economic rationale for a return to the nineteenth century liberal state. My prediction is that the state of the twenty-first century will remain a mixed regime. It will follow the track opened by the social-democratic state, but it will combine more clearly the positive aspects of liberalism and socialism. It will be a social-liberal state. It will be social because it will continue to protect social rights and to promote economic development. It will be liberal because it will continue to protect individual freedom, it will use more market and fewer administrative controls, it will carry out its social and scientific services mainly through competitive public non-state service organizations, it will promote human capital and technological development so as to allow its business enterprises to be more innovative and internationally competitive. It will be social-liberal because it will make labour markets more flexible while respecting basic social rights, which are a main socialist achievement of the twentieth century.

10

The Republican State

We saw in the previous chapter that the increased need for a strong and legitimate state has stemmed on the one hand from the increasing demands of society and on the other from the emergence of the global system. The new state that is emerging needs to be a strong liberal, democratic, and social state. A strong liberal state assures civil rights that protect life, property, and liberty, and assures that each citizen is treated with respect independently of wealth, gender, race, or culture. A strong democratic state assures political rights to all citizens, viewing each as equal to the others. A strong social state assures social rights, combating unemployment and economic inequality. But, to be strong in respect of the three classical human rights, the state needs to be able to assure republican rights, and to count upon citizens participating actively in political affairs. In other words, the state needs to be republican.

The republican state is a state strong enough to protect itself from private capture, defending the public patrimony against rent-seeking; it is a participatory state in which citizens organized in civil society take part in defining new policies and institutions and in exercising social accountability; it is a state that relies upon government officers who, although self-interested, are also concerned with the public interest; it is a state with an effective capacity to reform institutions and enforce the law; it is a state endowed with the necessary legitimacy to tax citizens in order to finance collective actions democratically decided; it is a state that is effective and efficient in performing the roles demanded of it. Summing up, the republican state is a polity that counts upon engaged citizens participating with politicians and civil servants in governing.

This definition of the republican state is related to the classical republican tradition, but I don't claim that it is faithful to it. The Greek and Roman republics were a reality and an ideal. The fourteenth and fifteenth-century Italian republics were also thought to be ideal. The eighteenth-century republicans based their own visions in the earlier ones. The twenty-first century republican state will necessarily be a different reality, which requires new concepts and new theoretical considerations, which involves specific values or ideologies.

The republican state is viable in the context of an active civil society in which the principles of liberal, social, and participatory or deliberative democracy are observed. Republican states will differ from country to country, reflecting their history and cultures, but they will share some basic and common values and institutions. Are we heading towards republican states? I believe so. Since the emergence of the modern state, democratic polities have been progressing: not linearly, not following a steady state, but through ups and downs, major advances and, sometimes, tragic retrogression. Advanced countries today count upon more effective institutions in making politicians and bureaucratic officials more accountable and in protecting the state against rent-seeking, on the one hand, and upon more educated and participatory citizens on the other. Republican rights, although constantly violated, are today better defined and protected. Institutional reform, and particularly public management reform, are advancing everywhere, which means that the state is becoming more capable. The recent ultra-liberal wave represented a major challenge and led to necessary state reform, but, given that its aim was to weaken the state, it failed and faded away. Thus, I believe that the opportunity to continue building the republican state is real today.

In the following analysis an empirical aspect and a normative aspect will be present. From a historical perspective, I believe it reasonable to predict the gradual rise of the republican state; from a normative one, I hope it will happen. This normative vein does not conflict with the historical one. On the contrary, they mutually reinforce each other. Historical developments point in this direction, and the challenges that collective action faces today require that institutions are invented and reformed in order to be consistent with this kind of state. I see things in this way, despite all the problems that advanced democracies face today. They are ripe for the emergence of the republican state, and so it is time to discuss how it will come about.

The same factors that gave rise to the social-liberal state—the crisis of the social-democratic state, the information technology revolution, globalization, and the misguided ultra-liberal response to these phenomena—are behind the emergence of the republican state. The social-liberal and the republican states are the same. Yet when I speak of republican state I am referring to the state's capacity not only to assure civil, political, and social rights but also to guarantee republican rights, and, in doing so, to protect itself from private capture. The concept of a republican state refers to the emergence of republican rights and to the revival of republicanism.

In the last quarter of the twentieth century, when republican rights acquired historical significance, while civil society organizations gained national and international relevance, it became obvious that a basic political challenge was to build a state capable of protecting itself from greedy and powerful individuals or corporations, while being able to organize collective action towards assuring citizenship rights. On the other hand, after the ultra-liberal offensive proved unable to eliminate or even reduce social rights, states became stronger politically, which, however did not mean a return to the social-democratic model. It became increasingly clear that such a model had been an excessive reaction against the classical liberal state, that free markets were an extraordinary powerful tool for promoting wealth and for guaranteeing freedom when duly regulated by the state. Thus, a middle-way solution now had its turn. Instead of a trade-off between liberal values and social rights, it became even more obvious that only a strong state could guarantee strong markets. It is also becoming evident that citizens who have their social rights judiciously protected behave more freely and more actively in markets than those who are not so protected. In this chapter I examine the social-liberal state that springs from this combination of state and markets, of individual pursuit of personal autonomy and citizens' demands for increased social security or for the protection of social rights. In the next chapter I will discuss at length the concepts of the republican state and of republican or participatory democracy.

In order to increase state capacity and build the republican state, modern societies will have to rely on politicians, civil servants, and citizens who are ready to participate in the political process, endowed with patriotism or civic virtues. Although concern for the protection of the *res publica* and civic participation are old phenomena, they became widespread—as a concern of the people and not only of the elites—only in the last quarter of the twentieth century. At the same time, the social-democratic state fell into crisis and market-oriented reforms became a central feature of globalization. Markets, whose role in resource allocation had been reduced during the era of the social democratic state, gained a new primacy but not to the extent that neo-liberals expected. Social rights, which came under severe attack during the neo-liberal wave, ended up being reaffirmed in almost all countries, as civil society rejected proposals for a minimal state. On the contrary, the role of the state in ensuring competitive markets, freedom, and social justice expanded. Instead of forcing its organization to return to bureaucratic public administration, consistent with the liberal state, or to the huge social bureaucracies developed by the social-democratic state, the state was involved in public management reform. And all this is possible as long as citizens, organized in civil society, are proving able to effectively take part in public affairs and to outline the framework of a participatory and republican democracy.

I say that the republican state will be democratic, liberal and social; however, we know that republican, liberal, democratic, and socialist ideals have been historically in mutual conflict. In Chapter 4, I argued that, although liberal and democratic ideals clashed in early nineteenth century, they eventually turned out to be compatible when liberals and democrats gave up their radical views. In the previous chapter I discussed and argued for a social-liberal polity, showing that, as long as we define liberalism as the affirmation of civil rights, of individual liberty and property rights, of toleration and pluralism, and define socialism as the effective protection of social rights with a central concern for social justice, the two may be compatible. In this chapter I will begin by acknowledging the classic conflict between republican and liberal ideals, and between republican and democratic ones, but I will again conclude that they can be made and are being made compatible provided that these ideals are not adopted radically. More than that: I will say that to the modern republican state corresponds a more advanced form of representative democracy, namely, participatory or deliberative democracy.

Republican Ideals

Republican and humanist ideals go back to the Greek and Roman republics. This is not the occasion for a survey of republicanism. Civic humanism or republican civic values emerged in Rome, with Cicero; reappeared in the northern Italian republics of the *quatrocento*, with Bruni; had their first 'modern' affirmation with Machiavelli; arrived in France with Montesquieu, in England with Harrington, and in the United States with Madison. Since republicanism preceded liberalism, political theorists often view republican values and duties as alternatives to liberal ones, although they rather complement each other, as we know from historians of ideas, like J. G. A. Pocock (1975) and Quentin Skinner (1978, 1998), or from political philosophers, such as Philip Pettit (1997), Richard Dagger (1997), and Newton Bignotto (2001). Republicanism stresses citizens' duties and political participation, and is based on the civic virtues required of citizens, while liberalism underlines rights and is based on the negative liberties of self-interested citizens. Yet, just as I do not see any necessary conflict between civil and social rights or between liberal and socialist ideals, so I do not any see absolute inconsistency between civil rights and civic virtues or between negative and positive freedom.

Historically, such values and the political currents behind them have clashed, but in contemporary advanced democracies we are learning to integrate values, to arrive at compromises or, more than that, quasi-consensus. The change from the liberal to the social-democratic state and finally to the social-liberal and republican state is a political development process through which citizen rights have been increasingly assured.

It is noteworthy that the political philosopher who most thoroughly discussed social-liberalism—Norberto Bobbio—has never been attracted by republicanism. For him, 'the republicans' republic is a form of ideal state, a "moral model" as it was called in Montesquieu's republic, which influenced the French revolutionary: an ideal state that does not exist anywhere'. Following most liberals, he calls himself a 'realist' in politics: 'In politics, I am a realist. It is only possible to speak of politics if one maintains a cold regard on history. Politics, be it monarchic or republican, is the fight for power' (Bobbio and Viroli 2001: 7–8). Yet I do not think that it is necessary to be an idealist to recognize the emergence of the republican state. It is enough to be clear that the republican state is not the ideal state; it is only a superior form of social and liberal democracy. It is not the state formed by virtuous citizens, but the state in which civic values are important. It is not the state that eliminates corruption and rent-seeking, but it develops effective weapons to protect itself from such threats. As the republican state guarantees republican rights, it is able to protect itself. In this way, the circle is completed.

In the past, when liberalism opposed democratic ideals and demanded an authoritarian state to protect individual liberties, it was assuming an all-powerful state and powerless individuals; now, when republicanism demands protection for the *res publica*, the assumption is the reverse. Yet, in both cases, the combination of self-interest and public interest is essential. Without a reasonably clear notion of public interest, it is impossible to define the *res publica*. In general, *res publica* is the public good; in a narrower sense, it is the public patrimony.[1] Without a republican perspective it is difficult to defend the public patrimony. If citizens lack clear notions of the public space and of the common good or public interest, the defence of the public patrimony is equally hopeless. As a more general concept of the public space, the *res publica* or 'the public' includes everything that is public, that belongs to the people, that is of and for everybody, that is manifest and therefore endowed with publicity, that is guaranteed or asserted through public law.[2] As an embodiment of the common good or of the public interest, the *res publica* assumes a normative character. When the people, instead of being mere observers, widen their allegiance to the common good or the public interest, they become better citizens.[3] Actually, it is impossible to defend the public patrimony if there is no republic, if citizens do not clearly understand the notion of public space, of common good or public interest.

The identification of the *res publica* with the state apparatus is misleading. The public patrimony includes more than what the state owns, while everything owned by the state is only nominally public; in practice, part of it may be captured by private interests. The public economic patrimony may be defined as the stock of public assets, but it is also and principally the flow of public resources—tax revenues on the one side, expenditures on the other. Revenues and expenditures of public non-state organizations should also be included. This flow of resources is more vulnerable than the stock of public assets because it is more easily subject to private appropriation. In the twentieth century, while the state and public non-state organizations burgeoned, the former in terms of its power to tax, the latter through voluntary contributions, the outright greed and consequent competition of interest groups for

---

[1] It is also possible to think of the *res publica* in terms of a political regime—the republican system—or in terms of the state itself.

[2] See Smend's analysis (1934) of the public and public thing problem.

[3] According to Janine Ribeiro (1994: 34), 'the more citizens are reduced to a public, to spectators of political decisions, the less will be the public character of adopted policies, the less will be its commitment to welfare, to the *res publica* which named the republican regime'.

those resources exploded as well. Thus, the protection of the *res publica*, which was already important before, became imperative.[4] In the republican state, concern for the protection of the public interest and of the public patrimony is central. Given the conflicting interests that exist in every society, the public interest will not always be evident. Democratic governance is the main process whereby modern polities define, on each issue, what the public interest is. Thus, the republican state is intrinsically democratic. But it is more than democratic because, just as it is able to protect individual citizens, so it is able to protect itself from conflicting interests: it possesses the institutions and the citizens that make for such protection.

Republicanism and Liberalism

From the standpoint of political theory, making liberalism and republicanism consistent is no simple task. First, we have to consider that liberalism is often identified with economic liberalism. While economic liberalism tends to stress self-interest and to be conservative, political liberalism tends to be progressive, ready to risk order in the name of social justice, and emphasizes solidarity. Sérgio Costa (2002: 22) observes that modern citizenship is characterized by economic citizenship defined in terms of property rights and contracts, and by political citizenship defined in terms of the right to participate. These two dimensions have as prototypes the figures of the *bourgeois* and the *citoyen*; and it is not from the former, who is part of a 'system of needs', that one can expect virtuous actions. Only from the political dimension, in the public sphere, can one expect to find virtuous citizens. We can have virtuous capitalists, but when they are so, they are acting according to the citizenship's logic, not with the market's one. Liberalism, as originally a bourgeois ideology, is interested in the protection of the liberties; economic liberalism in the guarantee of property rights and contracts, political liberalism, in the equality of all citizens and in individual freedom. It is difficult to reconcile republicanism with purely economic liberalism, while political liberalism is consistent with the republican tradition.

Second, we have to consider the two concepts of freedom. While the liberal tradition views freedom as 'negative' in the sense that the state should not interfere with the freedom and the property of citizens except to prevent harm to society, and has a limited conception of citizens' rights, republicanism views freedom as 'positive' and so has a broader concept of human rights.

---

[4] There is no estimate of this flow of resources if we include the revenues of public non-state entities. However, if we take into account only the fiscal burden, we know that, in developed countries, it grew from about 5–10% at the beginning of the 20th century to about 30–50% of GDP today. In fact, the tax exemptions that benefit certain groups should be included in the concept of *res publica*. Their inclusion is justified in so far as the revenue that the state does not collect does not benefit the whole of society, does not correspond to a general reduction of taxes, but to a benefit for certain groups.

Conceptually, liberty has two sides: the negative concept, which is associated with civil rights and liberalism, and the positive concept, which is associated with democracy in the case of political rights, with socialism in the case of social rights, and with full citizenship in the case of republican rights. Negative liberty is 'freedom from', while positive liberty is 'freedom to'. Citizens have the negative liberty of not being subject to restrictions on or interference with their legitimate wishes or interests; they have the positive liberty to participate in government, share in the public or the common good, and resist the attempts by private individuals to capture the public patrimony. To be consistent just with a negative concept of freedom, one has to reject the idea that the state is supposed to be oriented to the common good.

This distinction between negative and positive freedom owes its contemporary formulation to Isaiah Berlin.[5] Berlin wrote his essay on the two concepts of freedom at the height of the ideological conflict between liberals and Marxists. Despite being aware of the trade-offs between the two kinds of freedom, he praised negative freedom and emphasized the risks of positive freedom, which is 'at times, no better than a specious disguise for brutal tyranny' (Berlin 1958: 131). As a classical liberal—and mindful of the fact that liberalism rose in the seventeenth century—he was concerned with limiting the power of governments that, in principle, are authoritarian. In contrast to the liberal view, the republican tradition adopts a positive concept of freedom. The people in the ancient Athenian democracy and Roman republic were citizens, not just subjects, and were not oppressed by an absolute monarch as Benjamin Constant's moderns—the liberals—were. Berlin's concept of freedom as the absence of some element of constraint that inhibits the individual from acting in the pursuit of his or her chosen ends has its origin in Hobbes. In his contractual theory of the state, which would later be adopted by liberals, Hobbes assumes the state of nature, the war of all against all, and from this he deduces—his method is essentially hypothetical-deductive—the concept of freedom as absence of constraint. In contrast, positive theories of freedom have their origin in Aristotle, who proceeds from the assumption that man is essentially a moral being, a political animal. From these premises, one can derive only a positive concept of liberty and reject, as many modern rational-choice liberals do, the idea of the common good. Yet, John Locke, who may be viewed as the founder of liberalism, had no difficulty in adopting a negative concept of freedom ('liberty is to be free from restraint and violence from others') and in emphasizing that the condition for that liberty to be assured is that the laws are oriented to the common good. In his words:

Men, when they enter into society, give up the equality, liberty, and executive power they had in the state of nature, into the hands of the society, to be so far disposed of

---

[5] Berlin (1958). The classic formulation of this distinction is by Constant (1814). In Part II, Chapter VI, of *De L'Esprit de Conquête et de l'Usurpation*, he writes about 'la liberté des anciens et la liberté des modernes'.

by the legislative, as the good society shall require; yet . . . the society or legislative constituted by them, can never be supposed to extend farther than the common good.[6]

Skinner distinguishes two versions of contemporary republicanism. On one side we have authors like Skinner, who believe that political participation is a condition for assuring personal freedom; on the other side, Charles Taylor, who connects government with self-government: we will be truly free only if we are committed to public service. For Skinner, liberals do not properly distinguish between corruption and honesty so long as they espouse the concept of the invisible hand. Interests are legitimate but from interests one should infer duties and virtues like courage and prudence, not just self-interest. Skinner observes that the danger of political constraint or coercion that liberals signal is real, but it does not follow from this that a negative attitude towards freedom is necessary or advisable. On the contrary, positive action on the part of citizens endowed with civic virtue is necessary to protect liberty and is a condition of an agent's being fully or truly at liberty. In his words:

The maintenance of our public duties is indispensable to the maintenance of our own liberty. If it is nevertheless true that freedom depends on service, and hence on our willingness to cultivate the civic virtues, it follows that we may have to be coerced into virtue and thereby constrained into upholding a liberty which, left to ourselves, we would have undermined.[7]

Here Skinner demonstrates that he is a republican, though a 'defensive republican'. Citizens must act positively in order to protect their own freedom. Like the liberals, he would prefer that freedom could be just the absence of constraint, but he realizes that freedom must be conquered and defended. In other words, positive or republican freedom implies effective participation on public affairs on the part of each citizen. In contrast, Philip Pettit's republicanism is not so clear. He distinguishes not two but three forms of freedom. He follows Isaiah Berlin in recognizing positive freedom as mastery of oneself, and negative freedom as the absence of interference. But he adds a third form, which he calls republican: the absence of domination. He views this non-domination as real freedom, and discards political participation as an essential element in republican positive freedom. Thus, he practically adopts a negative concept of liberty. He sees a major difference between domination and interference: 'it is possible to have domination without interference and interference without domination'. The liberal seeks non-interference, but this is not enough. 'If there is domination but no interference, as in the case of the non-interfering master, only the ideal of non-domination will find

---

6 Locke (1690: 57; 131). Note that Locke here uses 'society' for state. In most of the book he uses 'civil society', 'political society', and 'commonwealth' to mean state. Sometimes Locke uses the word 'government' with this same sense, as it is often done in Anglo-American political theory, but in most of the times he attributes to this expression the same sense that I am giving to it: the group of people that govern, or the governing process.
7 Skinner (1990: 295). On this distinction, see the survey by Melo (2002a).

anything to denounce' (Pettit 1997: 23). In other words, if you are not now suffering from the interference of an enlightened or benign monarch, it does not mean that you will not suffer it in the future. Modern republicans as well as modern liberals would not dispute that. Yet, according to Pettit, classical republicans were not concerned with participation but with non-interference. Thus, he concludes, 'the republican conception of liberty is not a positive one . . . '.[8] With this claim, Pettit's republicanism loses most of its strength. He does not realize that eighteenth-century republicans were, in fact, a mixture of classical republicans and modern liberals, and removes from republicanism and from the concept of positive freedom its most specific ingredient: political participation.

Charles Taylor adopts a more affirmative theory of freedom and of republicanism. As a republican he believes that citizens pursue the public interest, but he starts by distancing himself from a common kind of moral or naïve republicanism that assumes altruistic behaviour on the part of men and women. The civic-humanist tradition to which he feels attached is 'patriotic'. And patriotism has here a precise meaning—the attachment to a principle that transcends egoism:

Patriotism is based on an identification with others in a particular common enterprise. I'm not dedicated to defending the liberty of just anyone, but I feel the bond of solidarity with my compatriots in our common enterprise, the common expression of our respective dignity. (Taylor 1995: 188)

Starting from this concept, he asserts that the republic is a society 'bonded by patriotism'. While the moral commitment to the well-being of all humans is frequently inoperative, the patriotic commitment to some common goods— our system of national health, our firefighting department, and the like—is an example of 'the bond of solidarity with my compatriots in a functioning republic . . . based on a sense of shared fate, where the sharing itself is of value' (Taylor 1995: 192).

This kind of reasoning, according to Taylor, is holistic, or, as I would call it, historical-deductive, not atomistic or hypothetical-deductive. The definition of republic adopted by Taylor requires such reasoning, which has origins in Aristotle, while the hypothetical-deductive one originates with Plato. If citizens in the republic have patriotic feelings it is because they live in a community, not in an atomistic society. From this reasoning, Taylor concludes that freedom is essentially positive: that the citizen is free only when he has a deep patriotic identification, and actively participates in the construction of the common well-being:

According to the civic-humanist tradition . . . the essential condition of a free (non-despotic) regime is that the citizens have a deeper patriotic identification . . . The citizen

---

[8] Pettit (1997: 27). The quotation's first phrase is in the title of the section, not in the text of the book.

was 'free' in the sense of having a say in decisions in the political domain, which could shape everyone's lives . . . The underlining reasoning of the thesis is that the disciplines that would be externally imposed by fear under a despotism have to be self-imposed in its absence, and only patriotic identification can provide the motivation. (Taylor 1995: 192–3)

In reconciling modern liberalism with modern republicanism, Skinner's conception of positive freedom is more helpful than Taylor's. Modern outstanding liberals like Rawls would probably feel more comfortable with Skinner's view. Others, like Dworkin, who adopt an aggressive negative concept of freedom, would reject both. Dworkin (2000: 120) says clearly that 'I mean by liberty what is sometimes called negative liberty—freedom from legal constraint—not freedom or power more generally'. On the other hand, he indiscriminately identifies the concern for civic virtue with communitarianism and conservatism.[9]

The Cost of Rights

Thus, in the political theory debate, liberals and republicans (and communitarians) diverge on the concept of liberty. Yet, when we see that this divergence is between Rawls and Skinner, or Taylor and Dworkin, we realize that, although it is theoretically strong, it is curiously weak in political terms. The four eminent political theorists are progressive, or 'liberals' in the American sense. They belong to the modern, social-democratic or social-liberal left. They are strongly opposed to all kinds of conservatism—that is, to the political view that systematically privileges social order at the expense of social justice. I am sure that they all would agree on the importance of protecting what I call republican rights. More than that, modern liberals (but not ultra- or neo-liberals) share with republicans (and democratic socialists) a recognition of the need to fight inequality and assert social rights.

Social rights can be understood as rights against other citizens, if we think, for instance, about workers' rights in relation to their employers. However, when we think about social rights as the right to a good life, education, culture, health care, these are rights against civil society and the state.[10] Such

---

[9] According to Dworkin (1985: 198): 'The conservative supposes that the good man would wish to be treated in accordance with the principles of a special sort of society, which I shall call the virtuous society . . . They treat the lives of other members of their community as part of their own lives.'

[10] I am using 'civil society' in its classic meaning, as a society organized and weighted according to the political powers possessed by individuals and groups, given their organization, wealth, or knowledge, and not as the collection of non-profit organizations. In recent times, given the increasing importance of public non-state (non-profit) organizations, this second meaning has also become usual. Civil society is often thought of in opposition to the state. This opposition, however, makes sense only when the government, which occupies state leadership, loses its legitimacy. Normally civil society and the state walk together: the government represents civil society within the state.

rights do not exist independently of the level of a country's economic development; they became protected rights in developed countries because those countries could afford them. In each society, social needs are transformed into social rights when minimum material resources are available to guarantee them. Class struggle, or, more mildly, the fight between left and right in each country in the last century took place around a central issue: the extent to which each nation-state should and could assert social rights. If the protection of civil and political rights implies costs, the affirmation of social rights involves additional costs and corresponding taxes. When we say that the state grew enormously in the twentieth century, we are essentially saying that taxes increased to finance military expenditures (which protect civil rights) and social expenditures. Rich and conservative individuals resist higher taxes everywhere, except those that protect property rights. They stress the importance of stimulating individual initiative and productive work. Yet, when it became clear that expenditures on education and health care were also investments, such arguments lost much of their appeal. They also argue against social welfare expenditures—minimum income systems, unemployment benefits—that would make labour more costly. However, in this case, the problem is to know which part of the salary should be paid directly to the worker, and which part indirectly. The higher the level of education and of income, the more able individuals are to provide for their own economic security. That is the reason why social security systems guarantee a minimum income. The complementary pension each individual requires for sustaining a standard of living above the minimum is supposed to be contracted individually with private pension funds.

Ultra-liberals, not liberals, are against positive social rights, arguing not only in terms of individual freedom but also in terms of costs: positive rights would be costly. Actually, in order to guarantee civil or liberal rights, particularly property rights, positive governmental action is also necessary, implying costs just as the protection of social rights does. Holmes and Sunstein, in *The Cost of Rights*, make this point in a compelling way. They do not use the expressions 'republican state' or 'republican political system', but, when they affirm that 'all rights are positive' because all rights involve costs and positive action on the part of the state, they are describing the republican state: the actual state that already exists in advanced democracies, the normative state that such democracies have as their goal. Their distinction between moral from descriptive rights corresponds to the classic distinction between natural and positive rights. They observe: 'an interest qualifies as a right when an effective legal system treats it as such by using collective resources to defend it . . . rights in the legal sense have "teeth" . . . When they are not backed by legal force, moral rights are toothless'. In other words, the legal system enacted by the state transforms moral rights into positive rights—into rights that may be defended in the courts and duly protected by the state. But, in this sense, they argue, 'rights cost money: rights cannot be protected or enforced without public funding' (Holmes and Sunstein 1999: 15–17). Not only social rights cost money. All rights, starting from the basic civil rights—freedom and property rights—have a cost. Military, police, penal, judiciary, and the tax collection costs are state expenditures directly related to the necessary protection of property rights. Individuals may go to court and defend their rights only if they have behind them the power of the state implicit in such costs. According to Holmes and Sunstein (1999: 220):

Private liberties have public costs. This is true not only of rights to Social Security, Medicare, and food stamps, but also of rights to private property, freedom of speech, immunity from police abuse, contractual liberty, free exercise of religion, and indeed of the full panoply of rights characteristic of the American tradition.

Services delivered by the state in a democracy are defined by the law, and, in principle, 'free'—that is, financed by taxes. It is this fact that makes them rights, not just needs, but this does not mean that they do not have a cost. It means only that the society has decided to share the costs. As soon as the law specifies a right, the delivery of an action or a service becomes necessary, and costs will be involved. Thus, government performance and its costs are essential to the concept of a republican state. It must be effective and efficient in enforcing rights, or in delivering services related to such rights. The state apparatus is not supposed just to be effective: it must also be efficient. Given the limited tax resources it can count on, the more efficient it is the more effective it will be able to be because it will be able to supply a larger quantity of services for the same cost. It is well known that the legitimacy of a government depends, among other things, on its capacity to raise taxes, but governments in democracies are able to tax only if citizens can see that the money is being well used. In other words, a state merits the name of 'republican' only if, besides protecting rights including republican rights, it does so in an efficient way. The republican state must be concerned with the protection of the public patrimony not only against corruption and milder forms of rent-seeking but also against inefficiency. All rights are democratically decided in the constitution and in the laws of each country, and have a cost. The assumption that positive and negative rights are distinct because the latter do not impose costs is false. Government always has a positive role, which is invariably costly. This positive role may protect or threaten liberty. It threatens liberty in the absolute state, it defends it in the democratic one (Holmes and Sunstein 1999: 50). In democracies, what the republican state is supposed to do—its positive action—depends on how strongly societies are to defend their human rights, and on the scope they accord them.

Although it is legitimate to think in a liberal and republican state, that in reconciling moderate versions of liberalism and republicanism, we should not take lightly the differences between the two ideologies and the dangers involved in liberalism. Liberalism can very easily turn excessively individualistic and lead to a weakening of the republic—of a polity living by the ideals of self-government and of a national and a cosmopolitan project. In his powerful book on the present crisis of American democracy, Michael Sandel starts by distinguishing republican theory, which asserts that liberty depends on sharing in self-government, from liberal political theory, which emphasises toleration and respect for individual rights. Despite their different emphases, he would have no reason to oppose one or the other. Yet, he notes:

The political philosophy by which we live (in the United States) is a certain version of liberal political theory. Its central idea is that government should be neutral toward the moral and religious views its citizens espouse . . . Since this liberalism asserts the priority of fair procedures over particular ends, the public life it informs might be called the procedural republic. (Sandel 1996: 5)

Sandel reminds us that, originally, the public philosophy that guided the United States was the republican one—a philosophy that 'requires a knowledge of public affairs, and a sense of belonging, a concern for the whole, a moral bond with the community whose fate is at stake'.[11] Later, however, liberalism predominated. Despite its positive aspects, the negative liberal vision of freedom presents a major problem: it lacks the civic resources to sustain self-government. He concludes:

A procedural republic that banishes moral and religious argument from political discourse makes for an impoverished civic life. It also fails to answer the aspiration for self-government; its image of citizens as free and independent selves, unencumbered by moral or civic ties they have not chosen, cannot sustain the public spirit that equips us for self-rule. (Sandel 1996: 349–50)

As we see, Sandel comes back to Taylor's powerful arguments. Political liberalism stands for toleration and pluralism, not for distrust and cynicism. In public debate, all kinds of arguments, including moral and religious ones, are legitimate, provided that they are tolerant and respectful of the others' ideas. And moral and religious values are decisive in uniting a community, in giving it a sense of direction, in providing for a republican and democratic state, provided that they are, as Rawls (1989, 1993) insistently demands, 'reasonable'. When classical or economic liberalism limits freedom to a negative conception, besides ceasing to be reasonable it takes the community out of the political society.

The Capacity to Tax

The republican state is a democratic state which derives its power and legitimacy from the support of civil society. It will assure negative freedom, but its

---

[11] Pocock (1975) wrote the classical book on the subject, showing the republican character of the American Revolution.

strength will depend on how willing its citizens, sharing a positive view of freedom, are to participate in civic affairs. Yet it is important to remember that, to assure life, property rights, and contracts that ground freedom, and the social rights that ground social justice, the state needs material resources—specifically, tax revenues. We have just seen, with Holmes and Sunstein, that rights have a cost. Therefore, a republican state is a state that is able democratically to tax citizens. Nobody likes to be taxed, but a good measure of a state's strength and of the government's legitimacy is its capacity to tax. I am not affirming that the higher the tax burden is, the stronger and more republican the state will be. But I am saying that a state that is unable to tax its citizens adequately, while these same citizens demand law and order and social services from it, is a weak state: it lacks political legitimacy, and will tend to fall into fiscal crisis. The modern state emerged in the late Middle Age, when rulers in the city-republics and monarchs in the kingdoms came to derive their revenues from taxes rather than from wars. As we read in *The New Encyclopædia Britannica* (1993: vol. 28: 399), 'taxes played a relatively minor role in the ancient world'. In Elias' *The Civilizing Process*, we have a fascinating account of how the constitution of the two central monopolies that define the modern state—the monopoly of legitimate force and the monopoly of taxation—led to the formation of the modern state between the thirteenth and the fifteenth centuries. There were forerunners of the monopoly control of taxes and the army, but it took an advanced division of functions, the emergence of a money economy in the cities, and the appearance of a new taxable class in these cities—the bourgeoisie—for this control to become stable. Through a long and gradual historical process, a large number of smaller social units come under the control of a larger one: the centralization of political power over relatively large territories in the figure of a monarch give rise to the modern state. 'Only when this complex apparatus has evolved does the control over army and taxation take its full monopoly character . . . A number of other monopolies crystallize those already mentioned. But these two are and remain the key monopolies' (Elias 1994: 268).

The process by which the monarchs achieved monopoly control over tax was long and difficult, marked by political strategies and all sort of struggles. 'The general belief of the kings themselves was that the rulers of a territory and their government should support themselves on the income from their domanial possessions in the narrower sense, that is, on the income from their own estates.'[12] Progress was slow. Even at the end of the eighteenth century, when Adam Smith founds modern political economy with *The Wealth of Nations*, he divides his chapter on the sources of revenues of the state into two parts: 'Of the Funds or Sources of Revenue which may peculiarly belong to the Sovereign or Commonwealth' and 'Of Taxes'. And he still considers it relevant

---

[12] Elias (1994: 345). Elias used the expression 'domanial possessions' to refer to the landed property and feudal rights involved.

to remark that, the first source supplying 'both improper and insufficient funds for defraying the necessary expense of any great and civilized state, it remains that this expense must, the greater part of it, be defrayed by taxes of one kind or another' (Smith 1776: ii 306).

Thus, in our first historical form of state—the absolutist state—a taxation system had just been precariously installed. Originally, its only legitimate purpose was to finance wars. Only when the state apparatus developed and began to offer other services, particularly security services, did their regular financing become another rational basis for taxation. With the liberal state, whose theoretical and ideological foundations were set out by Smith, the legitimacy of taxation was enhanced, but the services the state was able to provide were limited, and the tax burden correspondingly small. In most advanced countries, it was smaller than 10 per cent of GDP. It is only in the twentieth century, with the rise of the democratic state, that the tax burden and the state expenditures increase dramatically: first, because of the rising security costs involved in protecting liberties and property rights; second, because the state starts to play a major role in stabilizing the economy and promoting economic growth; and third, because the gradual transition from the liberal-democratic state to the social-democratic state involves huge new welfare and social costs. Thus, the tax burden increases as the state becomes stronger, more able to protect civil, political, and social rights. We usually think of taxes as an imposition, and in some way associate them with authoritarian rule. Yet history shows that high taxes are the outcome of democracy. In democratic regimes, people demand more from the state in terms of services, and in one way or another agree to pay more taxes. To be sure, they do so reluctantly. This disposition to pay taxes obviously has limits, which are related to those services civil society believes should be viewed as rights and financed by the state. The answer to this question is eminently political: the basic ideological divide between left and right turns on the extent to which the state should assure social rights and incur the associated costs. When the modern state faces fiscal crisis, this is an indication that state expenditures have increased too much, or that taxpayers are not ready to accept tax increases. When the nation-state faces balance-of-payments crises, this is a signal that the nation's expenditures exceed its capacity to generate foreign revenues. Public management reform is an answer to the first problem. Its central objective is to offer the same social protection at a lower cost.

We notice in advanced democratic societies that the upper limit to the tax burden is high. By that I do not mean that the more advanced and democratic a society is, the higher its tax burden will be, but that a high tax burden is one indication of the strength and republican character of the state. It is no accident that average tax burdens in developed countries are substantially higher than in intermediate countries, and higher in these than in poor countries. It is not without consequences that the United States has a tax burden of

30 per cent as against 44 per cent in the European Union and more than that in the more advanced northern European social democracies. Contrary to certain naïve perspectives, developed democracies do not follow a single economic model—the American market model. As we have already seen, there are at least three additional models: the European social model, the Asian or Japanese developmental model, and the Latin American mixed model of capitalism. When Goodin et al. (1999) found the 'social-democratic' model of welfare capitalism to be superior to the 'corporatist' and 'liberal' models, it would be impossible not to relate this finding to the greater taxation legitimacy achieved by the Netherlands and the Scandinavian countries. The neo-liberal ideological wave that began in the mid-1970s was an attempt to limit state expenditures and the tax burden. Its failure to achieve this goal is an indication that voters in modern democracies demand services from the state and are ready to pay for them. But it also indicates that advanced European societies have reached a kind of limit in this area. The social rights whose costs must be financed by taxes are, basically, already defined. The tax burden will probably increase further not because of new rights but because their costs—particularly health care costs—will tend to increase in relation to other costs, mainly of manufactured goods, as productivity gains in service industries are smaller. The challenge that public management reform faces is precisely that of increasing the quality and the efficiency of required services, thus limiting the tax burden.

11

Republican Democracy

The state that is emerging in the twenty-first century will be liberal, social, and republican, but above all it will remain democratic. What kind of democracy will it be? Not the liberal democracy that characterized the first half of the twentieth century, or the social democracy that became dominant in the more advanced countries in the second half of that century. In the era of its first incarnation—liberal democracy—democracy was elitist: although elected competitively, elites were not accountable to voters. The era of social-democracy was the period of public opinion democracy. As long as politicians followed public opinion, they began to be in some measure accountable. Representation, although limited, progressed substantially. By the end of the century, however, the increasing presence of social accountability organizations in the realm of civil society was clearly indicating that the democratic regimes in the more advanced societies, and in countries like Brazil and India, were reaching a new stage of political development.[1] Public debate broadened and its scope gained some depth. This new form of democracy has been called 'participatory democracy' and 'deliberative democracy'; I suggest it should also be called 'republican democracy'.

From Aristocratic Republicanism to Republican Democracy

Just as classical republicanism and classical liberalism conflicted in the past, so did republicanism and democracy. According to Cicero Araujo (2000), modern democratic citizenship involves three normative ideals—civism, pluralism, and plebeism—corresponding, respectively, to the republican, the liberal, and the democratic traditions. The republican tradition, besides being civic, is aristocratic. To Aristotle, aristocracy was the ideal regime, although he objectively realized that the true alternatives that Athens faced in his time

---

[1] This special condition of Brazil and India is one of the outcomes of the research project 'The Reinvention of Social Emancipation'. The papers are collected in Boaventura de Souza Santos (2002).

were oligarchy and privilege on the one hand, and democracy and political instability on the other. In the Roman republic, the idea that society should and could be governed by citizens endowed with public virtues gained currency. Cicero and Machiavelli, separated by 15 centuries, still clearly followed this same line of thought, despite all the setbacks that they themselves faced. And the eighteenth century political philosophers such as Montesquieu, Harrington, and Madison, although attracted by liberalism, or such as Rousseau, interested in democracy, remained essentially aristocratic republicans. They sought an aristocracy based not on blood but on virtue, competence, and wealth—the last subsuming the first two. Rousseau, who clearly distinguished republic from democracy, viewed the latter as practically unachievable by humans, and imposed severe restrictions on the admission of new citizens to his ideal community—the republic. To have some control over the expected virtue of their citizens, republicans accepted what all political thinkers for centuries had considered obviously right for ideological as well as for rational reasons: limitations on citizenship. Yet, after the capitalist revolution and an enormous increase in the middle classes created the conditions for modern democracy, those limitations ceased to be either rational or politically viable.

When liberalism challenged republicanism in the eighteenth century, it was not in the name of political equality—the plebeian principle—but in the name of liberty, since the two currents concurred in rejecting democracy as it is understood today, that is, giving full voting rights to all citizens, regardless of sex, education, religion, or wealth. As we saw in Chapter 4, only after the capitalist revolution and after a 'liberal period'—the nineteenth century—were more developed countries able to adopt universal suffrage and become democracies. Only at that moment were the elites in those countries reasonably persuaded that the poor did not represent a real threat to social order—that they would respect property rights and contracts. From that moment, elites had no alternative but to accept the political demands for democracy coming from the poor and from a large section of the middle classes. The advanced capitalist societies were ripe for modern democracy and universal suffrage.

However, even in the first part of the twentieth century, when universal suffrage had become a reality in the new democratic nation-states, political theorists remained attached to an elitist, anti-plebeian approach to democracy. I am not referring to Mosca's (1896) sociological and political theory of the circulation of elites, which are pre-democratic, but to Schumpeter's and Down's theory of competitive democracy. This theory, which I identify historically with the concept of liberal democracy, still has numerous followers in the United States, where the transition from liberal to social democracy has not been completed.[2] It views representative democracy merely as a competition

---

[2] See Chapter 4.

among elites for the support of the voters. Once this support is achieved, the elite, according to this concept of democracy, is entitled to make its own decisions independently of the voters' will.

When Schumpeter (1942) developed this theory in the first part of the twentieth century, it made sense. Today, citizens just do not accept such a limited concept of democracy. At first, public opinion became increasingly effective in making politicians in some measure accountable. Concomitantly, while workers became better organized in their unions, and centre-left political coalitions won their first general elections in several European countries, the state became social-democratic, that is, committed to the protection of social rights. More recently, with the increasing role played by social accountability organizations, each fighting for its interpretation of the public interest, democracy became increasingly participatory. The republican state and the corresponding republican democracy were gradually emerging. While the organizations of civil society were increasingly recognized by the legal system as valid political interlocutors and gained political legitimacy, the public space increased in density, creating the basic conditions for participatory democracy, and some countries or federal states started to experiment with several forms of direct democracy, including the recall of incumbents. Although political elites remain powerful, their power is increasingly checked by an active citizenship willing to have some degree of participation in political power. Although politicians in the more advanced democracies are far from examples of republicanism, Schumpeter's aristocratic disdain for politics and politicians who, instead of debating, would just tell untruths in order to achieve their objectives, cannot today be so easily accepted as a good description of politicians. In the same way that cannot be accepted as a good description of citizens, Anthony Downs' related theory (1957) justifying elitist democracy with the argument that voters act rationally, are just concerned with their own interests, and, so, will not engage in actions oriented to the public interest.

Modern republicanism responded to this historical change, and lost its old traits of aristocratic ideology. While economic liberalism remained elitist and became conservative, the only significant version of republicanism today is democratic and progressive, sponsoring participatory democracy. The more advanced existing forms of democracy are still far from effectively deliberative democracy, but we are also far from the classical model of liberal democracy.

Republican, Participatory, or Deliberative Democracy?

What is the difference between republican and deliberative democracy? The theoretical debate between the elitist or competitive theory of democracy and deliberative democracy is rich. Arguments for and against one or the other conception are still today at the centre of the Anglo-American political theory debate. This is essentially a normative and ideological debate. On the one side, we have social-liberal or politically liberal political theorists, headed by Habermas, Rawls, and Joshua Cohen, who defend a deliberative concept of democracy; on the other, classical liberals and rational-choice 'realists', who show the limits of representation and political accountability in contemporary democracies, and reject the deliberative ideal.

In this book on the building of the republican state, political theory is central but I avoid a normative approach. Rather, I adopt a sociological or historical approach in which normative theories are implicit. The issue is not what reason has to say about the central political problems of our time, but how modern societies, divided between the public interest and group interests, normatively view these problems. I am interested in ideal public reason, but in this book I am more concerned with an effective or viable concept of democracy. I know that there is a powerful link between the two approaches. Rawls (1997: 135) observes that the ideal of public reason is realized or satisfied whenever government officers follow public reason and explain their reasons to other citizens. This means that politicians and senior civil servants have no other option in a democracy but to explain rationally their views on a society's central political and moral values. It also means that a normative and hypothetical-deductive approach to politics is necessary. Yet I believe it is intellectually dangerous to rely essentially on a normative approach. I want it to be checked by reality, by the historical process.

From this point of view, if there are facts that have invalidated an elitist or competitive theory of democracy, there are other facts that should restrain us from speaking of deliberative democracy. In all democracies, including those that have recently completed their democratic transition, a majority of citizens may still be self-interested, and the participation costs may still be higher than the rewards they can obtain from active citizenship, but we already find a large enough number of republican citizens to make the classical model of elitist democracy unworkable. There are still many politicians who merely make trade-offs between the desire of being re-elected and the craving to become rich, but the political pressure on politicians to make trade-offs, rather, between the desire to be re-elected and the search for the public interest increases every decade. On the other hand, we must be realist enough to recognize that the historical conditions for deliberative democracy are not yet present in any country. This will be true even if we do not include among the conditions for public deliberation substantive equality and consensus among participants. This requirement was adopted by Joshua Cohen in his seminal paper on deliberative democracy. Based on Habermas, he was the first political philosopher to use the expression and discuss it fully, but he went further, and defined it ideally. His concept of 'ideal deliberation' involves five aspects. First, deliberation is supposed to be *free*, meaning that participants are bound only by the results of their deliberation; second, deliberation should be 'reasoned', in the sense that the parties are required to state their reasons for advancing, supporting, or criticizing proposals; third, deliberation should be 'formally equal', meaning that procedures do not single out participants; fourth, deliberation should be 'substantively equal': 'participants are substantively equal in that the existing distribution of power and resources does not shape their chances to contribute to deliberation'; and, fifth, 'ideal deliberation aims to arrive at a rationally motivated *consensus*' (Cohen 1989: 74–5). Although immediately after the quoted assertions Cohen adds that consensus may not be achieved and that compromise and voting may be required, the two requirements that participants be substantively equal and that they reach consensus are not even minimally realistic. The critiques that have been directed at deliberative democracy in large part derive from this idealism or lack of realism.

This is not a good reason to reject the concept of deliberative democracy, which opens a new normative space for the improvement of democracy. In the context of the present analysis, however, which intends to be historical rather than normative, it is a valid reason for asserting that the model of democracy emerging in the more advanced societies is less demanding: it is participatory or republican democracy. It is less demanding because it clearly does not require equal substantive power among participants of the public debate, nor does it suppose that consensus will be reached. It is contented that the debate involves a substantial participation from civil society's organizations, and that the debate follows minimal rules of communicative action, particularly mutual respect in offering reasoned arguments for each position. Decisions will ultimately be made by elected politicians in the parliament, in the context of a representative system, but each major decision will be preceded by a broad and lively public debate. Such debate will influence the setting of the agenda and the framing of the main alternatives to each decision. In some cases, the arguments presented will be strong enough to persuade the other party. In others, a new alternative arising from the debate will be able to satisfy the conflicting groups, and conflict will be overcome. Yet, in most cases, compromise will remain necessary, and majority voting will eventually decide the issue.

This type of democracy is participatory because it counts on the active participation of the organizations of the third sector (corporative organizations and, increasingly, public non-state social accountability organizations). The classic analysis of participatory democracy was made by Carole Pateman, from a left-wing point of view. She starts her analysis by criticizing the elitist and pluralist concepts of liberal democracy, discusses Rousseau's republican participatory system and G. D. W. Cole's socialist views of democracy, and on this basis builds her own theory. According to Pateman, participatory democracy involves socialization through participation. By this she means that the workplace or industry, as a political institution, must be democratized. Second, she defines participatory democracy thus:

One might characterize the participatory model as one where maximum input (participation) is required and where output includes not just policies (decisions) but also the development of the social and political capacities of each individual, so that there is a 'feedback' from output to input. (Pateman 1970: 43)

The concept of participatory democracy that I adopt here is less ambitious. It has its origin in a Latin American and Catholic tradition of political and social thought critical of classical and economic liberalism,[3] which gave birth to the Workers' Party (PT) in Brazil and attracted international attention because of Porto Alegre's 'Participatory Budget'.[4] This experience is just one of many institutional innovations in participatory democracy that are taking place in the world today.[5] This line of thought is well established in the Brazilian political and constitutional system.[6] The 1988 Constitution has several provisions referring to forms of participatory democracy, or social accountability.[7] Participatory democracy is more than just a Brazilian ideal; it is a Latin American one. Catalina Smulovitz and Henrique Peruzzotti, based on their Argentinean experience, contend that the nature of new democratic regimes and the scope of citizens' rights are being shaped by the 'politics of societal accountability', in which civic associations, NGOs, and social movements play a central role:

Citizen action aimed at overseeing political authorities is becoming a fact of life and is redefining the traditional concept of the relationship between citizens and their elected representatives. (Smulovitz and Peruzzotti 2000: 147)

According to Boaventura de Souza Santos and Leonardo Avritzer, participatory democracy is a central form through which social emancipation is being reinvented at the beginning of the twenty-first century. It has its theoretical foundation in Habermas's procedural concept of deliberation. Rather than remaining content with the opposition between a procedural and a substantive (usually Marxist) concept of democracy, Habermas adopts a procedural

---

[3] See, for instance, André Franco Montoro (1974). As well as a law professor, Montoro was a leading centre-left Catholic political leader in Brazil.

[4] The participatory budget was introduced by the mayor from the Workers' Party (PT), Olívio Dutra (1989–92), and continued by Tarso Genro and Raul Pont, from the same political party. On the experience, see Navarro (1998); Avritzer (2002*a*, *b*); Santos (2002); Baiocchi (2003).

[5] See on the subject Evelina Dagnino (2002), Santos (2002), and Fung and Wright (2003).

[6] The Brazilian Workers' Party (PT) does not have Marxist origins. Rather, it originated in Catholic social movements that, through Luiz Inácio Lula da Silva, were able in the late 1970s to control a major union in São Bernardo, in greater São Paulo, previously under the control of Communist union leaders. After the political party was created in 1980, some Communist groups adhered to it.

[7] See, for instance, Silva (1997). His textbook on constitutional law discusses democracy in three sections: representative democracy, plural democracy, and participatory democracy. Another Brazilian jurist, Moreira Neto (1992), dedicates a full book to the 'right of political participation'.

approach, but includes in it a social and deliberative criterion. In doing so, he recognizes that new players had to be considered in the democratic process, and makes clear that a procedural approach cannot be used to justify an elitist form of democracy. Souza Santos and Avritzer (2002: 53) conclude:

What the democratization process did through the introduction of new players in the political scene was to open a debate in favour of a meaning for democracy and for the constitution of a new social and institutional grammar for it.

The new emerging democracy is participatory or republican because the republican tradition is based on the participation of citizens in the political process. In the first part of the twentieth century, when unions and other corporative organizations gained political influence, the idea of participatory democracy reached a wider audience, but did not achieve the status of a new form of democracy in Anglo-American political theory. Yet, when an outstanding political philosopher such as Jürgen Habermas wrote about communicative action, and Joshua Cohen translated the notion into the concept of deliberative democracy, the idea immediately gained currency. As participatory democracy is a modern republican concept, deliberative democracy is equally so. Participatory democracy and deliberative democracy are almost synonyms. As Avritzer (2000: 43) observes, 'although participation and deliberation are not synonyms, it is interesting that all deliberative arrangements are amplified forms of participation'. Whereas participatory democracy did not achieved the status of a grand theory, deliberative democracy did so. Habermas, adopting in this case an analytical and normative approach rather than an historical and sociological one, prefers deliberative to republican democracy. According to him, 'the central element of the democratic process resides in the procedure of deliberative politics'. This reading of democracy differs from the liberal view 'of the state as a guardian of an economic society' and of democracy as a process 'effected exclusively in the form of compromise among interests'. It differs also 'from the republican concept of an ethical community institutionalized in the state' and from the republican view of democracy as 'equivalent to the political self-organization of society as a whole', which 'leads to an offensive understanding of politics directed against the state apparatus' (Habermas 1992: 296–7). Yet I understand deliberative democracy as a political ideal, and the contributions to it from political philosophers such as Habermas, Rawls, and Cohen are timely and profound. In historical terms, however, I believe that we should be more modest or more realist, and for the moment engage in building the republican state and a republican democracy.

In studying democracy today, political theorists have no alternative but to discuss, in practical terms, participative or republican democracy and, normatively, deliberative democracy. Yet resistance to it remains strong, especially among rational-choice theorists. As long as they profess a strong pessimism about the possibility of collective action, they resist acknowledging the existence of a number of republican citizens oriented to the public interest and committed to engage in some, however limited, participation in public affairs. The new republicanism, the revival of the ideas of public sphere and civil society, and the theory of deliberative democracy are today essentially the same thing. The constitutional state and the rule of law, preconditions of modern democracy, become effective only when an active civil society—originally a bourgeois civil society—is behind these two basic liberal institutions. Historically, in the words of Bignotto (2000: 63), 'civic humanism presented to its time the need to define values associated with the capacity of acting in the city in the name of the city'. Behind the construction of the modern republican state, a moral philosophy is necessary, oriented to the interests of the state. The sheer size of the modern state does not allow for the Greek *civitas*, but it is possible to think of a civil society, or a public sphere, in which citizens act civically. Before being a condition for the consolidation of democracy, the existence of an active civil society is central in ensuring the rule of law. Given the existence of an active civil society, rulers will not obey the law only because they are constrained to do so, or because they see that it is on their self-interest, or because they view the law as fair. As Catalina Smulovitz (2003) remarks, costs can be imposed on rulers who transgress the law in a decentralized manner by an autonomous and active civil society.

The transition from the social-democratic to the republican state is a historical and intellectual complex process, involving the reform of the state and the design and introduction of new institutions, including public management reform. This reform makes sense only in the realm of some form of democracy—specifically deliberative democracy—because it involves assigning to senior civil servants greater discretionary power, and thus depends on the existence of effective social accountability mechanisms to make them reasonably accountable. Such social accountability exists only in the context of a strong public sphere, in which an active civil society is present.

When I say that a republican democracy is emerging, I am supposing that citizens endowed with republican virtues are behind it. It is impossible to develop the values of, and build the institutions that support, the republican state without the existence of such men and women. They will not be saints, they will be also self-interested or display an enlightened self-interest; but the civic virtues intrinsic to republicanism will be present in some way. This republicanism will not be international. It will be national or communitarian, as Taylor suggested, associating it with patriotism. They may be liberals, but in this case they will be what Michael Walzer (2001: 176) calls 'liberal nationalists', referring to Isaiah Berlin's way of thinking:

Liberal nationalism is probably best understood as a species of liberal reformism. Its protagonists take the actually existing world of passionate attachments as given, and then they try to modify it—not so as to make all the attachments harmonious, a utopian rather than reformist project, but to make them sufficiently compatible to coexist in peace.

The existence of republican citizens is not just an assumption or a normative claim. It can be detected in all kinds of society. Despite the individualism or its opposite—conformism—that characterizes so many, it is impossible to understand the political and social progress achieved to date without considering the role of critical citizens, endowed with some public virtues and concerned with the public interest. An interesting empirical corroboration of what I am asserting is the political surveys published in *Critical Citizens*. In this book edited by Pipa Norris, a group of distinguished researchers, based on their own research and existing surveys of citizens' satisfaction with democracy, reject as conventional wisdom the idea that democracy is in crisis: on the contrary, it is very much alive. Political unhappiness is real and increasing, but not because there is a growing cynicism about democratic government, as the conventional wisdom suggests, but because citizens have become more critical. According to Norris (1999*a*: 21): 'Democratic values now command widespread acceptance as an ideal, but at the same time citizens have often become more critical of the workings of the core institutions of representative democracy'. On the other hand, she criticizes Robert Putnam's contention that American civic values have declined. Her critique is directed at these findings since, even there, although a reduction in informal associations could be verified, no decline in political participation could be. Studies of the pattern of political participation in the advanced democracies show that it is trendless. Yet one thing is clear: institutional confidence in democracy is significantly related to political participation (Norris 1999*b*: 260). Participatory citizens are confident but critical. They are republican citizens committed in one way or another to reform, and their political actions make a difference.

When I propose to call the democracy that is emerging republican, I do not adopt this communitarian concept of republicanism which, in its more extreme forms, supposes that it is possible to substitute civil society for the state. This goes against the core argument in this book. On the contrary, I understand modern republicanism as offering a view on how to strengthen the state through the active participation of the organizations of civil society. In the last quarter of the twentieth century, after pluralist or social democracy became consolidated in the more advanced countries, the new political problem was how to improve democracy. How to make representative democracy a better democracy. How to make politicians more accountable. The more obvious solution—to improve representation through institutional change—continues to occupy the attention of political scientists, as it is a central strategy for political development. Yet perhaps a more effective contribution to this problem came from society itself, as its organizations increased their role in the political process at the national and also the international level.

Social Accountability and the Republican Democracy

Thus, active and participating organizations of civil society are central in the transition to republican democracy. Society in mature democratic countries as well as in the new democracies is increasingly learning how to organize itself. While one of the two classic forms of corporative organization—the unions—lost ground after the 1970s, probably because they limited themselves to negotiating wages and work conditions, and the other—the business associations—just maintained their influence, a whole new set of civil society organizations, particularly social accountability organizations forming complex societal networks, emerged at the national and international levels. Political advocacy or social accountability became a new reality, responding to the increasing complexity of the political system and to the presence of a reasonable number of citizens ready to participate in civil society organizations.

The recognition of a public non-state space and the need for social accountability organizations became particularly important at a the moment when the crisis of the state intensified the state–market dichotomy, leading many to imagine that the only alternative to state property was private property, and that democracy can be only procedural and elitist. In fact, the public non-state form of ownership is an increasingly significant alternative not only because public non-state service organizations provide the social and scientific services, but especially because social accountability organizations make government officials accountable and participatory democracy more representative.

Recently, unions have begun to recover influence, showing that corporative and social accountability organizations support each other. At the moment when globalization and the state crisis demand a re-examination of the state–society and the state–market relationships, the public non-state space plays the role of intermediary. It is able to facilitate the appearance of state–private sector partnerships, or the rise of social accountability or forms of public advocacy, opening new perspectives for building a republican state. As Cunill Grau (1995: 3) observes, 'the introduction of "public" as a third dimension, surpasses the dichotic view that opposes in an absolute manner "state" with "private" '. Along similar lines, Bresser-Pereira and Cunill Grau (1998: 31) state that the existence of a public non-state space between the state and the market permits the constitution of a virtuous circle of democratic character:

On the one hand, civil society will be much more democratic as corporative organizations become more representative. However, it will be much more democratic to the extent that public non-state social accountability organizations, defending rights and practising social accountability, attain greater development.

Following the same line of thought, Vincent Ostrom develops the conception of 'open public space', identifying it with the conception of civil society, as a space that is public but outside state jurisdiction. Using Tocqueville's classic comparison between the American and French systems, he points out how this public space is part of Anglo-Saxon common law, opening the possibility for civil society to take an active part in contracts and to become a legitimate origin of law, independently of the state. From there, Ostrom (1991: 211) observes that 'it is open public space and the form by which it connects to more structured state forms that makes the process of government accessible to the citizenry'. In the public space, or in the public sphere, members of society learn what living in a democratic society means: public debate advances, public opinion becomes more and more relevant, public spirit is developed, and a culture of inquiry is established. In 1994, during a seminar in Brazil, Manuel Castells (1994) claimed that NGOs were quasi-public organizations. Indeed they are, to the extent that they are halfway between state and society. Public non-state organizations carry out public activities and are controlled directly by society through their boards of directors and associates. Other forms of social accountability involve direct participation by citizens in the public space, as we saw in the previous section.

Robert Putnam and associates have made an important contribution to understanding the role of public non-state social accountability and corporative organizations. They recovered the concept of 'social capital', originally developed by L. Judson Hanifan, and formally defined by James Coleman in the late 1980s.[8] In a book about Italy, Putnam stresses the importance of corporative and public non-state organizations.[9] In fact, his concept of social capital is broader, because it includes the informal social networks that cannot be viewed as organizations. The social capital of a given community or of a given nation-state will be greater the stronger are the social networks among individuals. Such networks may be exclusively social, involving family, friends, and associates, or political, including all kind of corporative and social accountability organizations. From this definition, Putnam and Kristin Goss derive a simple and obvious conclusion:

Social networks matter . . . Social interaction helps to resolve dilemmas of collective action, encouraging people to act in a trustworthy way when they might not otherwise do so . . . Social capital can be simultaneously a private and a public good.[10]

Within this broad concept of social capital, it is necessary to stress the civic associations that are part of the public sphere. Civil society organizations or social accountability organizations have gained a new political and administrative relevance, not as a substitute for classic representation but as a complement to it. Through their exertions, representative democracy has started

---

[8] Coleman (1990). Hanifan (1920) is referred in Putnam and Goss (2002).

[9] Putnam (1993). The author points to the importance of association, or 'social capital', already present in the 'choral societies' of the medieval period for the acceleration and consolidation of economic development. A large literature developed out of this seminal work.

[10] Putnam and Goss (2002: 6). See also Putnam (1993, 1995, 2000).

to display traits of participatory or republican democracy. Some authors that originally discussed participatory and deliberative democracy oppose it to representative democracy,[11] but they were probably thinking on representative democracy in its original, elitist or Schumpeterian, form. Using the concept of representative democracy in a broader sense, simply as the alternative to direct democracy, it remains the only real possibility for democracy. And social accountability organizations and deliberative or participatory mechanisms are not an alternative to but an improvement on representative democracy.

After the late 1970s, the idea of participatory democracy gained force in Latin America and in eastern Europe, while authoritarian rule was being challenged by civil society organizations. After democracy was achieved, these organizations increased their participatory and political accountability roles. At the same time, the idea thrived among the advanced democracies where the concepts of social capital and social networks gained broad currency. Social accountability did not emerge as an alternative but as a complement to state action. Along this line of thought, Stark and Bruszt (1998: 127) argue that the growth and modernization of an economy (or its 'transformative capacity') depends on 'the strength and cohesiveness of social networks in the economy itself'.

Political decentralization or devolution to sub-national units usually entails increased political participation or the use of social accountability mechanisms. When public policies are under the control of central government, social accountability is, by definition, precarious. The moment devolution takes place, social accountability becomes a possibility. Nuria Cunill Grau, surveying the theme in Latin America, found three models differentiated by its more or less formal character. While the Bolivian model, which delegated power to territorial organizations, would be more closed to citizens' participation, the Mexican system, as expressed in the National Solidarity Program, would be in an intermediary model, and the Colombian 'veedurías ciudadanas' would be the least formally institutionalized and the most open to participation by all types or citizens' organizations. Yet she observes that either formalization or lack of it is a good criterion to evaluate social accountability. To start with, it is necessary to have citizens and a state that recognizes them as such. Thus, 'independently of the formalization of the social accountability models, whenever the state decides to institutionalize social accountability, the effectiveness of the policy will depend on the effectiveness of the state itself: by definition, if the state is fragile, social accountability will also be so'. Consequently, Cunill Grau concludes that the conditions for effective social accountability are just beginning to exist in Latin America.[12]

In fact, decentralization and social accountability depend on the existence of citizen rights, beginning with the right to full disclosure of information on

---

[11] See, for instance, Jürgen Habermas (1992) and David Miller (1992). The real conflict is between deliberative democracy and rational choice theory, as Miller emphasizes in this same paper.
[12] Cunill Grau (2000: 284–92, 301, 322).

public agencies. In other words, it depends on the existence of the rule of law and, more broadly, on the advance of democracy. Democracy is no substitute for decentralization and social accountability, but the latter are outcomes of the democratization process and, at the same time, they are factors making for better democratic governance. The advance of democratization, the transition from the first stage of democracy, when free elections already exist but elites continue to exercise almost all power, to more advanced forms of democracy, depends essentially on increased public debate and on various forms of social accountability that spring up at the local level and are fuelled by devolution. In the 1970s and the 1980s, one of the key figures in the long process of transition to democracy in Brazil, André Franco Montoro—a politician and a law professor—distinguished himself not only by the democratic principles he promoted but also by always tying democracy to devolution and participation. Yet, evaluating the decentralization process in Latin America, Ivan Finot (1999: 74) came to the conclusion that 'only exceptionally citizens' participation in public management beyond elections has been achieved'. Along similar lines, Philip Oxhorn, who conducted extensive research on the popular sectors in Chile, observes that, after the democratization, while the number of grass-roots organizations continued to increase extraordinarily—they continue to double every two years—'the public presence of popular-sector organizational activity is extremely low . . . there has been no systematic efforts from within the popular sectors themselves to create any kind of popular social movement, or even influence governmental policies' (Oxhorn 1995: 273). In other words, social accountability, which would make government officers more account-able, is fragile in Latin America, including even in a relatively advanced country like Chile. To the extent that governments do not use civil society organizations as a tool to control the administration, as happened in Brazil—in Rio Grande do Sul's 'participatory budget', or in Minas Gerais's parents participation in running public schools—the capacity of communities to organize themselves is limited. When governments do use them, we have signs of public management reform.

Conservative liberals object to participatory mechanisms, asserting that such organizations do not have a voters' mandate—which is formally true. However, the limits imposed by formal representation remain huge. Despite all institutional strategies to reduce the hiatus between citizens and represent-atives, to make politicians more accountable, such hiatus has only increased as the size and complexity of the modern states have grown. Thus, the liberal argument fell into a void. Through political advocacy or social accountability mechanisms, society proved able to complement representation effectively. Civil society's organizations are present everywhere, fighting for their views, informing, arguing, debating. Elected politicians decide in parliament or in executive positions taking into consideration all that activity—an activity that makes representation more real. As Andrew Arato (2002: 97) observed, 'we are correct in considering the public sphere and civil society as intermediate between representatives and citizens. They reduce the distance and the tension between them'. Political advocacy organizations play an intermediary role between voters and representatives. These organizations may have suffered from all kinds of limitations, but eventually they confer on democracy a republican character.

II

Reforming Public Administration

12

Bureaucratic and Civil Service Reform

From the last chapter we conclude that the social-liberal and republican state will rely more on markets than the social democratic state, while remaining committed to the protection of social rights. It will be less protective, but governments in each nation-state will continue actively to promote commercial and technological policies. Globalization has increased nation-states' interdependence, but this does not mean that the national political realm is vanishing or that political decisions are losing relevance. On the contrary, as society and markets become more and more complex, and civil society more demanding and able to exert social accountability, the strategic character of national governments and of the political decisions they make increases.

Building the new social-liberal and republican state involves a continuous process of political and economic institutional reforms: trade reform, tax and fiscal reform, social security reform, labour reform, political reform, and public management reform. In this book, my concern is only with the last type of institutional reform that began in the 1980s in Britain, New Zealand, and Australia, and so far, with a few exceptions such as Brazil, has been limited to developed countries.

Public management reform intends to create new legal and organizational institutions that allow the transformation of the professional bureaucracy into public managers. Downsizing the state apparatus may be part of it, but the central objective is to rebuild state capacity, making government more efficient and more accountable. This reform does not underestimate the patrimonial and clientelist elements still existing in developing countries, nor the strength of bureaucratic and pork-barrel factors in the developed ones. It proceeds, however, from the assumption that the best way to fight patrimonialism, clientelism, the pork barrel, or sheer corruption is not to try to 'complete bureaucratic reform' but to take a step forward and engage in managerial public administration. In this chapter, I discuss the transition from bureaucratic public administration to public or new public management.

Bureaucratic Administration's Intrinsic Irrationality

Classic bureaucratic administration, based upon the Prussian army's administrative principles, resulted from a series of civil service reforms implemented in the second half of the nineteenth century in Germany, England, France, and the United States, examined in Part I of this book. Still in that century, we had the Japanese bureaucratic reform. At the beginning of the twentieth century, countries like Canada, New Zealand, and Australia engaged in civil service reform. In Brazil it began in the 1930s, during the first Vargas administration. In some major developing countries, like Mexico, the creation of a civil service career did not materialize, although a powerful professional bureaucracy developed.[1]

Capitalist and liberal economies adopted bureaucratic public administration, classically described by Max Weber as a rational–legal form of domination, between the eighteenth and the nineteenth centuries. It came to replace patrimonial administration—the traditional form of bureaucracy developed especially in the Chinese empire—that achieved its full character in Europe with the absolute monarchies. In patrimonial administration, public and private patrimonies were essentially fused; the state was conceived of as the sovereign's property. Public office was often the property of bureaucrats. An example is the *officiers*, the nobility charged with collecting rents in France. Also in France, *commissaires* were tantamount to a 'dynastic bureaucracy'. Within this framework, nepotism and corruption were the rule, although this did not prevent high-level patrimonial bureaucrats—who, together with the aristocracy, exercised a great deal of political power—from indulging in self-glorification and arrogance as the masters of technical rationality. This attitude, as described by Rosenberg, lasted until the nineteenth century, when the Prussian bureaucracy slowly ceased being dynastic (or patrimonial) and became civil service.[2]

Civil service reform came about because patrimonial administration proved inconsistent with industrial capitalism and liberal political parliamentary regimes, which appeared in the nineteenth century. The rule of law and a clear-cut separation between state and market are essential to capitalism. Business activities require institutions guaranteeing the rule of law, or property rights and contracts. Entrepreneurs will invest only if they can count on regulated markets and a predictable political environment, so that their

---

[1] On the Mexican bureaucracy see Miguel Ángel Centeno (1997).

[2] In the words of Rosenberg, who, in his study on Prussian bureaucracy, offers us a lively description of the distortions that may vitiate any bureaucracy (1968: 23–4): 'Prussian bureaucracy was not the only one in the nineteenth century to practice the vices of self-glorification and group arrogance . . . It built for itself a special place within the state services of the European world as it claimed to be the practical embodiment of the political teachings of German Idealism; as it operated behind a metaphysical smoke screen; as it persuaded many that public administration was "the" Government; the bureaucracy, "the" state; authority, freedom, privilege, equality of opportunities.'

profits will depend principally on the competitive advantages that they achieve. Bureaucratic public administration was one of those institutions. Civil service reform and the emergence of bureaucratic administration, based upon centralization, clear hierarchical lines, rigid routines, step-by-step control of administrative procedures, impersonal methods of recruiting personnel, and secrecy represented a higher level of instrumental rationality or efficiency. The conduct of state affairs by professional civil servants, specially recruited and trained, who follow well-defined careers, are endowed of a 'bureaucratic ethos' consonant with the public interest, and who respond to politicians in a neutral manner is also a way of guaranteeing property rights and contracts. Weber clearly realized that bureaucratic public administration was adopted because, in his time, it was the only possible way to effectively coordinate work within such a large and complex organization as the state. Silberman, proceeding from a rational choice perspective, comes to a similar conclusion: bureaucratic organization was the way to reduce uncertainty about the decision-making process and thus increase the possibility of foreseeing behaviour. Thus, the two explanations are complementary.[3] Civil service reform, the process of bureaucratization or rationalization, is a historical phenomenon deriving from the superior character of bureaucratic public administration vis-à-vis patrimonial administration. At that time, it was the best way to increase efficiency, eliminate nepotism, and reduce corruption.

Yet, the assumption of efficiency, upon which civil service reform rests, did not prove sound.[4] As the small nineteenth century liberal state was replaced by the twentieth century's large social-democratic state, this type of administration did not ensure that either good-quality or low-cost services were delivered to the public. Bureaucratic public administration, born within the framework of liberal capitalism—and not in that of liberal democracy, which became dominant only in the twentieth century—proved to be slow, expensive, self-centred, authoritarian, not geared to meet citizens' demands. For a long time, following Merton's and Gouldner's classical analyses, 'distortions' or 'dysfunction' explained the inefficiencies associated with bureaucratic administration.[5] Paperwork, regulatory rigidity, lack of initiative, secrecy, were all distortions of an organizational model which, in principle, was rational or efficient. In recent times, Gerald Caiden (1991b) has returned to this perspective, referring to 'bureau-pathologies' or to 'mis-administration'.

Yet, although within the same institutional bureaucratic framework there may be higher- or lower-quality management practices, it has become increasingly clear that bureaucratic public administration is inherently irrational or

---

[3] Silberman (1993). Although it may be possible to think that the second perspective is an alternative to the first one, it is in fact complementary, since Silberman, though choosing the theory of rational choice, which became dominant in American political science, adopts, as did Weber, the historical method rather than the logical-deductive one.

[4] Alvin Gouldner (1945) had made this clear already in his classic and pioneering book.

[5] Robert Merton (1949), Alvin Gouldner (1945).

inefficient. Weber described it as a type of domination—'rational-legal domination'—which would be characterized by technical superiority or efficiency. Its 'rational' character appeared in the form of instrumental rationality consisting in the adoption of the most appropriate means to reach the intended goals. Its 'legal' character meant that the law would define the most appropriate means to achieve the objectives also stated in the law. This system contained an intrinsic contradiction: in a world in continuous and progressively faster change, it is impossible to be at the same time rational and legal. It is impossible to be rational by defining, in law, the specific goals to be achieved and the means to be followed: the law can broadly define objectives and means, but its competent specification depends necessarily on case-by-case decision-making.

The Rise of Public Management

Such a contradiction was not serious while a small state prevailed, whose only role was to protect civil rights or to guarantee property rights and contracts. Strictly speaking, in the liberal state only four executive ministries were necessary: a Ministry of Justice, in charge of the police or domestic order; a Ministry of Defence, including the army and the navy; a Finance Ministry or Treasury; and a Foreign Relations Ministry. In this type of state, the most important public services aimed directly at maintaining law and order and at protecting the country against foreign enemies. The problem of efficiency was not, in fact, central. In the twentieth century, however, the state apparatus became the large social-democratic state, undertaking new social roles— education, health, transport, social security and social care, culture, scientific research—and new economic roles: macroeconomic stability, regulation of public services and monopolist activities, provision of public infrastructure, industrial and foreign trade policy. For this large and costly state organization, the problem of efficiency became serious. The demands for the delivery of good-quality and low-cost public services weighed upon politicians and bureaucrats, whose legitimacy started to depend on this variable. The way was open for public management reform.

Michel Crozier (1996) remarks that the two fundamental tendencies of our times are the growing complexity either of the world in which we live in or of the collective actions we have to carry out, and the demand for personal freedom or individual autonomy. One tendency reinforces the other: complexity offers opportunities for autonomy and innovation by individual agents, while autonomy increases the complexity of the system. Thus, the bureaucratic model, based upon the rigidity of norms and the discipline of civil servants, became incompatible with present needs. It had already proved to be badly suited to the period of mass production, but not so clearly, due to the standardization of activities that marked that time. Yet, after the world moved towards a cycle of high technology in production, chiefly in services, the bureaucratic paradigm, averse to innovation, became definitively obsolete.

Notwithstanding, after the Second World War bureaucratic values in public administration were renewed and reasserted, while, at the same time, and inconsistently, national governments' new commitments to economic development and social protection led them to seek more flexible and efficient forms of managing state agencies and state-owned enterprises. Consequently, the influence of management theories and practices, which developed explosively in business schools and business consultancies, soon began to be felt also in public administration. The ideas of withering out the adoption of strict administrative procedures, and of decentralization to more autonomous agencies, acquired a presence within all governments, together with a renewed confidence in budgetary planning. Yet, instead of proposing the reform of the whole structure of the state organization and of the method of rendering bureaucrats accountable, developmental reformers limited themselves to creating new autonomous agencies, to free them from some bureaucratic controls and to insulate them from politics. This was also the case in some developing countries, like Brazil, where we witnessed in the 1960s and 1970s development-oriented administrative reforms.[6]

Proper public management reform gained momentum only in the 1980s, with the neo-liberal wave and with Margaret Thatcher's election as prime minister of the United Kingdom. Yet it soon became clear that the reform was not necessarily neo-liberal. It depended on the form that it assumed. As Peter Aucoin remarks, Thatcher launched public management reform, but in the end it was 'adopted by governments formed by political parties from across the political spectrum, including parties on the traditional left, most notably Labour governments in Australia and New Zealand'. Public management reform emerged when globalization and the crisis of the state challenged the legitimacy of state bureaucracies and bureaucratic public administration. According to Aucoin, governments in all Western democracies were driven to pursue reform for three major causes: first, the need for 'restraint in public sector spending'—what I call 'the fiscal crisis'; second, the 'widespread decline of public confidence in the effectiveness of public policies and the quality of public services . . . ; and third, in the new international economic order, the impacts of what governments do and do not do, across a wide range of public policies areas are no longer regarded as merely internal or domestic matters having little or no effect on the global competitiveness of national economies' (Aucoin 1995: 2). Since then, public management reform has

---

[6] As we shall see, the 1968 Brazilian administrative reform fits this category. The idea is to transform the state and its bureaucracy into instruments for development, by means of increasing the state's planning capacity and of granting more autonomy to state-owned enterprises, agencies (called 'autharchies'), and public non-state organizations (called 'public foundations').

proved to be the second major administrative reform within the framework of industrial capitalism. As Christopher Pollitt and Geert Bouckaert (2000: 1) underline in a well-documented comparative analysis of ten OECD countries:

> The period since the 1980s has witnessed a pandemic of public management reforms, which has swept across much of the OECD world. The working lives of millions of public officials have been substantially altered (and in some tens of thousands of cases, prematurely terminated [...]. The ways and means of managing vast public budgets have been reshaped.

New public management came to the fore because bureaucratic public administration had exhausted its possibilities. Public management reform began in the 1980s, but presupposed civil service reform or, at least, the existence of a professional bureaucracy. It is impossible to have public management reform without establishing a body of senior professional civil servants with the capacity and the legal mandate to manage the state under the supervision of politicians and of civil society. A major reason for the adoption of public management reform was voters' pressure for two apparently contradictory objectives: smaller taxes and better-quality public services. The demand for more efficient ways of managing the state has been increasing in direct proportion to growing state expenditures and the corresponding tax burden. At the beginning of the twentieth century, when it did not surpass 10 per cent of GDP, pressure in this direction was limited; when this figure reached 30, 40, 50 per cent of GDP, pressure increased. This does not mean that citizens always elect political parties that promise to tax less. Conservative political parties' programmes permanently include tax reduction, but in the 1990s, when the limits of ultra-liberal reforms aimed at reducing the state organization became obvious, they lost rather than won elections. All political parties, however, are increasingly constrained to justify taxes with good social services. In January 2001, for instance, an editorial of *La Reppublica*, referring to the next national elections, had as its title: 'Who will know better how to reduce taxes?'[7] In the 2000 elections in the United States, large fiscal surpluses allowed the two contending candidates to include tax reductions in their political manifestos. Yet politicians' and the public's mood in relation to tax reductions was different from that of the 1994 elections, which had occurred at the peak of the neo-liberal wave: the proposed reductions were moderate.[8] In Britain, before the 2001 election, there was almost a consensus

---

[7] *La Reppublica*, 28 January, 2001. The original title is 'Chi saprá meglio ridurre le tasse?'. The editorial observes that tax reduction depends on expenditure reduction, and adds: 'To reduce expenditures radically is a slogan always repeated provided that specific indications of what will be cut are not mentioned.'

[8] Once elected, President George W. Bush became involved in huge tax cuts for the rich, while military expenditures were boosted. An explanation for such an irresponsible fiscal policy lies beyond the scope of this book.

that state expenditures had to be increased, given the clear gap between social services funding in Britain and that in other western European countries, but tax increases should be minimum, and outcomes maximum. In all rich countries the ultra-liberal drive to reduce state expenditures is over, but voters are increasing their demands for better use of fiscal resources. Governments of all ideological orientations, left or right, have responded to such challenges by engaging in public management reform.

The Persistence of Bureaucratic Administration

In Chapter 13 I will survey such reform in a few selected countries. Here, I want merely to note how historically persistent bureaucratic public administration has proved to be. Economic and political development is supposed to involve corresponding changes in public administration. Governance is a dynamic process through which political development takes place and through which civil society, the state organization, the state institutions, and government organize and manage public life. In principle, these four manifestations or 'instances' of the governing process should have equivalent qualities or levels of political development. The strength of civil society, the efficiency of the state organization, the adequacy of state institutions, the effectiveness in enforcing the law should be highly correlated variables. Yet it is necessary to acknowledge that bureaucratic public administration, although inefficient and unable to cope with the sheer dimension and increasing complexity of public services, has revealed itself to be more persistent than the hypothesis of the correlation of political instances would predict. When the political regime changed from authoritarian to liberal, the state organization duly changed from patrimonial to bureaucratic. Yet afterwards, when the political regime turned successively liberal-democratic and social-democratic, bureaucratic public administration remained practically unchanged.

After the 1930s, the liberal-democratic state started to transform itself into the social-democratic state. Yet, notwithstanding the new and increasing demands for an efficient state organization, change in the political regime did not involve change in public administration, which remained bureaucratic. In fact, the transition from the democratic to the social-democratic state led to a reaffirmation and enlargement of the bureaucratic system. Instead of limiting itself to exclusive activities of state, it hired new types of bureaucrats, and bureaucratic public administration was extended to social and scientific services, to public utilities, and, in certain cases, even to business enterprises, since the employees of state-owned enterprises were often viewed as civil servants. Thus, the definition of the civil service was radically broadened. All types of public-sector works were identified with civil servants, if not with statutory civil servants. In the liberal and in the liberal-democratic states, civil servants were only magistrates, prosecutors, military, police personnel, tax collectors, auditors, and policy-makers. They performed exclusively state activities. In the social-democratic or welfare state, the state took upon itself basic and university education, health care, social assistance, museums, and symphony orchestras. Thus, teachers and university professors, doctors and nurses, social workers, musicians and museum curators, all became statutory civil servants. The same happened even to employees of state-owned enterprises working in public utilities, like transport, energy generation and transmission, and communications. Such enlargement of the civil service concept became particularly apparent in European countries such as France, Germany, Austria, Belgium, Netherlands, the Scandinavian countries, and Canada, where social-democratic institutions were more advanced.

My explanation for this is related to the class character of the professional middle class. Within this class, the most cohesive group, socially and politically, is the state bureaucracy or techno-bureaucracy. With the rise of the social-democratic and the developmental state, this group increased and gained power. At first, and for a long period, their more outspoken representatives identified rationality and economic development with the hierarchical bureaucratic system that was behind them. It took at least five decades for that false identification to collapse: from the 1930s, when the social-democratic state begins to be put into practice, to the 1980s. At the moment when public management reform begins, the senior civil service and, more broadly, the professional middle class working for the state began to realize that their power and influence were being reduced rather than increased by the persistent reliance on bureaucratic public administration.

At the beginning of the twenty-first century, the resistance of bureaucratic public administration is waning: public management reform is under way. It is a gradual reform that will take years to be reasonably completed. In each country, one can specify the moment when the new reformist ideas begin to be really discussed and the first institutions set up. After that, however, there is a long and often contradictory way to go. In some countries, the short-term goal may be the dismissal of redundant civil servants; in others, decentralization and contracting-out social services may become dominant. In any case, increased concern for the citizen, now regarded also as a client, will be present. Lesser bureaucratic emphasis in state effectiveness and increased weight given to efficiency in public management, will be the tonic of a complex reform process, which is essentially a learning process.

The evaluation of public sector activities, their quality, the ratio of expenditure to goods produced and services provided, will deserve central attention. Yet, as Jean-Claude Thoenig (2001: 207) observed in Ireland, Norway, Canada and New Zealand, 'evaluation tends to emphasize what can be called the internal aspect, which concerns the performance management of staff and departments'. And he adds:

This general approach, which is more managerial than strategic, and more oriented towards efficiency than effectiveness, is intended to close the information loop, and keep policymakers informed about what is working and what is not.

In the same line, Hellmut Wollman (2001: 28) observed that the introduction of internal (agency-based) monitoring, information, and feedback loop mechanisms, which is an instrumental key component of public management reform 'has made remarkable advances. In most countries such procedures of internal monitoring and self-evaluation have been employed as a pivotal procedure'.

The reform process should not be thought of as a radical break from bureaucratic administration. Nor should the reform occur with the same intensity in all sectors. In fact, managerial public administration should be built on bureaucratic public administration, based on the existence of a professional and competent civil service. The combination of managerial and bureaucratic principles should vary according to the demands of each sector. The main values involved in bureaucratic public administration are professionalism, security, and effectiveness. That is why, in the strategic core, where these characteristics are important, they should still be present alongside managerial public administration. Nevertheless, in other sectors, where efficiency and a focus on clients are crucial because of the large number of civil servants and users involved, the weight of bureaucratic public administration should diminish until it virtually disappears in the state-owned enterprises as they are privatized or, where privatization does not apply or should be delayed, as they are 'corporatized'. As Roberto Cavalcanti de Albuquerque (1995) observes, it is doubtful whether this new paradigm should entirely replace the political-administrative model, particularly in the bodies that directly exercise the powers conferred on the state. Thus, it is not a case of ignoring the major advances involved in civil service reform, but of taking advantage of the positive aspects that it contains while eliminating what is no longer useful. In countries like Brazil, where clientelism is still a threat, the 1995–98 public management reform maintained and enhanced bureaucratic institutions such as public entrance examinations and the strengthening of formally structured careers. These institutions, however, should be flexible enough not to conflict with the principles of managerial public administration. They should, above all, not prevent the rewarding of personal merit, or limit the initiative and creativity of civil servants in managing human and material resources.

13

Public Management Reform in Practice

Public management reform started in Great Britain, New Zealand, and Australia in the 1980s.[1] In the United States the reform occurred mainly at local level, but the National Performance Review Program that Al Gore directed during the Clinton administration, following David Osborne and Ted Gaebler's *Reinventing Government* (1992), represented a major effort. Public management reform advanced also in the Scandinavian countries and in the Netherlands. In Canada the reform had to await a major fiscal adjustment programme that lasted most of the 1990s, but it is today under way. In Italy, it is beginning.[2] Among the developing countries, only in Brazil and Chile has public management reform gained ground. As public management reform spread, it became possible to understand its lasting and broad nature. Instead of small 'administrative reforms', each government in the advanced countries started to adopt structural reforms based on a new and relatively coherent view of public management—as coherent, at least, as it was bureaucratic public administration. Nevertheless, this does not mean that convergence was taking place on a single model of public management. As Patrick Dunleavy and Christopher Hood (1994) argue, politicians and the citizenry still hold the power to choose from a range of alternative standards for the future organization of public services. Although public management reform has a worldwide reach, its international impact is variable, depending upon the history, culture and political and administrative leaderships of different countries. Along similar lines, Elke Löffler (1996) remarks that similar political goals do not imply that the implementation of management reforms will be the same in all countries; and Pollitt and Bouckaert (2000: 167–92) argue that

---

[1] One of the best analyses of the British experience was written by a university professor at the request of the union of British civil servants (Fairbrother 1994). See also Tomkins (1978); Pyper and Robins (1995); Nunberg (1995); Plowden (1994). For criticisms, see among others Pollitt (1993); Clarke and Newman (1997).

[2] A study carried out by OECD/PUMA (1997: 28) classified the OECD countries in three categories: those adopting a managerial administration, or performance management (Australia, Canada, Denmark, the United States, Finland, Great Britain, New Zealand, and Sweden); mixed management (Germany, Austria, Belgium, France, Norway, and Switzerland); bureaucratic administration, or rule and norm management (Spain, Greece, Italy, and Portugal).

'the "new public management" (NPM) may have affected many countries, but some much more than others'.[3]

Why has public management reform had more impact on the Anglo-Saxon political cultures than on those of continental Europe? The general answer to this question is that the more advanced a country's bureaucratic model is, the more difficult it will be to undertake public management reform, not only because bureaucratic resistance is greater but also because, in so far as the civil service is reasonably efficient, the less pressing the need for change will be. This explains why, in the three countries that developed the bureaucratic model most formally and thoroughly—Germany, France, and Japan—public management reform lags behind. Although Great Britain and the United States had undergone civil service reforms, their bureaucratic system was never as formalized as in those three countries. This may also explain why some developing countries were able to initiate reforms before the 1980s, pointing towards a managerial approach. Since they did not have a strong bureaucratic system, they were able to implement 'development-oriented reforms', which may be seen as a transition to public management reform. These reforms, however, were incomplete and fragile since there was no consistent theoretical framework behind them. This was particularly the case with the 1968 reform in Brazil, which was a pioneer in adopting a public management perspective but ended up seeing it reversed.[4]

Although Silberman, in his study of the 'emergence of the rational state' in France, Japan, United States, and Great Britain, does not discuss public management reform, we may find in his central argument an explanation why some countries resist public management reform more than others. Silberman shows, first, that civil service reform was not as efficient and endowed with 'technical superiority' as Weber presupposed, and second, that it was not as convergent to the same pattern of public administration as a historical-functionalist perspective of bureaucratic modernization would presuppose. In fact, studying the four countries he finds two models or modes of bureaucratization: the British and American model, which he calls 'professional', and the French and Japanese, which he calls 'organizational'. The former is substantially more flexible than the latter. It is based on professionals whose education has been funded by their families: only after completing their education do they compete to enter the state apparatus, retaining, however, relative autonomy in relation to the state itself. The latter countries demand from the bureaucrat a prior commitment to the state, to the extent that his education, undertaken in schools specially designed for this purpose, is already a part of the

---

[3] On the different characteristics of political leadership in modern democracies, see also Elgie (1995). He studies particularly the ways in which the heads of government were able to control the decision-making process in six liberal democracies.

[4] The 1968 administrative reform, a 'developmental administrative reform', was enacted by a military regime. With the transition to democracy in 1985, the new regime tried to reject everything coming from the military. I discuss this event in this chapter, in the section on the 1995 Brazilian public management reform.

recruitment process. Thus, the dependence of the bureaucrat on the state is stronger, and specialized careers are also more rigid, making it more difficult to change career. Despite the rigidity of the specialized careers, the organizational model, with its common career path for its personnel and the same pay system for all, produces a relatively more homogeneous type of public official than the professional model. Additionally, according to Silberman (1993: 414), the concept of 'public' differs between the two models. In the professional model, the concept of 'the public' is closely linked to the concept of 'the social', that is, it is related to social institutions, particularly educational ones, seen as public. The bureaucrat becomes a public agent in so far he acquires knowledge, which should be at the same time technical and oriented to the promotion of the public interest. In contrast, in the organizational model, 'the public' is identified with political institutions, specifically with the state. Rigid norms define the procedures that the bureaucrats, including upper-level civil service, are supposed to follow. It is clear from this classification that the organizational model corresponds to the classic Weberian model, while the professional is a more flexible variant of this same model. Silberman discusses, throughout his book, the reason for this variation. Using a rational-choice model, he sees it as the outcome of political decisions made by the elites aimed at reducing uncertainty. As this uncertainty was historically greater in France and Japan, where bureaucratic rationalization or civil service reform occurred after two radical revolutions—the French Revolution and the Meiji Restoration—a more rigid model was chosen.

I have a different explanation, which is complementary rather than alternative to Silberman's hypothesis. The variation is associated with the late historical character of the French and Japanese industrializations in relation to the British, and with the fact that civil service reform preceded industrialization in the two former countries, whereas it followed it in Britain and the United States.[5] Civil service reform in France and Japan was associated with a national project. It was instrumental to industrialization in these countries, while in Britain and the United States it was a response to the need for coordination and reduction of uncertainty and of transaction costs in the state organizations of these two already industrialized countries. For one or, more likely, both of the reasons given above, the civil service was relatively less rigid in Britain and in the United States, particularly in the former, and this explains why Britain pioneered public management reform. Moreover, the legal systems in France and Germany are based on Roman law, which is more formal and so more susceptible to bureaucracy than British common law. The United Kingdom has a civil service of the highest quality, but it has never been as bureaucratized as those in France, Germany, and Japan.

---

[5] The classic analysis of backward industrialization among today's developed countries, and of the larger role performed by the state in these cases, is by Alexander Gerschenkron (1962). I add that civil service reform took place before industrialization in France, Germany, and Japan.

In the following sections I briefly review public management reform in some developed countries. The absence of some countries, like the Netherlands or Canada, does not mean that reform did not take place there. Among the Scandinavian countries I discuss only Sweden, although all the others are also involved in reform. Among the developed countries, I make no mention of public management reform in Germany, Japan, and Spain. In Italy, reform is just beginning.[6] I complete this chapter with a discussion of civil service reform and public management reform in Latin America.

Public Management Reform in Britain

Although the quality of public service delivery remains a major political issue, Britain probably presents the most balanced and successful case of public management reform. It is probably one of the reasons for the country's good economic performance since the 1990s. Concern with the modernization of the civil service goes back to the 1960s, culminating with the 1968 Fulton Report, which identified the lack of an adequate attitude on the part of public services managers as the central problem. The difficulties in making the civil service accountable by measuring performance in quantitative and financial terms appeared the main obstacle to the modernization of the state apparatus. The reforms carried out in the 1970s focused on the introduction of managerial controls in the public service domain. Already in that decade, we have the first attempts at importing techniques from the business world and fitting them into already existing administrative structures.

The quest for efficiency gained new momentum in 1979, when Margaret Thatcher became Prime Minister. Actually, the Conservatives were concerned rather with reducing taxes and tax-financed public services. Privatization was the answer to reducing state intervention but not to reducing taxes, since state-owned enterprises had their own revenues. On the other hand, resistance to cutbacks in free public services proved stronger than the new administration expected. Thus, it was soon recognized that the reduction of state expenditures and personnel depended on reform. The expression that was used to encapsulate this was 'value for money'. The main instrument to evaluate the effectiveness of public expenditure was the efficiency reviews carried out by the newly created Efficiency Unit. This organization selected public sector activities and submitted each of them to scrutiny guided by the following questions: What is it good for? How much does it cost? Which value does it add? The scrutiny involved a full evaluation of existing procedures, following a managerial approach. The outcomes of 'Rayner's scrutiny',[7]

---

[6] See Franco Bassanini (2000) for an account of the reform's first steps, beginning in 1999. Richard Locke and Lucio Baccaro (1996) report reforms in the Italian civil service that already point towards public management reform.   [7] Rayner was in charge of the scrutiny process.

although uneven, were significant in reducing costs and in promoting more efficiency in the delivery of services. Yet, given the pressure for more services and the increasing costs of some of them, particularly health care, the reduction in governmental expenditure was limited. In cultural terms, the scrutiny system played an important role in developing a managerial ethos that implied, concurrently, rupture and continuity in relation to the bureaucratic one: rupture as it rejected formalism; continuity as it strengthened civil servants.

A second major step in British public management reform was the introduction of the Financial Management Initiative, extending to the whole administration a new system of managerial administrative information. A group of senior Treasury officers, officers of the Management and Personnel Office, and external consultants implemented this initiative. While the goal of Conservative politicians in the government was to reduce the size of the state and the tax burden, the senior civil servants' aim was to redeem the prestige of the British civil service, which was undergoing a crisis caused in part by Britain's own economic crisis. A political alliance was therefore forged. This alliance failed to reduce the size of the state, given the political resistance by the British voters, but it was able to limit the tendency towards further growth and, eventually, it radically reformed British public administration.[8] The plans developed by senior civil servants and consultants called for the reorganization of departments around cost and budget centres, and for an increase in centralized managerial control. In addition, these plans required broad information systems in order to make performance measurement and evaluation work. The success achieved by this reorganization programme was uneven, revealing the administration's difficulties in reforming itself. The development of managerial information systems and the introduction of budgetary mechanisms based on cost centres were at the heart of the reorganization. Together with such developments, there was an attempt to fill the managerial echelons of the public services with new managers, who attended special training courses. Performance-related pay systems, as well as productivity schemes, were designed for them, particularly for those who reached senior level.

The Efficiency Unit scrutiny, the introduction of the Financial Management Initiative, and decentralized budgetary procedures were the first measures aimed at transforming the British civil service from a bureaucratic into a managerial administration. In this process, it became necessary for government to begin a structural reorganization of public service, so that those initial reforms might be consolidated and expanded. This was a job of the Next Steps Programme, which began in 1988 and played a crucial role in British public management reform.[9] The British reform has been based on devolution of

---

[8] I owe this political analysis to William Plowden.

[9] Kate Jenkins, who later would have a crucial role as a consultant in the Brazilian 1995 public management reform, led the Next Steps Programme. She would also have an important role in Mexico, where, however, resistance to reform proved greater.

authority and on management contracts. The executive agencies, created by the Next Steps Programme, are organizations endowed with autonomy and accountability. There is an emphasis on the clear definition of responsibilities, as well as on the appointment of responsible head officers and in paying them according to their true worth (Trosa 1995). One of the main changes introduced has to do with the process of selecting the head officers of these agencies, who are recruited by strictly competitive processes to which both civil and non-civil servants may apply. The management contract establishes the general principles according to which agencies must function and endows their managers with instruments against interference from the central administration in the management of public services delivered by them. In 1991, in John Major's administration, an emphasis on customer services became evident in two major programmes: the Citizen's Charter and Competing for Quality.

In the British public management reform, quasi-autonomous governmental organizations and public non-state organizations played an important role in rendering decentralization and managed competition feasible in the area of social and scientific services. For some time they enjoyed a poor reputation in Britain, given the accountability problems involved when decentralization is enforced. Yet the general outcome of this emphasis on public non-state service organizations performing social and scientific services was mostly favourable. Hospitals, universities, and other bodies became relatively autonomous, assuming a hybrid character between the state and the private sector: non-profit organizations without civil servants on their staffs, free from controls befitting the state administration, although included in the public budget. These institutions proved to be, in most—though not in all—cases, more autonomous and accountable, and consequently more efficient.

A key public management reform was introduced in the National Health System (NHS) in the late 1980s: the 'purchaser/provider system'. Britain's territory was divided into health authority areas, and a budget was assigned to each authority according to the population of its area. Health authorities contracted out, on a relatively competitive basis, the hospitals that would serve its population, from inside or outside the district. Also on a competitive basis, they used general practitioners (GPs) to screen patients. Each citizen in the district is supposed to choose a certified GP, who may authorize clinical examinations and surgery at endorsed hospitals. The hospitals compete for authorization by health authorities and endorsement by general practitioners, who compete for clients, under the tight cost control of the health authority. Thus, the purchaser-provider system is a classic example of managed competition—one of the central control systems adopted by public management reforms. This system proved so efficient that it is being adopted—with the necessary adaptations—by several other countries. Yet health care remained deficient in Britain because the Conservative administration kept the system seriously under-funded. According to *The Economist* of 15 March 1997, the NHS was 'threatened with privatization' (*sic*), given that it could not count on suffi-cient budgetary resources. By 'privatization', the newspaper meant the control of the health system by insurance companies and managed care companies. And, it added: while the British system is 'very efficient', if we want to know how inefficient a health system can be, 'just look at what happens in the United States'. To demonstrate this, the newspaper compared the American system (private, based on insurance companies), the French (state-owned), and the British (financed by the state but provided by competitive public non-state organizations). Costs per inhabitant/year were, in 1996, US$1,300 in Great Britain, against double ($2,600) for the French health system, and almost triple ($3,800) for the private American system. The United States expends 14.5 per cent of its GDP on health, against 6.8 per cent in Britain. For health care services whose quality is probably superior to those in the United States (in the US, 20 per cent of the population is not covered by health insur-ance), the British people spend seven percentage points of GDP less.[10] These data underline two things: first, the efficiency of competent public manage-ment; second, that it is a major mistake to trade-off efficiency for budget reductions. Increased efficiency in the use of public money is a way of increas-ing the quality and the coverage of the public services, not an excuse for reducing public spending on them. As soon as public management reform is distorted and transformed into a way of reducing taxes for the rich, a negat-ive built-in incentive to reform is created: the reform itself loses its rationale.

The leaders of the Labour Party criticized the purchaser provider system, but, after the 1997 elections it realized how efficient it was and maintained it, looking only to reduce excessive controls. Since 1999, the new administration has substantially increased public expenditure on the NHS—which was essential. In general, as Pollitt and Bouckaert (2000: 274) point out,

the new Labour government of 1997 reversed very little of what had gone before. Although ideologically more sympathetic to the public sector they did not reverse the private/purchase splits, although they took some steps to ameliorate the least popular consequences of the latter. If anything, they intensified the 'league table' system still further, 'rebranded' the Citizen's Charter programme and launched a Service First initiative. Many of their proposals shared the underlying assumptions which had been characteristic of their Conservative predecessors.[11]

Lynne Poole (2000), while looking at the changes introduced by New Labour in health care restructuring, recognizes that the managerial approach was essentially maintained. Yet, reform in Britain was not completed in this area. The distinction between the demand side and the supply side was not clearly

---

[10] *The Economist*, "Un Unhealthy Silence", 15 March 1997. More recent figures show an increase in the costs of health care in Britain, but British health care figures remain considerably smaller than the European Union average. In January 2000, Prime Minister Tony Blair made a pledge to raise the levels of health spending in Britain to the EU average by 2006. The 2002 British budget continued to point in this direction.   [11] Pollit and Bouckaert, 2000: 274.

established in institutional terms. Managers on the demand or control side should continue to be statutory civil servants, since they perform exclusive state activities, dispensing public money, while on the supply side hospitals should be fully autonomous, and have only private employees. The Labour administration oriented modestly its action in this direction, but found strong resistance from the NHS staff. In June 2001, Alan Milburn, the Health Secretary, said that the private sector should have an increased role in the health service, but added that 'the real stars of the show' would be the NHS's own staff.[12]

Public Management Reform in New Zealand

New Zealand presents an extreme case of public management reform. It started around 1984 under a Labour government, which designed the reform and began to implement it, but became radical after 1990 under a conservative administration. When the Labour Party returned to power in 1999, the new administration maintained the reform, but moderated it. When the conservatives came to office, public management reform was viewed as complementing the market-oriented economic reform programme undertaken during the same period in order to ensure the country's international competitiveness. The two main Labour targets were to increase the efficiency of the public sector and to improve the accountability of public services vis-à-vis the executive branch and the parliament. The conservative administration added a third explicit objective: to downsize the state. It also adopted a client orientation in the public services; granted elected officers more autonomy in the use of taxpayers' money; and increased the transparency of the public sector. The emphasis was on the strategic control, by ministers, of public policies through a clear definition of objectives for the managers of the decentralized public agencies. As John Halligan (2001: 75) observes,

one of the most startling innovations was the separation of political and managerial roles, through the association of outcomes with ministers and outputs with chief executives, the minister selecting the outcomes, and purchasing the outputs from the chief executives, who selects the necessary inputs.[13]

Thus, the two policies of separating policy formulation from execution, and purchasing from providing, were extensively applied. Contracting out was radicalized. Whenever possible, contracting out took place with private enterprises rather than only with public non-state organizations. Another option pursued was the creation of partnerships with the private sector. In the outsourcing system, performance standards were established and outputs specified. The idea was always to make agencies more competitive among themselves, and more accountable to citizens, through quasi-market mechanisms. Fixed-term contracts and performance-related pay systems were

---

[12] The *Guardian*, June 25, 2001.   [13] Halligan, 2001: 75.

adopted to recruit agencies' directors and executive officers, preferably from the private sector. State-owned enterprises had to make their targets, objectives, and performance criteria explicit in such a way that Parliament could follow up their actions. Thus, a radical transition in the public sector took place in New Zealand. In addition, it is unlikely that any other country was as aggressive as New Zealand in defining its privatization programme. To evaluate its performance, the New Zealand public sector used new legal instruments. As a result of the 1988 State Sector Act and of the 1989 Public Finance Act, it became equipped to answer such basic questions as: What is being bought? How much does it cost? What are the possible impacts on the treasury? And who is responsible?

Thus, the calculation of the government balance sheet showing the total cash position was transformed into an important indicator of the performance of the state sector. One of the main reasons why public management reform is often identified with ultra-liberal ideology and rational choice theory is the character it assumed in New Zealand. A small group of politicians in the economic ministries, senior civil servants and businessmen designed the reform around 1982. They and particularly their conservative successors looked for inspiration to rational choice theory,[14] to the related principal–agent assumption, and to business management literature (Richardson 1998). Enid Wistrich (1992), based upon documents such as the 1987 Treasury report *Government Management: Brief to the Incoming Government*, emphasizes that the Treasury, following an ultra-liberal view that was dominant throughout the second phase of the reform, acted broadly and successfully in the role of think-tank for the reform movement, supplying it with intellectual rigour and coherence. In other words, public management reform in New Zealand was controlled by the economists in the Treasury.

Public management reform may follow ultra-liberal tenets, as was the case of New Zealand under the Conservatives, but this ideological orientation is not intrinsic to it. On the contrary, as long as the main objective is strengthening state organization, it challenges the neo-liberal assumption that the state is per se inefficient.[15] When, in 1999, the Labour Party returned to power, it trimmed its excesses.

Public Management Reform in Australia

Australia, like the United States and Brazil, is a complex case due to its federal system, the states sometimes being under the control of different political

---

[14] Particularly, Buchanan and Tullock (1962) and Niskanen (1971).

[15] Social-democrat authors critical of neo-liberalism, such as Adam Przeworski, extensively use the tools of rational choice and of the agent–principal model to support public management. To do so, they need to fight against the fact that rational choice views officials just as self-interested individuals—something that is consistent with bureaucratic administration, not with public management. Their assumption that institutions may be independent of the moral quality of public officials that draw and approve them is another contradiction they have to face.

parties. A public management reform effort has been in place within the Australian public sector from the beginning of the 1980s, with many of its themes in evidence, such as market or quasi-market incentives and the use of private sector managerial techniques. According to Spencer Zifcak (1994), the reform began under the Labor Hawke administration with the White Paper *Reforming the Australian Public Service*, whose principal elements were embodied in legislation in the Public Service Reform Act (June 1984). The document was informed by merit and equal opportunity principles, as well as the search for efficiency. The second phase of the reform, coinciding with the government's second term, emphasized contracting out. In the third phase, starting in 1987, the reform focused on the machinery of government and personnel reduction. Administrative power shifted from the Public Service Board to the Department of Finance, that is, from the administrative bureaucracy to the economic bureaucracy. 'Politically and administratively, the balance of power had been tipped in favour of the reformers' (Zifcak 1994: 25). Caiden (1991a: 13) highlights the following basic principles that guided the Australian reform: (1) precise definition of each agencys' functions; (2) adoption of an entrepreneurial culture; (3) increased autonomy for executive agencies; (4) creation of the result-oriented Superior Executive Service; (5) reduction of regulations and forms; and (6) a performance-related pay system for executives.

One may observe two phases in the implementation of the reform. The first was in the early 1980s, which witnessed the rise of young technocrats operating as agents for the acceleration of reform (Halligan 1991). This movement coincided with Bob Hawke's Labor government, which undertook broad yet quite moderate reform. As the objectives of this first phase, we might cite the quest for a more sensitive and responsible administration vis-à-vis elected officers; an increase in the efficiency and effectiveness of services; the guarantee of equity in access to public employment; and the creation of a more independent and efficient system of protection for fundamental rights. The second phase of the reform, still under the Labor Party, was marked by fiscal crisis and globalization. Reform was deepened, particularly methods for purchasing goods and contracting out services. Managerial practices became dominant. In his detailed comparative analysis of the British Financial Management Initiative (FMI) and of Australia's Financial Management Improvement Programme (FMIP), Zifcak asserts that the Australian and British reforms, although adopted by prime ministers with different political orientations (Hawke and Thatcher), 'pursued agendas which were very similar . . . In both countries a clear and persistent determination by the prime minister to change the face of administration acted as a powerful incentive to innovation'. Yet, Spencer Zifcak found a major difference between the London and the Canberra reforms: 'the Hawke administration adopted a collaborative rather than conflictual approach to civil service reform . . . Canberra's bureaucrats were more willing than their counterparts in Whitehall to take risks.

This yielded them greater rewards' (Zifcak 1994: 172). Yet, in Britain, when the Next Steps Programme replaced the Financial Management Initiative, it was able to 'generate a momentum for change considerably beyond that which the FMI had engendered . . . the changes that the Thatcher government had made to the composition of the senior civil service ensured that the Next Steps, like the (Australian) FMIP, would be more favourably received within the administration than the (British) FMI had been' (Zifcak 1994: 173). Thus, eventually both reforms succeed as long as reformers were able to involve and commit civil servants to them. We will see that this variable was the key in the Brazilian reform. The return of a conservative political coalition brought changes to administrative programmes, but the basic ideas behind public management reform remained intact. According to Halligan (2001: 81–2), the 'reform era' is now based on 'the outcomes and outputs framework: agency heads are responsible for ensuring that their departments produce the necessary outputs in order to reach the outcomes that have been the subject of parliamentary appropriations'. Thus, as happened in public management reform elsewhere, budgeting and parliamentary control became an essential part of it also in Australia.

Public Management Reform in the United States

As we saw in Chapter 3, civil service reform in the United States was relatively belated. The Pendleton Civil Service Reform Act, which put in place a professional bureaucracy, was enacted in 1883, but became effective only during the first two decades of the twentieth century. By any measure, the American civil service reached the degree of formalism achieved by Germany, France, or Japan. In 1946, new legislation institutionalized the vision of a 'legislative-centred' federal administration, in which Congress treated the agencies as an extension of itself, and put the federal administration under the 'joint custody' of the Congress and the President (Rosenbloom 2001). These circumstances probably facilitated the continuation and affirmation of the managerial experience, particularly at local level. At the federal level, public management reform began in 1978, with the Civil Service Reform Act during the Carter administration. This law provided for the introduction of performance evaluation and merit-related pay systems for the American civil service, together with new procedures for downgrading and dismissal. With President Ronald Reagan, the most progressive aspects of Carter's programme were cut short or severely restricted, while all the emphasis was placed on downsizing. However, and just as happened in the United Kingdom, the new government's initial aim of drastically reducing the size of the state apparatus proved difficult to implement. The Grace Commission, which worked during the period 1982–4, presented proposals aiming at ensuring more efficient expenditure of budgetary appropriations by using the 'private sector best practice' as a model.

In the early 1990s, Osborne and Gaebler's book *Reinventing Government* (1992) supplied ideas and models for the new Clinton administration.[16] In September 1993, President Bill Clinton launched the National Performance Program, with Vice-President Al Gore as its head. The motto of this programme was 'to work better and cost less'—a managerial and pragmatic approach.[17] In contrast to what happened in Britain and Brazil, Al Gore's initial report *From Red Tape to Results* (1993) contained little theory and the largest possible amount of practical recommendations. The President's interest in the subject was great. Given the direct involvement of the Vice-President, the reform acquired political significance and involved a considerable communication effort on the part of the Democrat administration. The reform was successful, although facing difficulties stemming from the federal character of the American state, and resistance from a well-established bureaucracy. According to *The Economist*, 'attempts at reinventing government bore fruit'. The number of civil servants was reduced by more than 300,000 out of an initial total of 2.2 million. Although the share of public expenditure in GDP remained unchanged, a large number of services were 'semi-privatized', fostering competition and more efficiency within service-delivering organizations.[18] Contracting out public non-state service organizations (and, in some cases, business enterprises) gained a new momentum, following a model that already characterized practically all American universities and nearly 50 per cent of hospitals. Peter Drucker (1995) remarks that in the Clinton administration this initiative yielded effective results. [END]

The core idea of the National Performance Review was not to diminish the state at any cost but to 'reinvent it', to make it more efficient and geared to client-citizens. Its second phase, which started in 1995, was launched with Al Gore's document (1995) *Putting Customers First '95*. This document had no ultra-liberal character whatsoever. An alternative conservative proposal was presented by the Republican Party in 1994, under the leadership of Representative Newt Gingrich, the so-called Contract with America, an ultra-liberal programme proposing to reduce the state to a minimum, eliminating basic state-delivered social services. As noticed by Kettl and Dilulio (1995), while the National Performance Review mentioned 'reinventing' the state, the Contract with America had the goal of 'erasing' the state. Yet, they argued,

---

[16] The literature on National Performance is now extensive. I highlight here works by Kettl (1994); Kettl and Dilulio (1994, 1995); Glastris (1994); Khademian (1995); Kellam (1995). The last text presents a historical retrospect of the programme. A critical perspective, from a classical bureaucratic point of view, can be found, for instance, in Moe (1994); Rabell and Portillo (1996).

[17] On 3 March 1993, when he announced the programme to be officially launched in September of that year, President Bill Clinton stated: 'Our goal is to make the whole federal government less costly and more efficient and to change the culture of our national bureaucracy from complacence and legalism to initiative and autonomy' (epigraph of Gore 1993).

[18] *The Economist*, 24 January 1998: 20.

Republican representatives would soon learn that diminishing the state might have some popular support so long as it remained within the realm of general ideas; but the moment it started threatening rights, particularly those of the middle classes, the adverse reaction would be very strong. This analysis was confirmed in the 1996 presidential elections, when the unpopularity of Republican proposals for 'erasing government' and support for Clinton's public management reform contributed to his victory. Four years later, after the 2000 elections, the Republican Party returned to the White House, the political discourse remained conservative but had ceased to be ultra-liberal. In January 1999 Al Gore sponsored, in Washington, a World Forum on Reinventing Government, with a large number of countries represented. Through this initiative, the American administration was formally trying to extend reform to developing countries. Following Gore's suggestion, the Second World Forum was held in Brasilia in May 2000. The return of the Republican Party to the presidency in January 2001 did not change the general orientation towards public management reform in the American administration.

The initial effects of the initiatives of managerial reform to public administration in the United States were weaker than those in Great Britain. Christopher Pollitt (1993) cites as a cause of this weakness the pluralism that characterizes the US political system, and the well-organized special-interest groups that lobby to have their proposals approved. In contrast, political power in Britain in the 1980s was much more concentrated at cabinet level or even at prime ministerial level. The Clinton Gore National Performance Review tried to reduce this difference. In spite of the federal character of the American political system, which limits the scope of reforms emanating from Washington, I believe that the review was reasonably successful. I have already cited some authors, and personally observed the favourable climate surrounding the reform at the January 1999 World Forum on Reinventing Government. An academic evaluation of the reinventing laboratories identifies more successes than failures (Ingraham, Thompson, and Sanders 1998). Another evaluation that examines the changing relationship between executives and middle managers finds that 'both levels of managers are experiencing a shift from being primarily "directors" or "chiefs" to being primarily "team leaders" . . . Second, in their new roles as team leaders, executives and middle managers are expected to focus on facilitating and communicating . . . Third, executives and middle managers are finding that their positions require less technical expertise and more human resources management' (Ingraham and Jones 1999: 222–3). Christensen, Lægreid, and Wise (2001), assessing the American reform, conclude that a market orientation and market-based pay supplements have been introduced throughout government. The goals of achieving more autonomy and simplifying decision-making and procurement appear to have been achieved in different federal agencies. Service-providing agencies became clearly more customer-oriented and gained in efficiency.

Public Management Reform in Sweden

Sweden adopted public management reform relatively cautiously in the 1980s. There is some evidence that traditional values continued to inform the reorganization of the Swedish public sector in greater measure than in Britain. Analyses of the Swedish case highlight movements towards devolution to counties and municipalities, and towards increased autonomy and accountability for agencies (Fortin 1996; Gustafson 1995). Yet important differences remain: the social-democratic character of the Sweden government restrained radical changes of the type that were adopted in New Zealand; concern with efficiency was combined with an emphasis on humanitarian concerns; and quasi-market mechanisms received less emphasis than social accountability or democratic participation.

In 1991, the Swedish government initiated public management reform with a programme evaluating performance based on annual reports. Additionally, it adopted a three-years cycle of in-depth performance reviews. And to such results-oriented change reformers added an extensive process of decentralization. The reform was directly linked to the budgetary process. Strategic objectives and measured outcomes for each organization receiving resources from the national budget are now an integral part of this process. The fiscal crisis of the welfare state affected the priorities established for public expenditures, and created pressure for reform. As a PUMA report (OECD/PUMA 1997: 89) stresses,

> the overall public management reform of the early 1990s emphasizes management by results. The overall objective is to provide information needed by the government and Parliament to evaluate and prioritize different public activities . . . The recession of the early 1990s and the need to reduce the budget deficit resulted in a shift in priorities. The idea of results-based decision-making was modified as the focus shifted from the best means of achieving goals to the question of ends, i.e., whether a government agency should be involved in particular activities at all. Still, the basic thrust toward management by results has continued.

An outcome of reform was that productivity in the public sector, which lagged in the 1970s and 1980s, improved substantially in the 1990s. As Pollitt and Bouckaert (2000: 266) observe, Sweden's achievements in public management reform were 'substantial'. Yet major problems remain, particularly, 'the continuing concern that the central ministries lack the capability to set a really well-informed yet demanding set of performance targets for agencies in public management reform', combined with an absence of a clear interest on the part of the ministers in making use of the increased flow of performance data.

Christensen, Lægreid, and Wise (2001: 63–4) stress the major efforts to develop agency-based audits in Sweden (and also in the United States). They quote a study by Blomqvist and Rothstein, which 'concludes that the efficiency effects are lower than assumed by the reformers, that the reforms have a positive effect on the citizens' free choice of public services and a negative effect on 'creaming' and social segregation. Yet the three authors conclude that there is little systematic knowledge about the consequences of reforms. As in most of the other national cases reported, Sweden is involved in effective public management reform, but a complete and systematic evaluation of its outcomes is lacking.

Public Management Reform in France

In France, public management reform made little progress. It began in 1989 under the Rocard administration, and was mostly abandoned by the subsequent conservative and socialist administrations. Yet, outside the centre, various initiatives promoted reform. According to Serge Vallemont (1996), an 'evolutionary' modernization took place through successive experimentation with different instruments, such as total quality management and performance contracts. Later, in the short-lived Socialist administration headed by Michel Rocard, a circular dated 23 February 1989 announced the reform as a global project involving the various dimensions of administrative modernization. It included administrative decentralization (*déconcentration*) and management by results, improvement of client–public service relations, development of managers' accountability, and actions for measuring performance. According to Nicoletta Meldolesi (1996), rather than involving institutional change, the French reform concentrated primarily on the management dimension, the introduction of the changes step by step being a crucial factor as it allowed the agents to appropriate, in successive stages, the new management instruments. Such step-by-step progression also made room for experimentation, followed by evaluation and diffusion of the experiments. This strategy made it possible to achieve managerial results, even if only partial ones, without the introduction of new legislation, that is, without institutional reform. As the first results of modernization, Sylvie Trosa (1995) highlights civil servants' improved motivation and significant advances in professional training. Change from *a priori* to *a posteriori* budgetary control was successful in 90 per cent of cases. On the other hand, Trosa raises some unresolved issues in France's modernization process, particularly departments' limited autonomy: in staff recruitment, for example, public competitions and promotion processes are organized locally, however strictly according to the national statutory rules.

Given that there was no previous institutional reform, the new forms of management are tested within the existing legal frame, constituting the 'evolutionary' reform referred to by Vallemont, and cohabiting with the hierarchy of the central administrations of the ministries. Therefore, in the core French public administration, in the realm of the *fonction publique,* public management reform was rather limited. It advanced further in the area of the public utilities, where decentralization and competition naturally play a larger role (Boyé and Ropert 1994). The public non-state organizations sector received special attention. Regulated as early as 1901, the associations oriented towards health care, education, popular housing—what the French call the *économie sociale et solidaire*—represent today a sizable economic and social industry in France despite the notoriously overwhelming role that the French state is supposed to play. In 2000, the social-democratic Lionel Jospin administration created a state secretary exclusively to oversee social and solidary organizations.[19] A year later, the conservative Jean Pierre Raffarin administration initiated a bold decentralization programme, the French constitution was amended, and a large number of public servants were transferred to the regional administrations; but France remained far from real public management reform. Yet the French were not blind to successful experiences in other OECD countries with public management reform. The *hauts fonctionaires* formed in some major schools, particularly the École Nationale d'Administration (ENA), remained resistant to change, but even among them many began to realize that the reform could enhance their prestige rather than diminish it. As Bernard Brunhes (203: 33) remarks, all countries that got involved in public management reform gave major attention to senior civil servants' individual concerns, with their *'états d'âme'*. This was particularly true of Brazil. No public management reform is viable if it cannot count on the support of the senior civil service. In France, public management reform will progress when senior civil servants understand that it favours competent and republican civil servants.

Reform in Latin America

The literature on Latin America's 'administrative reforms' is as huge as the number of reform attempts in the region. Peter Spink's survey of the area starts with the observation that Latin American bureaucracies seem to be permanently engaged in administrative reform: 'The administrative reform theme and, more recently, the reform of the state, have maintained a visible presence in Latin America in most of the last 70 years' (Spink 1998: 5). In all cases studied, administrative reform either involved ordinary change of the central government organization chart, increasing or diminishing the number of ministries, or changing this or that department from one ministry to another, or insisted in completing civil service reform, having as a model the

---

[19] On this subject, see Lipietz (2000), Fourel (2001: 11–12). The latter observes that this sector located between the private and the public (state) sector was called in France 'third sector' in the 1970s, 'social economy' in the 1980s, and 'social and solidary economy' today.

American or the French bureaucratic model. The challenge was to overcome patrimonial rule, to turn public administration professional and rational-legal. Yet patrimonial rule has remained strong in the region, and the attempts to build a professional civil service often ended in protecting the corporatist interests of the local bureaucracies concerned with winning or retaining special privileges in relation to their respective labour markets. When competent professional bureaucracies have materialized, as we can observe in larger Latin American countries and in Costa Rica and Uruguay, they have little to do with the classic Weberian bureaucracy: they are more entrepreneurial, more technical, more flexible, more sensitive to the demands of state agencies and state-owned enterprises.

Governments in Latin America have been constantly involved in 'administrative reform', but, as Andrew Nickson observed (2002: 125, 131), "in most Latin American countries, the NPM initiatives were introduced in a hazardous and unsystematic way. The exception is Brazil, where the national government developed a concerted effort to conduce the reform of the public sector according to a consistent NPM paradigm". And he correctly observes that one of the reasons why the NPM initiatives in Latin America have made little progress is the "absence of a key factor required for its exit: the existence of a professional civil service". Brazil was again an exception in relation to that. It was one of the few Latin American countries to undertake full civil service reform, the 1936–8 reform of Getulio Vargas, undertaken by the Departamento Administrativo do Serviço Público (DASP). It is true that this reform was never completed, and Brazil, as could be expected, never achieved a civil service similar to the French or the American ones. During the 1930s, bureaucratic reform was influenced more by the American civil service than the French, but later, especially when Congress proposed and approved the 1988 Constitution, the country tended increasingly to treat the French administration and its ENA as a model.[20] From the 1930s to the 1980s, each new government attempted to 'deepen' the administrative reform, to make bureaucratic what hitherto was patrimonial or just clientelist. When, in 1995, the Cardoso administration decided to launch public management reform, Brazil's public administration remained a mixture of bureaucratic, corporatist, and patrimonial institutions and practices. One of the key strategies adopted by the new administration, while promoting public management reform, was to value and promote a professional and modern bureaucracy, opening for the first time yearly entrance examinations for all the 'state careers', whose candidates were supposed to have at least an undergraduate university degree,

---

[20] Brazilians and Latin Americans in general did not realize that teaching public administration is secondary at ENA. The prestige of this organization derives rather from its monopoly over recruiting and selecting some of the brightest French young students than from the quality of their teaching. When a student completes successfully the ENA basic course, he or she is automatically admitted to the French high bureaucracy.

and organizing a systematic training system for the new civil servants. The Brazilian reform was against bureaucratic administration, that should be replaced by public management, but favoured professional bureaucrats who are supposed to define and implement it.

It is difficult to know which Latin American countries, besides Brazil, have been engaged in anything close to civil service reform. My conclusion is that, although some interesting advances are taking place in Argentina, Uruguay, Mexico, and Colombia, only Chile may be included in this category. Oscar Oszlak does not address this question directly, but from his analysis of the personnel recruitment and selection systems in the Latin American countries it is possible to infer that only Argentina, besides Brazil and Chile, is experiencing some public management reform. He supposes four situations—(a) a generalized public competition system, (b) use of informal but relatively robust selection criteria, (c) a personal confidence criterion as the dominant one, and (d) a mixed system—and concludes that 'Argentina, Brazil and Chile are the only countries that report the generalized adoption of selection procedures as defined in (a). In other cases these procedures are only adopted as an exception, in specific jurisdictional realms like diplomacy or heath care services' (Oszlac 2001: 17). Except for Brazil, where a more formal process exists, the department head is solely responsible for recruitment and selection of the required personnel. Yet, although most Latin American countries have not undertaken effective civil service reform, Oszlak (2001: 20) reports that 'employment stability of public servants tends to be great'. In other words, to put it bluntly, we have the worst of all worlds—a perverse system of incentives, and no impersonal selection through public competitions but extended tenure rights.

Public management reform usually presupposes civil service reform that creates a professional civil service in the given country. Mexico might be an exception to this rule. Mexico never had true civil service reform, but there are attempts to execute public management reform. The country is experiencing two countervailing movements: on the one hand, steps are being taken towards modern management reforms; on the other, there seems to be an attempt to undertake a classic civil service reform, which might lead to a bureaucratic regression of the type that occurred in Brazil after its re-democratization in 1985. For many years Mexico could count on a competent and well-paid bureaucracy. When the rule of the Institutional Revolutionary Party (PRI) came under threat, discussions and efforts to implement bureaucratic reform increased. The main objective was life tenure. Yet, after President Vicente Fox defeated the PRI, but did not mount an attack on the civil service—something that was wholly expected given the healthy constraints existing in modern democracies, but something that bureaucrats always use as an argument for resisting reform and asking for tenure privileges—the outdated demand for civil service reform lost its priority.

How, then, can we explain so much talk about public sector reform in Latin America in the past 20 years, and so little action? There have been some administrative reforms, but they did not follow the public management model. Most of these reforms were conducted by economists—local economists and from international agencies like the World Bank—who have little familiarity with public management and have mixed feelings on the subject. On the one hand, they have an idea of a professional civil service as something good; on the other, they know that the era of classic bureaucracy is over. Given the dilemma, they tend to leave the question aside and reduce public sector reform to structural adjustment, privatization, downsizing, and fighting corruption. Argentina and Peru, two quite different countries but having in common the size of their foreign debt and the depth of their fiscal crisis, are examples of this. There has been no real reform in either, just drastic reductions in state personnel and some decentralization in Argentina. As highlighted by Ghio and Etchemendy (1998), in Argentina one of the objectives of the Menem administration beginning in 1989 was to undertake public management reform, but eventually downsizing has prevailed over more qualitative aspects.

Yet, contrary to the conventional wisdom, which attributes reforms in Latin America to international pressures, public management reform in these two countries was initiated by their governments, without the direct participation of the World Bank. Since the debt crisis and, specifically, since the 1985 Baker Plan officially defined American policy in relation to the highly indebted countries, market-oriented reforms have been attempted everywhere on the Latin American continent, particularly trade liberalization and privatization. The World Bank was the agency behind the reforms. In the early 1990s the idea emerged that it was time for a 'second generation' reform, which would include reforming the state. Yet its proposals diverge fundamentally from the public management reforms that I discuss in this book. For the World Bank, reforming the state in developing countries means, first, downsizing.[21] Additionally, it involves classic civil service reform and anti-corruption measures. When, in the late 1990s, economists at the Bank finally learned about public management reform and considered the possibility of adopting it, they ended up rejecting the idea with the 'sequencing argument'—a typical bureaucratic argument that I discuss in the last section of this chapter. Developing countries, including those at intermediate levels of development, would not be ready for it. It would be required, first, to downsize the state apparatus; second, to fight corruption; third, to 'complete'

---

[21] Martin Rama (1999: 1–3), who organized a 'Symposium Issue on Efficient Public Sector Downsizing', says: 'Downsizing is not a final goal of economic policy, but economic reforms may require mass layoffs . . . The World Bank indirectly supported more than 40 attempts to downsize the public sector in developing countries between early 1991 and late 1993'. For World Bank support for civil service reform instead of public management reform, see Nunberg and Nellis (1995).

civil service reform. Only after that would the Bank recommend public management reform.

Public management reform made little progress in Latin America, with the exception of Brazil and Chile, but devolution or political decentralization initiatives were effective in modernizing the state organization. According to Burki, Perry, and Dillinger (1999: 1), 'since 1983, all but one of the largest countries in the region have seen transfer of power, resources, and responsibilities to subnational units of government'.[22] In Brazil and Argentina, devolution started in the 1980s and was clearly an outcome of the transition to democracy. In Brazil, decentralization took the form of devolution of responsibilities from central government to the states and particularly to the municipalities. In Argentina, devolution, especially in basic education, was to the provinces.[23] As a reaction to the concentration of power in central government during the military regimes, the underlying idea was that central government should transfer to states and/or municipalities all social services except social security, so as to make them better adapted and more accountable to the local people.

An effect of the 1988 Brazilian Constitution has been to double the municipalities' share in the total tax revenues. For some time, mayors had difficulties in using this new money, since the states and the federal government continued to provide their habitually poor services. The 1988 Constitution has redefined the revenue shares but not the responsibilities of the different government levels. Yet gradually the municipalities have taken on their new social tasks. It was originally stipulated in the Constitution that 25 per cent of the municipalities' expenditures should be earmarked for education. A 1998 constitutional amendment requires that 60 per cent of this 25 per cent be spent on basic education. In Mexico, one of the major electoral commitments adopted by the Fox administration beginning in 2000 was decentralization. In Venezuela, decentralization began in the late 1980s, but largely failed. The Chavez administration adopted a re-centralization policy, arguing that devolution had benefited only a limited number of groups in Venezuelan society. I am not able to evaluate this argument, but there is almost no doubt that, given the large rents coming from the oil industry, political elites in Venezuela have been engaged predominantly in rent-seeking. It seems that the decentralization efforts since the late 1980s were not able to reverse this generalized political behaviour (Rivas 2000; Briceño Reyes 2000).

Another type of devolution—to Indian communities instead of to the regions—has been occurring in Bolivia. Some left-wing groups resisted decentralization, associating it with privatization and viewing devolution and privatization as endangering national autonomy. However, the nation-state has always been precarious in Bolivia, given the poverty of the country and the

---

[22] The exception is Peru. The study covers the 14 largest Latin American countries by population, from Brazil to Nicaragua and Paraguay.

[23] On the devolution of health care in Argentina, see Vassalo (2000).

fact that its two great Indian nations, the Quechua and the Aymara, have never been integrated into the Bolivian state, even today constituting quasi-states within the nation-state. A constitutional amendment and the Law of Popular Participation, both of 1994, have recognized these realities and initiated a devolution process to the local communities: the 'territorial organizations' (meaning Indian lands) have been recognized, political and administrative power has been devolved to municipal governments, and new forms of budget allocation have been defined. Besides, in each municipality, Local Committees of Economic Development (CODEL—Comisión de Desarrollo Económico Local) have been established, which 'are not an institutionalized organism but a space for public debate and agreement at municipal level'. In these committees all sorts of local citizens' organizations, NGOs, religious organizations, business, workers', and particularly indigenous associations participate (CEPAD 2000). As observed by Molina Saucedo (1994), who was directly involved in the Bolivian reform, this kind of 'participatory' devolution, which originally looked like an 'impossible decentralization', is today a successful reform in Latin America because it responded to major demands.

A major macroeconomic problem following decentralization can be the lack of fiscal discipline. In the 1980s central governments in Latin America finally realized that they had no alternative but to balance their budgets. Yet, as devolution was taking place, the next problem was to curb populist spending practices at state and local levels. Public services may be more efficient and responsive at local level, but the macroeconomic problems involved should not be dismissed. After the devolution promoted by the 1988 Brazilian Constitution, one of the major macroeconomic issues that had to be confronted was the imposition of fiscal discipline on the sub-national units. First, state banks had to be controlled, and most of them were privatized. Second, the debts of the states and of the large municipalities were consolidated. And third, a Fiscal Discipline Law, enacted in 2000, prescribed severe sanctions on governors and mayors who proved unable to control their accounts.

I discuss now, briefly, public management reform in Chile and Brazil. The economic and political transformations that took place in Chile were not accompanied by similar changes in the management of the state apparatus. Since 1982 Chile has not faced a critical or unmanageable situation that makes the adoption of drastic measures necessary. Furthermore, it does not face any of the problems that usually accompany state reform processes, such as fiscal crisis, widespread corruption, obvious inefficiencies, or serious questions about the appropriate size or scope of the state. Despite these trends, Mario Marcel (1997) points out that the recent administrative reforms in Chile are designed to address its most serious problems. In particular, civil society is placing new demands on public institutions, and the state is trying to respond with a reform agenda that uses its available resources most effectively. According to Marcel, the process of state modernization in Chile, whose implementation started in 1993, already under democratic rule, was developed around three axes. First, a new organizational culture emerged and was focused on results, in contrast with the traditional focus on procedures. Second, the adoption of a gradual and cumulative change strategy sought to produce long-term changes in public institutions. Third, reform efforts remained under the direct control of the executive branch: the central administration and executive agencies.

Yet, the initiative that makes me include Chile among the countries that began public management reform was the incorporation into the national budget of a system of performance indicators and targets. This innovation began in 1994, and after three years of application managed to reach approximately 70 state agencies and 300 performance indicators. A pilot programme, launched in 1993, was conceived on the assumption that, despite bureaucratic rules, public agencies were flexible enough to undertake public management initiatives and capable of defining their own functions and goals. The core of the programme was the development of strategic planning exercises. With the participation of directors, staff members, and clients, these exercises attempted to achieve a clear identification of the organizational mission, the objectives, the services to be delivered, and the main clients. After this analysis, specific management projects and a managerial information system would be developed. These projects, in turn, would establish specific management targets and commitments and permit internal and external reviews. Targets and commitments could then be turned into performance agreements or management contracts that would envisage incentives and rewards for good management. This programme was applied initially in five public agencies and later extended to five other agencies within the Ministry of Finance, all being completed in 1995. The experience of the pilot programme inspired a more comprehensive programme that consolidated a managerial perspective on state reform. In this sense, public management reform was viewed as a gradual process: feasible, partial initiatives were implemented without big legal changes. Moreover, incentives, demands, and guidelines directed at institutional managers would play a central role in the administrative reform. In line with this reform agenda, the new government under President Eduardo Frey established an Inter-Ministerial Committee, made up of the Ministries of the Interior and of Finance, and the General Secretariat of the Presidency. Its fundamental purpose would be the promotion, coordination, and planning of initiatives to be implemented in public agencies. In mid-1994, the first initiative developed by the committee was the signing of 'modernization commitments' between 43 public bodies and the central government, represented by President Frey. These commitments, proposed by the bodies themselves, covered a variety of fields and presented different levels of complexity. The evaluation of these commitments at the start of 1995 showed that they reached close to 80 per cent of the agreed targets. Nonetheless, the *Dirección de*

Presupuestos ("Budget Office") of the Ministry of Finance concluded that the gradualist and sequential focus adopted by the Pilot Programme was too slow to produce a significant effect on the public administration as a whole. It was decided to promote a more aggressive agenda, concentrating on the generation of performance indicators in order to integrate them into the budgetary process. During the preparation of the budget in the second half of 1994, some leading agencies were requested to identify performance indicators and targets for the year of 1995. Twenty-six public bodies responded to this request and 107 performance indicators were selected. This information was incorporated into the 1995 budget act and was favourably received by the National Congress and by the press. This system was extended to the following year, when it reached 67 institutions with 291 indicators.

The Chilean reform presented one central problem. It tried to reform management without changing institutions—specifically, without defining clearly the increased administrative autonomy accorded to agencies. The new Lagos administration (2000) maintained the programme involving strategic planning and control by outcomes through the national budget, but centred its attention on a 'complete institutional redesign of the state organization'. On the other hand, civil service reform, creating a professional civil service and defining bureaucratic careers, became a major objective. Thus, the socialist administration implied a return to the principles of bureaucratic public administration, although the new managerial tools were not rejected.[24]

The Brazilian 1995/1998 Public Management Reform

Public management reform was launched in Brazil in 1995 with a White Paper—the *Plano Diretor da Reforma do Aparelho do Estado*—and with a constitutional amendment aiming at making the 1988 Constitution consistent with the reform. Four years later, when the first Cardoso administration ended, its basic institutions, its managerial logic, and its central concern with rebuilding the state were completed, and a long process of implementation was beginning. Prior to the 1995/98 Public Management Reform, there were two significant administrative reforms, but the first was never completed, and the second, which already presented a managerial approach, was soon reversed. The first, beginning in 1936, was the bureaucratic reform that established a professional civil service and the principles of bureaucratic public administration. The second, established by the military regime through Decree-Law n° 200 (1967), was the developmental reform—a kind of pioneering public

---

[24] Lecture given by Hector Oyarce, 'Proyecto de Reforma y Modernización del Estado en Chile', representing the Chilean government at the conference Changing Governance and Public Sector Reform in the Americas. Ottawa: Canadian Centre for Management Development, 1–2 May 2001.

management reform—which was discontinued in 1985–8 with the transition to democracy and the promulgation of the 1988 Constitution.[25] I was personally involved in the reform between January 1995 and December 1998, in the Ministry of Federal Administration and Reform of the State (MARE) in the first Cardoso administration. The implementation of the reform continues, now under the new Ministry of Planning, Budgeting, and Management, that resulted from the merger of MARE with the Ministry of Planning and Budgeting.[26] It is important to distinguish public management reform, defined in the *Plano Diretor*, from the constitutional amendment that came to be called 'administrative reform'. The constitutional amendment was an important part of public management reform, because, besides creating the juridical conditions and establishing some basic principles for the reform, it stimulated a national debate that eventually changed the bureaucratic Brazilian views on public administration. After 34 months of debate and negotiation, the Congress finally approved the amendment, retaining most of its original propositions: quite a different fate from the other two major reforms sent to the Congress at the same time, the social security and the tax reforms.[27]

Managerial public administration was introduced as representing a superior stage to bureaucratic public administration. Its objectives were to achieve more efficiency and accountability in the state organization. Thus, besides attaching importance to classic forms of political accountability (procedural rules, auditing, and parliamentary review), the reform proposed three forms of managerial accountability: control by contracted outcomes, by managed competition, and by social accountability. Prior to the reform proposal, a diagnosis of Brazilian public administration at that moment was undertaken in the first months of 1995.[28] In the constitutional amendment, the essential idea was to make more flexible the existing full tenure system for civil servants, and to eliminate the single-law regime for hiring state personnel. The basic objective of the amendment was not to eliminate personnel redundancies—although this was also a legitimate objective—but to make public management more efficient and more accountable, by defining institutions that motivate competent professionals, and allow for imposing penalties on the ones not willing to work as they are supposed to.[29] The *Plano Diretor*, however, stressed that some of the institutional changes did not require formal constitutional

[25] For an analysis of the 1936–8 civil service reform, see Beatriz Wahrlich (1983, 1984); for the 1968 developmental reform, see Wahrlich (1970). For an account of the evolution of the Brazilian state from patrimonial rule to public management reform, see Bresser-Pereira (2001c).

[26] The *Plano Diretor* and other documents and papers related to the 1995–8 Public Management Reform are available at www.bresserpereira.org.br

[27] For an analysis of the debates and negotiations around the administrative reform, see Bresser-Pereira (2003a). For a comparative analysis of the three reforms, see Melo (2002b, 2003).

[28] For this diagnosis, I relied on a previous one that is summarized in Andrade and Jacoud (1993). Nevertheless, the paucity of data on the Brazilian public administration was a disgrace. One of the objectives of the reform was to increase substantially such information, making it available to the public through a monthly bulletin and the Internet.

[29] The tenure principle in the 1988 Constitution made this practically impossible.

amendments, in spite of the detailed character of the Brazilian constitutional system. When, for instance, the two basic organizational institutions of the reform, agencies (executive and regulatory) and the 'social organizations' (public non-state service organizations financed by the state), were formally created, it was not necessary to change the constitution.[30] Other important changes in public administration did not involve constitutional reform: an effective remuneration policy for civil servants; yearly recruitment and selection of new civil servants for the 'state careers';[31] and elimination of undue privileges that statutory civil servants had acquired by the law that had established the 'single public labour regime' (a requirement of the 1988 Constitution that the 1998 managerial amendment repealed).

In a critical study of the 1995 managerial reform, Celina Souza and Inaiá Carvalho (1999: 201) correctly observe that, although the reform emphasized decentralization to states and municipalities, it did not sufficiently recognize the regional complexities involved in implementation.[32] Indeed, devolution was a political and administrative process that preceded managerial reform and had its own autonomy. Thus, our team tried to develop a broader model of public management reform, in which devolution was a part but not central. We gave emphasis, rather, to administrative decentralization, understanding this expression broadly. Most significant was the definition of the roles of the state. We distinguished (a) the exclusive activities of the state— which should remain within the state apparatus—from (b) the social and scientific services—which should be contracted out to public non-state service organizations—and from (c) the production of goods and services for the market, which should be privately owned. Our basic concern was to change from bureaucratic to managerial public administration, making public managers more autonomous and more accountable through the creation of executive and regulatory agencies, and transforming social and scientific services in 'social organizations'. Finally, we wanted to improve the efficiency and quality of the public services, orienting them to the client-citizen instead of maintaining their orientation to the bureaucracy.

The institution that we called 'social organization' is key to the reform. A federal law was approved defining the social organizations and the process

---

[30] The creation of each new regulatory agency required legislation. The first three agencies regulated electric power, oil, and communications. A general law specified limited exemptions or waivers for organizations declared executive agencies. As to the provision of social and scientific services, two laws were enacted: the Social Organizations Law, establishing the rules for the transformation of state organizations into public non-state organizations, and the OSCIPs Law, permitting the recognition of public non-state organizations or social organizations. To benefit from federal budget allocations, the Brazilian state requires management contracts from social organizations and 'partnership agreement' from OSCIPs (Organizações da Sociedade Civil de Interesse Publico—Civil Society Public Interest Organizations). On the latter, see Augusto Franco (2002).

[31] By 'state careers' is meant the civil service careers that are engaged in the exclusive activities of state.

[32] Souza and Carvalho (1999: 201). Among other analyses and critiques of the 1995 reform, I cite Azevedo and Andrade (1997); Lima Jr. (1998); Cruz (1998); Gaetani (1998); Barreto (1999); Petrucci and Schwarz (1999).

through which state departments or agencies performing social and scientific services would be transformed into this new form of institutional organization. Yet we faced difficulties in implementing this part of the reform. This may be illustrated by the federal universities. At the beginning of the Cardoso administration, when I proposed the idea, the Ministry of Education that runs a large number of federal universities accepted it, but, in view of the strong reaction of various deans, who understood that 'the university was being privatized', the minister retreated.[33] As a rule, despite all the guarantees that were offered to bureaucrats working for departments or state agencies that were supposed to be transformed into social organizations, with some exceptions they tended to reject the change. Most senior civil servants approved of the idea theoretically, but did not want it applied to their own case. Yet, when the case was not one of transformation of a department into a social organization, but the qualification of an existing public non-state service organization or service NGO into a social organization (specifically OSCIPs), the reform proved much easier.[34]

As an economist, since 1987 I have been diagnosing the Brazilian (and the Latin American) crisis not only as a foreign debt crisis, but also as a fiscal crisis of the state. Thus, instead of viewing the 1995–8 public management reform as an exogenous constraint imposed by globalization, I view it rather as a consequence of the endogenous crisis of the state. I was not ignoring globalization, but my concern was rather with the crisis of the Latin American developmental state. The reform design expresses my insistent critique of the two opposite ideologies that have dominated the Brazilian scene for long: on the one hand the old statist ideas, on the other hand the conservative ultra-liberal credo imported from the developed countries that preached but not did not practise such ultra-liberalism.[35] The 1995–8 public management reform adopted a managerial approach to public management and a social-democratic and social-liberal approach to the role of the state. The reform is managerial because it draws inspiration from the management of private companies and because it adopts the promotion of public agencies' autonomy and accountability as its basic strategy to achieve more efficiency and higher quality. It is democratic because it presupposes democratic governance, makes social accountability by civil society a major form of political accountability, and requires transparency from public agencies. It is social-democratic

[33] Minister Paulo Renato de Souza, however, retained his own conviction on the need of more autonomous and accountable universities and, in the following year, presented a proposal for a constitutional amendment conceding effective administrative autonomy to the universities, particularly in relation to its personnel, who in Brazil are full civil servants, that in practical terms changed them into special social organizations. My ministry participated from the drawing of the amendment. Yet the constitutional amendment did not prosper. The federal universities remained in crisis.

[34] The law creating the OSCIPs was directly inspired by the law of social organizations. While President Cardoso's staff resisted and was able to impede the qualification of civil society's organizations as social organizations *sensu stricto*, according to the respective law, the OSCIP law that had the same objective did not face such resistance. Today, there are only around 30 formal social organizations resulting from the transformation of departments or state agencies—particularly large hospitals at state level, and scientific research centres in the federal government—while qualified OSCIPs exceed 1,500.　　　　[35] On this critique, see particularly Bresser-Pereira (1993, 1996).

because it asserts the role of the state in guaranteeing the effective protection of social rights. It is social-liberal because it believes in the market as an excellent but imperfect resource-allocating agent, and views contracting out services and managed competition as excellent accountability tools. Although it reasserts the duty of the state to protect the weak—the poor, children, young single mothers, and the elderly—it does not aim to be paternalistic. It does not underestimate their capacity to work and to defend their own rights of citizenship, so long as the state offers the right incentives and opportunities.

The reform was not on the agenda of the country or in the manifesto of the political coalition that won the 1994 elections. When the new ideas began to be exposed to public opinion in January 1995, opposition was, at first, widespread. Yet, as public debate continued, it gained increasing support in society and, finally, among senior civil servants. In the end, against all initial predictions, the Congress approved the administrative reform constitutional amendment in 1998.[36] At the beginning of 1998, realizing that the constitutional amendment was successful, I concluded that a small ministry like MARE, short of executive power, should not be responsible for implementing the reform. Considering other experiences using the administrative power existing in the Budget Office, I proposed that the implementation of the reform should be the responsibility of a new Ministry of Planning, Budget and Management (which would result from MARE's merger with the Ministry of Planning and Budget). The proposal coincided with other views in the administration, and President Cardoso adopted it for his second term beginning in 1999. Since that date, the Ministry of Planning, Budget and Management has been implementing the reform. Originally, it was not called 'public management reform', since this denomination was not yet widespread, but rather 'managerial reform'. The new minister changed its denomination to a similar name—'entrepreneurial reform'—but during the second four-year term of the Cardoso administration the public management reform had continuity. In 2003, after the Workers' Party won the presidential elections, it maintained the basic principles of the reform, despite its opposition to the reform during the previous administration.

Advances are happening, not only at federal but also at state and municipal levels, since the 1995 reform has changed the public administration agenda throughout the country. Transformations usually evolve gradually, which makes some people believe that the reforms have foundered. In fact, they have not failed. Major administrative reforms have a critical moment of institutional and cultural change, and a long and uncertain process of implementation.[37] What is important to know is whether the new

---

[36] For an account of the political strategies that I have used to approve the constitutional amendment, see Bresser-Pereira (2002*a*). A general presentation of the reform is in *Reforma do Estado para a Cidadania* (Bresser-Pereira 1998*a*). In English, see Bresser-Pereira (1997, 1999).

[37] On the implementation of the 1995 public management reform, see Regina Pacheco (1999, 2003); Bresser-Pereira (2001*a*); Nassuno (2000); Evelyn Levy (2002); Carlos Pacheco (2002); and Nassuno and Kamada (2002); Marini, 2002; Nickson (2002).

views have been accepted and become dominant in society and among senior civil servants, or, in other words, whether a cultural change has taken place. In the case of the 1995–8 public management reform, such a change was probably its most outstanding achievement.

I conclude this review of public management reform in Latin America with a reference to the Latin American Centre of Administration for Development (CLAD). This is a small multilateral Ibero-American organization formed by 25 member countries, with headquarters in Caracas. I was its president from 1995 to the end of 1997 and, since then, president of its Scientific Council.[38] During this period, I was able to change the organization's mission so that it became a major forum for debate on public management reform in the region. Since 1996 CLAD has organized major annual congresses, with support from Bank of Interamerican Development, and other international bodies.[39] During three days, a large number of participants discussed hundreds of papers in about one hundred panels. In the 1998 Congress, in Spain, the 26 ministers of public administration signed the Madrid Declaration, 'A New Public Management for Latin America'. Prepared by CLAD's Scientific Council, this document, which is available at CLAD's website, represents, in principle, a major change in Latin American views on administrative reforms: Latin Americans ceased to view them as civil service or bureaucratic reforms and started to understand them as public management reforms (CLAD 1998). This is clear, for instance, in the survey recently conducted by Peter Spink. New public management is a winning idea in Latin America, although Latin Americans remain highly concerned with poverty and inequality, and want to add to the managerial approach, a rights approach. As Spink underlines, following an approach that Bernardo Kliksberg has been championing for years in the region, 'the approach based on citizens, rights share most of managerial public administration's concerns, but besides emphasizing outcomes, underlines the relations that the state establishes with citizens, and their impact on social inclusion and poverty alleviation'. (Spink 2001: 34).[40]

The Sequencing Question

From the brief report on public management reform undertaken in this chapter, I believe it is licit to conclude that a major change is taking place in the forms of organizing and managing the state apparatus. The Anglo-Saxon and Scandinavian countries lead the reform, but it is already noticeable in other

---

[38] CLAD's Scientific Council comprises Luiz Carlos Bresser-Pereira (president), Nuria Cunill Grau (secretary), Adam Przeworski, Joan Prats y Català, Leonardo Garnier, and Oscar Oszlak.

[39] In 1995 BID's president, Enrique Iglesias, was one of the first persons to give full support to the reform ideas I was proposing. Since then, and specially to make possible the first congresses, BID's support, through the Office for State Reform, has been crucial.

[40] Bernardo Kliksberg's work on public management reform and its relation to poverty alleviation and social inclusion is central in Latin America. See, among others, Kliksberg (1994, 1997).

European countries and in at least two Latin American ones. In Latin America, institutional reforms, particularly public management reform, are strategic factors in overcoming the crisis of the state, which was predominantly severe in the region, and in promoting economic growth. Yet there is probably a correlation between income per capita and the governance stage. Thus, the managerial character of public management institutions and the professionalism of civil servants are active rather than passive factors in economic and political development when they prove to correspond to a higher governance level than the level that the country's or the region's existing per capita income leads us to predict.

For the moment, in spite of some advances, we cannot say that much was achieved by way of implementing public management reform. For sure, there is an increasing awareness that the classic bureaucratic model of public administration is inconsistent with the complexity and dynamism of modern capitalism. The 'Weberian civil service' has ceased to be an ideal. Instead, more flexible labour contracts and professional, competent, and more autonomous public managers are now required. Neither the developmental state nor the ultra-liberal minimal state any longer makes sense. The statist model of development is exhausted, damaged by a fiscal crisis, while the ultra-liberal alternative proposed (although not adopted) by the rich countries has not shown the promised results. The region badly needs better governance, better political and administrative institutions that will enable its governments to find their own ways of promoting economic development and reducing blatant social injustice: public management reform adapted to Latin American circumstances certainly has a role to play in this area.

Can public management reforms be successful at the present stage of economic growth? The defenders of the necessary 'sequencing' of the reforms claim that it cannot. The expression 'sequencing', used originally by economists and political scientists in discussing whether economic liberalization should precede political liberalization or vice versa, became increasingly used by international bureaucrats to evaluate the timing of reforms.[41] On a more general level, the issue of sequencing is controversial because, although its proponents have a point, sequencing can serve as a convenient excuse for not reforming. It was a pretext for the continuation of authoritarianism; now it is an excuse for not undertaking public management reform. First, it is argued, civil service reform should go through, and only after that should we think of public management reform. I have personal experience with this kind of conservative reasoning. International experts do not directly express their bureaucratic views, even when some new procedure has conclusively worked

---

[41] On the sequencing of economic and political liberalization, see particularly Armijo (1993); Jaquette (1993: 60). The latter states: 'we need to deal with all the cases simultaneously when managing economic and political liberalization, and, within this context, to concentrate our attention on its micro-sequencing'. This view is more dialectic and realistic than a linear sequencing.

elsewhere. The staff prefers to suggest that they agree, but there is a sequencing problem: 'one must not put the cart before the horse', they say; another formula is to say: 'first' it is necessary to do 'this and that' . . . and only after a series of conditions that probably will take years have been accomplished, to undertake the reform. Yet I learned while managing private and public organizations that on certain occasions it is necessary to put the cart before the horse, or, in mathematical terms, that we often have to solve simultaneous equations systems. Rapid change might create needs or raise problems that one should face and tackle at the same time. For example, if an organization decides to devolve authority only after having fully trained the managers, decentralization will never occur because the training of managers will be completed only through the exercise of their new authority.

In countries like Brazil, Chile, and particularly Mexico, the problem of sequencing appeared in the demands for undertaking or completing civil service reform, and only after that confronting public management reform. In Mexico, this attitude was clear on the eve of the electoral defeat of the Institutional Revolutionary Party (PRI) as the Mexican bureaucracy, including its more competent officials, felt threatened and looked for more stability. It is doubtful, however, that more stability for bureaucracy, in any form, will be useful to that country at present (Arellano 2002). Yet, as the victory of President Fox did not lead to the feared massive dismissals,[42] these fears have probably diminished, and the door for public management reform is open. Actually, the enactment of bureaucratic tenure would only create more privileges, as it was seen in Brazil in the 1988 Constitution. The idea that a change of government would lead to mass dismissals in the public sector is mistaken. This did not happen in Brazil in 1985, with the transition to democracy, or in Mexico in 2000, with the inauguration of the first non-PRI government in 80 years, because both countries had already achieved a stage of democratic governance inconsistent with such patrimonial practices. However, public management reform is a more effective way to fight nepotism and clientelism in democracies than bureaucratization, in so far as the autonomy of public sector managers and the demand for more public sector efficiency make new public management even more incompatible with such practices than bureaucratic public administration. Often, the best way to solve a problem is to jump over the obstacle instead of just confronting it.

---

[42] Confirming what I emphatically predicted in a conference in Mexico City in 1988.

14

Public Management Reform Defined

We are now ready to define public management reform. As conceived in this book, it encompasses more than what is usually understood by 'new public management' (NPM).[1] It not only involves new management practices and new managerial institutions, but it also assigns a major role to social accountability mechanisms and redefines the logic of the state organization and of the state functions. The four distinct relevant forms of ownership in contemporary capitalism—state, public non-state, corporative, and private—and the three basic types of activity in which the state is often involved—exclusive activities of the state, social and scientific activities, and production of goods and services for the market—are central to public management reform.[2] The basic idea is that activities that use state power should be within the state organization; social, cultural, and scientific activities involving externalities and dealing with basic human rights should be mainly financed by the state while executed by public non-state service organizations. Additionally, public management reform is concerned with the democratic character of government officials' decisions. Thus, while it emphasizes more autonomy for government officials in their decisions, given the complexity of the problems that government faces today and the speed required for some decisions, it demands, as a trade-off, greater transparency and accountability in the decision-making process. Finally, the objective of public management reform is not just to make the state organization more efficient, but to build state capacity.

Among the ways of making state officials accountable, public management reform emphasizes control by contracted outcomes, managed competition for excellence, and direct social accountability, besides the classic forms of control: direct supervision, checks and balances, and parliamentary review. As public managers become more autonomous, the assumption is that they

---

[1] There is already an extensive literature on new public management, since the pioneering works by Kooiman and Eliassen (1987) and Aucoin (1990). I draw on and quote some of this literature in the following pages. Here, I cite just a few books, which present a general view of the subject: Barzelay (1992, 2001); Pollitt (1993); Troas (1995); Crozier (1996); Ferlie et al. (1996); Bresser-Pereira (1998*a*); Lane (2000); Pollit and Bouckaert (2000); Kettl (2000).

[2] There is a fourth type of property—corporative ownership—which is socially and politically important, since it includes unions and all kind of organizations representing interests, but it will not be used in the model of public management reform presented in this book.

will be more motivated to work creatively. Such motivation will derive from an incentive system which is practically impossible in bureaucratic public administration but which is central to new public management. Although bureaucrats are always proposing to implement incentive systems, and notwithstanding that rational-choice principal–agent models demonstrate the superiority of such systems, they are not adopted because conflict with the whole monopolist and tenure-oriented character of bureaucratic administration. In contrast, when we have a public management system in action, an incentive system is a natural part of it, coupled with the demand for a republican ethos on the part of government officers.

Thus, we should avoid adopting a narrow view of public management reform as just one of the worn-out administrative reforms. Politicians and senior civil servants use such expressions to describe the organizational changes they make when assuming an executive position. In this sense, administrative reforms become meaningless: what is routine cannot be reform. We may speak of 'real' administrative reform but, in this case, in modern times they should be limited to just two major ones: civil service or bureaucratic reform, and public management or managerial reform. Reforms only are worthy of the name when they involve the creation of new and noteworthy institutions. Most 'administrative reforms', including the World Bank's second generation of reforms, are intended to 'complete' civil service reform, to make it more professional, more impersonal, and more procedural. Public management reforms, which began in the developed world in the 1980s and gathered momentum in the 1990s and 2000s, have a wholly different and broader orientation.

Public management reforms should also not be confused with the adoption of new management practices or strategies without the corresponding changes in institutions. They cannot, for instance, be understood as 'operative improvements in the administrative institutions of the executive branch' (Longo and Echebarria 2001: 101). This kind of change is not operative when rigid bureaucratic institutions have not been reformed, and are just routine after public management reform has taken place. Good managers are continually looking for better ways of managing their organizations. The search for quality and efficiency in management is a daily, permanent process. One of the most important managerial principles is that there is no steady state growth path or 'automatic pilot' mechanism for organizations. It is a false optimism of inexperienced managers—and of bureaucratic officials—to believe that they will find a formula that will stand on its own, valid in all situations at all times. In management, what is right today might become obsolete tomorrow: new facts, or the simple disorganization or entropy of existing ones, will continuously demand new executive decisions. Hence, it is important not to confuse reform with change in managerial strategies. 'Total quality control' or 'reengineering' are managerial strategies. The former is being increasingly used by governments involved in public management reform. Yet, although quite appropriate as a management strategy, it should be clearly distinguished from reform itself.

Finally, the public management model that I am discussing is broader than the NPM theories that were developed principally in Britain in the 1990s. I see two basic dimensions in public management reform: one dimension involving the structural reform of the state organization, the other defining the new principles or strategies required to manage that organization. Privatization may be seen as part of the first dimension of public management reform, although the distinction between exclusive activities of state and social and scientific services that the government chooses to finance is more relevant. The key terms in the second dimension are 'autonomy' and 'accountability'. NPM theories deal more with the second than with the first dimension of public management reform.

The main purpose of reform is to make the state organization more efficient and effective. More broadly, it is to improve public governance—the whole process involving government, institutions, civil society, and markets. By making the state organization more effective and efficient, public management reform is an essential element in governance, together with civil society and other institutions. Civil society debates public issues in the public sphere, providing the basic conditions for competent and legitimate rules of the game. The institutions are the rules of the game: on them will depend much of the political development of a society. The state apparatus is one such institution that I single out due to its central role in good governance. Public management reform is gradually changing the state organization, establishing rational limits to its actions, creating new roles for it, increasing its ability to protect the *res publica*, and making public managers more efficient and accountable. In other words, it is building state capacity. Privatizing state-owned enterprises, outsourcing business enterprises' auxiliary services, and contracting non-profit organizations to deliver social and scientific services are reforms aiming to strengthen state capacity by depriving it of functions that do not belong to it. Public management reform is changing the state organization everywhere, and restoring the idea of public administration to public management.

Defining Characteristics

We can better understand public management reform by examining its objectives and characteristics. There are many definitions of it. Arigapudi Premchand (1998), for instance, highlights eight characteristics that will prevail around the year 2020: smaller and more flexible state agencies; clear separation between departments defining public policies and agencies implementing them; well-defined public ethical standards for both bureaucrats and politicians;

transparency, with widespread publication of statistics and results; clear budgetary processes, with a medium-term perspective, and a short-term detailing of performance indicators; abolition of civil servants' tenure; completely electronic payments; and managerial public accounting systems. Hood (1991: 4) lists seven characteristics of the new public management: professional administration, explicit performance indicators, more emphasis on control by results, breakdown of public organizations into smaller units, more competition between units, emphasis on the use of management practices originating in the private sector, and emphasis on greater discipline and parsimony in the use of resources.

Public management reform is the institutional, cultural, and managerial transition from bureaucratic public administration to modern public management. It involves changing institutions, particularly the state organization, the administrative culture, and management strategies. It imports practices from private management while maintaining its essentially public and political character. Amongst its basic strategies, it has made agencies and their public managers more autonomous and accountable, controlling through contracted outcomes and managed competition rather than through procedural control and close supervision.

Public management reform aims to improve the quality of the executive decisions taken by government officers. The assumption is that the more decentralized and autonomous the decision-makers are, the more competent— more consistent with the objectives—will be the decisions taken. Given the assumption that the problems faced by government are increasingly complex and change rapidly, public management reform assures a limited but effective amount of discretionary power to public managers. The increase in autonomy is supposed to be checked by the increase in accountability: the transparency requirement and the use of citizens' control or social accountability is key in this trade-off. In this matter, public management reform is just going along a general tendency of empowering consumers or clients in relation to producers of goods and services—consumers who, in the case of public management, are also, above all, citizens.[3] More analytically, public management reform involves:

- decentralizing power and resources to regulatory and executive agencies that perform exclusive activities of the state, while increasing the power of the strategic core of the state over outcomes and of policy-making secretaries over institutional reforms and policies;[4]

---

[3] *The Economist* (3 February 2001: 24), after reporting on the increasing scrutiny to which the medical profession is being subjected by society, concludes: 'In many areas of life outside the surgery and the hospital—shopping, banking, government services, for instance—power is shifting from producer to the consumer'. This shift is still limited, but the difference from the recent past—the 1950s, for instance—is already enormous.

[4] Decentralization or devolution to sub-national units (states and local governments) is not necessarily a characteristic of public management reform.

- contracting out to public non-state service organizations, recognized as 'social organizations', the social and scientific services that society decides to finance with state resources because they involve high externalities and basic human rights;
- outsourcing to business enterprises support or auxiliary activities that do not involve either state power (and are performed by agencies) or basic human rights (which should be provided by social organizations);
- making agencies and social organizations accountable through control of contracted outcomes, managed competition, and social accountability, that involve high transparency, rather than through classic bureaucratic controls (procedural rules, auditing, and parliamentary review);
- staffing agencies and social organizations differently: while agencies will have civil servants, social organizations will work with private employees;
- strengthening the civil service, which will be limited to performing the exclusive activities of the state, and will continue to be organized into careers or 'bodies';[5]
- requiring from civil servants not only technical competence and ethical behaviour but reasonable autonomy to decide, and political capacity;
- establishing an incentive system, involving pay differentials, transparent performance evaluation, and real opportunities for training and career advancement; and
- extensively adopting information technology and particularly Internet technology, for auditing, purchasing, payment, and all kinds of official registers.

Public management reform presupposes a democratic state and the existence of active organizations of civil society. In so far as it limits the use of bureaucratic controls, to be effective it depends on a strong social accountability system. It is impossible to have a public management reform without such organizations. They are also essential for a second reason: communications. The democratic process is a permanent two-way communication system between politicians and citizens, and, besides the media, associations, unions, and NGOs are channels for it. As William Plowden (1997: 4) stresses:

The character and state of development of civil society are relevant to/impinge upon the character of public administration in several and different ways. First, the institutions that comprise civil society greatly enhance the quantity and the quality of two-way communication between government and citizen . . . In the second place, these institutions are channels though which governments, in their turn, can interrogate or inform groups of citizens with specific interests.

Public management reform should not be confused with 'regulatory reform', even though it involves decentralization to regulatory agencies.

---

[5] Public management reform implies the substitution of managerial public administration for bureaucratic public administration. This, however, does not imply decreasing the role of state bureaucracy. On the contrary, as the reform assigns a greater managerial autonomy to it, it takes on an increasingly strategic role in managing the state apparatus.

Regulatory reform emerged at about the same time as public management reform, but was clearly an expression of the neo-liberal wave aiming at reducing the size of the state. It is a complement of privatization, justifying the sale of state-owned business enterprises operating in monopolistic or quasi-monopolistic industries, like the electricity industry, water supply, and sewage disposal. Instead of remaining a 'producer state', the state should privatize all these enterprises and create agencies to regulate the sector and, principally, to set prices as if a market existed. I am fully in favour of public management reform, but I have many reservations about regulatory reform, since I do not believe that regulators are able to act as 'technically' as this kind of reform expects. When the market is monopolistic or quasi-monopolistic, I believe that state ownership remains the best option, despite all the problems involved in that type of ownership.

Public management reform should also not be confused with good government. It is able to improve only the quality of executive decisions and consequently the efficiency of the state organization, but not the quality of the strategic decisions involving the framing of new policies and new institutions. In other words, public management reform is no substitute for good government. Strategic decisions taken at the strategic core of the state by the head of government, ministries, politicians in parliament, senior magistrates, and senior civil servants define how good the government is and, more broadly, governance.[6] In modern democracies, the quality of such decisions depends on the strength of civil society, on the level of public debate existing in society, on the quality of institutions, and on the democratic legitimacy of decision-makers. Thus, good government depends on a complex set of variables which go beyond the reach of public management, even when we understand them in broad terms, as I do in this book.

Public management reform should also not to be identified with democratic administration, although it is viable only in modern democracies. Administration and democracy are in principle contradictory. Administration involves hierarchy, democracy involves representation and participation. After the Second World War, the rise of the social-democratic state involved an enormous increase in bureaucracy. Looking at this trend, many liberal analysts feared that bureaucracy would destroy democracy. Samuel Krislov and David Rosenbloom (1981: 1), for instance, writing in the early 1980s, expressed clearly this concern: 'Nowhere is the rise of the bureaucratic state more perplexing than in democratic nations.' This concern was perfectly reasonable. Yet it was based on a false assumption: that the power of bureaucracy was greater than the strength of democracy. According to this line of thought, the two authors continued: 'Whereas modern democratic governments are unable to function without well-developed bureaucratic components, bureaucratic governments

---

[6] On public managers' strategic decisions, see particularly the works by Dror (1994, 1997); Crozier (1996); Crozier and Tilliette (1995).

have little need for democratic political institutions.' This analysis is consistent with what Alford and Friedland (1985), writing approximately at the same time, refer to as the 'managerial world view' which, beginning in the analysis of the growing role of bureaucratic organizations at business and state levels, and from the technical capacity of organizations to manage complex tasks, ends with the capacity of powerful elites running such organizations to dominate the social and political system.[7]

Yet what the following 20 years presented was a different picture. Bureaucracy proved inefficient and had to be changed, while democracy proved again and again to be the more sensible political regime—a regime strong enough to establish the conditions in which bureaucrats, now better called public managers, are supposed to operate. In fact, public management reform is possible only in the realm of democratic regimes, when its first historical expression— the elitist model of democracy—progresses towards a republican model of democracy, counting on an active civil society, a participatory citizenry.

While civil service reform is the outcome of the liberal yet authoritarian state, public management reform is possible only when democracy is consolidated. While classic bureaucrats' main concern is asserting the legitimacy and effectiveness of state power, modern public managers assume state power as existing, and look for more efficiency and more quality. Thus, accountability becomes a central problem in managerial public administration. The public managers are supposed to be accountable to the elected politicians who head them, to the members of parliament, particularly to the members of the political opposition, to the media, and to the formal and informal representatives of civil society, who occupy the public space, participate in public debate, and adopt several mechanisms of social accountability or citizenry's participation. The public manager in democracies is necessarily oriented towards the user-citizen or client-citizen,[8] rather than maintaining the self-centred attitude that characterizes bureaucratic public administration.

To sum up, public management reform means reforming the state organization so that it becomes not only more efficient and effective, but also more in accordance with the democratic regime of which it is supposed to be a tool. It means rendering the state organization more efficient by making possible the effective use of the most adequate means to reach the intended ends; and more democratic because it is citizen-oriented, and because it depends on mechanisms of social accountability. Naturally, critics may say the opposite: that

---

[7] Alford and Friedland (1985). On this subject, I wrote: decentralization 'rather than decreasing control over companies, aims at increasing it . . . its objective is the objective of all rational managerial actions: to increase the efficiency of corporations, while firmly keeping control in the hands of management' (Bresser-Pereira 1981: 115).

[8] I use the two expressions as synonyms. It is possible, however, to make a distinction between them: the user-citizen does not pay for the services delivered to him, while the client-citizen does. The distinction may be useful because some state services involve universal rights (basic education, for instance) while others do not. It is foolish if it presumes that the citizen should always be a user, never paying for services delivered by the state.

public management reform leads to a more authoritarian administration to the extent that public managers are allowed discretion, that is, are allowed to take decisions rather than simply applying the law. According to this reasoning, new public management would be infringing the principle of the universality of procedures that characterizes the rule of law and civil service reform. In fact, there is no violation of this principle. Public managers are assured more autonomy within the limits established by the law. To this end, it is necessary to count on the existence of a democratic regime in which the direct control of society over more autonomous agencies assumes a strategic nature. That is why public management reform, beyond a reform *for* citizenship and democracy, is a reform *in* democracy, which presumes the existence of the democratic regime.

Bureaucrats' Accountability

A major political problem of modern democracies is the accountability of government officials, particularly of public servants. Public management reform has a specific answer to this. It is possible to distinguish control, in which the administration's perspective is dominant, from accountability, in which what is relevant is to know how government officials are accountable to society. Although control goes downward from top government officials to the lower ranks, and accountability upward from the people to government officials, in democracies the two mechanisms end up as being similar. We must distinguish how governments are accountable, from the control and accountability of public managers directing state secretaries and agencies. A central question in public management reform is how to control bureaucrats, so that they use their autonomy to act in accordance with the public interest. In other words, the question is the accountability of public managers to society.

The bureaucratic answer to this question is as simple as it is unsatisfactory: accountability will be assured in so far as bureaucrats observe the restrictions imposed by the law and the administrative procedures. Such legal and procedural control on bureaucrats' accountability leads to all the bureaucratic distortions that we have being analysing in this book. The adoption of principal–agent theory is only an interesting generalization, and does not solve the problem. If it is enormously difficult to make politicians accountable to society, the trouble in making public organizations' managers accountable to politicians and society is as great.[9] It is a formalist mistake to think that the public manager is responsible only to politicians and to the law: he is also

---

[9] According to Przeworski's definition (1996: 32), 'governments are "accountable" if citizens can discern whether governments are acting in their best interests and sanction them appropriately, so that those incumbents who act in the best interest of citizens win elections and those who do not lose them'. It is clear from this definition how difficult it is to reach this democratic objective.

responsible to society, since as well as being a bureaucratic agent he is a political agent, exercising a political role.[10] Another mistake is to imagine that it is up to the politician, as representative of the people, to formulate public policies, while the task of the public manager is to carry them out. Research by Aberbach, Putnam, and Rockman (1981) on this subject is definitive. These authors distinguish four activities in relation to public policies: articulation of political ideals, intermediation of interests, formulation, and implementation. The first activity would be exclusive to politicians, the last a task only for bureaucrats, while the middle two are shared by the two groups.[11]

A more sophisticated—or ideological—answer to this question is to assume that bureaucrats would be endowed with a public ethos that would make them behave according to moral principles and promote the public interest. In these matters, bureaucrats would be more dependable than politicians ... Although I have been demanding and affirming the possibility of republican behaviour on the part of government officers—bureaucrats or politicians—it is obvious that we cannot just count on that. Public management reform uses hierarchical and political mechanisms to control bureaucrats, but the latter has precedence in democracies. One cannot legitimize public policies only in terms of the technical competence argument. It is up to society, directly or through its political representatives, to define objectives, and then to make government officers accountable. For the control of politicians, civil society counts on a specific form of control, namely, the vote; for the control of bureaucrats, it disposes also of an identifiable institution—social accountability—besides the indirect control it exercises through politicians and other bureaucrats (the judiciary, auditors). As Sutherland (1993: 25) observes, one of the functions performed by institutions is to 'compel the government to carry out the public will'.

Judith Gruber (1987) examines the problem of the democratic control of bureaucrats from the viewpoint of the existing 'restraints': controls have either a procedural character, if they establish the form or process of public policy decisions, or a substantive character, if they define the objectives or scope of public managers' action. All decisions involve a procedural and a substantive aspect, and may be accountable by means of specific mechanisms of varying degrees of strictness. Thus, she builds a model with two coordinates: the vertical, indicating the procedural restraints, and the horizontal, indicating the substantive restraints. Depending on the degree of utilization of these restraints and of their combination, five types of control are defined: (1) control through participation, (2) control through clientele relations, (3) control through pursuit of the public interest, (4) control through accountability, and (5) self-control.

---

[10] Peters (1996: 15), for example, among ideas that are 'no longer truthful', includes the presupposition of a non-partisan public service.

[11] For an empirical verification of bureaucrats' political autonomy, according to the principal–agent model, see Wood (1988).

The proponents of participatory accountability would stress the procedural aspect of decision-making, emphasizing the importance of citizen participation. Those who defend control through client relations are more interested in the results of the decisions or of the public policies, and in how well they serve citizen interests. The advocates of control through the search for the public interest count on the control of politicians over bureaucrats in order to guarantee, substantively, the public interest. The proponents of control through accountability give priority to procedural controls that involve methods of auditing, ombudsmen, boards of directors, and transparency. Finally, in the case of self-control, its defenders count on the professional standards of public managers. Democratic accountability of bureaucrats involves a combination of all these controls. In democracy, citizens cannot presuppose that public managers represent their interests, or that politicians will do so, although with elected politicians there exists at least the presumption that they represent the voters' interests.

Controlling the bureaucracy may prove costly, either because the controls themselves are expensive or because they impose unsupportable rigidities on the work to be done. If controls have a mainly procedural or legal character, they directly result in less efficient public services. If they involve extensive *a posteriori* auditing, we have the cost of contracting bureaucrats to control bureaucrats, as well as rigidities since auditing is essentially a procedural control. If controls are by results, the delivery of services may become more efficient, but one should not minimize the costs involved in dealing with management contracts and results. The same may be said of managed competition. When it is viable, service delivery may gain in efficiency, but one needs to control the costs involved in managing competition (which limited the success of the innovative purchaser-provider system adopted in the early 1990s by the British National Health Service). On the other hand, controls may purport to rely only on the public spirit of politicians and on their authority over bureaucrats, or on the bureaucrats' self-control. But this is not realistic: it would be naïve republicanism. Finally, we have social accountability systems that may be efficient in policy evaluation but have limited effectiveness. Public management reform involves all these controls, but requires a pragmatic perspective, which counts on the initiative and public spirit of bureaucrats and on the efficiency of formally contracted results, managed competition, and the participation of citizens, but without eliminating direct supervision and auditing.

Social accountability mechanisms, ranging from boards to citizens' councils, NGOs, advocacy groups, social movements, and grass-roots organizations, are public non-state social accountability institutions.[12] They exhibit different

---

[12] Bresser-Pereira and Cunill Grau (1998). This book is based on the presence of two kinds of institution in the non-state public sector: those oriented to social accountability and those oriented to the production of social services. The paper that serves as a reference for the book (Bresser-Pereira and Cunill Grau 1998) makes this distinction clear.

degrees of formal existence, but in contemporary democracies, especially at local level, they are acquiring a growing importance to the extent that they successfully control bureaucracy. The increasing decentralization of state activities to the local level is in part a response to this. The control of public services by elected representatives at national level is always a democratic guarantee, which advocacy groups complement with the decentralized units at local level. As Kaboolian (1999: 313) remarks, social advocacy typically takes two forms: lobbying and litigating. In either case, 'the definition and shape of public services is greatly affected by these actions'. NGOs also became influential at the international level, but, in this case, they seek to make governments accountable rather than just bureaucrats. Their increasing influence has led critics to argue that they are not democratic because they lack formal representation. Yet their influence depends partially on how 'representative' they are, since numerous middle-class citizens, rather than a small number of wealthy people, finance the bigger NGOs. We still may argue that this is not the ideal form of representation, but to think in ideal terms in this matter makes little sense. As Manin, Przerworski, and Stokes (1999) show, democratic representation is always relative, imperfect. Precisely because representation is imperfect, social accountability or advocacy mechanisms improve rather than threaten it.

The Logic of the Range of Accountability Mechanisms

In order to understand the accountability issue and the role played by public management reform, we need a theoretical framework. I suggest that the concept of a 'range of accountability mechanisms' offers such a model.[13] Every society uses three encompassing institutional coordinating mechanisms: the state, civil society, and the market. The state includes the legal or judicial system, constituted by legal norms and fundamental institutions of society, and the state apparatus with its government or administration. The legal system is the most general coordinating mechanism to the extent that it establishes the basic principles for the other mechanisms to function minimally. The market, in its turn, coordinates or, to use economists' terminology, allocates resources through competition. Finally, civil society—which I understand as society's political dimension, in which power is proportional to the relative weight of various social groups—constitutes a third basic mechanism of control. In civil society, the weight of each interest group or individual depends on its organizational, wealth, or knowledge capacity. While the state coordinates society through law and government, and markets through competition,

---

[13] These ideas were first developed in Bresser-Pereira (1998*b*). For an extension of this approach see the book edited by CLAD's Scientific Council (2000) *La responsabilización en la nueva gestión pública latinoamericana.*

civil society's members participate with public debate, and give life to the public sphere in which, in democracies, governments' legitimacy is tested.[14] Governments in each state act either by approving new legislation though the parliament or by framing public policies and taking decisions at executive level. In modern democracies, voters, individually and flexibly organized in civil society networks, control government, which, in its turn, holds state power, manages the state organization, and decides on economic transfers to the poor or to selected industries.

Government on one side and society on the other enforce the law and make effective and efficient public policies through a variety of control or accountability mechanisms that range from the hierarchical or administrative to market competition and social accountability. These institutions have a double character: they are not only control mechanisms that allow government to rule, they are also democratic devices making government officials more accountable to society. In democracies, all politicians and civil servants have to be accountable. The range of controls that society has at its disposal goes from the most concentrated to the most general, from those dependent on decisions or administration to the automatic ones. At societal level, this range of accountability goes from executive decision-making that frames policies to the more general institutional mechanisms: the legal system, which is part of the state, and the market system. Within the state organization, the range of controls goes again from the more specific to the more general: from hierarchical controls to managed competition and social accountability mechanisms. There is a logic in this range of institutional accountability mechanisms—a logic that orients public management reform. The general principle is that the accountability mechanism that is more generic, more diffuse, or more automatic is to be preferred. For that reason, at societal level the constitutional or legal system and the market are the best institutions—the ones that most broadly guarantee the control of actions and the accountability of actors. First among the accountability mechanisms comes the constitutional and legal system of the state, and, more broadly, the whole institutional system, including unwritten law. Second are markets. State institutions come before markets because markets are impracticable without a prior legal guarantee of property rights and contracts. Markets emerge as the preferable control mechanism whenever objectives are clear-cut, information is available at low cost, positive or negative externalities are not relevant, and monopoly power is limited. That is why, ideally, markets control business enterprises that have a well-defined objective—profit—and, in most industries, that face

---

[14] In this study, I do not engage in the issue of the relative importance of these three institutional accountability mechanisms. Clearly, the perspective of neoclassic economists, who attribute to the market a predominant role, is a reductionist one. The critical perspective of the evolutionary economists, expressed very well by Delorme (1995), is more provocative. It emphasizes the role of institutions and organizations, and the dynamic character marked by the diversity of accountability mechanisms and of the context in which they operate.

real competition; whereas markets are ineffective in controlling actions or organizations that do not have clear and measurable objectives such as profit. Most actions involving values that cannot be measured in money terms makes market coordination imperfect if not simply impossible. Only the state, through the legal system, is able to regulate these actions.

At the state organization level, as well as inside all organizations, accountability mechanisms will have to be administrative or organizational. The government at the strategic core of the state will have to use a combination of organizational accountability mechanisms that also follow the same principle: the more diffuse ones are preferable. We have two kinds of administrative mechanisms: the classic bureaucratic and the public management mechanisms. The public management mechanisms are more diffuse and automatic than the bureaucratic ones. By 'bureaucratic control mechanism' I mean the detailed definition of bureaucratic procedures, direct supervision, parliamentary review, and auditing or horizontal accountability. By 'public management control mechanism' I understand management by contracted outcomes, social accountability mechanisms, and managed competition.

The administrative or organizational accountability mechanisms may be organized on a spectrum from the most diffuse and automatic to the least. The general definition of objectives or policies by the parliament or through executive policy-making precedes these organizational accountability mechanism. Thereafter, the social accountability mechanisms are the most diffuse among the control mechanisms. Social accountability is to the organizational level what democracy is to the political one. Democracy as a political system is an accountability mechanism opposed to authoritarianism, or guardians' rule.[15] Through social accountability, society organizes itself formally and informally to control public and private organizations. This can also happen at a political, direct democracy level, through plebiscites or referendums. At the public organization level, social accountability can operate in two ways: informally, when society organizes itself politically to control or influence institutions over which citizens have no formal power; or formally, when Congress drafting laws or the administration framing policy create boards of directors or auditing councils. Social accountability is a vertical rather than a horizontal form of accountability. It is an essential tool of public management reform. As long as agencies and social organizations are autonomous, hierarchical controls are not enough, and should be complemented by social ones. Yet the limits of this kind of control are obvious. They may work only as complements of each other.

In our range of organizational accountability mechanisms, after social accountability we have quasi-markets or managed competition. Bureaucrats have enormous difficulty in understanding this form of control. They immediately

---

[15] I limit myself to this reference to democracy and guardianship. On the subject see Chapter 15 of Robert Dahl (1989).

imagine agencies and social organizations competing for profits ... Yet managed competition is applicable precisely where profits do not exist, or where they are not the basic goal to be pursued. The most general form of managed competition is competition for excellence. Similar organizations producing the same services compete to meet the excellence criteria defined by top management: usually a basket of weighted standards or of performance indicators. The managers of each competing organization have access to the results achieved by the others, and receive moral and/or financial incentives according to their relative success. When there are comparable organizations, this is a preferable control mechanism in relation to management by results, in which a management contract sets the performance indicators, because they become relative. There are other forms of managed competition, but they often involve distortions. In those nearer to real markets, organizations compete for clients. Yet, if an organization could not or should not compete for profit, it probably also should not compete for clients.

Management by results through management contracts comes next in the range of accountability mechanisms. Like the previous ones, it is a public management mechanism, but it differs from them in already being a form of hierarchical control. The main problems this mechanism faces are the definition of performance indicators and the relative value to assign to each indicator. Finally, we have the other hierarchical mechanisms—direct supervision and auditing. Provided that they are used moderately and reasonably, they are essential management tools. Under a managerial approach, direct supervision should principally assume the character of leadership supervision, in which the manager is concerned with the needs of his personnel and is able to motivate them positively. Auditing, meanwhile, should be more concerned with controlling outcomes than procedures.

15

The Basic Model

Public management reform requires a redefinition of the roles of the state. In defining these roles, economics use the concept of public goods, coupled with the concept of externalities. Instead of referring primarily to these concepts, I discuss the roles of the state in terms of the relevant forms of ownership and the corresponding forms of organization existing in modern societies. And I will relate the ownership forms to the efficient, managerial, administration of the state organization. I will ask what the exclusive activities or roles that the state performs are, and distinguish them from social and scientific activities, which the state is interested in financing but does not need to execute, and from the production of other goods and services in the market. Throughout this book I have been distinguishing bureaucratic administration from public management. In this chapter, I use these concepts to present a model of public management reform.

Forms of Property

Beyond private property and state property, there are third and fourth forms of ownership relevant to modern capitalism: public non-state property and corporate property. Usually, social theory refers only to public property, understood as a synonym of state property, and private property. This simplification originated from the dual character of legal theory, according to which organizations conform either to public or to private law. Instead of the legal criterion I suggest another to distinguish the ownership forms of organizations: the objectives criterion. Which interests are organizations oriented towards: public interest, corporative interest, or private interest? Accordingly, we have three types of ownership and corresponding forms of organizations: public, private, and corporative. They are public when their direct aim is the public interest; private, when they serve the interests of individuals and their families; corporative, when they represent group interests, as is the case with unions and associations. Among public organizations, it is necessary to distinguish the state organization or apparatus from public non-state organizations (which also aim at the common good) and public non-state service organizations form public non-state social accountability (or political advocacy) organizations.

It is important not to limit the definition of public organizations to state organizations. This is a classical bureaucratic ideology legitimized by administrative law. Bureaucrats aspire to monopolize the quality of being 'public'. Equally misleading is labelling public non-state organizations 'private'. This happens where state bureaucracies are particularly dominant. They were created according to private law but, as long as they are genuinely oriented to the public interest, they are public.

Public non-state organizations are oriented to the public interest, but they are not part of the state apparatus; they do not answer directly to the heads of branches of the state; and their personnel are not statutory civil servants. It is not always easy to distinguish public organizations that are inside the state apparatus from those that are outside. There is a grey area—organizations that are quasi-state. The definition will depend on the administrative law principles regulating the matter in each country. To simplify, I understand the quasi-state as public non-state organizations.

What I call public non-state organizations, Mintzberg (1996) calls 'non-owned organizations'.[1] Why shouldn't we call such organizations just 'non-profit' or 'third sector' organizations—two expressions that are part of common parlance? I use the expression 'public non-state organizations' because it is more precise; because the expressions 'non-profit' and 'third sector' include organizations that are not public, not directly oriented to the public interest, but exist to protect corporative interests, which are not far from private interests. What distinguishes corporative organizations from business enterprises (and cooperatives) is that the latter, being for-profit organizations, may be coordinated principally by the market, while corporative organizations (like public ones) cannot be.

Public non-state organizations are, in principle, oriented to the public interest as much as state organizations. People call these organizations 'private', probably for legal reasons, but in fact, in terms of their objectives, they are public. Oxford or Harvard Universities, for instance, are as public as the University of California or the University of Montreal. The difference is that the former are public non-state while the latter are officially state universities. In fact, American and Canadian 'state' universities, unlike French, German, or Brazilian state universities, are also public non-state organizations, since they are fully autonomous administratively, and their teaching staff and other

---

[1] Mintzberg (1996: 76) sees four types of organization in modern capitalism: private, public (or state-owned), non-owned, and cooperative. The non-owned organization corresponds to my public non-state organization. The cooperative organization, however, does not correspond to corporate organization. It is a form of private property in so far as its members share the profits or surplus it produces. The corporate organization, on the other hand, is non-profit, but is not directly oriented towards the public interest: it defends the interests of its associates.

employees are not civil servants. They receive larger budget allocations from the states, but are managed in a similar way to the 'private' universities. We certainly may have distortions: individuals may capture public non-state organizations and use them in their own interest, but the same may, and often does, happen to state organizations. The major challenge that modern democracies confront is precisely to protect the public patrimony from that fate: to avoid disrespect to republican rights.

The 'public' is not to be confused with the state. Public interest and public space are broader concepts than state interest and state space. State interests are formally defended by state lawyers, while public interests are formally defended by state prosecutors. Although the state is public by definition, in practice it often is not: the pre-capitalist state was, ultimately, private, since it existed to serve the needs of the prince. In modern democracies, there is a clear distinction between the public and the private but, as observed in the discussion of republican rights, attempts to capture the public patrimony are always present. The public sphere is the space of everyone for everyone; the state is a specific form of public space, namely, the space of the state apparatus.

Among public non-state organizations it is important to distinguish those that are basically oriented to providing social and scientific services—the public non-state service organizations—from those specially engaged in social advocacy or social accountability. Although the expression NGO is often used as a synonym for what I call public non-state organizations in general, NGOs are typically public non-state social accountability organizations, while non-profit organizations providing, for instance, health care, education, social assistance, are public non-state service organizations.[2]

Exclusive and Non-Exclusive Activities

The definition of exclusive state activities derives from the definition of state organization. The state is the only organization possessing 'extroverse' power, that is, power over individuals or citizens who are not part of the state organization itself but are members of the nation-state. In the process of using or applying extroverse power, the state, as the expression of collective action, is supposed to promote or to guarantee the fundamental political objectives that modern societies have set for themselves: social order, political freedom, equality or social justice, and well-being or economic development. This concept is essential in order to distinguish those activities that are exclusive to the state from those that are not, those involving the use of state power from those that do not. Private and non-profit or third sector organizations

---

[2] I prefer 'public non-state organization' to 'NGO' because I want to emphasize its public nature and its 'non-state' rather than 'non-governmental' character. In this way, I avoid the imprecise identification of government with state.

hold power only over their employees, while the state has power outside itself: it has the exclusive power of law-making, and imposing taxes. The specifically economic state activity is to promote resource transfers, while the corresponding private activity is resource exchange.

The concept of public goods is often used to define the roles of the state. Yet it tends to unduly limit such roles. The state deals mostly with public goods that cannot be subject to exchange, while the private sector deals with private goods. The state is supposed to ensure basic public goods such as social order, the defence of the country against foreign enemies, freedom, justice, and protection of the environment, while the private sector would provide all other goods and services. This is neo-liberal ideology, not reality. Democratic societies require that the state, additionally, provide the quasi-public goods necessary to economic and social development. With this objective, the state complements the market by means of economic transfers. While the market operates through the exchange of equivalent values, the state does so through economic transfers financed by taxes—transfers principally oriented to social protection, but also to economic development.

The state is a monopolist entity by definition. It is for no other reason that Weber defines it as an organization that holds a legitimate monopoly of violence. Yet exclusive state activities are just monopolist activities. The central monopolistic roles involving the use of state power are defining laws and public policies, imposing and collecting taxes, maintaining order and warranting justice, defending the country in war, to represent it in peace. These roles do not allow for competition. Imagine, for instance, a nation-state that appoints two ambassadors to represent it in another country, just to see who does it better . . . Or that allows two judges to judge the same case simultaneously . . . Or that sets two inspectors the task of inspecting competitively the same taxpayer . . . Such possibilities are obviously absurd.

There are, however, other activities that are exclusive but not monopolistic. Budgetary transfers fall into this category. They are not exclusive activities, although, through their scope, they define the social-democratic and the social-liberal state. They are not exclusive because private individuals also make donations or transfers. They do not involve the provision of public goods but of quasi-public goods, like education, health care, welfare, environmental protection, protection of the cultural patrimony, and incentives for the arts. Yet policy-making in these areas and the corresponding budgetary process should also be included among the exclusive activities of the state, since they involve the use of taxpayers' money, and so involve state power. It is true that private donations amount to little when compared with state transfers, but this does not affect the non-exclusive character of the latter.

A third major kind of exclusive activity of state is economic policy-making. Microeconomic policies are normally part of the basic legal system of a modern democracy. They deal with property rights, enforcement of contracts, and the protection of competition, and so we would be tempted to conclude that it is not the case of singling them out. Yet they recently gained a new relevance to the extent that the privatization of state-owned enterprises working in quasi-monopolistic markets required the creation of new regulatory agencies. In this way, regulatory activity was delegated to autonomous agencies, whose influence increased substantially. On the other hand, since Keynes established in the 1930s the basis of macroeconomic theory and policy, policy-making in such areas became a major form of exclusive state activity. Finance ministries, central banks, and international organizations like the International Monetary Fund and the Basle Bank of International Settlements, are actively involved in controlling the money supply and interest rates, the budget deficit, the international accounts and the exchange rate, in order to guarantee macroeconomic stability at national and international levels. To this end, the creation of central banks in the twentieth century was critical. The increasing concern with avoiding international financial crisis and stabilizing the international financial system is at present a major objective that will only increase the strategic role played by macroeconomic policy-making. All such actions are exclusive activities of state. International organizations share state power and practice exclusive state activities in so far as these are delegated to them by member nation-states.

It is central to public management reform that, within the exclusive activities, policy-making should be clearly distinguished from execution. While autonomy is given to the latter, the former is centralized in the strategic core of the state, be it at federal, state, or municipal level. 'Departments' directly tied to ministers perform policy-making, whose execution is delegated to executive and regulatory agencies.[3] This distinction suggests that ministries at the strategic core define policies; agencies execute them. In practice, this is not always true. Regulatory agencies in particular tend to have some policy-making power. But in terms of the model, this distinction is convenient. I discuss the agencies below.

State activities are not limited to the exclusive ones. They comprise also non-exclusive activities, particularly basic social and scientific services and the production of goods and services. It is important to distinguish these two types of non-exclusive activities, because public management reform treats them differently. Social, cultural, and scientific services are supposed to be run according to managerial principles but, to the extent that they are subsidized by the state, being delivered to citizens free or quasi-free of charge, they should not be privately owned. Besides, they deal with central human rights that should not be trusted to profit-oriented business enterprises. Among the social and scientific services, modern democracies provide schools, universities,

---

[3] The expressions 'executive' and 'regulatory' agencies are becoming usual. In relation to the 'policymaking departments', however, there is less consensus. In each country, these departments have a different name.

scientific and technological research centres, hospitals, day-care centres, out-patient care centres, entities assisting the under-aged, the deficient and elderly, museums, symphony orchestras, public radio and television broadcasting stations, and so on. There is a whole set of reasons for the state to use public money to finance such services. The main economic argument justifying it is that these services involve important positive externalities, which, by definition, markets do not duly remunerate. The ethical argument is that these activities involve basic human rights, which any society should guarantee for its citizens.

A major political objective of modern democracies is social justice, or, in a more limited way, equality of opportunity. The universal rights to basic education, to health care, and to a minimum income are essential for such equality. Using Michael Walzer's concepts of 'complex equality' and 'spheres of justice', we learn that the central normative principle is that the 'spheres' of justice frontiers are not crossed. Or, in practical terms, that money is not used to 'buy' the social goods pertaining to other spheres of justice, such as education, health care, political power, social prestige, divine grace, and so forth (Walzer 1983). Thus, the modern social-democratic as well as the social-liberal and republican state are supposed to provide such services free or almost free of charge and to finance them out of tax revenues: not because it would not be practical to finance them through private charity, but because the state in virtually all advanced democracies assures such rights.[4]

Third, we have the market production of goods and services. We have already seen that, in principle, public management reform implies privatization of such activities. But we may find within the state apparatus different types of activity—the auxiliary ones—that should be outsourced rather than privatized. For the state's exclusive activities or core functions to be carried out, the support of a series of auxiliary services is necessary. Some are complex, like architectural projects, construction, consulting; others are quite simple, such as cleaning, security, transportation, catering, and data processing services. All involve some specialization. Increasingly, the modern state buys them competitively. The idea that statutory civil servants should directly provide such services became at least odd.

The Matrix

I am now able to present a simple matrix that puts together the forms of ownership, the discussion of the roles of the state according to their exclusive or non-exclusive character, and the principles of public management reform. Table 15.1 is self-explanatory. In the rows, we have the activities classified by

[4] An exception is the United States, which does not have a universal health care system.

TABLE 15.1. *The basic model*

		Forms of ownership			Management forms		Organizational forms
			Public				
		State	non-state	Private	Bureaucratic	Managerial	
Exclusive Activities	Strategic core:	◯				◯	Policy-making departments
	Executive & regulatory agencies:	◯				◯	Executive and regulatory agencies
	Non-exclusive social and scientific services:		◯			◯	Social organizations
	Other products and services to the market			◯		◯	Private enterprises

their nature: the exclusive state activities, which may take place either in the strategic core or in the decentralized agencies, the social and scientific services, and the market production of goods and services; in the columns, three of the four forms of ownership, and the models of administration (managerial or bureaucratic) according to each case.[5]

The strategic core of the state corresponds to the elite that heads the state: the presidency, the ministers and policy-making departments, the parliament, and the high judicial courts. In the strategic core, politicians and senior civil servants take the specific government decisions: on legislation, legal judgments, and policy. This is the realm of politics, but also of public management. It is here that, as well as politicians, senior civil servants act more politically. The strategic core is supposed to be small, that is, staffed by a small number of highly qualified government officers. Political theory, political science, and economics are their major intellectual tools. In the executive branch, the typical core of the state's organizational institution is the policy-making departments, and management contracts the specific management tool. There are corresponding strategic cores at state and municipal levels.

[5] This table was first presented in the *Plano Diretor* (Ministry of Federal Administration and Reform of the State—MARE, 1995).

In addition to the activities in the strategic core, we have exclusive activities in the decentralized agencies which enforce the law and execute government policies. Typical activities are regulation, policing, auditing, promotion of commercial and industrial policies, and promotion and evaluation of social and scientific activities, particularly education, health care, social security, and social assistance.

There are two basic decentralized units in the model: regulatory and executive agencies. Regulatory agencies execute the state's policies as defined by the law and decide on prices in the regulated monopolistic markets, while executive agencies execute government policies that are not necessarily defined in law. Thus, regulatory agencies are supposed to be more independent than the executive agencies. Ministers in the strategic core control executive agencies through management contracts—contracts that are not required in the case of regulatory agencies, since the law already defines their objectives or basic policies. In principle, regulatory agencies control the prices of privatized monopolistic sectors with the objective of establishing prices that would obtain if perfect market competition existed. The law may also define executive agencies' objectives, but in a broader way, leaving room for the incumbent government or administration to decide which policies to follow.

In managing the strategic core, the distinction between bureaucratic administration and public management is not always clear, while in the decentralized agencies there is no doubt that the administration must be managerial. In fact, although bureaucratic systems may have 'agencies', rather they will be bureaucratic departments. The modern concept of agency derives directly from public management reform that started in Britain, when the Next Steps Programme defined executive agencies.

In the third row, we have the social and scientific services: schools, universities, research centres, hospitals, day-care centres, social assistance organizations, museums, symphony orchestras, and so on. The activities involved are exclusively state ones, but they are central since the modern social-democratic state chooses to finance them. The state should not provide the service directly, but contract them out to public non-state service organizations. Since they are not exclusive activities, because public non-state service organizations and private enterprises may perform them as well, the matrix tells us that the state should not perform them through civil servants. These are competitive activities that should not be treated as monopolies: they should not remain within the state apparatus. To be performed efficiently, these services require a large degree of autonomy that is impossible to assure within the state apparatus, even within the framework of new public management. On the other hand, these activities should not be privately owned, to the extent that they are strongly subsidized by the state, in addition to relying on voluntary work and donations from society. In some cases, such as chartered primary schools, the state finances them fully provided that they are free to the students. Policy-making departments and agencies will deal with the regulation, financing and control of such services, but public non-profit organizations will take care of them.

I call the public non-state service organizations that perform social and scientific services substantially financed by the state 'social organizations'.[6] To qualify as social organizations, their managers must be accountable for the public resources they receive. When the organization is large and the funds sizeable, one of the accountability mechanisms adopted should be the requirement of a management contract with the government. In most cases (but not necessarily all), besides public resources, they may and should count on their own revenues and on private donations.

In the last row, we have the market production of goods and services not included in the previous two categories. In principle, business enterprises should perform such activities in a capitalist economy. Yet, in the twentieth century, the state intervened strongly in this area, not just in the monopolistic or quasi-monopolistic area of public services, but also in manufacturing and mining undertakings involving large economies of scale. The main reason for state intervention in this area was not ideological but practical, and of a double character: on the one hand, the state invested in sectors where investments were too large for the private sector to make them; on the other, it invested in monopolistic sectors which could be self-financed by their own high profits. Thus, what explains the emergence of a large number of state-owned enterprises in the early and mid-twentieth century may also explain why many of these enterprises were privatized in the 1980s and 1990s: capital requirements. From the 1930s to the 1970s, the state was able to impose forced savings, to realize in this way public savings, and thus to invest in some basic industries. With the fiscal crisis of the state that broke in the early 1980s, public savings became negative or near zero, the state lost financial capacity, while the private sector—particularly in the advanced economies— was systematically acquiring it. Thus, privatization was, initially, a means to deal with the fiscal crisis of the state. The rich countries, in which the crisis was less severe, also privatized less. However, there is another major reason. It became increasingly evident that business activity does not belong to the state. First, wherever the possibility of competition exists, markets are more efficient than states in coordinating the economy. Second, the system of incentives and penalties used to motivate workers and principally business executives, cannot be easily transferred to state-owned enterprises. Third, management in state-owned enterprises is often subject to political criteria, which by definition impairs efficient resource allocation. Privatization was the object of extensive ideological debate. For some time, there was relative consensus on the necessity of privatization (given the fiscal crisis) and on the

[6] In Brazil, a 1997 federal law defines in quite specific terms a social organization ('organização social'), and several states and municipalities have also enacted social organizations laws.

gains from privatization (given the greater efficiency and lesser subordination to political factors of privatized companies). Yet privatization of natural monopolies is debatable: in principle, it should not happen. In order to privatize them, it is necessary to establish autonomous regulatory agencies able to impose the prices that would prevail if there were a market. This is an almost impossible task. Regulatory distortions will tend to be worse than state inefficiencies. Additionally, monopolistic industries and certain mining industries involve Ricardian rents that permit the state-owned enterprise to realize huge profits and to self-finance investment. If this is the case, privatization will be harmful to economic development. It is true that the state has the alternative of taxing the activity instead of keeping it under its control, as it does in some oil producing countries. Yet it is interesting to note that Chile, which was involved in ultra-liberal reforms, never privatized its copper industry. In Brazil, state investments in steel production and petrochemicals may be explained by the large investments required, while in telecommunications, electrical power, and oil we also have to consider the possibility of self-finance as a major reason for the state investments. Probably for that reason, oil and most electrical production remain state-owned in Brazil.

In the following chapters I discuss the model summarized in this table, which is both normative, because it shows how it should be, and descriptive, because many of these ideas are already being practised in contemporary nation-states in which public management reform is under way.

The Resulting Size of the State Organization

In this book, I am both an interpreter of what is actually happening in public management reforms and someone with his own normative ideas about them. According to the model of public management reform, as we have just seen, the state should itself undertake the exclusive state activities. Social and scientific services should be contracted out to 'social organizations', while auxiliary services should in principle be outsourced, that is, they should be submitted to a public bidding process and contracted out to business enterprises. With some exceptions, the production of goods and services in the market should be private. Table 15.2 shows the 'size' of the state resulting from such reform. In the columns we have the tree types of activities that we have been discussing. In the rows, we have the respective core activities and the auxiliary activities that in principle should be outsourced.

The size of the state measured in terms of the number of statutory civil servants and military is limited to quadrant 1, where we have the policy-making departments and agencies (and the armed forces). It is small. Yet the size of the state in terms of expenditures is much bigger. It includes the whole shaded area (quadrants 1, 2, 4, and 5), since it covers columns one (exclusive

TABLE 15.2. *Size of the state resulting from public management reform*

	Exclusive state activities	Social and scientific services	Goods and services for the market
Organizations performing respective core activities	1 Policymaking departments & Executive and regulatory agencies	2 Social organizations (contracted out)	3 Business enterprises (privatized)
Auxiliary activities	4 Business enterprises (outsourced)	5 Business enterprises (outsourced)	6 Business enterprises (outsourced)

activities) and two (contracted-out social and scientific services), and the respective auxiliary services depicted in row two. Only the production of goods and services for the market stays out of the state organization, as it does the auxiliary activities of the three basic types of activities.

This is a model without grey areas. In reality, they are many. The distinction between core activities (in the state organization, social organizations, and business enterprises) and auxiliary ones is often difficult to draw. I would say, for instance, that managing the state's physical assets is an auxiliary activity, but there are legitimate doubts about this view. There will be activities whose proximity to exclusive activities cautions against outsourcing. Outsourcing of auxiliary services began in the mid-twentieth century, when public works were outsourced. At the beginning of that century, it was still usual for the state to carry out directly its architectural and engineering projects and construction works. Today, this practice has almost disappeared. This outsourcing process gained a new name and a new format, Public–Private Partnerships (PPPs)—a strategy to finance public assets with private funds. It is an alternative funding mechanism that proceeds from the same assumption that stimulated privatization: the increasing limitations that public budgets face everywhere. Edward Sternberg (1993) called these state-business enterprises and state-public non-state associations, 'public–private hybrid organizations'. Collaboration between state and the private sector, such as university–industry, and military industrial alliances, is increasing its scope in the United States, and seeks to direct important sectors of society according to a political criterion—the public interest—and private methods.

While auxiliary services should be outsourced to business enterprises, social and scientific services should be contracted out with public non-state service organizations. I am distinguishing outsourcing from contracting out just to emphasize one thing is to provide social and scientific services dealing directly with basic human rights, another thing is to buy other services from business enterprises.

There are also grey areas between what should be directly performed by the state and what should be financed by taxes but contracted out with social organizations. Public primary education, for instance, is a major question. In the model, we have a clear-cut distinction between statutory civil servants, who perform the exclusive activities of state, and employees of private and public non-state service organizations. In practice, we may have intermediate situations. Personnel in the British NHS, for instance: are they statutory civil servants, public employees, or private employees?

Overall, this model says that, in the emerging social-liberal state, the state should perform directly only the core exclusive activities. In terms of personnel, it will be a small state, but, as long as social and scientific activities remain essentially a state responsibility, it will be large in terms of expenditures in relation to GDP.[7] The state is supposed to guarantee universal rights and to have a developed welfare system, but is it not supposed to directly perform the respective activities. While public management reform reduces the size of the state in terms of personnel, it does not necessarily reduce total state expenditures. This becomes clear when we examine the numbers in most countries undergoing public management reform: public expenditures in relation to GDP have not fallen but, on the contrary, have continued to rise.

---

[7] In measuring the size of the state, we could possibly include state-owned enterprises. In this case, however, we would incur a series of difficulties, since the companies are not financed by taxes but by their sales revenues, and it is unthinkable to add taxes to sales. Anyway, this theme has lost part of its relevance as privatization has became a generalized process.

16

Devolution and Decentralization

Besides decentralization to executive agencies and social organizations, public management reform involves devolution to sub-national units of activities and the corresponding fiscal resources to finance them. It involves also making public managers more autonomous and more accountable. In synthesis, decentralization—delegating authority to lower levels—is crucial to managerial public administration. Before speaking about public management reform, people in public administration for a long time used to identify reform with decentralization, which is a central problem to all kinds of organization, public and private. It is through decentralization that one expects to impart greater flexibility to management and greater adaptability to local conditions. Thus, decentralization has been the classical strategy adopted by organizations as they grow and, especially, as they are supposed to have agencies throughout a large territory. Through decentralization, organizations search to overcome the diseconomies of scale inherent in their growth. Small organizations, including a small state apparatus, may be efficient if kept centralized, but large ones cannot be: they often have no alternative but to decentralize.

Public management reform involves a wholesale change of attitudes towards how to manage the state. It implies more than just decentralization, because it implies devolution—the political dimension of decentralization. Devolution is political decentralization: it is more than just a provisional delegation of authority to lower levels that can be always taken back, as is usual within business enterprises; it is the lawful transfer of revenues and responsibilities to sub-national levels: to states or provinces, and counties or municipalities. The United Nations has been stressing the role of decentralization on human development.[1]

Decentralization in large business enterprises follows broadly the 'decentralized functional organization' model that Alfred Sloan adopted in General Motors during the first decade of the twentieth century. It is a strategy of delegation of authority which, in order to prevent loss of control, breaks away from the principle of unity of command, originating in military organizations

[1] For a report of nine case studies on decentralized governance and an attempt to define the relationship between decentralized governance and social participation, see Cheema and Tabet (2000).

and adopted by 'scientific management' in the late nineteenth century. Instead, it adopts the principle of duality of command: line authority and functional authority coexist. I call this model 'decentralized functional organization', although it has been called by other terms such as 'divisional organization' and 'matricial organization'. The essential idea is to have duality of command by subordinating the decentralized functional manager to the respective central functional vice-president and to the regional or product-line vice-president of the decentralized unit. Alfred Chandler (1962) made the classic analysis of this flexible and contradictory organization model, which still today is dominant in private organizations. When I discuss decentralization to executive agencies and social organizations, I am not referring to this type of decentralization, adopted by large business enterprises, but to a specifically public management strategy that has some similarity with it.

A wholly different thing is political decentralization to sub-national and local levels. At the extreme, it leads to federalism, with confederation as an intermediate stage. For a long time, centralization rather than decentralization characterized the historical formation of the modern nation-state. In reality, the nation-state was often the outcome of the centralization of the power of smaller nations, often having similar languages. The United States was a case of centralization—of the transfer of powers from the states to the Union—but this transfer was freely decided by the confederated states. Brazil represents a third case: a centralized country that, in 1892, just after the fall of the monarchy and the beginning of the republican regime, decided to turn into a federation.

In the last quarter of the twentieth century, however, probably as a response to globalization, a change occurred in the direction of devolution. According to Castells, the nation-state, facing globalization, defends itself from the resulting loss of autonomy in defining policies within its territory, moving in two opposite directions: in one direction, it organizes itself internationally in regional economic blocs, in free trade zones, or in cartelized customs unions; in the other, it is involved in devolution to regional or local units. Castells (1999: 161) observes that:

In face of the increasing complexity of the global operative system, citizens and groups need more easily verifiable criteria on how their values are represented and their interests defended. Their capacity for everyday political control, besides elections every four years, is more easily organized at local level. Thus, one may observe a worldwide movement of decentralization of state institutions, partly as a response to local and regional demands, to collective expressions of identity, but partly, also, as a result of a conscious effort of the Nation-State to find alternative formulas to the rigidity of centralization and to the legitimacy crisis which emanates from the distrust of citizens.

Thus, decentralization is a public management strategy, while devolution is a political decision with managerial consequences. Decentralization is often decided top-down, and is a strategy for increasing the head-offices' capacity to achieve proposed objectives, while devolution is usually a response to demands for more local or regional autonomy to which government officials in the central government reluctantly accede. Devolution is the outcome of political negotiations around the division of powers among levels of government. Large countries have no alternative but to have federal systems. Medium-sized countries that in the past established themselves as centralized nation-states—such as Britain, France, Italy, and Spain—have no democratic alternative but to opt for some form of federal organization. In any case, with devolution democratic governance is being improved.

Centralization is the usual initial situation of a new nation-state. The United States is a clear exception in this respect. In Europe, several smaller 'nations' were transformed into single 'nation-states'. Anderson (1991) proposed that nations should be thought of as 'imagined communities', not as given and definitive ones. Historically, nation-states were imposed on smaller nations but, eventually, they came to constitute genuine new nations. Nevertheless, when democratic governance becomes dominant in these countries while the fear of wars among them diminishes, we see devolution become a central issue in state reform. Now, in the case of the European Union, we are seeing a voluntary process of centralization and state formation. In this respect, the European Union is a major historical demonstration of what political engineering may achieve when capitalism and the market economy become dominant, when states become strong and government legitimate, when the exploration of other countries loses its rationale, and the advantages of peace and economic integration are realized. Yet the economic and political integration of Europe stimulates devolution at sub-national level. When done voluntarily, as in the case of the European Union, centralization to the Union level and devolution to regional level may be conjointly negotiated. Nation-states transfer to the Union responsibilities that they cannot perform effectively in their own territory: national defence, common norms on trade, financial and labour markets, and now, with the Euro, a single currency. The subsidiarity principle—what can be done at a lower level should not be done at a higher one—prevails.[2] There is no clear criterion by which to define what is supposed to be centralized to the Union, what is supposed to remain with the nation-states, and what should be object of devolution. Public debate and gradual advances are the only options.

We have two cases of imposed centralization: the European case—centralization forced on smaller nations—and the Brazilian case, in which centralization was imposed on the regions. In both cases, the outcome was

---

[2] André Franco Montoro, the first elected governor in the state of São Paulo, Brazil (1983–86), after many years of authoritarianism repeated insistently a sentence that he tried to turn into reality in his administration: 'what can be done by the municipality should not be done by the state; what can be done by the state should not be done by the central government.'

eventually a new nation—a new imagined community. Yet, while in the former case the old nations remain, in the latter the regions lose most of their particularities. The difficulties faced by devolution in public management reform vary according to the form the initial centralization took. If it was voluntary, as in the United States, devolution is built into the system: difficulties are minor. If centralization was forced, but it was a centralization of regions, not of nations, difficulties with devolution are medium. Finally, if centralization was originally imposed on nations, devolution to these same nations often involves great difficulties.

The logic behind devolution and the subsidiarity principle is that which informs public management reform: social activities, such as basic education, health care, social work, and policing can be more accountable to citizens if they are carried out in a decentralized manner, at local, or, at most, at regional level. Bureaucratic argument in favour of centralization is based on the incapacity of governors and, mainly, of mayors to spend resources 'rationally'; instead, they dedicate themselves to clientelism and nepotism. This, however, is an authoritarian view of the capacity of local governments. It does not take into account the fact that the empowerment of communities to control the services delivered locally by the state has increased extraordinarily in democracies. Manuel Castells (1979) acknowledges this fact and gives it an historic dimension. The increasing complexity of public administration in a global world leads to the threat of political crisis taking the form of citizens' distrust of their governments. The only way to recover trust is decentralization and citizens' empowerment, or social accountability of public services—two major tenets in public management reform. In this process, administrative decentralization to agencies and social organizations on the one hand and devolution to sub-national units on the other are complementary. Even when there is no devolution and an agency remains under central government, decentralization combined with management by results make social accountability strategic. Obviously, when political devolution is included in the process of public management reform, the role of social accountability becomes even more decisive.

The assertion that decentralization is a means of democratization is dubious. When decentralization is an administrative strategy that does not imply devolution, this thesis does not make sense once the objective is just greater management effectiveness and efficiency. Gary Miller observes, in relation to organizations, that delegation only occurs in practice because it achieves this result. Within organizations, delegation is not a democratic achievement or loss of control. It is simply a management strategy aimed at increasing the manager's control over outcomes. However, when decentralization means devolution, when it is political and involves territorial distribution of power, there is a clear relationship with democracy. In fact, as demonstrated by Tocqueville, American democracy was born out of local power, emerging from the ideals of equality in New England communities. At first, there were local democratic communities; then, from this base, the 13 American states formed a new nation-state. The movement was, thus, the inverse to devolution but highlights its importance at the present moment of history. It did not flow from the centre to the periphery, as is peculiar to devolution, but from local communities to central power. In most countries, however, including Brazil, which began as a centralized nation-state, devolution is a means by which the poorest and least educated citizens express, at local level, their effective citizens' rights. Evelyn Levy (1997: 65) questions this relationship between political decentralization, increased local power, and democracy by quoting authors such as David Slater (1990), according to whom decentralization may lead to parochialism, submission, and the exercise of oligarchic power by the local elite. There is no doubt that this may happen, and that it has occurred in history. Democracies usually originate in the centre rather than in the periphery of nation-states, in the struggle of the middle class and workers for more freedom and voice in political issues. Democracies originating in local government, as in the case of the United States, are the exception. However, when democracy has its origin in the state and not in the community, the path towards its consolidation tends to be long and difficult. The 'enlightened' elite, which claims to speak in the name of democracy, is initially so distant from the people that it is not difficult for them to betray this same people.

It is only when citizens, at local and national levels, manage to attain a minimum measure of equality in relation to the elites that democracy stops being oligarchic and becomes real. Political devolution and administrative decentralization are signs that this democratic process is under way. When decentralization is made according to the principles of managerial public administration, involving increasing competition among agencies and especially among social organizations, and enhanced social accountability mechanisms, we will be heading in the desired direction. In the next two chapters, I discuss decentralization (not devolution) to the two major organizational institutions in the model of public management reform that I am presenting here: agencies, executing exclusive state activities, and social organizations, charged with delivering social and scientific services.

17

Executive and Regulatory Agencies

Historically, bureaucratic reform aimed at granting the civil service independence from political pressure in recruiting personnel. Public management reform decentralizes administrative decision-making to autonomous or decentralized agencies. All countries involved in public management reform stress agencies' autonomy. Allen Schick (2002: 2) suggestively observes that, while 'departments were the building blocks of the twentieth century state, the disestablishment of agencies may be a hallmark of the post-modern twenty first century'. Yet we should distinguish clearly the two types of decentralized agencies, and have a precise conception of the extent and limit of the autonomy that they are supposed to have.

Executive and regulatory agencies are decentralized state organizations that implement policies. When the law clearly defines the policy, we have a state policy; when it leaves the precise definition to the incumbent administration, we have a government policy. Regulatory agencies are supposed to execute state policies and be more autonomous from the administration, while executive agencies will be less autonomous politically but equally independent in administrative terms. Policies introduced by executive agencies are supposed to change the moment that the opposition political party or political coalition wins an election and a new administration begins, while the policies introduced by regulatory policies do not change so easily. Government policies may be changed either by the parliament or by the executive, while state policies may be changed only by the parliament. Congressmen will define state policies in such a way—in precise terms—so as to prevent the administration from changing them in the light of its electoral commitments.

When we discuss agencies' autonomy, we should consider three forms of autonomy: administrative, judicial, and political. In this chapter, proceeding from the assumption that agencies are, by definition, administratively autonomous, I suggest that, unlike executive agencies, regulatory agencies are supposed to have judicial autonomy. Yet neither one nor the other should have political autonomy, that is, authority for policy formulation. In some special cases such authority may be delegated to regulatory agencies, provided that the problem is strictly technical and so not the object of public debate.

By administrative autonomy I mean the autonomy to decide on personnel, organizational, and financial issues involving the organization; by judicial, the autonomy to decide case by case, on the basis of the law or of executive policies; and by policy, the autonomy to decide on rules of the game. According to another criterion, while executive agencies are never autonomous in relation to the head of the executive power, agencies may receive a limited delegation directly from the parliament. In both cases autonomy is delegated, but delegation in the latter case is stronger than in the former.

Administrative Autonomy

Executive agencies roles' are diverse. They go from police to tax collection, social security and social assistance to science and technology support. In the reform process, they often result from the decentralization process, and so, from the transformation of bureaucratic departments, they will receive special 'administrative autonomies'. Such autonomies or exemptions, following the usual bureaucratic rules, are usually related to three areas: budgeting and finances, human resources management, and purchasing. The law that regulates agencies will define them. The underlying logic is that agencies will require greater independence for making decisions on the means to achieve the contracted results. The ministers will discuss with the agencies the 'what', leaving to them the decisions on 'how'. Thus, public management reform avoids a vicious circle in which the service organizations' heads argue that they are unable to deliver better results because they do not have control of the 'means', while the holders of the 'means' argue that they cannot transfer their authority to the decentralized organizations because they are not delivering results.

With reference to the budgetary-financial aspect, executive agencies should have their budgets arranged in a more aggregated manner, with resources allocated to only one project or sub-activity. Besides, in order for the agreed outcomes to be efficiently realized, it is necessary to guarantee that the budget allocations be effectively available to the agency, with no possibility of cuts or contingencies. With respect to human resources management, a relationship with civil servants must be sought based on performance and merit, with financial mechanisms of recognition specified, such as performance-related remuneration. Hiring should also take place at the agency level. As for purchasing, the reform will concede to agencies' higher thresholds of exemption from formal bidding procedures. Agencies' autonomy will also include more flexibility in day-to-day decisions, such as on travel and maintenance expenditures. Finally, agencies will have significant freedom to determine their organizational structure.

In relation to human resources policy, agencies are supposed to have as employees statutory civil servants as long as they perform exclusive activities of state. The head of the agency, however, may be hired from the private sector. Auxiliary functions involving quasi-routine work should be outsourced. In public management reform, the civil service should be restricted to people able to perform highly skilled managerial or staff work. All people working in the agency are supposed to be subject to a system of incentives and penalties or to a principal–agent approach, but in the civil servants' incentive system the public interest will necessarily play a major role—a role that is not required in lower-level functions. The civil service ethos means precisely an explicit commitment with the public interest—which, although often forgotten or betrayed by civil servants, nevertheless remains central to the definition of the civil servant.

The centrality of executive agencies to public management reform arises from the fact that the programme that began such reform in Britain—the Next Steps Programme—was a programme that conceded increased autonomy to executive agencies. Yet agencies present a major managerial challenge when compared with the social organizations that we will discuss in the next chapter. As happens with all exclusive state activities, they are, by definition, monopolistic. Thus, although some forms of managed competition may still be used to control them, the basic method of making them accountable is management by results and social accountability.

The law that creates each executive agency should be sufficiently broad to permit the adoption of different public policies, depending on the elected government. This is the case with police agencies, or agencies dealing with education, health care, welfare, scientific research, arts and cultural support, and industrial and technological policy. We have already seen that the social and scientific services should be executed by non-profit social organizations, but their financing and evaluation may be performed by executive agencies, leaving policy-making secretariats time to decide on specific policies for the area.

Regulatory agencies are supposed to have somewhat greater administrative autonomy than executive agencies. First, while managers in regulatory agencies should always have a definite time mandate, managers in executive agencies should be susceptible to dismissal at any time. Chief executive officers may be dismissed before their mandates expire, but this will usually depend on parliamentary approval after verified wrongdoing. An opposition party's electoral victory will not legitimize the dismissal of a regulator, while such changes will be viewed as normal in the case of heads of executive agencies. Second, while management contracts are the major accountability mechanism controlling executive agencies, such devices make no sense with regulatory agencies. In the management contract, the minister, assisted by the policy-making secretary, will set the objectives and performance indicators for the agency. This is the classic strategy of managing by results: the minister uses the management contract to make the executive agencies' autonomy consistent with the objectives and policies that he establishes. In relation to regulatory agencies, however, it is not the minister but the law that sets up the major objectives and policies, making the management contract unnecessary.

Judicial and Political Autonomy

While executive agencies are not supposed to have judicial or political autonomy, regulatory agencies are supposed to granted broad judicial autonomy and limited political autonomy. Regulatory agencies have judicial autonomy to the extent that their managers are supposed to have the power to take on specific cases. In some cases, similarly to what happens in the judicial branch of the state, the manager arbitrates conflicts; in most cases, he authorizes or forbids actions by private individuals or organizations. The law that creates each regulatory agency should, in principle, perform a double strategy that is often not understood. On the one hand, it should be more rigid or stable in defining the general policy to be followed; on the other hand, it should delegate to the managers of the agency effective judicial autonomy. Regulatory agencies exist in principle to regulate private quasi-monopolistic and state-owned monopolistic industries. Yet, as even fully monopolistic industries have been privatized, particularly in developing countries, these agencies have gained a central role. Whether in the case of monopolistic or quasi-monopolistic industries, regulatory agencies are supposed to perform the difficult task of creating a surrogate competitive market. They are supposed to set prices as if a competitive market existed. This policy is a typical state policy that, in principle, should be enshrined in law. It does not change as governments change. Businessmen need this guarantee to invest in such industries. The price decisions taken by the regulatory agencies according to this rule are judicial decisions.

Judicial autonomy involves other types of decisions. For instance, a communications agency may decide which international digital pattern to use in the country. Regulatory agencies may have the power to grant public concessions: to decide on oil, or on radio and television channel concessions. This will vary from country to country. In Britain, for instance, unlike in Brazil, the decision on oil concessions comes from an executive agency rather than a regulatory one.

While administrative autonomy is essential to public management reform, and judicial autonomy a condition for the existence of a regulatory agency, political autonomy is not. The privatization of monopolistic industries, starting in the 1980s, required some political autonomy on the part of the regulatory agencies. Such autonomy was essential for investors, whose investment decisions depend on price-setting independently of political considerations.

Yet such autonomy was often extended well beyond price determination. Agencies were also expected to define policies—in democracies, a prerogative of elected politicians. The ultra-liberal ideology emerging in the late 1970s transformed such political autonomy into a central requirement, particularly for developing countries. Politicians would be all rent-seekers, or populist, if not corrupt—and this 'fact' made agencies' political autonomy 'necessary'.

Even in the developed countries, such political autonomy was never achieved. A certain degree of autonomy was granted over policy formulation, but this autonomy was delegated by elected politicians who are supposed to have the final say. When Parliament believes that such delegation should occur, it should be given, in principle, to the elected head of government, who, in turn, will decide how much he or she will delegate to the agency. Alternatively, we may have a kind of joint responsibility—of the parliament and the head of government. What is important is that they must always be ready to intervene—particularly when agencies fail and public disapproval grows—because theirs is the final democratic responsibility. Yet their intervention will not always be welcome. *The Economist*, for instance, reported in 2003 that 'the recent turbulence in government policy on industries spanning telecoms, energy, finance and the media suggests that politicians are exerting their influence over regulatory decisions more than ever before'.[1]

In any case, delegation should be limited to the formulation of 'technical' policies for the industry. What is a technical policy? I don't believe that there is an objective definition of this term. It is not legitimate to say merely that technical policies are those that require specialized knowledge or technical expertise. A policy is technical only if society, if the public, acknowledges its own incapacity and also the incapacity of elected politicians to evaluate the issue, and delegate decisions on it to experts. Thus, whenever an issue assumes a political character, whenever it becomes the object of public discussion, the decision ceases to be technical: it becomes political and must be decided politically. What determines whether a decision is technical or political is not its content, but whether or not it became subject to public debate. If this happens, if the issue is included on the national, regional, or local agenda, this problem must eventually be decided by elected politicians. They will look for technical advice, but they cannot avoid the responsibility of deciding.

I wrote normatively on the subject in the last few paragraphs. Yet my normative views do not conflict with effective practices in the more developed countries. The ideal that regulatory agencies should not be autonomous in political terms is the option effectively adopted by governments. As Stephen Breyer (1982: 3) observes,

it proved illusory to look to regulators as 'scientists', professionals, or technical experts . . . There is no scientific discipline of regulation, nor are those persons appointed

---

to regulatory offices necessarily experts. Indeed, some of the most successful—as well as some of the least successful—regulators have had political backgrounds and have lacked experience in regulatory fields.

Central banks are also normally viewed as regulatory agencies, and are supposed to have some political autonomy. They are supposed to pursue two objectives: to control inflation and to keep unemployment low—objectives that are often contradictory. The American Federal Reserve clearly has these two objectives. In the case of the European Central Bank, the decentralized character of the European Union led their founders to drop the second object-ive. Since it is relatively easier (although still very difficult) to assure price stability than full employment, this decision assured the European Bank greater political autonomy than the Fed has. Is this a good thing? I don't believe so. Despite being less autonomous than the European Bank, the Fed has been more effective in assuring economic growth with price stability—the golden rule of monetary policy. Take another case. Since the late 1980s, the Central Bank of Brazil has adopted a basic interest rate that is, in real terms, three or four times higher than the basic interest rates in countries with similar country risk classifications. In 2001 this practice finally came to the attention of society, and began to be the object of vigorous public debate. From this moment, interest rate policy stopped being just technical and became also political. It ceased to be just a responsibility of the Central Bank's directors, and became also a responsibility of the elected politicians, particularly of the president.

In sum, agencies require general administrative autonomy, regulatory agencies require judicial autonomy as well to make decisions on the prices of the products of monopolistic firms as if there were competitive markets. Yet administrative and judicial autonomy should not be confused with political autonomy—with autonomy to define policies, which is the prerogative of elected politicians, particularly when a given issue becomes the object of public debate.

Autonomy or Insulation?

How does 'bureaucratic insulation' fit into this approach? While the expres-sion 'regulatory reform' is related to the neo-liberal ideological wave, and often means delegating to agencies' policy formulation in an authoritarian manner, the word 'insulation' is associated with an authoritarian bureaucratic vision of the state, although it is not necessarily authoritarian, as regulatory reform is not necessarily neo-liberal. The concept of bureaucratic insulation became particularly popular among political scientists studying the twentieth century developmental state in intermediate developing countries such as Brazil and India. They were concerned with the developmental reform of the state apparatus, one of whose key aspects would be the bureaucratic insulation of some agencies more directly concerned with macroeconomic stability and the promotion of economic development. Bureaucratic insulation thus constituted a strategic tool against patrimonial domination. Bureaucratic insulation may be defined as a form of granting to some selected agencies not political autonomy in deciding policies, nor public management autonomy in the form that I define in this book, but autonomy from political interference. It happened historically in developing countries where developmental bureaucracies were able to promote economic development through state action. Bureaucratic insulation makes strategic agencies free from clientelism or pork barrel, particularly in hiring personnel. In semi-authoritarian regimes and in new democracies, politicians are less accountable than in established ones, so that it is practically impossible to make all agencies fully professional, immune from pork-barrel or clientelist practices. Since some strategic agencies absolutely must have such independence, they are chosen to be insulated from politics. Politicians and senior civil servants take this initiative, sometimes from the start, sometimes after disgraceful episodes. In this way, the political system limits its own power as a way of assuring minimum governance standards.

This increased autonomy and independence generally begins with the strategic agencies, in which technical knowledge is more important and in which the danger of generalized crisis in the event of poor management is greater. Slowly it spreads to other agencies. The agencies left behind are those in which clientelism or pork-barrel politics is less demoralizing to politicians. Generally, the agencies that are left behind are those providing health, education, and other social benefits, not only because they are viewed as less strategic by politicians but also because everybody feels competent to make decisions in this area, and any damage, unlike what may happen with incompetent decisions in a central bank, for instance, although serious, tends to be localized. The legitimacy of agencies' autonomy depends on presuppositions about the technical competence of its professional managers. To the extent that these agencies perform strategic roles in their respective national societies, the concession of autonomy by politicians is a question of political survival.

Peter Evans, referring to developing countries, calls bureaucratic autonomy an 'embedded autonomy' to emphasize that the bureaucracies of the developmental states, such as those of Korea, Brazil, or India (which he contrasts with the 'predatory' states), although relatively autonomous, should be and generally are embedded in society. According to Evans, state capacity will depend on the ability of state bureaucrats to establish networks with businessmen and other members of society:

The internal organization of the developmental states comes much closer to approximating a Weberian bureaucracy. Highly selective meritocratic recruitment and long-term career rewards create commitment and a sense of corporate coherence. Corporate coherence gives these apparatus a certain kind of 'autonomy'. They are not, however, insulated from society as Weber suggested they should be. To the contrary, they are embedded in a concrete set of social ties that binds the state to society and provides institutionalized channels for the continual negotiation and re-negotiation of goals and policies. (Evans 1995: 12)

Ben Ross Schneider (1995) carried out research in the early 1980s that proceeded from the assumption that bureaucratic autonomy contributed to making state intervention more effective. Yet he concluded that there was a 'need to revise the argument': government on the lines of Evans's 'embedded state' is more effective as long as a close collaboration between the bureaucracy and businessmen takes place. Evans calls the successful embedded bureaucracies 'Weberian', although their members have little to do with the authoritarian and rigid bureaucrat described by Weber at the beginning of the twentieth century. They are, rather, developmental bureaucracies, which were dominant between the 1930s and 1970s in Latin America, and successfully promoted economic growth. Today, after a major crisis, they are increasingly managerial bureaucracies. 'Weberian' would be a correct characterization of such modern bureaucracies only if by that we meant simply a corps of professional civil servants, recruited by merit and promoted according to a career path. Now, the bureaucracy that Weber had in mind is more than only that: it was authoritarian, supported by secrecy, dependent on rigid norms, rational–legal in the strictest sense of the term. 'Weberian', for instance, applies to the bureaucracy to which Putnam refers in research undertaken in 1971 on the Italian bureaucratic elite: 'the typical member of the Italian bureaucratic elite is the essence of the classic bureaucrat—legalist, illiberal, elitist, hostile to the usage and practices of pluralist policy, fundamentally non democratic' (Putnam 1993: 50–1). The bureaucracy that Peter Evans (1979) studied in Brazil in the 1970s, and that Ben Ross Schneider (1991, 1995) and Gilda P. Gouvêa (1994) analysed in the 1990s, is quite different from that. It is not legalist but entrepreneurial and, as Schneider well demonstrates, its career, although reflecting principles of merit, is far from the classic bureaucratic career. Besides, developmental or managerial bureaucracies, embedded in society as Evans points out, have not only a technical but also a political character. One of the roles they play, apart from the merely technical, is to develop strategies of articulation between the apparatus of state and that of society as a form of neutralizing client-oriented pressures, and of amplifying their resources. In this sense, civil servants are political agents acting in a democratic context, and taking advantage of the tools democracy offers. Public managers follow elected politicians' decisions while developing legitimacy strategies through which they obtain autonomy from politicians themselves, according to the demands or the support of society.

In the case of Brazil, legitimate concerns about clientelism led some authors to the unnecessary, if not contradictory, identification of bureaucratic public administration with bureaucratic insulation, and the latter with agency autonomy. Edson Nunes, for instance, in his study on Brazilian public administration, remarks that 'universality of procedures and bureaucratic insulation are perceived many times as appropriate forms of counterbalancing clientelism (Nunes 1984: 33–4).[2] Yet, although the universality of procedures is an essential characteristic of democratic regimes, it does not require a bureaucratic form of public administration. New public management is also consistent with the rule of law, without limiting the public manager to obedience to rigid bureaucratic norms. Insulated agencies are independent from politicians but, so long as they often follow bureaucratic rigid rules, their managers are not autonomous in the public management sense.

If bureaucratic insulation grants just administrative autonomy to agencies, it is a positive strategy to protect a feeble state. Yet, if it involves political autonomy in taking policy decisions, it is an authoritarian tool. In consolidated democracies, the parliament grants autonomy to agencies. On the other hand, and unlike in the case of bureaucratic insulation, parliament requires senior civil servants to be accountable to itself and to society. While only some strategic agencies acquire relative autonomy from politicians, we have a partial public management reform. The reform is complete only when all agencies, not only the strategic ones, are at the same time independent and accountable, but this is the same as to say that reform is complete when democracy consolidates.

Bureaucratic insulation is an issue related to the bureaucracy's 'relative autonomy', one of the central themes of political and sociological theory after the Second World War. The question is: to what extent is bureaucracy an autonomous form of capitalist class? It is not appropriate to revisit this discussion now. It is clear today that public and private bureaucracy, or the new professional class, is a social class in contemporary capitalism, deriving its power and influence from the monopoly of technical and organizational knowledge.[3] Yet the question of economic rationality and bureaucracy remains central, particularly in developing countries. In order to assure rationality to public policies, how autonomous should bureaucracy be from voters? This question receives a reasonable answer in advanced democracies, as long as they require, to a reasonable degree, politicians' and senior civil servants' accountability. In developing countries, however, it remains central.

---

[2] On the same line of thought, see also Peter Evans (1989), Stephan Haggard (1990).

[3] This theme is extensively treated in my studies on techno-bureaucracy as a social class in modern mixed capitalist societies (Bresser-Pereira 1981).

18

Social Organizations

In the public management reform model that I am presenting, social organizations are probably the more interesting organizational institution. The idea, in reform terms, is to transform social and scientific services provided directly by the state into quasi-state or public non-state service entities of a special kind, which will be part of the state budget but not part of the state apparatus, and so will not have statutory civil servants working for them. I propose to call these institutions 'social organizations'. In legal terms, social organizations will be private, since they will be subject to the same regulations as apply to the private sector; in political terms, they will remain public as long as they are oriented to the public interest. To qualify as a social organization and to openly receive budgetary allocations, it is a necessary condition that the institution's managers be clearly accountable for the public resources received. When such funds are substantial, besides other forms of accountability, the organization should sign a management contract with the respective supervisory ministry or secretariat in which the performance indicators are supposed to be clearly defined. When funds are relatively small, other less administratively demanding accountability mechanisms will be sufficient. In principle, any new public non-state organization can qualify as a social organization, although in the reform process the more important task is to transform existing entities performing social and scientific services into social organizations.

Social organizations may originate in the transformation of existing state departments or agencies into public non-state organizations or in the qualification of existing public non-state service organizations as 'social organizations'. In Brazil, for instance, the number of state organizations transformed into social organizations has been small, but a large number of service NGOs are qualifying as social organizations. They perform a wide array of social and scientific services partially subsidized by the state.[1]

We have already seen that in contemporary capitalism there are not only two relevant forms of property—private and public ownership—but four: private,

---

[1] The Brazilian law calls such organizations Organização da Sociedade Civil de Interesse Público (OCIPs, Civil Society's Public Interest Organizations).

state, public non-state, and corporative property. Social organizations are the prototype of public non-state service organizations. They are devoted to the public interest, but they are not part of the state apparatus, and do not have civil servants in their labour force. Social organizations are just one of the possible forms of public non-state service entities. They are typically service organizations, acting in the education, health care, culture, sport, and social assistance areas. They differ from public non-state social accountability or public advocacy organizations. The best-known non-governmental organizations, such as GreenPeace, Amnesty International, or Transparency International, are not mainly service organizations but public advocacy organizations. Foundations in the American style, like the Ford Foundation, combine service and social advocacy: essentially they finance social and cultural projects performed by NGOs or by public non-state service organizations.

Some public non-state service organizations should not qualify as social organizations, and thus should not receive partial finance from state subsidies. Hospitals serving the rich, for instance, may be authentically non-profit, and so public non-state, and finance themselves solely from the fees they charge patients and insurance companies. To be considered a social organization, it is not enough for the organization to have public objectives in its statutes. It is required to be in fact public, that is, oriented to the public interest. In countries where there are tax exemptions for non-profit organizations, there are fake public non-state service organizations which in fact are owned by a family, or by a group of individuals, and serve their interests. Just as private interests may capture state organizations, so they may seize formally public non-state ones. It is not always easy to distinguish the false from the true public non-state organization, because we often have to deal with grey areas.

On the other hand, there are public non-state service organizations subsidized by the state that are not really social organizations. This is the case with organizations whose employees, although not statutory civil servants, are treated in practical terms as such, and whose accounts are controlled by the states' auditing system with the same centralized rigour as regular state agencies. They should not be included in the social organizations category. And we have many mixed cases. Take, for instance, the British National Health Service. Its hospitals have managerial autonomy that would entitle them to be considered social organizations. Yet their employees are treated similarly to civil servants. These hospitals will be true social organizations when they achieve autonomy and an accountability that they do not have today.

Social organizations exist as a result of a political decision of society: the decision to finance with state resources social and scientific services that it believes cannot or should not be fully financed by the market. When the activity depends on state subsidies and on private donations and voluntary work, public non-state ownership is the natural solution. The fiscal crisis of the social-democratic state did not lead citizens to suspend their support to such services, but to require from their delivery better quality with less money. In other words, they were demanding higher efficiency. For some time, in the 1980s and 1990s, it became usual to hear that, due to the fiscal crisis of the state, it had no alternative but to eliminate social and scientific services. This is nonsense. If society considers the service relevant, it will accept the corresponding taxation. The real question is how to provide such a service: directly or through social organizations. Public non-state service organizations, specifically social organizations, are the solution for the delivery of social and scientific services because they are more flexible, autonomous, and so more efficient than the direct delivery of the service by statutory civil servants. The pressure for reforming the state and making it more efficient and more citizen-oriented opened the way for the delivery of social and scientific services through public non-state organizations.

Public management reform sees this as a strategic form of ownership. The growth of public non-state service organizations stems from the better quality and greater efficiency of the social and scientific services they provide. Services that do not involve exclusive state activity, do not employ state power, and therefore are not intrinsically monopolistic do not need to be inside the state apparatus. Nor should they be, since the more appropriate form of property for them is public non-state and not state ownership. In this manner, they can enjoy the greater management flexibility that characterizes private organizations. On the other hand, the strategy of administered competition, which is a precarious form of control in the case of state entities that are monopolistic by nature, is appropriate for public non-state service organizations.

Why not provide such services directly through private enterprises? Why use a public non-state type of organization? Because they deal directly with fundamental human rights, such as education and health, where the profit criterion is not adequate to guarantee quality of service. These types of services involve trust, dedication, solidarity, which will only be consistent with the profit criterion if the client-citizen has full information on price and quality, on inputs and outputs of the services,[2] and, if not satisfied, full capacity to 'exit' in Hirschman terms.[3] These two efficient markets' conditions are not present in a satisfactory way in this type of service. When we enrol a child in a school, the information about it is limited, imprecise; our competence to control the quality of its service still more limited, and the exit possibility is small. When we enter a hospital, our capacity of information and of exit is even more limited: most of the time this capacity comes too late. In choosing a restaurant, a spoon, or a car, we have ample information and exit capacity, while in fundamental services, such as education and health, apart from information, we need to be able to count upon the

---

[2] Rose-Ackerman, 1996; Weisbrod, 1988.   [3] Hirschman, 1970.

assumption that the members of the organization are mostly motivated by public interest rather than private profit.[4] As Mintzberg observes:

> It is not clear whether those professional services widely accepted as public—certain minimum levels of education and health, for example—are particularly effective when offered directly by the state and principally by private enterprises. Neither of the two is capable of dealing with all the differing requisites present in these professional services. Markets are insensitive, hierarchies are crude. Organizations without proprietors, or, in certain cases, cooperatives can serve us better in these cases, if financed by the state in order to assure fairness of distribution.

Thus, besides affirming the superiority of public non-state service organizations in terms of quality and efficiency in the delivery of education and health care, Mintzberg does not hesitate in claiming state financing for them.

The expansion of social organizations originates in society, which is continuously setting up new service NGOs that may receive partial finance from the state, and in the state itself to the extent that public management reform transforms departments and agencies into social organizations, or creates incentives to promote new non-profit service organizations. This has occurred in New Zealand, Australia, and United Kingdom. It is also happening in various European countries and, more recently, in the United States, where, for instance, communities build and the state finances 'chartered schools'. These schools, in spite of the opposition of the state school unions, are expanding because they use scarce resources more efficiently and offer more freedom of choice to parents. The Clinton administration gave strong support to them as an alternative to the voucher system, which involves state support to fee-paying schools. The chartered schools are public schools, not only because they are non-profit but also because they are fully free: their running costs are covered by the government. Yet they are managed either by managers chosen by the community or by private enterprises that charge a fee for their work. I, personally, do not favour the private management of the schools, preferring the first alternative; but as long as the universality principle is assured, and the schools remain open to all and follow the supervision of a public body of citizens, this question is secondary. In the United Kingdom, the universities, which were state-owned, are today quasi-state if not altogether public non-state services. The reform of the British university system in the 1980s, along these lines, was particularly successful: academic standards were maintained if not improved due to the managed competition that the higher education funds created through peer evaluations. In his second term, Prime Minister Blair is giving priority to service delivery which follows a central idea: to increase funding for services like health and basic

---

[4] I know very well that this reasoning does not make sense to a neoclassic economist, or to an economist or a political scientist of the rational choice school, for whom the idea of public spirit does not exist. However, this is not the occasion to discuss this theme. We have already done so in the first two chapters of this book.

education that will be kept universal, 'but their delivery will increasingly depend on competition between providers from either the public or the private sector'.[5]

In Brazil, public management reform envisaged the transformation of state agencies into social organizations and is qualifying as such existing public non-state service organizations. According to the 1995 *White Paper on the Reform of the State Apparatus*, the non-exclusive social and scientific services delivered by the state should be transformed gradually into social organizations. The 1998 constitutional amendment defined a special form of social organization for military organizations, while two 1998 laws defined new organizational institutions. One law, which expressly defined the 'social organizations', adopted a narrow concept, requiring management contracts, while the other defined them more broadly, so that existing public non-state service organizations could be qualified as such.[6] Although the expression 'social organization' designated originally a specifically Brazilian organizational institution, I believe that we should define as social organizations all public non-state or non-profit service organizations which provide social and scientific services financed by the state, and are accountable not only to society but also to the administration. In principle, accountability to the administration should be institutionalized through management contracts, which will establish the objectives and performance indicators to be observed. Yet there is a myriad of small social-assistance and education organizations, often related to a church, that receive support from the state but do not justify a management contract. Nevertheless, I believe that they should equally be viewed as social organizations.[7]

If we envisage a spectrum from private to state ownership, social organizations are nearer to the state than other public non-state organizations: they are quasi-state organizations. Modesto acknowledges that the character of the social organizations model is neither private nor state, with a negative and a positive argument. The negative argument is that social organizations are not veiled state departments, they do not have any prerogatives of public law, and law will not institute them. The positive argument is that social organizations are state-society partnerships:

In a comprehensive sense, social organizations represent a form of partnership of the state with private institutions of public purpose (*ex-parte principe* perspective), or, from another angle, a form of popular participation in administrative management (*ex-parte populi* perspective). (Modesto 1997: 31–4)

---

[5] *The Economist*, Bagehot, 'Whatever Works', 4 May 2002: 56.

[6] In Brazil, one law is known as 'the social organization's law' while the other is 'the OSCIPs' law' (OSCIP is the Portuguese abbreviation for Public Interest Organizations of Civil Society).

[7] Originally, I had a more restricted definition of 'social organization', believing that a management contract with the administration would be essential. Actually, social organizations may be made accountable in several forms. Management contracts are an excellent accountability mechanism, but they involve costs that small organizations do not justify.

Social accountability is particularly important in the case of social organizations. The existence of a large and representative board of directors will be an endogenous form of social control. Yet it is necessary to consider other forms. As Maria Inês Barreto stresses, social participation is of extreme relevance in the organization model, because it is up to civil society to 'play a double role: on one hand, act as a channel for making explicit and affirming social rights; on the other, to be an important element of restraint in the actions of public or private interest groups' (Barreto 1999: 140).[8] In this sense, it is necessary to consider the problems of collective action involved in the operation of social organizations. Besides the use of social accountability mechanisms, accountability will be assured in social organization through the essentially flexible and autonomous character of its management. Second, transparency is essential. Communication channels between public service users and politicians must flow in such a way as to permit the latter to be informally socially accountable to the former. The role of the media here is strategic. As Marianne Nassuno (1997, 1998), discussing social organizations' accountability, has underlined, information will assist politicians in the control of institutions, placing the associated problems in a wider sphere of discussion. Besides the risk of private capture, social organizations face the risk of 'feudalization'. I understand by 'feudalization' of a public non-state organization the fact that it is under permanent control of a given group, independently of its ability to manage it. This group does not privatize the institution, does not use it for its own enrichment, but retains power over it even if it exercises that power badly, even if its directors have lost the legitimacy to continue in power. Thus, when regulating social organizations, it is necessary to include conditions guaranteeing its public character and avoiding feudalization.

The transformation of state services into social organizations faces initial rejection on the part of civil servants. In Brazil, this happened even though the project had been subject to ample debate and received generalized public support. Resistance to change came from corporative sectors in the civil service and from jurists involved in a strictly bureaucratic view of public administration. Yet support came from all quarters. A well-known social activist, Herbert (Betinho) de Souza (1995: 3), for instance, understood the basic meaning of the social organization model:

Here you have something new that could work. In fact, these social organizations of a public nature form a new type of NGO, originating in the state and not in society, with strong state support and the participation of civil society. There could be advantages for both sides and we could be freed from the private x state trap. (Betinho de Souza 1995: 3)

Reform towards social organization should occur gradually, and in different formats, according to the country, the region, and the service. Given its

---

[8] On social organizations, see also Nassuno (1997), Morales (1998), Pacheco (2002).

inherent superiority to the bureaucratic model, each social or scientific service supported by the state will tend to evolve towards it. It will be in the interests of its public and eventually of its employees. Given natural resistance to change, the civil servants that experience the change will argue that the entity will lose the 'state's protection' and will be more vulnerable. In fact, it is in principle easier to extinguish a state organization than to take a social organization out of the budget. In the first case, a decree is often enough, while in the second it is necessary first to discuss the subject in Congress.

Autonomy for a social organization means that it is responsible for its personnel. Management takes the decisions on pay and on hiring independently of government approval. After a state entity is transformed into a social organization, its managers, while looking for additional revenues and for expenditure cuts, will fight in Congress for greater budget allocations, not for higher salaries. Given a budget allocation, salaries will be higher if the same service output is performed with fewer personnel. Thus, every employee begins to feel responsible—up to a certain point he starts to 'own' the organization. He knows that if a co-worker is not working hard, he is a victim of theft. This is an entirely different situation from the one existing in state organizations, where the Treasury is very far from them, becoming difficult to establish that relation.

Social organizations usually charge for their services, but it is not a necessary condition for their existence that they do so. Chartered schools, for instance, are social organizations that are free of charge. In any case, the price demanded from clients will not cover all costs, so that they must look for donations, voluntary work, and participation in the state budget. As they are more efficient, social organizations save taxpayers' money. But this should not mean that the transformation of agencies or departments into social organizations would entitle the economic authorities to reduce state expenditures on those sectors. Which sectors should count on greater or lesser state resources is a political decision that parliaments are supposed to take. If government reduces the state budget of each activity in which performance improves, there will be a negative incentive to make better use of scarce resources. This may be a bureaucratic, but never a managerial, strategy. Yet the fact that social organizations can count on other sources of revenue besides the state budget has led economic authorities to support the idea of viewing the creation of social organizations as a direct strategy for reducing state costs and balancing the budget. This is a mistaken view. Social organizations may have this effect, but because of their superior efficiency, not because government rejects its commitments to social and scientific services. If social organizations cost less, the adoption of the model will permit the state to do more with the same money, thus responding to increasing social demands. In Britain, for instance, the reform of the universities did not lead the state to spend less on university teaching and research, but allowed it to increase substantially the number of students without a proportional increase in costs.

19

Managing from the Strategic Core

The state is politically and administratively managed from the strategic core. Government decisions involve legislation, policy formulation, and high judicial decisions. The management process involves day-to-day decisions in each organization related to its finance and control, to its personnel and other inputs, and to its outputs. Both exceed the scope of this book, which is not on government, nor on management, but on reform—reform that is designed to make government decision-making more effective and management of the state organizations more efficient and accountable. Thus, I will not discuss government policy-making here. In relation to management, I will limit this chapter to discussion of the strategic plan that each organization is required to have, and the managerial strategy that each public management reform will choose. I could discuss other relevant topics, like information technology and personnel. The information revolution, and particularly the Internet, is playing and will continue to play a major role in public management reform, which, on the other hand, depends essentially on the formation of a new type of personnel, more qualified and more able than the classic civil servants to make decisions independently. Yet I will limit myself to the cultural and organizational dimensions of the reform. I know that it also involves a management dimension, chiefly in the implementation process, but there are so many possibilities that I believe it more appropriate to leave such subjects to public management books.

The clear separation between departments in the strategic core formulating policies and supervising management contracts, and the agencies and social organizations executing services, is central to public management reform. When the delivery of services takes place at the ministry or department level, combining policy formulation with execution, it is necessary to encourage discussion on the possibility of transferring them to an existing decentralized institution acting in a compatible area, thus avoiding the unnecessary creation of new institutions. In the event that it is impossible to aggregate them in an existing institution, the creation of a decentralized organization becomes necessary. Unburdened of executive activities, the strategic core will be in a better condition to dedicate itself to its managerial activities, which involve the formulation and evaluation of public policies, and accompaniment or control of the decentralized institutions under its supervision. Thus, officials in the strategic core will have more time to take government and management decisions.

In principle, public organizations that have not undergone public management reform, that is, that have not been transformed into agencies or social organizations, may nevertheless have strategic plans and a management strategy. They have not benefited from reform, but this does not legitimize giving up the use of managerial tools. Without prior institutional reform, the organizations will have more difficulty in achieving their objectives, but they will have even more difficulty if they cling to classic bureaucratic procedures.

Strategic Plan

In public management reform, each public organization has a strategic plan, even when it is not supposed to have a management contract with the supervisory ministry, as in the case of the regulatory agencies. Such a plan is the basic document that defines the structure and orients the action of each agency or social organization. Policy-making departments could also have strategic plans, but this is not essential. The plans classically begin with a diagnosis, and have as their basic elements, on the one hand the definition of the mission, the objectives, and the targets or performance indicators, and, on the other, the organization's structure, the personnel requirements, and the policies to be followed. The strategic plan serves as a basis for the management contract, but has an intrinsic value as long as it involves the participation of all the organization's members and represents a commitment on their part.

The diagnosis of the organization's main problems comes first. It is essential to distinguish the problems that are within the scope of managers' authority to resolve, from those that depend on institutional reforms, such as, for instance, the transformation of a department into an agency or into a social organization. A classic temptation in the diagnosis process is to say that the personnel and the institutional setting are inadequate, and to add that changes in such areas depend on external factors—which leads to paralysis. Such radicalism leads nowhere. Often it is possible to get much more from the existing personnel and the existing structure that one would initially suppose.

It became fashionable and almost routine to define private and public organizations' missions. Yet one should not underestimate the importance of doing so. Each organization must have a core business and it must be well-defined. Too broad or too narrow a mission may cause serious problems. In public organizations, the definition of the client-citizen involves special consideration. He or she is not just a client but principally a citizen, to the extent that he or she has rights. The client has rights when he pays for the service, while the citizen's rights exist independently of payment. It should follow logically from this that client-citizens usually receive better treatment than clients do, but it is not so. Bureaucratic organizations are classically self-centred or self-regarding. It is a major challenge to transform them into managerial organizations, in which the client is important. The greatest difficulty is in specifying performance indicators. In business enterprises this is relatively simple, as long as profit is the bottom line. In public enterprises, managers will have to refer to other indicators—some final, like customer satisfaction or reduction in mortality rates, others intermediate, such as the time involved in each service, or costs.

With regard to the organization's structure, it is essential to consider functional authority. In other words, it is necessary to overlook the unity of the command principle, and use matricial[1] authority whenever this applies. Such a directive will naturally involve a greater demand for cooperation among the managers with different specialities and still more different personalities, but one of the secrets of good management is precisely that: making a team out of a group of different and often competing individuals.

Implementation problems in the strategic plan merit special attention. The plan should be characterized by sequencing, or definition of steps, although the manager will realize that concomitant actions are often more effective than sequential ones. A problem in the implementation process is how to reconcile two frequently hostile dimensions. On the one hand, some concrete improvements must be obtained in the short run; on the other, the cultural change of the organization must be put into focus. In both cases, perhaps the most difficult issue to handle involves the sensibility of civil servants and employees in relation to the proposals of the plan. In this sense, a major effort has to be devoted to progressively involving the personnel in the plan's objectives and policies. Apart from this, care in the communication process and transparency in the decision-making process are extremely important, since the individuals who contest change tend to mobilize and make their opposition clear, while those favourable to reform tend to be less vocal.

Management Strategies

In public management reform, agencies' strategic plans should be part of a broader management strategy. Peter Drucker developed the management-by-results strategy in the 1950s as a corollary of the decentralization design that he called 'divisional decentralization'. This decentralization design, originally

---

[1] This term is defined a little later in the text.

developed by Alfred Sloan in the 1910s for General Motors, thereafter became standard with most major American business enterprises (Drucker 1954, 1964). The basic idea is to combine strong headquarters in which functional vice-presidents define policies with strong divisions (product or regional divisions), and line vice-presidents (with equal status to the functional ones) who manage executively. After the 1970s this decentralization design began also to be called 'matricial' organization. It uses throughout the organization a double authority pattern: line and functional. Drucker proposes to control the decentralized divisions through management by results. The simple idea is to require from decentralized divisions, as a trade-off for the increased autonomy they are granted, the precise definition of objectives and goals, and then to control the decentralized units by the results achieved. I believe it fair to say that, if we have to choose just one characteristic of public management reform, it is management by results. Several studies evaluating the strategy conclude that it works well.[2]

In the private sector, there are countless competing management strategies, all following, in one way or another, the principles of management by results. Re-engineering, score cards, and total quality management are among the best-known. These strategies emphasize control of processes, which, however, does not mean a return to bureaucratic administration, a denial of management of results. We must not oppose control of outcomes to the permanent definition and redefinition of the processes of production, which is a managerial strategy par excellence, but contrast it to the strict observance of procedures that characterizes bureaucratic administration. Among business management strategies, probably the most successful has been total quality management, which, originating in the works of Edward Deming, was developed after the 1950s in Japan, and afterwards systematized by the Japanese themselves, mainly through the Japanese Union of Scientists and Engineers (JUSE).[3] Another influential management strategy is re-engineering, systematized by Michael Hammer and James Champy.[4] Of these two strategies, quality control is the one that most management reforms in the OECD countries (Löffler 1996, 1997) and in Brazil have been adopting. This is because it has an interesting rationale, and chiefly because, in the evaluation process, it is not limited to the profit objective but sets a number of other criteria, which, being qualitative, adapt well to public management. The basic message is that it is not enough to ground management on results. As Greg Davidson (1997: 31)

---

[2] Among studies on efficiency and appraisal of results, see Zapico and Mayne (1995); OECD/PUMA (1996, 1997).

[3] Deming (1982). He was a statistician and engineer, business consultant, and professor at New York University. Based on Walter Shewhart's research, in Japan, on control of statistical quality of processes of production, he began to develop a management strategy which the Japanese, who developed it, call TQC—Total Quality Control. For an account of how these ideas came about and were developed, see Mann (1985).

[4] Hammer (1990); Hammer and Champy (1993, 1995).

observes, a focus on results is necessary but not sufficient; organizations also need a profound understanding of the formal (and informal) processes they use to produce results, and their employees need to have the capacity and conditions to monitor and adjust these processes. On the same subject, Deming is emphatic. Among the 14 points he developed on total quality management, the eleventh, in the 1985 version, says: 'Use statistical methods to continue bettering quality and productivity, and eliminate standards of labour that prescribe numerical quotas'. In the 1986 version, he radicalizes: 'Eliminate administration by objectives' (quoted in Mann 1985: 27–9). In fact, Deming has nothing against administration by results, and he does not ignore the need for definition of quantitative performance indicators. Nevertheless, he considers unacceptable the definition of objectives or of results for a worker, a department, or a company, without management having clearly defined the improvements in processes that make it possible to reach these objectives. According to Falconi Campos (1992: 19), the items selected in a control system are numerical indicators measuring the total quality of each process; thus, one should never choose an indicator over which it is impossible to exercise control because the required changes in processes are still unknown.

The continuous revision of work processes in the search for higher productivity, the so-called 'Deming cycle', is essential. The expression 'total' in the denomination of the strategy emphasizes the central role played by improvement processes in each stage of goods and services production. Engineers and statisticians developed this management strategy, but this did not blind them to the importance of workers' participation in the definition of the process. Their objective in that respect was to engage and motivate personnel. Quality management, given its origin, is essentially a strategy developed for manufacturing. Strategic planning, with its definition of mission, objectives, and performance indicators, is part of it, but the emphasis is on quality control, that is, on the revision of work processes 'until a statistical quality control is reached'. When strategic planning alone assumes the role of management strategy, it is usual to focus on great objectives and let slide the essentials, that is, the increase in productivity. In business administration, we traditionally have a production, financial, or marketing approach. Quality management adopts a production approach, although it does not underestimate the others, particularly marketing. As Falconi Campos observes, 'the real criterion of quality is the *consumer's preference*. Quality is directly connected to the satisfaction of the internal and external client' (Falconi Campos 1992: 2–14, author's emphasis). Despite this, the main message which the private sector received from Deming and his associates, and which, more recently, the public sector has been receiving, is that excellence in production is necessary and possible through the continuous revision of work processes and the use of statistical techniques to control quality.

Public management reform tends to prefer total quality control as a management strategy because of its adaptability to the multiples objectives and criteria that governments have to observe in presiding over their respective states. With quality control the risk of falling into the classic bureaucratic 'one size fits all' mistake is smaller. Yet I want to conclude this chapter by remarking that the key problem in reform is not choosing among management strategies, but creating organizational institutions and a management culture that allow the effective adoption of those strategies. In the private and in the public non-state sectors, this previous problem does not exist, since business enterprises and non-profit organizations are inherently autonomous: their managers have just to choose and implement, case by case, the most appropriate management strategies. In the public sector, by contrast, the first task is to create the institutional conditions to provide the necessary autonomy for the agency. These conditions will necessarily differ from those in the private sector. The state does not operate through the exchange of goods or services in the market, but through unilateral resource transfers financed by tax revenues. The control mechanism is not the market but the administration and democratic governance. The central criterion is not profit, which does not even exist, but the public interest. The interests of politicians, civil servants, and citizens will count in the definition of the public interest, which will be, as far as possible, characterized as law. The law will broadly define the administrative rules or institutional conditions, which will be similar to those existing in the private sector and even more similar to those prevailing in the public non-state sector. They may be similar to the extent that public management reform decentralizes decision-making authority; creates autonomy for public managers; establishes performance standards for all public organizations; forms quasi-markets and other mechanisms to promote competition among public organizations; and develops ways to measure the productivity of public organizations.

Management Contracts

Public management reform transferred the management-by-results strategy from the private to the public sector, including the idea of the management contract, which business enterprises do not use, and assigning more importance to qualitative performance indicators, which business enterprises do not need. We have already seen that Deming developed an alternative strategy— total quality control—and criticized management by results. Although correct in demanding precise definition of processes, his strategy is eventually one of the many possibilities of management by results; it is just a more detailed or specific one.

In public management reform, management contracts are documents through which the decentralized organization—agency or social organization—is tied to the supervisory ministry with a set of performance indicators and, more broadly, with a strategic plan. A typical management contract will include: (1) the organization's mission, strategic objectives, and goals; (2) performance indicators; (3) means and conditions necessary for execution of pledged commitments, particularly personnel and budget allocations; (4) evaluation processes to be followed by the organization and the supervisory ministry; and (5) mechanisms of transparency and social accountability. The goals having been identified, it will be possible to define performance indicators, expressed in units of measurement that will be more meaningful for those who utilize them, whether for evaluation purposes or to support decision-making based on the information gathered from them. A performance indicator is usually a number or percentage that indicates the unit of measurement and its magnitude. To measure institutional performance it is necessary to collect data. However, since the development of new data can be costly, public managers will engage in cost-benefit analysis, limiting their enthusiasm for the construction of new data or information systems. Normally, improvement of the existing systems of data collection/processing will do the job. The problem will be, rather, to know how to use the data that already exist. Performance indicators having been defined, we are able to draw up the management contract through which the supervising ministry will follow up and evaluate the institutional performance of decentralized agencies, whether executive agencies or social organizations. To guarantee the implementation of public policies formulated by the strategic core and their compliance with the demands and expectations of society, the dynamics of monitoring management contracts makes it possible to identify—preferably sooner rather than later—of eventual difficulties or deviations in time to make the necessary modifications in the conditions, objectives, and goals or in the method of their implementation. In drawing up the management contract, the institution and the supervising ministry seek assurance that the objectives and goals are consistent with the institutional mission, that the basic sources of data that make it possible to define and to follow up performance indicators have been identified, and that the contract's 'language' can be understood by all, including the organization's client-citizens.

In the execution of the management contract, an essential element is the partial report of results. The report will link information on attained performance to the mission and to the strategic objectives. Unless they understand this link, the users of information may not be capable of judging progress towards expected results. Information in reports should adhere to questions relative to the fulfilment of the institutional mission and be presented in a manner that is concise and comprehensible, including by those not belonging to the institution, so to increase administrative transparency and facilitate social accountability. Special attention must be given to the reasons why time limits or results may have diverged from the established goals. In the event of non-fulfilment of goals, this explanation is necessary so that the decentralized unit, the supervising ministry, Congress, and other public institutions can decide what to do. In the event of targets being exceeded, the information can serve as an example of best practice. Apart from explaining the reasons for not fulfilling goals and meeting agreed time limits, the report should contain information on the actions that will be taken by the organization to correct these deviations.

Part III

A Discussion of the Reform

20

Theoretical Approaches to New Public Management

New public management—the new discipline that serves as an intellectual basis for public management reform—is far from constituting a unified intellectual field. Its adherents, although sharing some common traits, such as client-orientation, contracting out services, and greater autonomy and accountability for agencies, have different intellectual and ideological allegiances. In this chapter, I distinguish three theoretical/ideological approaches in the new public management field. My objective is not to undertake a complete survey, but to stress that there are different theoretical and ideological orientations on how public management reform should take place, and to differentiate them from the approach I take in this book. There are many ways of organizing the field. Jacques Chevallier (1996), for instance, finds the origins of the 'managerial model' as far back as in the 1960s, which he opposes to the 'legal model' and to the 'sociological model'. The legal model corresponds to bureaucratic public administration; the sociological model, to the 'theory of organizations', originated with Max Weber (1922) and Chester Barnard (1938). Yet, it would be more interesting to put these two models under one title, the sociological or historical approach, and oppose it to the economic approach—the 'rational choice model', originating in neoclassical economics. New public management is often related to public or rational choice critiques of bureaucracy and state intervention, in so far as some conservative politicians and consultants involved in public management reform, particularly in New Zealand, invoked rational choice. Yet new public management is not intrinsically related either to rational choice or to the theory of organizations. I believe that the theory of organizations is often less ideological and more useful in understanding the state organization and how it should be managed, but a rational choice approach may also help us to understand the same questions from a different perspective.

New public management theoretical–ideological orientations vary also according to the different national realities that analysts face. We have, for instance, an Anglo-Saxon, a Continental European, and a Scandinavian tradition of approaching government and the state. They also vary according to the level of economic development and of democratic governance. Yet probably the more relevant way of distinguishing new public management approaches is the distance of each of them from bureaucratic public administration on the one hand, and from business administration on the other. We may also use as distinguishing criteria their conservative or progressive ideological content, and the type of control or form of accountability that reformers favour.

We could plot the various new public management theoretical–ideological approaches on a graph in which the horizontal coordinate represents a continuum from bureaucratic public administration to the business administration approach, while the vertical one would move from a politically progressive to a conservative approach. Yet this method would be misleading because there is no reason to identify bureaucracy and bureaucratic public administration with progressive ideas, and businessmen and business administration with conservative thinking. When bureaucrats engage in politics, they tend to be 'statists', interested in increasing the state organization power and their own power, rather than socialists, as the case of the Soviet Union demonstrates. They may also be just conservatives. On the other hand, although businessmen tend to be conservative, they are not necessarily so. The degree of identification of public management with management of private companies denotes the gradual distancing from the typically bureaucratic approach. Yet this does not mean that the more distant from bureaucratic and the nearer to business administration the reform is, the more 'authentic' it will be. New Zealand's reform in the 1990s, for instance, closely approximated public administration to private administration, but this fact did not make public management reform more authentic in New Zealand: it made it only more radical.

The Political Approach

It is possible to discern at least three orientations in the literature on managerial public administration, which I propose to call the 'technical', 'economic', and 'political and sociological' approaches. The technical orientation is typical of management consultants and recent converted bureaucrats; the economic approach, of economists and rational-choice theorists; and the political and sociological approach is the one that I adopt in this book. All of them limit the role of the classic forms of control (hierarchy, procedures, and parliamentary review) and adopt control by results as the main accountability strategy. But, while the technical approach limits itself to this still hierarchical form of control, the economic approach includes managed competition or quasi-markets control, and the political adds a democratic form of accountability— social accountability—giving to it a strategic role. Besides, while the technical approach does not have a specific strategy to motivate personnel, the economic approach uses principal–agent reasoning to propose essentially economic incentives and penalties, while the political and sociological approach, disregarding economic incentives, emphasizes moral or organizational incentives besides straightforwardly political incentives: the republican ethos.

The distance between new public management and bureaucratic administration is apparently higher in the economic than in the other two approaches because it tends to confer on quasi-markets an overwhelming importance. Yet, paradoxically, the principal–agent model that it uses often leads to centralizing activities, in clear conflict with a central idea in public management. Besides, the economic orientation tends also to use rational-choice reasoning, which assimilates political actors—the actors involved in public management— to economic actors—those involved in business management and real markets. In contrast, the political approach is fully distinct from bureaucratic public management as it decentralizes and relies, on the one hand, on managed competition and social accountability mechanisms, and, on the other, on republican values on the part of public officials. The technical orientation, although more pragmatic, may make similar mistakes to the economic orientation, while the political one claims that an essential difference exists between the private space and the public space: the private or business realm is the space of markets; the public realm, the space of politics. Compared with a bureaucratic view, the three public management approaches have a liberal character because they attribute importance to the market in the coordination of the economy, and because even the technical orientation backs managed competition. Some new public management analysts and practitioners, particularly those espousing the economic orientation, are ultra-liberal. The second phase of the New Zealand reform was clearly ultra-liberal. Yet, as I will discuss later, radical liberalism is ultimately incompatible with managerial public administration.

Instead of trying to further distinguish these orientations, I believe it more practical to theoretically and ideologically define the particular kind of political approach that I have adopted in practice and have generalized in this book. First, it is not just a management approach: it also involves a new form of analysing the roles of the state and of the organizational institutions that play these roles. The distinctions between exclusive and non-exclusive activities, and between private, public non-state, and state ownership are crucial. Second, this orientation has its foundation in the republican tradition of political thought: it is based on the conviction that self-interest and control mechanisms must be—and, in practice, are—complemented by republican or civic virtues on the part of government officials. Third, it is not enough to rely on the classic forms—vertical and horizontal, elections and control by other agencies—to make the administration accountable: all forms of social accountability or of democratic civic participation are crucial to making agencies autonomous and accountable. A republican state merits this adjective not only because it assures republican rights but because it relies on the civic participation of its citizens. Fourth, although preaching an approximation of private and public labour markets, it reserves the exclusive activities of the state to civil servants. Their careers, although more flexible, should conserve the ideas of public selection and merit promotion. Full tenure is unthinkable, but a greater degree of labour stability than there is in the private sector is advisable. Fifth, although it demands more extensive use of quasi-markets, competition is not for clients, but for excellence (efficiency and quality) in public services. Clients have demands; citizens have rights. Sixth, public management legitimacy is also economic, but essentially political: given the democratic constraint assumption, the final criterion is always political. Seventh, public management may have similarities with business management, but is essentially different. While in private management the mechanism of coordination is the market, and the objective is profit, in public management this mechanism is political, and the objective the public interest. The real question is not about exporting organizational and institutional practices and concepts from one sector to the other. Instead, it is necessary to filter and critically re-elaborate each concept, each technique.

The political approach warrants this name because it is based on the idea of the public sector's irreducible specificity, it is considered eminently political, ruled by the principles of power and legitimacy, while the private sector is mainly economic, ruled by the market and the principle of profit. In this context, the value given to citizens' participation in the management of the public thing takes on high relevance. The client-citizen is a whole citizen, who is both object and subject of public services as he participates in the formation of public policies and in the evaluation of results. As Schedler (1996: 8) observes, the classic notion of citizenship confers on the citizen the right to decide what activities the state should exercise and the policies it should carry out, as well as their extension and effects, while the client-citizen 'exerts influence over the *results* of these activities (that is, over their actual outputs)'. Consequently, it increases the accountability of public managers before citizens.

The political approach to public management reform implies the conscious adaptation of administrative techniques and ideas of the private sector to the public sector. It requires and stimulates an ethical revival on the part of public managers, who start viewing the citizen as a client and partner, and establishing better quality at reduced cost as a new mission for state services. The increased concern over service quality reflects an approach guided by values, based on a mission, and directed towards reaching excellence in public services. This allows more attention to the concerns and values of the client-citizen, as well as attention to the 'voice' of the citizen. The development of 'social learning' about the supply of routine services (for example, community development work, evaluation of social needs) is also widely considered. In this way, a continuous set of tasks and values that are distinctive to public service is established, with an emphasis on ensuring the participation of citizens and the accountability of public managers. The idea of the citizen as client-citizen is central to public management reform. However, criticism of this view is often heard, the argument being that it would reduce the citizen, first, to the status of taxpayer, and then to that of client, when he is much more than that: he is a citizen who has political rights and duties. This argument does not make sense. No doubt, the true citizen has effective rights, including the right to respect by the deliverers of state services. The client orientation imported from the administration of companies means exactly that: to fulfil the needs of the client, to respect him. But this does not mean that the citizen's right to participate is being left aside, or that the importance of social accountability mechanisms and institutions is being underestimated. On the contrary, civic participation is an essential element of political and democratic approaches to public management reform.[1]

Public management reform requires theoretical tools. The more general is political theory. Two other tools, however, dispute the second position: organization theory, which has its origin in sociology, and public choice, which borrows from neoclassical economics. Both theories view the organization, including the state apparatus, as a rational structure which responds to an economic logic or follows an instrumental rationality. Yet they use different methods, and reach different conclusions.

Public Choice

Any form of administration, public or private, includes a system of incentives and penalties, or a system of positive and negative motivation. Since Hawthorn's studies, led by Elton Mayo in the beginning of the 1930s, which gave rise to the school of human relations and, more broadly, to organization theory, the central theme of business administration has been motivation: that is, how to establish an incentive system that motivates workers to perform their tasks well. In the private sector, performance-related bonuses, merit-based promotion systems, management by results, management by performance indicators, and managed competition follow this basic idea. More recently, political science has developed, within the rational or public choice school, principal–agent theory as an alternative to organization theory. Given its more abstract character, this approach, besides allowing the study of hierarchical subordination and horizontal cooperation within organizations, is also useful in the analysis of the relationship between voters and

---

[1] Mário Covas, governor of the State of São Paulo 1995–8, well-known for his commitment to public interest, during a lecture in Brasília remarked that total quality management is particularly suitable for the public sector because assuring the quality of public services through social accountability is a way of strengthening citizenship.

elected politicians, or between shareholders and chief executive officers. The central problem, however, remains the same: which incentive and penalty system is most successful in leading the agent to observe the guidelines or decisions set by the principal?

This theory, which, in principle, could mean a step forward due to its degree of generalization, in practice means a step back, to the extent that its proponents tend to return to old Taylorist scientific administration ideas, or to bureaucratic public administration. The difference is that, while scientific administration adopts an engineering perspective, as Taylor's did, principal–agent theory uses a public choice, or economic, approach borrowed from neoclassical economics, and logically deduces the 'rational' behaviour of government officials. Following the opening by Ronald Coase (1937, 1988), the simple existence of all organizations, including the state organization, is logically deduced from the concept of transaction costs. Agencies in the executive branch have some autonomy as long they receive a congressional delegation from legislators who 'cede substantive discretionary authority to the bureaucracy in policy areas where the legislative process is less efficient relative to bureaucratic decision making' (Epstein and O'Halloran 1999: 14). This hypothetical-deductive approach faces serious limitations when applied to politics and the management of organizations. The assumption that agents and principals act in a 'rational' or self-interested way involves deducing their behaviour rationally from the *homo economicus* model. This inference process is useful for neoclassical economic theory, which works at a high level of abstraction, and where the objectives are themselves economic. Yet, even among economists, the debate over this assumption is intense. I am persuaded that macroeconomic theory in particular encounters serious problems when this kind of approach is applied to it. A historical approach is essential (Bresser-Pereira 2003*b*). However, in the case of public management this economic and aprioristic approach is less applicable. Public management operates necessarily at a lower level of abstraction, and works with institutions and agents whose basic objectives are not economic but political.

It is not my intention in this book to undertake an analysis of public choice theory and the principal–agent sub-theory. Both imply transferring to political theory and public administration the methods and principles of neoclassical microeconomics, which are already the object of discussion among economists given their radical logical-deductive and abstract rather than historical-deductive character. However, as the objective of economic agents in the market is rightly to maximize profits, the explanatory power of neoclassical theory is strong when the objective is explain abstractly how a market-coordinated economic system works. In the case of political behaviour, however, the maximization of self-interest assumption is far from universally accepted. On the contrary, I would say that classical political philosophy rejects the assumption, without adopting an opposite and naïve approach to the effect that political behaviour is only public interest-oriented. In addition to this is the fact that political and particularly administrative phenomena are more concrete and particularized than market economic relationships described by the neoclassical general equilibrium theory. That is why I consider the heuristic capacity of public choice to be limited. Nevertheless, it may be useful in understanding political behaviour, as, for instance, Adam Przeworski's work (1985) on social democracy demonstrates.

In this book, my aim is not to criticize rational choice and principal–agent theory but to argue that, given their pessimistic conception of human nature, these theories are incompatible with public management reform, while ultimately consistent with the bureaucratic approach to public administration. I know that my claim is contrary to the conventional wisdom among new public management critics. As they saw rational choice being invoked by practitioners in the second phase of the New Zealand reform, they conclude that public management reform was deduced from rational choice. Yet works by political scientists who are representative of this theoretical perspective, such as Jean Tirole (1994), Terry Moe (1990), and McCubbins, Noll, and Weingast (1987), illustrate my view. They are interested in learning how elected politicians can control bureaucrats—a typical agency problem, that is, a problem that principal–agent theory would be able to solve. How do they solve the problem? Significantly, they find the solution in a more intensive use of administrative procedures . . . In other words, in the late twentieth century, they rediscovered bureaucratic public administration principles! According to them, politicians may control bureaucrats in two ways: through the oversight mechanism, which involves monitoring, reward, and penalty, or through the administrative procedures mechanism. For many years, they said, 'positive political theory' ignored this last alternative, limiting itself to undertake expensive and inefficient research on and analysis of the oversight mechanism.[2] McCubbins, Noll, and Weingast (1987: 255) discovered or rationally deduced the usefulness of legal administrative rules, adapting them to the terms of rational choice theory:

By structuring the rules of the game for the agency, administrative procedures sequence agency activity, regulate its information collection and dissemination, limit its available choices, and define its strategic advantage.

We also find this return to the past with the use of apparently modern instruments in Tirole (1994). Using neoclassical economics to understand the internal workings of the state, he assumes that politicians and civil servants are self-interested and thus exclusively motivated by monetary incentives or opportunities for career advancement. On the other hand, he observes that,

---

[2] 'Positive political theory' is an expression that rational choice political scientists use to describe their approach, probably inspired on Friedman's 'positive economic theory' (1953)—a paradoxical defence of the neoclassical hypothetical-deductive method.

unlike what occurs in private companies, whose aim is clearly to maximize profit, governmental agencies have multiple objectives that are generally hard to measure and are ultimately contradictory. Given this difficulty, private interest groups are permanently seeking to capture public managers. In order to deal with this threat, a regulatory system is set up, which, however, private interests may also capture—thus requiring the setting up of additional checks and balances. Tirole concludes, in a strictly bureaucratic way, that, rather than relying on the supervision of bureaucracy by politicians, it is better to reduce the size of the state and the economic interests it deals with, and rely on a rule-book to prevent public administration from taking decisions with relative autonomy. In his words:

To reduce the government officials' temptation to be captured, one may reduce the stakes interest groups have in the regulatory decision. This means relying less on the information held by the government officials and regulating instead by the rule-book. In our view, the central feature of a bureaucracy is that its members are not trusted to make use of information that affects members other than themselves, and that decisions are therefore based on rigid rules. (Tirole 1994: 14)

More interesting is Moe's analysis (1990). He also uses neoclassical instruments borrowed by neo-institutionalism and rational-choice theory to gain an understanding of public administration. He starts from the Olsonian assumption of radical pessimism in relation to the possibility of effective collective action (Mancur Olson 1965). Although beginning his paper declaring that 'public agencies are the business firms of the public sector', later he clearly distinguishes private from public organizations. These differences lead to the lack of rationality or efficiency in public administration (Moe 1990: 223). Moe seeks inspiration from Coase's and Williamson's economic theories to understand the state and public administration (Coase 1937; Williamson 1985). The premise of his theory is that autonomous economic agents cooperate freely in organizations, establishing contracts to this end, and thus overcoming their problems of collective action, as long as this implies lower transaction costs than those occurring in the market if each individual decides not to cooperate and to act individually. Yet he observes that this theory is a poor explanation for the existence of public organizations, since participation in them is not voluntary: there is no exit possibility for citizens, unless one considers emigration or electoral fall-out. While in private competitive organizations there is always some exit possibility, in public organizations this is only partly possible and, in the state as a whole, it is impossible. Citizens, instead of exiting, must participate. In any circumstance, they have to bind to the state institutions.

Next, to explain cooperation in public organizations, Moe resorts to principal–agent theory, which also attempts to solve the collective action problem (that is, the cooperation problems existing in society). He remarks that this theory would be in theory more useful, as principals define the contractual structures with incentives and penalties, which, in turn, leads agents to comply with the objectives sought by the principal. Yet results are also poor: the agency problems are insurmountable. In both cases—in the economic theory of organizations and in principal–agent theory—Moe is loyal to methodological individualism. Organizations are seen not as a historical phenomenon, as Weber analysed them, but as the logical-deductive outcome of economic agents' decisions to cooperate. Moe concludes that these theories need to be adapted to the particular conditions of the state and politics. Politics is not exactly the world of voluntary exchanges, but rather the realm of the exercise of public authority to perform economic transfers and redistribute income. That is why the theory of transaction costs is of little use, and principal–agent theory, or simply agency theory, may be applied, but with limitations. Agency theory is concerned with the subordination of the agent to the principal, and with the guarantee that the agent does his work as effectively as possible. In this process, the principal's decisions, which result in organizational structures, are of great importance. The basic problem is taking structural decisions to allow the construction of an organization or an institution that works. The problem is not choosing procedures or controls, but building organizations that are capable of fulfilling their respective missions. However, Moe observes that the fulfilment of this objective in the public sector is much more difficult than in the private sector, if not altogether impossible. In companies, property is clear and firm; in state agencies, command is transitory. That is why political parties in power seek to build organizations that are reasonably insulated from government, so that, when they lose control of the state, the new government is not able to change significantly the institutional arrangement and policies of public agencies. Moe observes that, in doing so, the insulating mechanisms are created precisely by those who *do not want* an effectively democratic control structure. Unlike what occurs in the market, the notion of loser and winner is not clear. Today's winners may be tomorrow's losers. And they are always within the system, without the alternative of exit. Therefore, Moe (1990: 230) says:

There are winners and losers, and the losers cannot leave—but instead, trapped within the system, they participate in the design of agencies and programs that they oppose, and they use what power they have to create organizations that cannot do their jobs.

In this process, the control of the principal (the voter) over the politician (the agent) is relative. Equally relative is the other step in the principal–agent chain: the control of the principal (the politician) over the public manager (the agent). The public manager acquires an autonomy that reduces clientelism and, mainly, responds to the demands of politicians to neutralize future opposition governments. On the other hand, it escapes democratic control, and may lead the bureaucrat to pursue his own interests instead of seeking the interests of the politicians who gave autonomy to the organization. In this case, the public interest is also overlooked. Through this process, Moe is describing the process of the division of power, or of checks and balances, that characterizes modern democracies. But he does so to highlight its perverse aspect. In modern countries, legislators do not have a view of the whole, which, according to him, only the heads of state can ultimately enjoy. Their basic concern is to protect themselves. And to this end, although we may find perfectly rational explanations for it,

Legislators gladly build a bureaucracy, piece by piece, that makes no sense whatever as an organizational whole ... The result, by most any reasonable standard of organization, is a structural nightmare. American public bureaucracy is an organizational mess. (Moe 1990: 237–8)

This pessimistic view leads Moe into an ultra-liberal stance.[3] Not even rigid bureaucratic rules are a solution, given the irrationality of politicians, who want to protect themselves. The only alternative would be the minimal state. Although Moe's analysis is provocative, it ends up in a dead-end. Between new public management and bureaucratic public administration, he does not choose the latter, as did the other rational choice political scientists cited above, but an idealist ultra-liberal goal: the minimal state, the same ideological stance adopted by public choice conservative economists like James Buchanan, Gordon Tullock, and William Niskanen.[4]

Essentially, rational choice analysis is unable to understand public management reform, and remains attached to bureaucratic administration because, proceeding from the assumption that there is an inherent tension between effectiveness and responsiveness, it considers a 'puzzle' the delegation of 'broad decision-making authority' to professional civil service since the 1930s (Epstein and O'Halloran 1999: 5): a delegation that would be contradictory to the accountability or responsiveness that modern democracies require. If this was a puzzle in the era of bureaucratic public administration, what to say of the era of public management? Public management reform substantially increases delegation to public managers, but this does not represent a threat to democracy because democracy itself is progressing, is becoming participatory and republican—something that pure rational choice theorists cannot acknowledge.

Organization Theory

The motivation system differs in organizations depending on variables such as the nature of the work, organizational culture, and the country in which

---

[3] For a less pessimistic use of principal–agent theory in public administration, see Melo (1996) and Przeworski (1999). The approach is not so pessimistic, but still limited.

[4] Buchanan and Tullock (1962); Niskanen (1971).

the organization is situated. We may accept the fact that, among politicians, the desire to be elected has precedence over their preferences in terms of the public interest, while, among bureaucrats, the wish to be promoted is stronger than that to defend the common good, which, however, does not mean that public interest or the common good are always relegated to second place. Motivations of 'moral' character, related to job satisfaction, team spirit, or the feeling of fulfilling a mission, especially one of a public nature, are powerful motivating factors, and are not necessarily selfish. In the analysis of public organizations, to go back to an engineer's view, like the Taylorist, or to an economist's view, like public choice, is to espouse an approach that sociological organization theory long ago criticized and refuted. After Weber's analysis of bureaucratic organization, which Talcott Parsons introduced into the American sociological literature, and after the Hawthorn studies, lead by Elton Mayo in the 1920s, organization theory became the core of business administration theory, following a sociological rather than economic approach.[5] The economic approach continued to be central to business administration, but particularly developed in the area of corporate finance, not as a tool to manage personnel. To understand the organization and how managers and workers behave and are motivated, theories borrowed from sociology and social psychology formed the core of organization theory. The new theory retained an essential economic element, so long as instrumental rationality was followed, but the engineering and purely economic-oriented perspectives were discarded.[6]

Although it is possible to distinguish many schools of thought in organization theory,[7] its most general premise is that organizations are a type of social system: a formal social system deliberately oriented to fulfilling objectives, in which instrumental rationality is dominant. As a formal organization, it is the outcome of rational decisions, or of 'administrative behaviour', whose bases were set up by Herbert Simon and James March in the 1940s and 1950s.[8] As a social system, it is a system in which the whole is greater than the sum of its parts. Therefore, it is not possible to reduce organizations to decisions of individual agents, such as the rational choice school presumes; or to identify decisions taken within the organization according to a 'bounded rationality' with the maximization hypothesis used in neoclassical economics; or even to limit

---

[5] These studies were undertaken at the Western Electric factory, in Hawthorne, Chicago, between 1927 and 1932. The classic report on these studies was made by Roethlisberger and Dickson (1939). From Mayo see *The Human Problems of an Industrial Civilization* (1946).

[6] Alberto Guerreiro-Ramos (1981). While teaching at the University of South California, he tried to develop a 'substantive' alternative to the 'formal' organization theory, which he views as excessively dependent on an 'economic' approach. Yet he was unable to reach to a satisfactory conclusion, probably because organization theory essentially combines a sociological approach and an economic approach.

[7] See, for instance, the surveys by Charles Perrow (1986) and Fernando Prestes Motta (1998); for an edited book with the classical works on the subject, D. S. Pugh (1971).

[8] Simon (1947); March and Simon (1958).

motivation to material incentives, or to selfish ones, although their relevance cannot be ignored.

In relation to incentives, which organization theory has been studying for decades, long before public choice theory appeared, there is a general consensus about the importance of non-economic or social incentives. As Amitai Etzioni (1964: 32) observes, the school of human relations found that the efficiency and rationality of organizations do not depend on the physical capacity but on the 'social capacity' of the workers, and that non-economic rewards play a central role in determining their motivation and happiness. Chester Barnard (1938), who, together with Mayo, may be considered the founder of the theory of organizations, insisted on the importance of cooperation and moral incentives in organizations. In a work that is today a classic in the area, Abraham Maslow (1943, 1970) proposes a hierarchy of motivations, starting from self-fulfilment at work, proceeding to self-esteem derived from autonomy and responsibility in the execution of tasks, participation in the social group, and safety offered by the organization, and ending with the 'physiological' motivation, which includes salary and monetary incentives. The emphasis given by Mayo and Barnard to cooperation factors in job motivation was later criticized as excessive by theorists of organizations, but the general idea was not challenged. To reduce the system of incentives in an organization to selfish incentives of material gain and career promotion is unthinkable. Today, in terms of organization theory, motivation is only one of the aspects studied.

The central concern is to understand the organization as a social system from various angles or perspectives. Gareth Morgan (1986), whose book on organization theory is probably the most highly regarded today, proposes that organizations may be viewed by means of a combination of eight metaphors: organizations as machines, as organisms, as the brain, as cultures, as political systems, as psychic prisons, as flow and transformation, and as domination instruments. Most organizations are lively and dynamic social systems, made up of economic and financial assets, processes, and technologies, and staffed mainly by men and women endowed with selfish and altruistic or social motives, and with contradictory views, of love and hate, in relation to the organization in which they work.[9] Through a process that Max Pagès et al. (1986) call 'mediation', we have the contradictory combination, within each organization, of privileges or advantages offered to motivate employees, and the constraints or coercion imposed on them by the organization. Pagès et al. carry out their research in, and arrive at their theory as a result of studying, business corporations, in which these contradictions are particularly acute.

---

[9] The literature on the theory of organizations is extensive. It is taught principally in business schools. The common ground of this theory is the work of Max Weber on bureaucracy and the works of Parsons (1937, 1960) and March and Simon (1958).

They also exist in public management, although in a less accentuated form. While the private employee is always doubtful whether his work is promoting the general interest, the civil servant is, in principle, always oriented to the public interest. For the private employee, it is necessary to believe, according to Adam Smith, that when he seeks the corporation's private interests, market competition guarantees the general interest. In contrast, the only doubt the public servant may have is whether the politicians in power are oriented mainly to public interest.

Gary Miller (1992), using systematically the tools of rational choice and principal–agent theory, makes a devastating critique of the 'economic theory of organizations' or 'organizational economics', opposing to it organization theory, whose basic ground is sociological, and, in the case of public management, principally political. What is interesting in Miller's work is that he makes internal criticisms, working with the assumptions of the theory he criticizes. Miller opposes markets to 'hierarchies' or organizations, and explains the existence of the latter in terms of Coase's theory: organizations emerge as transaction costs render inefficient the market coordination of individual activities in relation to the alternative administrative coordination that characterizes organizations. Thus, institutional rules, the system of incentives that govern an organization, should be different from those that preside over the working of markets. Nevertheless, and contrarily, the economic theory of organizations attempts to extend to organizations the same incentive systems, mainly of a pecuniary character, that work in markets. When adopting this strategy, however, organizational economists, supported by principal–agent theory, face insoluble anomalies. Within organizations, their predictions of rational behaviour oriented to personal gain are not consistent with what in fact happens. A large amount of research demonstrates that group work, cooperation, leadership, and corporate organizational culture produce results far more efficient than a system of 'rational' incentives can. In fact, Miller explains, this does not mean that members of organizations act irrationally: it simply indicates that the existing institutions within the organization lead them to rational behaviour that is not merely individualistic, oriented to personal gain. Whereas in markets exchanges are impersonal, in organizations they are personalized.

In conclusion, in the process of public management reform, the sociological theory of organizations has greater predictive capacity than the economic theory of organizations. Although rational choice uses social-mechanism reasoning more explicitly than organizational theory, the social mechanisms developed by the latter are stronger. If motivation of social and moral character is important in private organizations, it is still more relevant in the state organization. Civil servants make trade-offs between the wish to be promoted and to gain more power on the one hand, and the wish to serve the public interest on the other. The former motivation is probably more important than the latter, but is not the only one. There are also those civil servants who make the perverse trade-off between rent-seeking and the wish to be promoted, but this second type of civil servant, who is the rule for the economic theory of organizations (rational choice), is the exception for organization theory. In general, civil servants choose the public profession because it is more secure, more stable, and allows them to work directly for the public interest, not because they aspire to power, much less to wealth.

21

Critics of Reform

Public management reform or new public management has been object of many critical analyses. Such critiques have been mostly ideological. Although it is common among certain critics to classify new public management as neo-liberal, I argue in this chapter that the ultra-liberal ideology is ultimately consistent, not with the managerial approach, but with the bureaucratic perspective of public administration. First, I will discuss the general critique. In a second section I will analyse Stewart and Ransom's critique.

A Neo-Liberal Reform?

Authors such as Christopher Pollitt (1993), Peter Fairbrother (1994), Vincent Wright (1994), Sylvie Trosa (1995), Nuria Cunill Grau (1997), and Clarke and Newman (1997) criticize new public management for being conservative. Wright, for example, asserts that the reforms that have been occurring in western Europe reveal, among other characteristics:

the general paradigm shift, with its strong ideological prejudice against the state, big government, bloated bureaucracies, universalistic solutions. In terms of the administration, the paradigm has been fed not only by Chicago-style market-oriented economics, but also by public choice theories (with their simplistic notions of bureaucratic behaviour), by principal-agent theory, by new theories of property rights and by economic analyses of the failure of the public sector. (Wright 1994: 105)

In this way, Wright identifies public management reform with neo-liberal ideology, which was dominant in the 1980s and 1990s. It is true that public management reform began in Britain under the Thatcher administration, and that in New Zealand, at a certain moment, it took a radically liberal form. It is also true that some proponents of the reform are ultra-liberals. Yet, in other countries where social-democratic or labour political parties ruled, public management reform was also undertaken, as in the first and the third phases of New Zealand' reform, and in the first phase of the Australian reform. The Brazilian reform definitely was not neo-liberal.

Some people have in mind, implicitly or explicitly, a multiple identity sequence according to which 'Thatcher government = neo-liberalism = rational choice = public management reform'. This equation, however, is true only in its first term. The Thatcher government was neo-liberal or ultra-liberal. The second term is arguable: there is a whole school of political scientists who use the instruments of rational choice, but are not conservatives; rather, they are social democrats. The third term of the equation (rational choice = public management reform) is also mistaken. The Thatcher government adopted public management reform, not for ideological reasons but for pragmatic ones. Thatcher, like any competent politician, was at that time making a political agreement to achieve results rather than being dogmatic. If she had been dogmatic, she would not have become involved in a reform that presupposes collective action. True neo-liberals, to the extent that they are radical liberals and ultra-individualistic, do not believe in the possibility of efficient collective action. That is why they do not believe in the possibility of the state—which consolidates collective action—acting efficiently in the economic area or even in the social area. Their real proposal is the minimal state, the withdrawal of the state from all areas except those guaranteeing property and contracts. Thus, they also propose for the production of public goods, from which it is impossible to exclude the state, the establishment of institutions that are so solid and so resistant to corruption, rent-seeking, and nepotism that they do not depend on the moral qualities of individual politicians and public managers. Which institutions are these? In public administration, they are rigid bureaucratic controls. Nevertheless, Thatcher made an alliance with consultants and public managers, who were anxious to overcome the crisis of the British civil service, so that both parties could reach their objectives. Thatcher did not eliminate social services from the state, but reduced their weight in the budget; public management reformers succeeded in making these services more efficient and thus partially restored the prestige of the civil service.

In fact, conservative and neo-liberal views of society and politics are essentially based on a pessimistic view of human nature, while progressive views tend to be more optimistic, keeping faith in human beings, which is essential for sociability and social cooperation. Public management reform, although occurring during a historic phase that was conservative because it was pessimistic, rests on this minimal optimism. After the optimism that rationalism, the Enlightenment, and, more broadly, modernity, brought to the world, in the last 30 years we have been living in post-modern times, in which doubts, fragmentation of identities, and lack of faith in reason are everywhere.[1] In the context of modernity, as March and Olsen (1995) observe, political order is seen as a matter of choice, as the result of the human reason seeking to build a more rational society. In post-modern thought, a concept of politics based

---

[1] See, among others, Jean François Lyotard (1979); Boaventura de Souza Santos (1995a, 1995b); Stuart Hall (1996).

on individualism and self-interest has recently replaced this democratic optimism. March and Olsen, in spite of using many of the methodological resources of individualism, rebel against this view of democracy:

Ideas of governors pursuing an autonomous public virtue and collective purpose have been subordinated to ideas of negotiation, political coalition, and competition . . . Nevertheless we, in company with many others, believe that individualism and exchange theories of democracy provide incomplete bases for thinking about governance. (March and Olsen 1995: 5–6)

In the same way as for March and Olsen, and unlike in modern conservative thinking, public management reform is supported by a more optimistic view of human nature than that adopted by rational choice: it assumes that politicians and public managers, albeit more interested in their selfish objectives, are also motivated by public interest. Managerial public administration relies on delegation of authority, autonomy of managers, and *a posteriori* control, because it relies on control by results, quasi-markets, and democratic controls, and also because it believes in the possibility of cooperation and in the pursuit of the public interest. It harbours no idyllic vision of human nature, and knows that controls are essential, that self-interest and selfless cooperation are always in unstable balance: without vigilance, not only administrative but also democratic, the balance falls on the side of self-interest. But it holds that, for administration to be public, it needs to be oriented to the public interest. We may have—and indeed do have—some authors that adopt an ultra-liberal view while supporting public management reform. But they are a minority. Reformers believe in the possibility of efficient state action. When certain authors attempt to equate business and public administration under the name of public management reform, they make the conservative mistake of not distinguishing the different logics that, in organizations, govern the private and the public realms. Public management reform derives inspiration from business management, in the decision-making autonomy enjoyed by managers of companies. Nevertheless, the differences between public administration and business administration, derived from the different natures of private and public organizations, need to be clear. There are two basic differences, from which all others derive. First, the business organization has owners and seeks profit, while the public organization belongs to everyone and pursues the public interest. Second, the company is governed or coordinated by the market, which is studied by economic theory, while the state is ruled by politics, which is analysed by political science and law.

Ranson and Stewart's Critique

Among the critics of public management reform, Stewart Ranson and John Stewart deserve special mention. They vigorously insist on the uniqueness of the public domain, which, they do not doubt, cannot be reduced to the principles of private administration. They state, 'In the public domain any notion of management which cannot encompass the recognition of politics and conflict as constitutive of a public organization rather than as an obstacle to it is barren'. In other words, they maintain that the efficiency criterion in the public realm is subordinate to the democratic criterion. For this, it is necessary to envisage a new public administration that fulfils both criteria, while preserving the priority of the latter. However, they do not have a clear idea of what this alternative would be. They perceive acutely that it is necessary to seek an alternative capable of out-performing both the social-democratic or corporative perspective and the neo-liberal approach. In the former, 'a conception of public management reflected a belief that the power of professional expertise, reinforced by the rules of fairness administered by welfare bureaucracies, could deliver the good society'. In the latter, by contrast, the belief is in 'contract management as best suited to deliver alternative purposes of public choice and accountability'. Ranson and Stewart's alternative must respect the fact that 'the rationale of action in the public domain rests upon the organizing principle of public discourse, leading to collective choices based on public consent'. The challenge is 'restoring the public to the polity', to develop a 'learning society', in which public discourse and social learning are dominant (Ranson and Stewart 1994: 110, 15, 153).

My answer to these critics is to fully agree with them. I believe that, in this book, I have been defending a similar approach, which is aligned to Habermasian views of 'communicative action' (Habermas 1981*a*, 1981*b*). However, when they try to define the ongoing historical process, and the seeds or roots of this alternative, Ranson and Stewart are not successful. They identify the conservative character of Thatcherism with public management reform. This is due, to a large extent, to their mistaken identification of consumerism with the notion of 'client-citizen', which is central to managerial public administration. According to them, 'the public in the new polity can be and need only be a customer' and this would be implicit (Ranson and Stewart 1994: 15). For these authors, the consequence of not distinguishing clearly the public field from the private, public from private administration, would be this orientation towards the client, the consumerist heresy, which would reduce the citizen to the status of consumer or client. I shall not discuss the appropriateness of the term again. I would simply comment that, although it is unacceptable to identify public with private administration, this does not mean that it is wrong to view the citizen as a client-citizen. What is wrong is to see citizens as mere clients, and forget their citizenship dimension. But this makes no sense in democracies. To view the citizen as a client-citizen is an advance, not a retrogression, in the consolidation of citizenship. To view the citizen as a client means simply to give him the attention that is his right, to accord him the respect he does not get from the practices of self-centred bureaucratic public administration. The business enterprise views the individual as a client because it is in its interest to do so; government and its bureaucracy view, or should view, the individual as a client because as a citizen he has a right to be viewed as a client. Moreover, the fact that one has rights as a client does not mean that one does not have rights as a citizen, that one is not supposed to take part in political decision-making, be it as a voter in representative democracy or as a member of civil society or the public sphere, in deliberative or participatory democracy.[2] The disparaging of the notion of client-citizen is just a cliché, which overlooks how bureaucratic officials mistreat citizens in classic public administration. Ranson and Stewart (1994: 15) end up casting doubt on some of the central characteristics of public management reform, such as the client-citizen orientation, the formation of quasi-markets, the establishment of contractual relationships between government and agencies, performance indicators, and flexibility in remuneration systems.

Thus, in spite of their beautiful defence of the political uniqueness of the public domain and of public administration, Ranson and Stewart limit themselves to a series of generous recommendations to render public administration more democratic and participatory. I agree with these recommendations, but judge that they lack objectivity to the extent that they do not contain clear definitions of the new institutions and new management tools that would characterize the reform and improve democratic governance. What I have been doing in this book is exactly that: to offer to discussion these institutional and managerial tools.

---

[2] On deliberative democracy, see Cohen (1989); Bohman and Rehg (1997); Elster (1998).

22

The Democratic Constraint

Modern societies seek administrative efficiency and democracy, but conventional wisdom considers them contradictory: a trade-off would exist between the two, if not in old democracies, probably in new ones. This is a false trade-off. Public management reform is an institutional reform involving a set of new institutions, which presuppose the existence of some kind of participatory democracy and, as long as these new institutions become reality, they contribute to democracy's improvement. Public management reform succeeded in more advanced democracies and in a few new democracies. In the former, democracy is probably facilitating new public management, while in the latter it is part of the process of democratic consolidation. Public management reform seeks to increase the quality and efficiency of public services, to enhance the civil service. Political scientists and consultants working in this field tend to understand this in terms of endowing the state organization with improved rationality, concluding that, in making choices, government officials should use economy or efficiency as the major criterion. In this chapter, I first show that public management reform may be successful only in democracies, and second, I discuss and challenge the bureaucratic ideology implicit in the efficiency criterion. Instrumental rationality and the consequent economic criterion are obviously important in capitalist societies, but, in democracies, there is a prior and more important criterion: the democratic constraint. Economists often use the word 'constraint' to mean the limitations that policy-makers face. They speak of a budget constraint, or a balance of payments constraint, and, particularly, of an efficiency constraint. I do not dispute that these exist. I just suggest that policy-makers also face a basic democratic constraint.

A Necessarily Democratic Reform

Public management reform makes no sense outside the democratic framework. While civil service reform took place in advanced countries in the nineteenth century, and thus in semi-authoritarian regimes in which liberal but still non-democratic ideas prevailed, public management reform is occurring only in liberal democracies, like the United States, or in social democracies, like the European countries. While bureaucratic public administration may indulge its self-centred preferences, new public management is necessarily citizen-oriented. Both approaches draw on authority, but whereas for the former hierarchical authority is all, for the latter it is just one of several possibilities that include management by results, social accountability, and managed competition. While classic bureaucracy preaches and practises secrecy, and seeks above all to be as distant as possible from politics, present-day public management is required to be transparent, and public managers are expected to assume their political responsibilities. William Richardson (1997: 13) wrote about the 'unsettled relations between democracy and bureaucracy', due to the 'essentially elitist or hierarchical nature of the rationale constructed by administrative theorists to legitimate power and authority of professional managers'. Public management reform is, among other things, a response to this unsettled question. It views civil servants as an elite sharing with politicians the strategic core of the state, demanding from them, besides technical competence, republican virtues, but this makes sense only when its government officials are fully accountable to a republican democracy, formed by a reasonable number of participatory citizens. Richardson (1997: 60) observes, referring to the United States, that 'it has been a long time since civil servants have been held in high esteem by the general citizenry'. Yet this should not be interpreted as a sign of decay in the American civil service, but as the outcome of the existence of more demanding citizens.

We have already seen that a client-citizen orientation is central for new public management. Government officials, whether politicians or senior civil servants, do not opt for a client-citizen orientation simply because they believe that this is the right thing to do, but because quality and efficiency in the delivery of public service has become a central political issue in modern democracies. Citizens in contemporary democracies are more severe with government officials than they were in the past. They demand more from the public services that are financed with taxes that they pay. For instance, Tony Blair, in the 2001 re-election campaign, focused his message on the pledge to improve the quality of health care, education, transportation, and police. It is not important to know here whether or not he was able to stand by his commitment. The relevant point is that he decided to commit himself in this matter rather than in others because he realized that public management—and its outcome, the delivery of public services—had become a central issue with voters. In Britain, as in most advanced democratic societies, voters continue to vote ideologically, but they also decide according to practical issues such as public-service delivery.

Classical political issues, like freedom, social justice, economic stability, economic growth, and a sensible foreign policy, able to protect the national interest, remain significant, but in a competitive world, in which economic constraints are overwhelming, such questions require specific answers. Given that the fiscal constraint is central and the demand for higher consumption standards is universal, economic development—and all the factors determining it, such as savings and capital accumulation, technological progress, investments in education and health care, and reforms creating adequate institutions—is the obvious response. Bureaucratic reform was one of these economic growth factors to the extent that it was based on the assumption that the rule of law assured civil servants some autonomy in relation to politicians. Yet, to the extent that the bureaucratic ethos is self-centred, it had little to do with the idea of improved democratic governance or of political development that was emerging in advanced democracies. Since the 1980s, however, the resolution of this contradiction has begun in so far as public management reform proved to be not only an economic development tool but also an answer in itself to voters' increasing demands. This is so because public management makes possible a greater quantity and a better quality of public services without increasing public expenditures.

Politicians in modern democracies must offer voters a credible vision of the future; they have to persuade them of the feasibility of their commitments. Thus, they have to demonstrate that they are able to do more with less, to make taxpayers' money produce more value. It is not enough for politicians to be honest and to commit themselves to the majority of the people—to the poor in poor countries, to the middle class in rich ones. At elections politicians, and between elections politicians and senior civil servants, have to explain how they are going to protect the public interest, how they are going to do more with less. Politicians have to tell voters before elections, and public managers have to tell citizens when they come to office, how they will make the best use of scarce tax resources. And, in their speeches and in their practice, they will increasingly have to include public management reform. They may use another expression for such a choice, but the more advanced democracy is, the more politicians at elections, and politicians and senior civil servants in between elections, have to specify the means to achieve the objectives. In modern democracies, the efficient delivery of public services have become a major political issue, and public management reform the best way to respond to it.

Tom Christensen and Per Lægreid (2001: 17) distinguish two concepts of democracy—an 'individually based' and a 'socially centered' democracy, which grossly correspond to the concepts of liberal and social-liberal democracies, and also to a sociological approach to democracy, or to a rational-choice one. They conclude that 'NPM contributes to strengthening the individually based interpretation of democracy and weakening the socially centered one'. This view mixes up the crisis of the social-democratic state that we discussed in the first part of this book, and the neo-liberal wave that begins in the early 1980s with public management reform that also emerged at the same time. In fact, public management reform may be individually centered, as it was for a certain time, to the limit, in New Zealand, or socially oriented, as I believe it was in Brazil. Depending on the ideology of the respective administration, new public management will stress either individual choices and preferences or the sharing of common values and norms, while striving for attending both legitimate demands.

Public management reform may work only in democracy. If an authoritarian regime tries to introduce public management reform, it has a different meaning from the one I am using in this book. First, due to a question of intrinsic inconsistency, public management is not able to use social accountability mechanisms as a major accountability tool. Second, since authoritarianism implies the negation of citizenship, public management may be client-oriented but not client-citizen-oriented. In an authoritarian regime, the client is an object of the reform, while in democracy the client is a citizen, the person to whom the reform is accountable.

The Economic and the Democratic Constraints

Although the initial motivation for today's worldwide public management reform has been economic, the constraint imposed by efficiency is not the only one to guide it. There is also the democratic constraint: if we live in a democracy, the nature and extent of state intervention, and the orientation and character of government policies and reforms, depend on the will of the citizens. The efficiency constraint often seems to be the only relevant one. The logic of using resources rationally became dominant with the emergence of capitalism, playing a fundamental role in contemporary world. The process of globalization imposes an unprecedentedly high degree of competition on countries and businesses enterprises, requiring of their respective states standards of efficiency never previously imagined. However, if this logic, which has the market and management as its main tools, is far from guaranteeing the desired efficient outcomes, it is even further from providing an acceptable criterion for the choice of ends and priorities of government action. An alternative and higher constraint in modern societies is the democratic constraint.

We live nowadays, principally in Europe and in the Americas, in democracies. This was the great political triumph of the twentieth century. In democratic regimes the economic constraint cannot be sovereign. It will always be of utmost importance, but the democratic constraint must prevail when collective action through the state is at stake. It is not enough that decisions are 'rational', that is, that they choose the most adequate means to achieve the desired ends. They also must be democratic, that is, they must respond to voters' demands or decisions.

Each constraint corresponds to a different logic. While instrumental rationality presides over the economic constraint, substantive rationality may eventually arise from public debate and the formation of consensus. The economic constraint cannot be ignored, but there is no reason to believe that economists or managers are the best fitted to take major political decisions. Notwithstanding the permanent claims of bureaucratic intellectuals, a strong argument may be developed to the effect that technicians have no monopoly of reason, that they often make major policy mistakes, and so that the best way to assure rational decisions is to submit them to public debate.

The political constraint is usually overlooked and wrongly understood by public servants, economists, and businessmen. They often suppose that the efficiency constraint is the only legitimate one: it would be the only 'rational' way of making decisions. Thus, they understand political influence on public decisions not as a legitimate constraint but as an obstacle. According to this approach, politicians would always be self-interested populists or worse. Instead of acting according to what is rational, they would be paying lip service to poorly informed voters while pandering to interest-group pressures. Although such critiques may have a point, they contain an elitist and anti-democratic bias. If we choose democracy as the best way to collectively achieve our political objectives—order, freedom, justice, and well-being—the first thing we have to do is to understand the rules of the game. Now, the first rule in democracy is that the citizens have the final word. Reason may and will be used, but it will be used as an argument for a given decision that someone will have to take. This someone will not be the bureaucrat but the politician, elected by and accountable to the people.

Thus, as long as we live in democracies, reforms will proceed only if they have the support of society, of the citizens with the power to vote. Perhaps this difficulty in understanding the democratic constraint is a result of the fact that democracy is historically a recent phenomenon.[1] Even though we can talk of 'Greek democracy', this was entirely different from what we understand today as a genuinely democratic regime. The universal right to vote and be elected is a phenomenon of the twentieth century. Even in the more politically advanced countries, the democratic regime became dominant only in that century. In the nineteenth century one could speak of democracy as the political regime in Britain, the United States, and France, but these were really liberal regimes, not democratic ones, since the right to vote was not universal. These 'democracies' were restricted and male-dominated democracies, in which the right to vote and to be elected was restricted to male property-owners. Only in the twentieth century was democracy generalized as a political regime: in the first half of the century in developed countries, and in the second half in developing countries.

---

[1] Ancient Greek 'democracy' does not fulfil the minimum requirements of the modern concept of democracy.

The political constraint precedes economic ones to the extent that the state precedes the market and conditions administrative decisions. Market and public administration can work well only if state institutions guarantee political legitimacy and property rights. When the political regime is democratic, the political constraint becomes decisive, since it becomes the ultimate source of legitimacy. In Plato's regime of rule by guardians, legitimacy could originate solely in reason. In more realistic authoritarian regimes, divine grace, or just sheer force, could serve to legitimize power. In democracies, however, both forms of legitimacy are unacceptable.

Does this mean that public management reform in democracies is less rational than it is in authoritarian regimes? On the contrary, one of the reasons why democracy became the dominant political regime in the twentieth century is that it assures better decisions than the authoritarian alternative. We may always have an 'enlightened' dictatorship, but today few would count on that. We may also have enlightened technocrats, but there is no reason why they will make more rational decisions than politicians. On the contrary, despite the central concern of public management reform to make technocrats accountable, they are less accountable to voters than politicians; they may bend to special interests more easily than politicians. Bureaucrats, especially the good ones, do not like to hear that. They often look upon politicians with disdain, as businessmen do—often with some reason. Yet they know that there is no alternative to political decision-making. In democracies, the political process may be hindered by self-interest and all the pitfalls of collective action, but, as a trade-off, it allows for more competent decisions as long as politicians may benefit from technical advice and from the learning process involved in extensive public debate.

Public management reform is exclusively consistent with some form of participatory democracy because it depends on the effectiveness of social accountability performed by citizens. Citizens' councils are called to play a major role, not only in making government officials more accountable but also in helping them to make decisions. In the liberal, elitist, model of democracy voters delegate to politicians political power for the term of their mandates. In participatory democracy delegation is limited to the extent that citizens are supposed to participate in the decision-making process. This does not mean that deliberative democracy will be dominant. Modern democracies are still far from that. They have, however, participatory mechanisms to improve the quality of political decisions as well as to check the decisions taken by politicians and managers. If these decisions do not take into consideration the economic constraints, the outcomes will be poor. Yet, in any circumstance, the democratic constraint will prevail as long as decisions are taken by politicians or by managers who will necessarily take into consideration what voters express in elections and in the participatory process.

Autonomy and Morality

If, historically, the democratic constraint is a new factor in determining government action, and shapes public management reform, the moral constraint is an old one. While bureaucratic or civil service reforms presuppose a liberal but still authoritarian regime, public management reform presupposes and encourages moral behaviour on the part of public officials. Liberal ideas guided the transition from patrimonial forms of domination to capitalism, offering an ideological legitimization for the separation between the state's and the prince's patrimony, while requiring the guarantee of property rights and contracts. For this separation to be complete, however, it was necessary to protect the state against nepotism and corruption. Civil service reform had this as its central objective. Through it, a corps of professional functionaries, chosen by merit and endowed with stability and continuity in their careers, would administer the state with the minimum possible autonomy, just applying the law. In this way, bureaucratic public administration would assure ethical conduct. This approach made historical sense because when most civil service reforms took place there were no democratic institutions, such as a free press, an active opposition, or a free and active citizenry, to control politicians' power. Therefore, bureaucrats, relatively free from politics but with little autonomy in decision-making, were used for the protection of the state patrimony against corruption and nepotism. It was up to the bureaucrats to administer 'by the terms of the law', according to the principle of universality of procedures, without using their discretion.

Yet an intrinsic contradiction was involved. At the same time as bureaucrats were assigned a strategic moral role, their autonomy in protecting republican rights was taken away. The guarantee of public morality was the responsibility of the law or, more amply, of an institutional system both liberal and bureaucratic, based on strict and detailed norms and on a system of division of powers, checks and balances, and internal and external auditing. It was also the civic duty of bureaucrats, to the extent that, supported by security of tenure, they would be able to defy corruption and the client-oriented nepotism of the politicians or their bureaucratic bosses. With this, however, the state and the public managers lost an important part of their control over the bureaucrats, who could use their security of tenure to protect from pressures, as well as not to do their jobs, not to cooperate.

Public management reform does not deny the role of the formal control system based on the principle of checks and balances and on a significant role for auditing agencies to avoid corruption and assure reasonable standards of public morality. It does not reject, either, the need for laws and regulations to help guarantee public morality. It just states that the trade-off between autonomy and corruption is less accentuated than is usually supposed. The greater the autonomy is, the more controls are *a posteriori*, by results and by administered competition, the greater may be the risk of corruption. Yet this does not mean that 'the greater will be actual corruption'. Modern societies rely on a range of accountability mechanisms that limit the possibility of corruption on the part of public managers. Their greater autonomy not only results in greater efficiency but also favours higher standards of public morality. The behavioural presupposition behind this statement is that autonomy stimulates respect for ethical values. The moment that the public manager receives managerial autonomy and becomes accountable by results, it becomes much more difficult for his superiors, bureaucrats or politicians, to justify clientelism and the pork barrel. They are formally incompatible with bureaucratic public administration, and substantively in contradiction with autonomy and managerial responsibility. As for sheer corruption, the transparency requirements that are central to public management reform and the range of accountability mechanisms will do their work.

Guillermo O'Donnell (1998) formulated the concept of 'horizontal accountability' and defines it as the existence of state agencies that are empowered, and factually willing and able, to take actions that range from routine oversight to criminal sanctions or impeachment in relation to actions or omissions by other agents or agencies of the state that can be qualified as unlawful. O'Donnell claims that this concept is liberal and republican. Yet, as Marc Plattner (1999: 65) observes, this concept stems primarily from the liberal tradition. In fact, it is a bureaucratic concept that remains valid. The strengthening of democracy and the fight against corruption requires this type of control. Yet, as it is not novel, and as it has the same pitfalls as the agencies to be controlled, I do not believe that the 'introduction' of such controls is the basic remedy that will improve new democracies, as has been suggested.[2] In Brazil, which I know better, such agencies exist and perform their anti-corruption role, but they are also a major source of bureaucratic inefficiency. The novel and interesting form of horizontal accountability is managed competition. The novel and more important form of accountability is upward accountability, that is, social accountability, provided that the organizations of civil society that perform it are backed by the law and by the judiciary power, including the public prosecutor's offices. As Philippe Schimitter (1999: 60) remarks,

The most glaring limitation is to restrict the notion to 'state' agencies and thereby exclude the possibility that horizontal accountability might also be exercised by non-state actors—media organizations, party secretariats, trade union confederations, business peak associations, lawyers' guilds, and mass social movements.

Vertical, horizontal, and classic forms of accountability and the modern, specifically republican form of it—social accountability—are all required to strengthen democracy and build an effective and efficient state. Democracy is

---

[2] See, for instance, Diamond, Plattner, and Schedler (1999).

a condition for the existence of such control, and its improvement a result of it. Yet public management reform does not repose only in controls: it relies also on the engagement of people. Even if we have a cynical view of human nature, such as that it is motivated only by opportunistic interest, it is not difficult to perceive that, when society gives someone autonomy and responsibility, this triggers the motivation to achieve that exists in every human being, and he or she starts to have a mission. He or she tends to become more interested in demonstrating good performance as much on the level of efficiency as morally. On the other hand, if, more realistically, we admit that the people have noble motives, that the public interest also can be a motivating factor for politicians and civil servants, the fact that we have a reasonable degree of autonomy and of corresponding responsibility leads us to pursue social objectives with more zeal.

Conclusion

This book discussed the emergence of the social-liberal and republican state in modern democracies and the role played by public management reform in this historical process. The discussion adopted a historical as well as a deductive and normative method. It borrowed concepts and theories from political science and political theory, from public management and business administration, from sociology and economics. Sometimes it was normative, although, whenever possible, I preferred to identify the tendencies present in the political process. First, I analysed the formation of the modern state and the challenges that it faces today; second, I showed that these challenges, particularly globalization, require a strong and legitimate democratic state; third, I discussed public management reform as one of the strategies to make the modern state strong and effective. In analysing this reform and the consequent new public management, I am part of a global movement that has already achieved major changes and continues to change the way the state is organized and managed. Yet I based my view of such reform, which draws on my own experience in Brazil, on my knowledge of what is taking place in other countries, and on my personal values and convictions.

State capacity depends, most of all, on its democratic institutions. It depends on how vigorous and diversified its civil society is, or its public sphere. It depends on how effective its institutions are in assuring representation and good governance, individual and social justice, the guarantee of property rights and contracts, the protection to political and social rights, the defence of the national interests. These major issues go beyond the objectives of this book. Nevertheless, an effective and efficient democratic state depends also on a good state organization, on an efficient management strategy, and on competent government officials, able to make trade-offs between their legitimate personal objectives and the public interest. These were central themes in this book. As it was central, a third variable on which a strong state depends is its capacity to protect citizens' republican rights or, in other words, its capacity to guard the public patrimony against the permanent rent-seeking efforts coming from all parts of society.

Approaches to public management reform may vary. The one that I adopt is democratic, liberal, social, and republican. I do not see these adjectives as intrinsically contradictory, although the political history of mankind is in many ways the history of the conflict between such ideologies. They may have been conflicting historically, and they may still present major differences, but, provided that they are understood reasonably, they end up being complementary: successive political achievements.

In the framework of public management reform, politicians make the basic decisions, but civil servants, particularly senior civil servants, play a strategic role. Even in the United States, where the fiction of a non-political bureaucracy is strong, Larry Hill (1992: 16) observed that 'public bureaucracy has emerged as a significant political phenomenon in recent decades'. We saw that a managerial response to the increasing complexity of the state requires greater autonomy and accountability on the part of public managers. We may also imagine a response to this problem in a strictly political sense. In the new social-liberal and republican state, the public servant remains non-partisan, but is required to be political and to display republican virtues.

First, he or she will be asked to act more politically. We are used to thinking that the senior public servant is a bureaucrat or an expert. This is correct if we mean that he is a professional possessing technical or organizational knowledge. However, the idea of the neutral bureaucrat, who just executes the law or follows the policies defined by elected politicians—an idea that was central to bureaucratic public administration—no longer makes sense. Among government officials, we distinguish elected politicians from senior civil servants, but all are 'politicians' in the sense that all are policy-makers who directly participate in defining and operating the political institutions. When I say that senior public managers are supposed to be more autonomous, I mean that they are supposed to take decisions, to have some discretionary power—the discretionary power that classical liberalism and bureaucratic (administrative) theory abhors. As their role changes, they will have to substitute the ethics of responsibility for the classic bureaucratic ethics of discipline. They will also be accountable to society, as their role ceases to be formally technical and becomes also political.

In contemporary democracies, elected politicians continue to have the central authority and the major responsibility. They continue to respond to citizens, who have the choice of not re-electing them, through the political process. However, they cannot be the only ones held responsible for the enormous political power involved in the modern state. Elected politicians are engaged in partisan politics and, although committed to the public interest, they are also supposed to represent groups or regional interests. Senior public managers share political power with elected politicians, and are as normatively committed to the public interest as elected politicians are.

Second, in modern democracies government officials—public managers as well as elected politicians—although also looking out for their own interests, are supposed to share republican virtues, to be committed to the general interest and to the protection of the public patrimony. In this way, they will be acting as guardians of republican rights. It is not a pure coincidence that public management reform took shape almost concomitantly with the emergence of such rights. Concern with corruption and nepotism remain present, but they are old issues. Sophisticated forms of capturing public resources received attention. 'Rent-seeking' or the 'privatization of the state' takes on many forms, among which the inefficiency and poor quality of bureaucratic public administration was paramount. It became clear that it is not enough to protect citizens against the abusive power of the state: it is also crucial to protect the state against powerful and greedy individuals. Civil rights and liberalism spoke out for the protection of the individual against the state, republican rights, and the new republicanism claim for the protection of public patrimony against mischievous individuals. Republicanism is as old as ancient Greece and Rome, but in modern social-liberal democracies a new republicanism, a new call for republican virtues in governing the state, became an essential requirement. Republicanism is not here to replace the rule of law, checks and balances, judicial review, parliamentary review, public auditing, and all the other institutions establishing systems of incentives and penalties, or to replace managerial strategies of making the state organization more efficient and more accountable. Republicanism is here to add, not to subtract.

There is a breed of new institutionalism, of a rational choice character, which believes—as classical liberalism and bureaucratic law believed—that what is required to govern is just an effective institutional system of incentives. As Guy Peters observes, 'rational choice version (of institutionalism) takes institutions as givens, or as something that can be easily created, rather than the consequence of an historical and differentiated process'.[1] The belief in the miraculous potentialities of the law and of several forms of auditing—or of 'horizontal accountability'—is common to both new institutionalism and classical liberalism. They share a belief in an independent and neutral civil service enforcing the law, although with different arguments. Classical liberal thinkers and administrative lawyers believed in the law because the main challenge that they faced was to establish the rule of law to protect citizens from an encroaching state. The new institutionalists believe in institutions because they 'discovered it', and expect, through them, to establish the required incentive and penalty system.

Modern republicanism assumes the rule of law, and acknowledges how important institutions and incentive systems are, but is also aware of their limits. For that reason, it relies on government officials endowed with civic values and committed to the public interest. In doing so, republicanism is not being utopian, but just acknowledging that in modern democracies voters

---

[1] Peters (1999: 54). Peters views Terry Moe as a typical sponsor of such an approach.

require politicians and senior civil servants to be endowed with republican virtues. To be sure, not all politicians and civil servants will conform to the political republican demand. Yet I believe that there is a tendency in this direction because, as Robert Dahl (1989) rightly remarks, democracy possesses the capacity of self-improvement. Citizens may sometimes seem uninterested in politics but, as they become more educated, better informed, and realize how much their lives depend on good governance, they tend to learn more about their citizens' rights and obligations. In this book, I may have taken, at times, a normative approach, but I was not dealing with utopian dreams. The social-democratic state, which, in the span of our lives became old, was already democratic; the emerging social-liberal and republican state is even more democratic. Despite all set-backs that are inevitable, in the new state that is emerging in the more advanced democracies, citizens as well as public officials will be required to be actively democratic, liberal, social, and republican.

The developing countries, one way or another, will follow their lead, promoting public management reform and building state capacity in so far as their elites and their people are able to import and adapt the institutions to their realities. The insistence of some developed countries and international organizations, like the World Bank and IMF, on exporting institutions while keeping technologies carefully protected is usually a recipe for failure. Institutions cannot be exported, but developing countries can import them in the same way as they import knowledge and technology—not just accepting the institutions and policies that are prescribed to them if not imposed on them, but building their own state organizations and institutions according to their own values and needs.

Although a citizen of a developing country I wrote this book with the developed ones principally in mind, because the ideas developed here have a strong normative character and because I believe that some of them are relatively new even for these countries. To write a book on building state capacity and reforming public management in the developing countries would require me to lower my aspirations and become involved in casuistic and sub-optimal solutions. My potential critics may claim that the ideas on the state and democracy that I defend here are not realistic for Muslim countries. I definitely do not agree with this view. In the past, and even today, certain versions of Christianity were, or are, as authoritarian as certain versions of Islam. The dominance of these views among the Muslim countries is a consequence of economic and social backwardness rather than of religion.

In writing about the state and democracy in the more advanced societies, I searched for an ideal, but I was permanently concerned with the best achievable, with reforms that are already taking place as a consequence of new historical facts that have made them possible or desirable. Marx's classic statement that societies pose problems to themselves only when they have some capacity to solve them may be viewed as just a debatable historical statement or as a methodological one. I opt for the second alternative. In the normative process of discussing how society should be transformed by men and women, one should always combine desire with prospect, what we want for the good of society with what new facts allow us to realistically aspire to and strive for.

REFERENCES

Aberbach, Joel D., Robert D. Putnam and Bert A. Rockman (1981) *Bureaucrats & Politicians in Western Democracies*. Cambridge, Ma.: Harvard University Press.

Aglietta, Michel (1979) *The Theory of Capitalist Regulation*. London: NLB.

Albert, Michel (1991) *Capitalisme Contre Capitalisme*. Paris: Éditions du Seuil.

Albuquerque, Roberto Cavalcanti de (1995) "Reconstrução e Reforma do Estado". *In* Velloso and Cavalcanti de Albuquerque, eds. (1995): 129–98.

Almond, Gabriel A. and Sidney (1963) *The Civic Culture*. Princeton, NJ: Princeton University Press.

Altvater, Elmar (1991) *The Future of the Market*. London: Verso, 1993. Originally published in German, 1991.

Amin, Ash and Jerzy Hausner (1997) "Interactive Governance and Social Complexity". In Amin, Ash and Jerzy Hausner, eds. (1997): 1–31.

——,——, eds. (1997) *Beyond Market and Hierarchy*. Cheltenham: Elgar Press.

Anderson, Benedict (1991) *Imagined Communities*. London: Verso, second edition, 1991.

Andrade, Regis e L. Jacoud, orgs. (1993) *Estrutura e Organização do Poder Executivo—Volume 2*. Brasília: Escola Nacional de Administração Pública—ENAP.

Arato, Andrew (2002) "Representação e *Accountability*". *Lua Nova*, n°.55/56, 2002: 85–104.

Araujo, Cícero (2000) "República e Democracia". *Lua Nova—Revista de Cultura Política*, n°.51, 2000: 5–30.

—— (2002) "Estado, Revolução e Democracia". University of São Paulo, Department of Political Science, copy.

Arellano, David and Juan Pablo Guerrero (2003) "Stalled Administrative Reforms of the Mexican State". In Ben Ross Schneider and Blanca Heredia, eds. (2003): 151–79.

Armijo, Leslie Elliot (1993) "Trade-offs Implicit in Alternative Roads do Democracy and Markets". In Leslie E. Armijo, ed. (1993).

——, ed. (1993) *Conversations about Democratization and Economic Reform: Working Papers on the Southern California Seminar*. Los Angeles: University of Southern California, School of International Relations, Center for International Studies.

Arquidiocese de São Paulo (1985) *Brasil: Nunca Mais*. São Paulo: Editora Vozes (elaborated under the coordination of Dom Paulo Evaristo Arns.

Aucoin, Peter (1990) "Administrative Reform in Public Management: Paradigms, Principles, Paradoxes and Pendulums". *Governance*, 1990 (3): 114–135.

—— (1995) *The New Public Management in Canada*. Montreal: Institute for Research on Public Policy.

Avritzer, Leonardo (2000) "Teoria Democrática e Deliberação Pública". *Lua Nova—Revista de Cultura Política*, n°.50, 2000: 22–46.

—— (2002a) *Democracy and the Public Space in Latin America*. Princeton: Princeton University Press.

—— (2002b) "Modelos de Deliberação Democrática: Uma Análise do Orçamento Participativo no Brasil". In Souza Santos, ed. (2002: 561–98).

Azevedo, Sérgio de and Luiz Aureliano G. de Andrade (1997) "A Reforma do Estado e a Questão Federalista: Reflexões sobre a Proposta Bresser-Pereira". In Eli Diniz e Sérgio de Azevedo, orgs. (1997) *Reforma do Estado e Democracia*. Brasília: Editora da Universidade de Brasília: 55–82.

Baiocchi, Gianpaolo (2003) "Participation, Activism, and Politics: The Porto Alegre Experiment". In Fung and Wright, eds. (2003: 45–76).

Ball, Terence, James Farr and Russell L. Hanson, eds. (1989) *Political Innovation and Conceptual Change*. Cambridge: Cambridge University Press.

Bardhan, Pranab and John E. Roemer, eds. (1993) *Market Socialism: The Current Debate*. Oxford: Oxford University Press, 1993.

—— and John Roemer (1992) "Market Socialism: a Case for Rejuvenation". *The Journal of Economic Perspectives*, 6(3) Summer 1992: 101–16.

Barnard, Chester (1938) *The Functions of the Executive*. Cambridge, Mass.: Harvard University Press.

Barnet, Richard J. and Ronald E. Müller (1974) *Global Reach*. New York: Simon and Schuster.

Barreto, Maria Inês (1999) "As Organizações Sociais na Reforma do Estado Brasileiro". In Bresser-Pereira e Cunill Grau, eds. (1998): 107–50.

Barry, Brian (1978) *Sociologists, Economists and Democracy*. Chicago, Ill: The University of Chicago Press.

Barzelay, Michael (1992) *Breaking Through Bureaucracy*. Berkeley: University of California Press.

—— (2001) *New Public Management*. Berkeley: University of California Press.

Bassanini, Franco (2000) "Government Reform in Italy". Paper presented to the Vth CLAD's International Congress, Santo Domingo, 24–27 October, 2000.

Bauman, Zygmunt (2003) "A Sociedade Líquida". Interview to Maria Lucia Palhares-Buke in *Folha de S. Paulo—Mais!*, October 19, 2003: 4–9.

Beetham, D. (1987) *Bureaucracy*. Milton Keynes: Open University Press (quoted in Ranson and Stewart, 1994.

Berger, Peter L. (1986) *The Capitalist Revolution*. New York: Basic Books.

—— and Samuel P. Huntington, eds. (2002) *Many Globalizations*. Oxford: Oxford University Press.

Berlin, Isaiah (1958) "Two Concepts of Liberty". In Isaiah Berlin (1969) *Four Essays on Liberty*. Oxford: Oxford University Press: 118–72. Originally published in 1958.

Bignotto, Newton (2000) "Humanismo Cívico Hoje". In Newton Bignotto, org. (2000: 49–70.

—— (2001) *Origens do Republicanismo Moderno*. Belo Horizonte: Editora UFMG.

—— Org. (2000) *Pensar a República*. Belo Horizonte: Editora UFMG.

Bishop, Matthew, John Kay and Colin Mayer, eds. (1995) *The Regulatory Challenge*. Oxford: Oxford University Press.

Bobbio, Norberto (1984) *The Future of Democracy*. Minneapolis: University of Minnesota Press, 1987. (Original Italian edition, 1984).

—— (1985) *Democracy and Dictatorship*. Cambridge: Polity Press, 1989. Originally published in Italian as *Stato, Governo, Società*, 1985.

—— (1988) *Liberalismo e Democracia*. São Paulo: Editora Brasiliense.

—— (1990) *Profilo Ideologico del '900*. Milão: Gazanti.

—— (1992) *L'Età dei Diritti*. Turin: Einaudi.

—— (1993) "Bobbio Defende Compromisso entre Liberalismo e Socialismo" (1993). Norberto Bobbio's interview to L. C. Bresser-Pereira. *Folha de S. Paulo, Mais!*, 5 de dezembro, 1993. Republished in Adriano Schwartz, ed. (2003) *Memórias do Presente*. São Paulo: Publifolhas: 222–32.

—— and Maurizio Viroli (2001) *Dialogo Intorno alla Repubblica*. Roma: Editori Laterza.

Bock, Gisela, Quentin Skinner & Maurizio Viroli, eds. (1990). *Machiavelli and Republicanism: Ideas in Context*. Cambridge: Cambridge University Press.

Bohman, James and William Rehg, eds. (1997) *Essays on Reason and Politics: Deliberative Democracy*. Cambridge, Ma.: The MIT Press.

Borcherding, Thomas E. (1985) "The Causes of Government Expenditure Growth: a Survey of U.S. Evidence", *Journal of Public Economics*, vol.28, no.3, December 1985: 359–82.

Bourdieu, Pierre (1989) *La Noblesse d'État*. Paris: Les Éditions de Minuit.

Boyé, Michel and Gerard Ropert (1994) *Gérer les Compétences dans les Services Publics*. Paris: Les Éditions d'Organization.

Boyer, Robert (1990) *The Regulation School: A Critical Introduction*. New York: Columbia University Press.

Bresser-Pereira, Luiz Carlos (1978) *O Colapso de uma Aliança de Classes*. São Paulo: Editora Brasiliense.

—— (1981) *A Sociedade Estatal e a Tecnoburocracia*. São Paulo: Editora Brasiliense.

—— (1984) *Development and Crisis in Brazil: 1930–1983*. Boulder: Westview Press, 1984.

—— (1985) *Pactos Políticos: Do Populismo à Redemocratização*. São Paulo: Editora Brasiliense.

—— (1986) *Lucro, Acumulação e Crise*. São Paulo: Editora Brasiliense.

—— (1988) "Economic Reforms and Cycles of State Intervention". *World Development*, 21(8) August 1993: 1337–1353. Originally published in Portuguese, 1988.

—— (1993) "Economic Reforms and Economic Growth: Efficiency and Politics in Latin America". Chapter 1 of Luiz Carlos Bresser-Pereira, José María Maravall and Adam Przeworski (1993) *Economic Reforms in New Democracies*. Cambridge: Cambridge University Press: 15–76.

—— (1996) *Economic Crisis and State Reform in Brazil*. Boulder, Co: Lynne Rienner Publishers.

—— (1997) "Managerial Public Administration: Strategy and Structure for a New State". *Journal of Post-Keynesian Economics*, 20(1) Fall, 1997: 7–23.

—— (1998a) "Reform of the State in the 90s: Logic and Control Mechanisms". *In* Leonardo Burlamaqui, Ana Célia Castro and Ha-Joon Chang, eds. (2000: 175–219). Originally published in Portuguese, 1998.

—— (1998b) *Reforma do Estado para a Cidadania*. São Paulo: Editora 34.

—— (1999) "From Bureaucratic to Managerial Public Administration". In Bresser-Pereira and Spink, eds. (1999): 115–46.

—— (2001a) "New Public Management Reform: Now in the Latin American Agenda, and Yet . . . " *International Journal of Political Studies*, n°.3, September 2001: 143–66.

—— (2001b) "The New Left Viewed from the South". *In* Anthony Giddens, ed. (2001): 258–371.

Bresser-Pereira, Luiz Carlos (2001*c*) "Do Estado Patrimonial ao Gerencial". In Paulo Sérgio Pinheiro, Ignacy Sachs e Jorge Wilheim, orgs. (2001) *Brasil: Um Século de Transformações*. São Paulo: Companhia das Letras: 222–59. (2001*d*) "Self-Interest and Incompetence". *Journal of Post Keynesian Economics* 23(3), Spring 2001: 363–373.

—— (2002*a*) "Citizenship and *Res Publica*: The Emergence of Republican Rights". *Citizenship Studies*, 6(2) 2002: 145–64.

—— (2002*b*) "Latin America's Quasi-Stagnation". *In* Paul Davidson, ed. (2002) *A Post Keynesian Perspective on 21st Century Economic Problems*. Cheltenham: Edward Elgar Press: 1–28.

—— (2002*c*) "After Balance of Powers Diplomacy, Globalization's Politics". *In* Eric Hershberg and Kevin W. Moore. eds., *Terrorism and the International Order: Global Perspectives on September 11 and its Aftermath*. New York: The New Press, 2002: 109–30.

—— (2003*a*) "The 1995 Public Management Reform in Brazil: Reflections of a Reformer". *In* Schneider and Heredia, eds. (2003) *Reinventing Leviathan*. Miami: North-South Center Press, 2002: 89–111.

—— (2003*b*) "Economics' Two Methods". Paper presented at the European Association for Evolutionary Political Economy XVth Annual Conference, Maastricht, November 7–10, 2003. Available at www.bresserpereira.org.br.

—— (2003*c*) "O Gigante Fora do Tempo: A Guerra do Iraque e o Sistema Global", *Política Externa*, 12(1), Junho/Julho/Agosto de 2003: 43–62.

—— and Nuria Cunill Grau (1998) "Entre el Mercado y el Estado: Lo Público No-Estatal". *In* Bresser-Pereira e Cunill Grau, eds. (1998): Buenos Aires: Editorial Paidos: 1–32.

——, eds. (1998) *Lo Público No-Estatal en la Reforma del Estado*. Buenos Aires: Editorial Paidos.

——, —— and Peter Spink, eds. (1999) *Reforming the State*. Boulder, Co.: Lynne Rienner Publishers, 1999.

——, —— and Yoshiaki Nakano (2002) "Economic Growth with Foreign Savings?". Paper presented to the Seventh International Post Keynesian Workshop, "Fighting Recession in a Globalized World: Problems of Developed and Developing Countries". Kansas City, Missouri, June 28–July 3, 2002. Available at www. bresserpereira.org.br.

——, José María Maravall and Adam Przeworski (1993) *Economic Reforms in New Democracies*. Cambridge: Cambridge University Press.

Brewer, John (1988) *The Sinews of Power*. Cambridge, MA: Harvard University Press.

Breyer, Stephen (1982) *Regulation and Reform*. Cambridge, MA: Harvard University Press.

Briceño Reyes, Dimitri R. (2000) "Los Efectos de la Descentralización desde una Perspectiva Regional". Paper presented to the Vth International Congress of CLAD, Dominican Republic, October 2000.

Brinkley, Alan (1998) *Liberalism and Its Discontents*. Cambridge, MA: Harvard University Press.

Brunhes, Bernard (2003) "Modernizar l'État, Modernizar le Service Public". *Futuribles*, n°.287, June 2003: 29–40.

Buchanan, James and Gordon Tullock (1962) *The Cauculus of Consent*. Ann Arbor: University of Michigan Press.

Burki, Shahid J., Guillermo Perry and William Dillinger (1999) *Beyond the Center: Decentralizing the State*. Washington, D.C.: The World Bank, World Bank Latin American and Caribbean Studies, 1999.

Burlamaqui, Leonardo, Ana Célia Castro and Ha-Joon Chang, eds. (2000) *Institutions and the Role of the State*. Cheltenham: Edward Elgar.

Caiden, Gerald E. (1991*a*) *Administrative Reform Come to Age*. Berlin: De Gruyter.

—— (1991*b*) "What is Really Public Maladministration?". *Public Administration Review*, 51(6) November 1991: 486–92.

Calogero, Guido (1968) *Le Regole della Democrazia e le Ragioni del Socialismo*. Roma: Edizioni dell'Ateneo.

Canitrot, Adolfo (1975) "A Experiência Populista de Redistribuição de Renda". In Bresser-Pereira, org. (1991) *Populismo Econômico*. São Paulo: Nobel, 1991. Originally published in 1975: 11–36.

Cardia, Nancy (1994) "Percepção dos Direitos Humanos: Ausência de Cidadania e a Exclusão Moral". In Mary Jane Paris Spink, ed. (1994).

Cardoso de Oliveira, Luís (1996) "Entre o Justo e o Solidário: Os Dilemas dos Direitos de Cidadania no Brasil e nos EUA". *Revista Brasileira de Ciências Sociais*, 31(11) junho 1996: 67–81.

Cardoso, Fernando Henrique and Luciano Martins, eds. (1994) *O Brasil e as Tendências Econômicas e Políticas Contemporâneas*. Anais do seminário com esse título realizado em Brasília, 2–3 December, 1994. Brasília: Fundação Alexandre de Gusmão, 1995.

Cardoso, Ruth (1994) "A Trajetória dos Movimentos Sociais". In Evelina Dagnino, ed. (1994).

Castells, Manuel (1994) "Comentário no Seminário *O Brasil e as Tendências Econômicas e Políticas Contemporâneas*". *In* Cardoso, Fernando Henrique and Luciano Martins, eds. (1994).

—— (1999) "Para o Estado-Rede: Globalização Econômica e Instituições Políticas na Era da Informação". *In* Jorge Wilheim, Lourdes Sola and Luiz Carlos Bresser-Pereira, eds. (1999: 147–71).

Centeno, Miguel Ángel (1997) *Democracy within Reason*. Second Edition. University Park: The Pennsylvania University Press.

CEPAD (2000) "Comisión de Desarrollo Económico Local, CODEL: El Principio del Desarrollo". Santa Cruz de la Sierra: CEPAD—Centro para la Participación y el Desarrollo Humano Sostenible, 2000.

Chandler, Alfred D. (1962) *Strategy and Structure*. Massachusetts: The MIT Press, 1986. First edition, 1962.

Cheema, G. Shabbir and Monir Tabet (2000) "Decentralized Governance for Human Development". In Ramesh Thakur and Edward Newman, eds. (2000): 261–95.

Chevalier, Jacques (1996) "Public Administration in Statist France". *Public Management Review*, 56(1) January 1996.

Christensen, Tom and Per Lægreid (2000) "New Public Management—Puzzles of Democracy and Influence of Citizens". Paper presented at the IPSA World Congress, Quebec, August 1–6 2000, SOG-panel "Management, Democracy and Citizens' Rights". Copy.

Christensen, Tom, Per Lægreid and Lois. R. Wise (2001) "Assessing Public Management Reform in Norway, Sweden and the United States of America". *International Journal of Political Studies*, n°.3, September 2001: 41–70.

CLAD (1998) *A New Public Management for Latin America*. Caracas: CLAD—Centro Latinoamericano de Administración para el Desarrollo, 1998.

CLAD's Scientific Council, ed. (2000) *La Responsabilización en la Nueva Gestión Pública Latinoamericana*. Buenos Aires and Caracas: EUDEBA and Centro Latinoamericano de Administración para el Desarrollo—CLAD.

Clarke, John and Janet Newman (1997) *The Managerial State*. London: Sage Publications.

Clarke, Sharon Gewirtz and Eugene McLaughlin, eds. (2000) *New Managerialism, New Welfare?* London: Sage Publications.

Coase, Ronald (1937) "The Nature of the Firm". *Economica*, n°.4, 1937: 386–405.

—— (1988) *The Firm, the Market, and the Law*. Chicago: Chicago University Press.

Cohen, Jean L. and Andrew Arato (1992) *Civil Society and Political Theory*. Cambridge, Ma.: The MIT Press.

Cohen, Joshua (1989) "Deliberation and Democratic Legitimacy". In James Bohman and William Rehg, eds. (1997): 67–92. Paper originally published in 1989.

Coleman, James (1990) *Foundations of Social Theory*. Cambridge, MA: Harvard University Press.

Constant, Benjamin (1814) *De L'Esprit de Conquête et de l'Usurpation*. Originally published in 1814. In Benjamin Constant (1997) *Écrits Politiques*. Paris: Gallimard.

Copp, David, Jean Hampton, and John E. Roemer, eds. (1993) *The Idea of Democracy*. Cambridge: Cambridge University Press.

Costa, Sérgio (2002) *As Cores de Ercília*. Belo Horizonte: Editora UFMG.

Coutinho, Carlos Nelson (1980) *A Democracia como Valor Universal*. São Paulo: Livraria Editora Ciências Humanas.

Crozier, Michel (1996) "The Transition from the Bureaucratic Paradigm to a Public Management Culture". Caracas: Consejo Latinoamericano de Administración para el Desarrollo, Document n°.3, November 1996. Paper presented to CLAD's First Interamerican Congress, Rio de Janeiro, October 1996.

—— and Bruno Tilliette (1995) *La Crise de L'Intelligence*. Paris: InterEditions.

Cruz, Sebastião and C. Velasco (1998) "Alguns Argumentos sobre Reformas para o Mercado". *Lua Nova—Revista de Cultura e Política*, n°.45, 1998: 5–27.

Cunill Grau, Nuria (1995) "La Rearticulación de las Relaciones Estado-Sociedad: en Busqueda de Nuevos Sentidos". *Revista del CLAD Reforma y Democracia*, n°.4, July 1995: 25–58.

—— (1997) *Repensando lo Público a través de la Sociedad*. Caracas: Editorial Nueva Sociedad and Centro Latinoamericano de Administración para el Desarrollo.

—— (2000) "Responsabilización por el Control Social". *In* CLAD'S Scientific Council, ed. (2000): 269–328.

Dagger, Richard (1997) *Civic Virtues*. Oxford: Oxford University Press.

Dagnino, Evelina, ed. (1994) *Anos 90: Política e Sociedade no Brasil*. São Paulo: Editora Brasiliense.

—— (2002) *Sociedade Civil e Espaços Públicos no Brasil*. São Paulo: Paz e Terra.

Dahl, Robert A. (1956) *A Preface to Democratic Theory*. Chicago: Chicago University Press.

—— (1961) *Who Governs? Democracy and Power in an American City*. New Haven, CT: Yale University Press.

—— (1971) *Polyarchy*. New Haven, CT: Yale University Press.

—— (1978) "Pluralism Revisited". *Comparative Politics*, 10(2), 1978: 191–203.

—— (1989) *Democracy and its Critics*. New Haven, CT: Yale University Press.

Davidson, Greg (1997) "Managing by Process in Private and Public Organizations: Scientific Management in the Information Revolution". *Journal of Post Keynesian Economics*, 20(1) Fall 1997: 25–45.

—— and Paul Davidson (1996) *Economics for a Civilized Society* (2nd edition), 1996. London: Macmillan.

Delorme, Robert (1995) "An Alternative Theoretical Framework for State-Economy Interaction in Transforming Economies". *Emergo: Journal of Transforming Economies and Societies*. 2(4), Autumn 1995: 05–24.

—— and Kurt Dopfer, eds. (1994) *The Political Economy of Diversity*. Aldershot: Edward Elgar Publishing House and European Association for Evolutionary Political Economy.

Deming, W. Edward (1982) *Quality, Productivity, and Competitive Position*. Cambridge, MA: The MIT Press.

Diamond, Larry, Marc F. Plattner, and Andreas Schedler (1999) "Introduction". In Diamond, Plattner, and Schedler, eds. (1999: 1–12).

—— (1999) *The Self-Restraining State*. Boulder: Lynne Rienner Publishers.

Dimenstein, Gilberto (1990) *A Guerra dos Meninos*. São Paulo: Editora Brasiliense.

—— (1996) *Democracia em Pedaços: Direitos Humanos no Brasil*. São Paulo: Companhia das Letras.

Downs, Anthony (1957) *An Economic Theory of Democracy*. Nova York. Harper & Brothers Publishers.

Dror, Yehezkel (1994) *La Capacidad de Governar: Informe al Club de Roma*. Barcelona: Círculo de Lectores and Galaxia Gutenberg.

—— (1997) "Delta-type Senior Civil Service for the 21st Century". *International Review of Administrative Sciences*, v.63(1), 1997: 7–23.

Drucker, Peter (1954) *The Practice of Management*. New York: Harper & Brothers Publishers.

—— (1964) *Managing for Results*. New York: HarperCollins Publishers.

—— (1995) "Really Reinventing Government". *The Atlantic Monthly*, February 1995: 49–61.

Dunleavy, Patrick and Christopher Hood (1994) "From Old Public Administration to New Public Management". *Public Money and Management*, 14(3) July 1994: 9–17.

Durham, Eunice (1984) "Movimentos Sociais: A Construção da Cidadania". *Novos Estudos Cebrap*, n°.10, October 1984: 24–30.

Dworkin, Ronald (1977) *Taking Rights Seriously*. London: Duckworth.

—— (1985) *A Matter of Principle*. Cambridge, MA: Harvard University Press.

—— (2000) *Sovereign Virtue*. Cambridge, MA: Harvard University Press.

Easton, David (1965) *A Framework for Political Analysis*. Englewood Cliffs: Prentice-Hall.

Elgie, Robert (1995) *Political Leadership in Liberal Democracies*. London: Macmillan.

Elias, Norberto (1994) *The Civilizing Process*. Oxford: Blackwell Publishers.

Elster, Jon (1998) "A Plea for Mechanisms". In Peter Hedström and Richard Swedberg, eds. (1998): 45–73.

—— ed. (1998) *Deliberative Democracy*. Cambridge: Cambridge University Press.

Encyclopædia Britannica, The New (1993) "Taxation". Chicago: *The New Encyclopædia Britannica, Macropædia*, vol.28: 397–421.

Epstein, David and Sharyn O'Halloran (1999) *Delegating Powers*. Cambridge: Cambridge University Press.

Esping-Andersen, Gøsta (1990) *The Three Worlds of Welfare Capitalism*. Princeton, NJ: Princeton University Press.

Etzioni, Amitai (1964) *Modern Organizations*. Englewood Cliffs: Prentice-Hall.

Evans, Peter (1979) *The Alliance of Multinational, State and Local Capital in Brazil*. New Jersey: Princeton University Press.

—— (1989) "Predatory, Developmental and other Apparatuses". *Sociological Forum*, n°.4, December 1989: 561–87.

—— (1995) *Embedded Autonomy*. Princeton, NJ: Princeton University Press.

——, D. Rueschmeyer, and Theda Skocpcol (1985) *Bringing the State Back In*. Cambridge: Cambridge University Press.

Fairbrother, Peter (1994) *Politics and the State as Employer*. London: Mansell.

Falconi Campos, Vicente (1992) *TQC—Controle de Qualidade Total (No Estilo Japonês*. Belo Horizonte: Fundação Christiano Ottoni da Universidade Federal de Minas Gerais.

Faoro, Raymundo (1975) *Os Donos do Poder*, second edition. Porto Alegre/São Paulo: Editora Globo e Editora da Universidade de São Paulo, 1975.

Federal Reserve Bank of Atlanta (2000) *Sustainable Public Sector Finance in Latin America*. Atlanta: Research Department, Federal Reserve Bank of Atlanta.

Ferlie, Ewan, Andrew Pettigrew, Lynn Ashburner and Louise Fitzgerald (1996) *The New Public Management in Action*. Oxford: Oxford University Press.

Finer, S. E. (1997) *The History of Government from the Earliest Times*. Oxford: Oxford University Press.

Finot, Ivan (1999) "Elementos para una Reorientación de las Políticas de Descentralización y Participación en América Latina". *Revista del CLAD Reforma y Democracia*, n°.15, October 1999: 71–110.

Forte, F. and Peacock, A., ed. (1985) *Public Expenditure and Government Growth*. Oxford: Basil Blackwell.

Fortin, Yvonne (1996) "Autonomy, Responsibility and Control—The Case of Central Government Agencies in Sweden". *In* OECD/PUMA (1996) *Performance Management in Government: Contemporary Illustrations*.

Fourel, Christophe (2001) "Le Gout des Autres et le Capital Social: Les Engeux de la Nouvelle Économie Sociale". *In* Christophe Fourel, ed. (2001): 7–27.

——, ed. (2001) *La Nouvelle Économie Sociale*. Paris: Éditions La Découverte e Syros.

Franco, Augusto (2002) "O Primeiro Passo de uma Reforma do Terceiro Setor". In Nassuno and Kamada, eds. (2002): 61–7.

Franz, Howard (1996) "The New Public Management and the New Political Economy: Missing Pieces in Each Other's Puzzles". Paper presented at the Conference "New Public Management in International Perspective", University of St. Gallen, Switzerland, July 1996. In International Public Management Network (www.willamette.org/ipmn/research/conference/index.html.

Frederickson, George H. and Jocelyn M. Johnston, eds. (1999) *Public Management Reform and Innovation*. Tuscaloosa: The University of Indiana Press.

Frederickson, H. George (1996) "Comparing the Reinventing Government Movement with the New Public Administration". *Public Administration Review*, 56(3) May/June 1996: 263–270.

Friedman, Milton (1953) "The Methodology of Positive Economics". In Milton Friedman, *Essays in Positive Economics*. Chicago: University of Chicago Press.

—— (1962) *Capitalism and Freedom*. Chicago: The University of Chicago Press.

Friedman, Thomas (2000) *The Lexus and the Olive Tree*. Second edition. New York: Random House.

Fung, Archon and Erik Olin Wright, eds. (2003) *Deepening Democracy*. London: Verso.

Gaetani, Francisco (1998) "A Reforma do Estado no Contexto Latino-Americano: Comentários sobre Alguns Impasses e Possíveis Desdobramentos". *Revista do Serviço Público*, 49(2) April 1998: 85–104.

Gerschenkron, Alexander N. (1962) *Economic Backwardness in Historical Perspective*. Cambridge, Mass.: Harvard University Press.

Ghio, José María e Sebastián Echemendy (1998) "Fugindo do Perigo: A Política de Reforma Administrativa na Argentina de Menem". *Revista do Serviço Público*, 49(2) abril 1998: 33–55.

Giddens, Anthony, ed. (2001) *The Global Third Way Debate*. Cambridge: Polity Press.

Glastris, Paul (1994) "A Reinventing Government Triumph". *The New Republic*, 21.11.94

Goodin, Robert E. and Julian Le Grand (1987) "Introduction". In Goodin, Robert E. and Julian Le Grand, eds. (1987): 3–16.

——, ——, eds. (1987) *Not Only the Poor: The Middle Classes and the Welfare State*. London: Allen & Unwin.

——., Bruce Headey, Ruud Muffels and Henk-Jan Dirven (1999) *The Real Worlds of Welfare Capitalism*. Cambridge: Cambridge University Press.

Gore, Al (1993) *From Red Tape do Results: Creating a Government that Works Better and Costs Less*. Washington, DC: Presidency of the United States, *National Performance Review*, September 1993.

—— (1995) *Putting Customers First '95*. Washington, DC: United States Presidency, *National Performance Review*, September 1995.

Gouldner, Alvin W. (1945) *Patterns of Industrial Bureaucracy*. Glencoe, Il.: The Free Press.

Gouvêa, Gilda P. (1994) *Burocracia e Elites Dominantes do País*. São Paulo: Paulicéia.

Gray, John (1993) *Beyond the New Right*. London: Routledge

Greider, William (1997) *One World, Ready or Not*. New York: Simon & Schuster.

Gruber, Judith E. (1987) *Controlling Bureaucracies*. Berkeley: University of California Press.

Guerreiro Ramos, Alberto (1981) *A Nova Ciência das Organizações*. Rio de Janeiro: Editora da Fundação Getúlio Vargas.

Gustafsson, Lennart. (1995) "Participación y Racionalización en el Área de Recursos Humanos: Reforma de la Gestión y el Empleo Público en Suecia", *GAPP*, n°.2. enero–Abril 1995: 53–61.

Habermas, Jürgen (1961) *Mudança Estrutural da Esfera Pública*. Rio de Janeiro: Tempo Brasileiro, 1984. Originally published in German, 1961.

Habermas, Jürgen (1981*a*) *The Theory of Communicative Action. Volume I: Reason and Rationalization of Society.* Boston: Beacon Press, 1984. Originally published in German, 1981.

—— (1981*b*) *The Theory of Communicative Action. Volume II: Lifeworld and System—A Critique of Functionalist Reason.* Boston: Beacon Press, 1987. Originally published in German, 1981.

—— (1992) *Between Facts and Norms.* Cambridge, Ma.: The MIT Press, 1996. Originally published in German, 1992.

Haggard, Stephan (1990) *Pathways from the Periphery: The Politics of Growth in the Newly Industrializing Countries.* Ithaca: Cornell University Press.

Hall, John A. ed. (1986) *States in History.* Oxford: Basil Blackwell.

Hall, Peter A. and David Soskice (2001) "An Introduction to Varieties of Capitalism". *In* Hall and Soskice, eds. (2001: 1–70).

——, —— and ——, eds. (2001) *Varieties of Capitalism.* Oxford: Oxford University Press.

Hall, Stuart (1996) "The Question of Cultural Identity". *In* Stuart Hall et al., eds. (1996): 595–634.

——, David Held, Don Hub and Kenneth Thompson, eds. (1996) *Modernity.* Oxford: Blackwell Publishers.

Halligan, John (1991) "Función Pública y Reforma Administrativa en Australia". *Revista Internacional de Ciencias Administrativas*, Madrid: v. 57, n°.3, septiembre 1991.

—— (2001) "Public Sector Modernization in Australia and New Zealand—An Evaluative Perspective". *International Journal of Political Studies*, n°.3. September 2001: 71–92.

Hammer, Michael (1990) "Reengineering Work: Don't Automate, Obliterate". *Harvard Business Review* 68(4) July 1990: 104–13.

—— and James Champy (1993) *Reengineering the Corporation.* New York: HarperCollins Publishers.

—— and —— (1995) *Reengineering Management.* New York: HarperCollins Publishers.

Hampton, Jean (1993) "The Moral Commitments of Liberalism". *In* Copp, Hampton, and Roemer, eds. (1993: 292–313)

Hanifan, L. J. (1920) *The Community Center.* Boston: Burdett.

Hayek, Friedrich A. (1935) *Collectivist Economic Planning: Critical Studies in the Possibilities of Socialism.* London: George Routledge & Sons.

—— (1944) *The Road to Serfdom.* Chicago, Ill: The University of Chicago Press.

—— (1948) *Individualism and Economic Order.* Chicago, Ill: The University of Chicago Press.

Hedström, Peter and Richard Swedberg, eds. (1998) *Social Mechanisms.* Cambridge: Cambridge University Press.

Held, David (1996) *Models of Democracy.* Second edition. Stanford, Cal.: Stanford University Press.

—— and Anthony McGrew (2002) "Introduction". In Held and McGrew, eds. (2002: 1–25).

—— and —— eds. (2002) *Governing Globalization.* Cambridge: Polity Press.

Heredia, Blanca and Ben Ross Schneider (2003) "The Political Economy of Administrative Reform in Developing Countries". In Schneider and Heredia, eds. (2003: 01–29).

Hershberg, Eric and Kevin W. Moore. eds. (2002) *Terrorism and the International Order: Global Perspectives on September 11 and its Aftermath.* New York: The New Press, 2002.

Hill, Larry B. (1992) "Public Bureaucracy and the American State". In Larry B. Hill, ed. (1992): 1–14.

—— ed. (1992) *The State of Public Bureaucracy*. Armonk: M. E. Sharpe.

Hirschman, Albert O. (1970) *Exit, Voice, and Loyalty*. Cambridge, MA: Harvard University Press.

Holmes, Stephen (1993) *The Anatomy of Antiliberalism*. Cambridge, MA: Harvard University Press.

—— and Cass. R. Sunstein (1999) *The Cost of Rights*. New York: W. W. Norton.

Hood, Christopher (1991) "A Public Management for All Seasons?", *Public Administration*, 69(1) Spring 1991: 3–19.

Huber, Evelyne, ed. (2002) *Models of Capitalism: Lessons for Latin America*. Pennsylvania: Penn State University Press.

Huntington, Samuel P. (1991) *The Third Wave*. Norman: University of Oklahoma Press.

Ihering, Rudolf Von (1872) *A Luta pelo Direito*. Rio de Janeiro: Editora Liber Juris, 1987. First German Edition, 1872.

Ingraham, Patricia and Vernon Dale Jones (1999) "The Pain of Organizational Change: Managing Reinvention". In Frederickson and Johnston, eds. (1999): 211–29.

——, J. Thompson and P. Sanders (1998) "Introduction". *In* Ingraham, Thompson and Sanders, eds. (1998) *Transforming Government: Lessons from the Reinventing Laboratories*. San Francisco: Josey-Boss.

Instituto de Estudos Políticos (1997) "Os Formadores de Opinião no País e a Reforma do Estado". Brasilia: Instituto Brasileiro de Estudos Políticos, February 1997.

Jacoby, Henry (1969) *La Burocratización del Mundo*. Mexico: Siglo Veintiuno, 1972. First German edition, 1969.

Janine Ribeiro, Renato (1994) "A Política como Espetáculo". In Evelina Dagnino, ed. (1994).

Jaquette, Jane S. (1993) "Some Thoughts on Sequencing". In Leslie E. Armijo, ed. (1993).

Jelin, Elisabeth and Eric Hershberg, 'Introduction to Constructing Democracy' (1996. In Elisabeth Jelin and Eric Hershberg, eds. (1996): 1–12.

——, —— and, eds. *Constructing Democracy* (1996). Boulder, Co.: Westview Press.

Jessop, Bob (1993) "Towards a Schumpeterian Work Fare State?". *Studies in Political Economy*, n°.40, Spring 1993: 7–39.

—— (1994) "Changing Forms and Functions of the State in an Era of Globalization and Regionalization". *In* Robert Delorme and Kurt Dopfer, eds. (1994): 102–125.

Jordan, Bill (1996) *A Theory of Poverty and Social Exclusion*. Cambridge: Polity Press.

Kaboolian, Linda (1999) "Dialogue between Advocates and Executive Agencies". In Frederickson and Johnston, eds. (1999): 312–28.

Kellam, Susan (1995) "Reinventing Government". *Congressional Quarterly Researcher*, 5(7) February 1995.

Kettl, Donald F. (1994) *Reinventing Government? Appraising the National Performance Review*. Washington: The Brookings Institution, Center for Public Management, August 1994.

—— (2000) *The Global Public Management Revolution*. Washington, D.C.: Brookings Institution Press.

—— and John Dilulio Jr (1994) *Inside the Reinvention Machine: Appraising Governmental Reform*. Washington, DC: The Brookings Institution, Center for Public Management.

——, —— (1995) *Cutting Government*. Washington, DC: The Brookings Institution, Center for Public Management.

Kettl, Donald F. and H. Brinton Milward, eds. (1996) *The State of Public Management*. Baltimore: Johns Hopkins University Press.

Khademian, Anne M. (1995) "Reinventing a Government Corporation: Professional Priorities and a Clear Bottom Line". *Public Administration Review*, 55(1) January 1995: 17–28.

Kliksberg, Bernardo (1994) "The 'Necessary State': An Agenda for Discussion". *International Review of Administrative Sciences*, n°.60, 1994: 7–58.

—— (1997) "Repensando el Estado para el Desarrollo Social: Más Allá de Convencionalismos y Dogmas". *Revista del CLAD Reforma y Democracia*, n°.8, 1997: 121–62.

Kooiman, Jan and Kjell A. Eliassen (1987) "Public Management in Europe". *In* Kooiman and Eliassen, eds. (1987) *Managing the Public Sector in Europe*. London: Sage (1987).

Kozak, David C. (1988) "The Bureaucratic Politics Approach: The Evolution of the Paradigm". In Kozak and Keagle, eds. (1988: 2–15).

—— and James M. Keagle, eds. (1988) *Bureaucratic Politics and National Security*. Boulder, Co.: Lynne Rienner Publishers.

Krislov, Samuel and David H. Rosenbloom (1981) *Representative Bureaucracy and the American Political System*. New York: Praeger Publishers.

Krueger, Anne (1974) "The Political Economy of the Rent-seeking Society". *American Economic Review* 64(3), June 1974: 291–303.

Lane, Jan-Erik, (1985) "Public-Policy or Market? The Demarcation Problem". In Jan-Erik Lane, ed. (1985): 3–52.

—— (2000) *New Public Management*. London: Routledge.

——, ed. (1985) *State and Market: The Politics of Public and Private*. London: Sage Publications.

Lange, Oskar (1936–37) "On the Economic Theory of Socialism". *Review of Economic Studies* 4(1): 53–71; 4(2): 123–42.

—— and F. M. Taylor (1938) *On the Economic Theory of Socialism*. Minneapolis: Minnesota University Press.

Latour, Bruno (2002) *La Fabrique du Droit*. Paris: La Découverte.

Levy, Evelyn (1997) Democracia nas Cidades Globais. São Paulo: Studio Nobel.

—— (1998) "Controle Social e Controle de Resultados: Um Balanço dos Argumentos e da Experiência Recente". *In* Bresser-Pereira and Cunill Grau", eds. (1998) 387–403.

—— (2002) "O Fortalecimento Institucional do Núcleo Estratégico". *In* Nassuno and Kamada, eds. (2002): 37–46.

Lilla, Mark, Ronald Dworkin and Robert B. Silvers, eds. (2001) *The Legacy of Isaiah Berlin*. New York: New York Review of Books.

Lima Jr., Olavo Brasil de (1998) "As Reformas Administrativas no Brasil: Modelos, Sucessos e Fracassos". *Revista do Serviço Público*, 49(2) April 1998: 5–31.

Lipietz, Alain (2000) *Pour le Tiers Secteur*. Paris: La Documentation Française/Éditions La Découverte.

Lipsky, Michael (1980) *Street Level Bureaucracy*. New York: Russell Sage Foundation.

Locke, John (1690) *Second Treatise of Government*. Cambridge: Hackett Publishing Co., 1980. Originally published in 1690.

Locke, Richard M. and Lucio Baccaro (1996) "Learning from Past Mistakes? Recent Reforms in Italian Industrial Relations". *Industrial Relations Journal*, 27(4), 1996: 275–303.

Löffler, Elke (1996) *The Modernization of the Public Sector in an International Comparative Perspective: Concepts and Methods.* Speyer: Forschungsinstitut für Offentliche Werwaltung, Forschungsberichte, n°.151, 1996.

—— (1997) *The Modernization of the Public Sector in an International Comparative Perspective: Implementation Strategies in Germany, Great Britain and United States.* Speyer: Forschungsinstitut für Offentliche Werwaltung, Forschungsberichte, n°.174, 1997.

Longo, Francisco and Koldo Echebarria (2001) "La Nueva Gestión Pública en la Reforma del Núcleo Estratégico del Gobierno: Experiencias Latinoamericanas". *In* Peter Spink et al. (2001): 97–152.

Love, Joseph (1996) *Crafting the Third World: Theorizing Underdevelopment in Rumania and Brazil.* Stanford: Stanford University Press.

Lyotard, Jean-François (1979) *La Condition Postmoderne.* Paris: Les Éditions de Minuit.

MacIntyre, Alasdair (1981) *After Virtues: A Study in Moral Theory.* London: Duckworth.

Majone, Giandomenico (1996) *Regulating Europe.* London: Routledge.

Man, Michael (1986) "The Autonomous Power of the State: Its Mechanisms, Origins, and Results". In John A. Hall, ed. (1986: 107–153).

Mandel, Ernest (1972)—*Late Capitalism.* London: Verso Edition, 1978 (first German edition, 1972.

Manin, Bernard, Adam Przeworski, and Susan C. Stokes (1999) *Democracy, Accountability and Representation.* Cambridge: Cambridge University Press.

Mann, Nancy R. (1985) *Deming—As Chaves da Excelência.* São Paulo: Makron Books do Brasil. Edição original em inglês, 1985.

Maravall, José María and Adam Przeworski, eds. (2003) *Democracy and the Rule of Law.* Cambridge: Cambridge University Press.

Marcel, Mario (1997) *Modernización del Estado y Indicadores de Desempeño en el Sector Publico: La Experiencia Chilena.* Copy, April 1997.

March, James G. and Herbert A. Simon (1958) *Organizations.* New York: John Wiley & Sons.

March, James G. and Johan P. Olsen (1995) *Democratic Governance.* New York: The Free Press.

March, James G. and Johan P. Olsen (1984) "The New Institutionalism". *American Political Science Review*, 78, pp.734–749.

Marglin, Stephen A. (1990) "Lessons of the Golden Age: An Overview". In Marglin and Schor, eds. (1990: 1–38).

—— and Juliet B. Schor, eds. (1990) *The Golden Age of Capitalism.* Oxford: Clarendon Press.

Marini, Caio (2002) "O Contexto Contemporâneo da Administração Pública na América Latina". *Revista do Serviço Público*, 53(4) outubro 2002: 31–52.

Marshall, T. H. (1950) "Citizenship and Social Class". In T. H. Marshall and Tom Botomore (1992) *Citizenship and Social Class.* London: Pluto Press. Originally published in 1950: 1–51.

Martins, Luciano (1976) *Pouvoir et Développement Économique.* Paris: Éditions Anthropos, 1976.

—— (1978) " 'Estatização' da Economia ou 'Privatização' do Estado". *Ensaios de Opinião* 2(9), 1978: 30–7.

Maslow, Abraham H. (1943) "A Theory of Human Motivation". *Psychological Review*, n°.50, 1943: 370–96. Quoted in Morgan (1986).

—— (1970) *Motivation and Personality.* New York: Harper & Row. Segunda edição.

Maurois, André (1947) *Histoire de la France*. Paris: Éditions Dominique Wapler.

Mayo, Elton (1946) *The Human Problems of an Industrial Civilization*. Boston: Graduate School of Business Administration of Harvard University.

McCubbins, Mathew D. (1991) *The Logic of Delegation*. Chicago: The University of Chicago Press.

—— Roger G. Noll and Barry R. Weingast (1987) "Administrative Procedures as Instruments of Political Control". *Journal of Law, Economics and Organization*, 3(2) Fall 1987: 243–77.

Meldolesi, Nicoletta Stame (1996) "Avaliação de Políticas Públicas na França". *Revista do Serviço Público*, 47(1) January 1996: 83–111.

Melo, Marcus André (1996) "Governance e a Reforma do Estado: O Paradigma Agente-Principal". *Revista do Serviço Público*, 47(1), January 1996: 67–81.

—— (2002*a*) "Republicanismo, Liberalismo e Racionalidade". *Lua Nova—Revista de Cultura Política*, n°.55–56: 57–84.

—— (2002*b*) *Reformas Constitucionais no Brasil*. Rio de Janeiro: Editora Revan.

—— (2003) "When Institutions Matter: A Comparison of the Politics of Administrative, Social Security, and Tax Reform in Brazil". *In* Schneider and Heredia, eds. (2003): 211–50.

——, ed. (1999) *Reforma do Estado e Mudança Institucional no Brasil*. Recife: Fundação Joaquim Nabuco e Editora Massangana.

Merquior, José Guilherme (1991) *Liberalism: Old and New*. Boston: Twayne Publishers.

Merton, Robert K. (1949) *Social Theory and Social Structure*. Glencoe, Il.: The Free Press.

Mill, Stuart (1859) *On Liberty*. Upper Saddle River: Prentice Hall, 1956. Originally published in 1859.

Miller, David (1992) "Deliberative Democracy and Social Choice". *Political Studies*, n°.40, 1992: 54–67.

Miller, Gary J. (1992) *Managerial Dilemmas*. Cambridge: Cambridge University Press.

Ministry of Federal Administration and Reform of the State—MARE (1995) *Plano Diretor da Reforma do Aparelho do Estado*. Brasilia: Imprensa Nacional, November 1995. An English version, *White Paper on the Reform of the State Apparatus*, was also published, and is available at www.bresserpereira.org.br.

Mintzberg, Henry (1996) "Managing Government—Governing Management". *Harvard Business Review*, May 1996.

Modesto, Paulo E. G. (1997) "Reforma Administrativa e Marco Legal das Organizações Sociais". *Revista do Serviço Público*, 48(2) May 1997: 27–57.

Moe, Ronald C. (1994) "The Reinventing Government Exercise: Misinterpreting the Problem, Misjudging the Consequences". *Public Administration Review*, 54(2) March 1994.

Moe, Terry M. (1990) "Political Institutions: The Neglected Side of the Story". *Journal of Law, Economics, and Organization*. n°.6, 1990: 213–53.

Molina Saucedo, Carlos Hugo (1994) *La Descentralización Imposible y la Alternativa Municipal*. Santa Cruz de la Sierra: Ediciones de *El País*, 1994 (second edition).

Franco Montoro, André (1974) *Da 'Democracia' que Temos para a Democracia que Queremos*. Rio de Janeiro: Editora Paz e Terra.

Moore Jr., Barrington (1966) *Social Origins of Dictatorship and Democracy: Lord and Peasant in Making the Modern World*. Boston: Beacon Press.

Morales, Carlos Antonio (1998) "Provisão de Serviços Sociais através de Organizações Públicas Não-Estatais". *In* Bresser-Pereira and Cunill Grau, eds. (1998): 51–86.

Moreira Neto, Diogo de Figueiredo (1992) *Direito da Participação Política*. Rio de Janeiro: Renovar.

Morgan, Gareth (1986) *Imagens da Organização*. São Paulo: Editora Atlas, 1995. Publicado originalmente em ngles, 1986.

Morin, Edgar (1990) *Science avec Conscience*. Second edition. Paris: Éditions du Seuil.

Mueller, D. and Murrell, P. (1985) "Interest Groups and the Political Economy of Government Size". *In* Forte and Peacock, eds. (1985: 13–36).

Mueller, Dennis C. (1987) "The growth of government: a public choice perspective". *Staff Papers*, IMF, vol.34, no.1, March 1987.

Nassuno, Marianne (1997) "Organização dos Usuários, Participação na Gestão e Controle das Organizações Sociais". *Revista do Serviço Público*, 48(1), January 1997: 27–41.

—— (1998) "O Controle Social nas Organizações Sociais no Brasil". *In* Bresser-Pereira and Cunill Grau, eds. (1998): 335–61.

—— (2000) "A Administração com Foco no Usuário-Cidadão: Realizações no Governo Federal Brasileiro nos Últimos 5 Anos". Paper presented to the Vth International Congress of CLAD, Dominican Republic, October 2000. *Revista do Serviço Público*, 51(4), October 2000: 61–98.

—— and Priscilla H. Kamada, eds. (2002) *Balanço da Reforma do Estado no Brasil: A Nova Gestão Pública*. Brasília: Ministério do Planejamento, Orçamento e Gestão, Secretaria da Gestão, 2002.

Navarro, Zander (1998) "Democracia e Controle Social de Fundos Públicos: O Caso do 'Orçamento Participativo' de Porto Alegre". *In* Bresser-Pereira and Cunill Grau, eds. (1998): 293–334.

Negri, Antonio e Michael Hardt (2000) *Empire*. Cambridge, MA: Harvard University Press.

Nelissen, Nico et al. (1999) *Renewing Government: Innovative and Inspiring Visions*. Utrecht: International Books.

Nickson, Andrew (2002) "Transferencia de Políticas y Reforma de la Gestión del Sector Público en América Latina: El Caso del 'New Public Management' ". *Revista del CLAD Reforma y Democracia* n°.24, October 2002: 113–40.

Niskanen, William A. (1971) *Bureaucracy and Representative Government*. Chicago: University of Chicago Press..

Norris, Pipa (1999*a*) "Introduction: The Growth of Critic Citizens?" *In* Pipa Norris, ed. (1999: 1–30).

—— (1999*b*) "Conclusion: The Growth of Critical Citizens and Its Consequences". *In* Pipa Norris, ed. (1999: 257–72).

——, ed. (1999) *Critical Citizens*. Oxford: Oxford University Press.

Nozick, Robert (1974) *Anarchy, State, and Utopia*. New York: Basic Books Publishers.

Nunberg, Barbara (1995) "Managing the Civil Service—Reform Lessons from Advanced Industrialized Countries". Washington, DC: World Bank Discussion Paper n.204, April 1995.

—— and J. Nellis (1995) "Civil Service Reform and the World Bank". Washington, DC: World Bank Discussion Paper n°.161, May 1995.

Nunes, Edson de Oliveira (1984) *Bureaucratic Insulation and Clientelism in Contemporary Brazil: Uneven State Building and the Taming of Modernity*. PhD dissertation, University of California at Berkeley, Department of Political Science, 1984. Published in Portuguese as *A Gramática Política do Brasil*. Rio de Janeiro: Zahar Editores, 1997.

O'Connor, James (1973) *The Fiscal Crisis of the State*. New York: St. Martin Press.

O'Donnell, Guillermo (1977) "State and Alliances in Argentina, 1956–1976". *In* Guillermo O'Donnell (1999). Originally published in *Desarollo Económico*, January 1977.

—— (1998) "Horizontal Accountability in New Democracies". *Journal of Democracy*, 9(3) July 1998.

—— (1999) *Counterpoints—Selected Essays on Authoritarianism and Democratization*. Notre Dame: Indiana University Press.

——, Philippe Schimitter and Laurence Whitehead, eds. (1986) *Transitions from Authoritarian Rule*. Baltimore: The Johns Hopkins University Press.

OECD/PUMA (1996) *Performance Management in Government: Contemporary Illustrations*. Paris: OECD/Public Management (PUMA).

—— (1997) *In Search of Results: Performance Management Practices*. Paris: OECD/Public Management (PUMA).

Offe, Claus (1973) "The Abolition of Market Control and the Problem of Legitimacy". *Kapitalestate*, n.1–2.

—— (1980) "Some Contradictions of the Modern Welfare State", in Offe (1984): 147–61.

—— (1984) *Contradictions of the Welfare State* (edited by John Keane. Cambridge: The MIT Press.

Ohmae, Kenich (1985) *Triad Power*. New York: The Free Press.

—— (1990) *The Borderless World*. New York: HarperCollins Publishers.

Olson, Mancur (1965) *The Logic of Collective Action*. Cambridge: Harvard University Press.

Osborne, David and Ted Gaebler (1992) *Reinventing Government*. Reading, Mass.: Addison-Wesley.

Ostrom, Vincent (1989) *The Intellectual Crisis of American Public Administration*. Segunda edição. Tucaloosa: University of Alabama Press.

—— (1991) *The Meaning of American Federalism in Constituting a Self-Governing Society*. São Francisco, Ca.: Institute for Contemporary Studies.

Oszlak, Oscar (2001) "El Servicio Civil en América Latina y el Caribe: Situación y Retos Futuros". Washington, DC: Interamerican Development Bank, copy, April 1, 2001.

Oxhorn, Philip D. (1995) *Organizing Civil Society: The Popular Sectors and the Struggle for Democracy in Chile*. Pennsylvania: The Pennsylvania State University Press.

Pacheco, Carlos Américo (2002) "O Modelo de Organizações Sociais e a Experiência do MCT". *In* Nassuno and Kamada, eds. (2002): 53–60.

Pacheco, Regina (1999) "Reforma da Administração Pública no Brasil: Eficiência a *Accountability* Democrática". *In* Marcus André Melo, org. (1999).

—— (2003) "Cambios en el Perfil de los Dirigentes Públicos en Brasil y Desarrollo de Competencias de Dirección". *Revista del CLAD Reforma y Democracia* n°.26 May 2003: 165–98.

Pagès, Max, Michel Bonetti, Vincent de Gaulejac and Daniel Descendre (1986) *O Poder das Organizações*. São Paulo: Editora Atlas, 1987. Publicado originalmente em francês, 1986.

Parsons, Talcott (1937) *The Structure of Social Action*. New York: The Free Press. Primeira edição em *paperback*, 1968.

—— (1960) *Structure and Process in Modern Societies*. Glencoe: The Free Press.

Pateman, Carole (1970) *Participation and Democratic Theory*. Cambridge Univ. Press.

Paulani, Leda Maria 'Hayek e o Individualismo no Discurso Econômico' (1996). *Lua Nova—Revista de Cultura e Política*, n°38, 1996: 97–124.

Perrow, Charles (1986) *Complex Organizations*. New York: McGraw-Hill. 3rd edition.

Peters, B. Guy (1996) "Models of Governance for the 1990". *In* Kettl and Milward, eds. (1996): 15–46.

—— (1999) *Institutional Theory in Political Science*. London: Pinter.

Petrucci, Vera and Letícia Schwarz, eds. (1999) *Administração Pública Gerencial: A Reforma de 1995*. Brasília: Editora da Universidade de Brasília.

Pettit, Philip (1997) *Republicanism*. Oxford: Oxford University Press.

Pinheiro, Paulo Sérgio (1996) "O Passado não Está Morto: Nem Passado é Ainda". Foreword to Gilberto Dimenstein (1996).

—— and Eric Braun, eds (1986). *Democracia x Violência*. Rio de Janeiro: Paz e Terra.

Plattner, Marc F. (1999) "Traditions of Accountability". *In* Diamond, Plattner, and Schedler, eds. (1999: 63–7).

Plowden, William (1994) *Ministers and Mandarins*. London: Institute for Public Policy Research.

—— (1997) "Public Administration and Civil Society". Paper presented to the conference 'Governance in the Euro-Med Region', The Hague, March 1997. Copy.

Pocock, J. G. A. (1975) *The Machiavellian Moment: Florentine Political Theory and the Atlantic Republican Tradition*. Princeton, NJ: Princeton University Press.

Polanyi, Karl (1944) *The Great Transformation*. Boston: Beacon Press, 1957. First edition, 1944.

Pollitt, Christopher (1993) *Managerialism and the Public Service*. 2nd edition. Oxford: Blackwell.

—— and Geert Bouckaert (2000) *Public Management Reform*. Oxford: Oxford University Press.

—— (2001) "Evaluation Public Management Reforms: An International Perspective". *International Journal of Political Studies* Special, September, 2001: 167–92.

Poole, Lynne (2000) "Health Care: New Labour's NHS". *In* John Clarke, Sharon Gewirtz and Eugene McLaughlin, eds. (2000): 102–21.

Pordominisky, Miguel Gandour and Luis Bernardo Mejia Guinarnd, eds. (1999) *Hacia el Rediseño del Estado*. Bogotá: Tercer Mundo Editores and Departamento Nacional de Planeación.

Prebisch, Raúl (1950) *The Economic Development of Latin America and its Principal Problems*. New York: United Nations, Dept. of Economic Affairs.

Premchand, Arigapudi (1998) "Themes and Issues in Public Expenditure Management". *In* Pordominisky and Guinand, eds. (1999: 158–80). Paper presented to the seminar "Hacia el Rediseño del Estado", sponsored by the Ministry of Planning of Colombia, Bogotá, April 27–29, 1998.

Prestes Motta, Fernando and Luiz Carlos Bresser-Pereira (1980) *Introdução à Organização Burocrática*. São Paulo: Editora Brasiliense.

——, Fernando C. (1998) *Teoria Geral da Administração: Uma Introdução*. São Paulo: Editora Pioneira. Segunda edição atualizada (Primeira edição, 1974).

Przeworski, Adam (1985) *Capitalism and Social Democracy*. Cambridge: Cambridge University Press.

Przeworski, Adam (1990) *The State and the Economy under Capitalism*. Chur: Harwood Academic Publishers.

—— (1991) *Democracy and the Market*. Cambridge: Cambridge University Press.

—— (1995) "O que os Países Civilizados Têm em Comum". *Folha de S. Paulo*, 2 de abril, 1995.

—— (1996) "Reforma do Estado: Responsabilidade Política e Intervenção Econômica". *Revista Brasileira de Ciências Sociais*, 32(11) October 1996: 13–40.

—— (1997) "Democracy and Representation". Paper prepared for the II Interamerican Congress of CLAD, Margarita Island, October 1997.

—— (1999) "On the Design of the State: A Principal-Agent Perspective". *In* Bresser-Pereira and Spink, eds. (1999): 15–39.

—— Susan C. Stokes and Eduard Manin (2000) *Democracy, Accountability, and Repesentation*. Cambridge: Cambridge University Press.

Pugh, D. S., ed. (1971) *Organization Theory*. Harmondsworth: Penguin Books.

Putnam, Robert D. (1993) *Making Democracy Work*. Princeton, NJ: Princeton University Press.

—— (1995) "Bowling Alone: America's Declining Social Capital". *Journal of Democracy*, 6(1) January 1993: 65–78.

—— (2000) *Bowling Alone: Collapse and Revival of American Community*. New York: Simon and Schuster.

—— and Kristin A. Goss (2002) "Introduction". *In* Robert D. Putnam, ed. (2002): 3–19.

——, ed. (2002) *Democracies in Flux*. Oxford: Oxford University Press.

Pyper, R. and L. Robins, eds. (1995) *Governing the UK in the 1990s*. London: Macmillan.

Rabell, L. Santana and M. Negrón Portillo (1996) " 'Reinventing Government': Nueva Retórica, Viejos Problemas". *Revista del Clad: Reforma y Democracia*, n°.6 July 1996: 147–64.

Rama, Martín (1999) "Public Sector Downsizing: An Introduction". *The World Bank Review*, 13(1) January 1999: 1–22.

Ranson, Stewart and John Stewart (1994) *Management for the Public Domain*. London: The Macmillan Press.

Rapaczynski, Andrzej (1996) "The Roles of the State and the Market in Establishing Property Rights". *Journal of Economic Perspectives*, 10(2), Spring 1996: 87–103.

Rawls, John (1989) "The Domain of the Political and Overlapping Consensus". *In* Copp, Hampton, and Roemer, eds. (1993: 245–69). Originally published in the *New York University Law Review* 2, May 1989: 233–55.

—— (1993) *Political Liberalism*. New York, Columbia University Press.

—— (1997) "The Idea of Public Reason Revisited". *In* John Rawls (1999: 129–80). Originally published in 1997.

—— (1999) *The Law of Peoples*. Cambridge, MA: Harvard University Press.

Rego, Walkiria Domingues Leão (2001) *Em Busca do Socialismo Democrático*. Campinas: Editora da UNICAMP.

Reis, Fábio Wanderley (1990) "Cidadania Democrática, Corporativismo e Política Social no Brasil". In *Para a Década de 90: Prioridades e Perspectivas de Políticas Públicas*. Vol. 4—*Políticas Sociais e Organização do Trabalho*. Brasília: IPEA/IPLAN.

Richardson, Ruth (1998) "As Reformas do Setor Público na Nova Zelândia". In Bresser-Pereira, Luiz Carlos and Peter Spink, eds. (1998) *Reforma do Estado e Administração Pública Gerencial*. Rio de Janeiro: Editora Fundação Getúlio Vargas.

Richardson, William D. (1997) *Democracy, Bureaucracy, & Character*. Lawrence: University of Kansas Press.

Rivas, Luis A. Angulo (2000) "Venezuela, Cambio Político y Rescentralización Unitaria". Paper presented to the Vth International Congress of CLAD, Dominican Republic, October 2000.

Rockman, Bert A. (1992) "Bureaucracy, Power, Policy and the State". *In* Larry B. Hill, ed. (1992): 141–70.

Roethlisberger, F. J. and William J. Dickson (1939) *Management and the Worker*. Cambridge, MA: Harvard University Press.

Rosanvallon, Pierre (1992) *La Crise de l'État-providence*. Paris: Éditions du Seuil.

Rose-Ackerman, Susan (1996). "Altruism, Nonprofits, and Economic Theory." In *Journal of Economic Literature*. 34 (2), June 1996: 701–28.

Rosenberg, Hans (1958) *Bureaucracy, Aristocracy & Autocracy*. Cambridge, MA: Harvard University Press.

Rosenbloom, David H. (2001) " 'Whose Bureaucracy is This Anyway?' Congress" 1946 Answer". *Political Science and Politics* 34(4) December 2001: 773–7.

Rosselli, Carlo (1924) "Liberalismo Socialista". *In* Piero Gobetti, ed. (1924) *Rivoluzione Liberale*. Turin: 1924. Republished in Carlo Rosselli (1992), *Liberalismo Socialista e Socialismo Liberale*. Salerno: Edizione Galzerano, Collettanea Socialismo Liberale.

—— (1930) *Socialismo Liberale*. Written in Italian, in 1930. First published in French, 1931. There is a recent English translation.

Sachs, Jeffrey D. (1989) "Social Conflict and Populist Policies in Latin America". *In* R. Brunetta and C. Dell-Arringa, eds. (1989) *Labor Relations and Economic Performance*. London: Macmillan Press.

Sandel, Michael J. (1996) *Democracy's Discontent: America in Search of a Public Philosophy*. Cambridge, MA: Harvard University Press.

Santos, Wanderley Guilherme dos (1988) *Paradoxos do Liberalismo*. São Paulo: Edições Vértice.

—— (1998) "Poliarquia em 3D". *Dados*, 41(2) 1998: 207–82.

Saunders, P. and Klau, F. (1985) *The Role of the Public Sector: Causes and Consequences of the Growth of Government*, OECD Economic Studies no. 4. Paris: Organization for Economic Cooperation and Development.

Schedler, Kuno (1996) "Legitimation as Granted by the Consumer: Reflections on the Compatibility of New Public Management and (Direct) Democracy". University of St. Gallen, Switzerland, July 1996. In *International Public Management Network* www.willamette.org.ipmn/research/conference/index.html.

Schick, Allen (2002) "Agencies in Search of Principles". Paper presented to the 25th Session of the Public Management Committee, Paris, March 21–22, 2002. OECD/ PUMA (2002)6.

Schimitter, Philippe C. (1999) "The Limits of Horizontal Accountability". *In* Diamond, Plattner, and Schedler, eds. (1999: 59–62).

—— (1974) "Still the Century of Corporatism?". *Review of Politics* 36(1): 7–52. Reproduced *in* P. Schimitter and G. Lembruch, orgs. (1979) *Trends Toward Corporatist Intermediation*.

Schneider, Ben Ross (1991) *Bureaucracy and Industrial Policy in Brazil*. Pittsburgh: Pittsburgh University Press.

—— (1995) "A Conexão da Carreira: Uma Análise Comparativa de Preferências e Insulamento Burocrático". *Revista do Serviço Público*, ano 46, vol.119, n°.1, January 1995: 9–43.

—— (2000) "The Politics of Administrative Reform: Intractable Dilemmas and Improbable Solutions". *In* Federal Reserve Bank of Atlanta (2000: 53–72).

—— and Blanca Heredia, eds, (2003) *Reinventing Leviathan*. Miami: North-South Center Press.

Schultz, David and Robert Maranto (1998) *The Politics of Civil Service Reform*. New York: Peter Lang.

Schumpeter, Joseph A. (1942) *Capitalism, Socialism and Democracy*. New York, Harper & Brother.

Shonfield, Andrew (1969) *Modern Capitalism*. Oxford: Oxford University Press.

Silberman, Bernard S. (1993) *The Cages of Reason*. Chicago: Chicago University Press.

Silva Pereira, Eduardo da (1997) "Organizações Sociais, Instituições Federais de Ensino Superior e Autonomia Universitária". *Revista do Serviço Público*, 48(2), May 1997: 59–79.

Silva Telles, Vera da (1994) "Os Movimentos Sociais e a Emergência de uma Nova Noção de Cidadania". *In* Evelina Dagnino, (ed. 1994).

Silva, José Afonso da (1997) *Curso de Direito Constitucional Positivo*. São Paulo: Malheiros Editores.

Simon, Herbert A (1947) *Administrative Behavior*. New York: Macmillan.

Singer, Hans (1950) "The Distribution of Gains between Investing and Borrowing Countries". *American Economic Review* 40, May 1950, 473–85.

Skinner, Quentin (1978) *The Foundations of Modern Political Thought*. Cambridge: Cambridge University Press.

—— (1989) "The State". *In* Ball, Farr and Hanson, eds. (1989: 90–131).

—— (1990) "The Republican Ideal of Liberty". In Bock, Skinner, and Viroli, eds. (1990): 292–309.

—— (1998) *Liberty Before Liberalism*. Cambridge: Cambridge University Press.

Skopol, Theda (1979) *States and Social Revolutions*. Cambridge: Cambridge University Press.

—— ed. (1998) *Democracy, Revolution, and History*. Ithaca, NY: Cornell University Press.

Slater, D. (1990) "Debating Decentralization—A Reply to Rondinelli". *Development and Change*, vol. 21, 1990. Quoted by Levy, 1997.

Smend, Rudolf (1934) "Sobre el Problema de lo Público y la 'Cosa Publica' ". *In* Rudolf Smend (1985) *Constitución y Derecho Constitucional*. Madrid: Centro de Estudios Constitucionales. Essay originally published in German 1934.

Smith, Adam (1776) *The Wealth of Nations*. London: Everyman's Library, 1960. First edition, 1776.

Smulovitz, Catalina (2003) "How Can the Rule of Law Rule? Cost Imposition through Decentralized Mechanisms". *In* Maravall and Przeworski, eds. (2003: 168–187).

—— and Henrique Peruzzotti (2000) *"Societal Accountability in Latin America". Journal of Democracy*, 11(4), October 2000: 147–158.

Souza Santos, Boaventura de (1995a) *Pela Mão de Alice: O Social e o Político na Pós-Modernidade*. São Paulo: Cortez Editora.

—— (1995b) *Toward a New Common Sense*. London: Routledge.

—— (2002) "Orçamento Participativo de Porto Alegre: Para uma Democracia Redistributiva". In Souza Santos, ed. (2002: 455–560).

—— and Leonardo Avritzer (2002) "Para Ampliar o Cânone Democrático". In Souza Santos, ed. (2002: 39–82).

——, ed. (2002) *Democratizar a Democracia*. Rio de Janeiro: Civilização Brasileira.

Souza, Celina and Inaiá M. Carvalho (1999) "Reforma do Estado, Descentralização e Desigualdade". *Lua Nova—Revista de Cultura Política*, n°.48, 1999: 187–212.

Souza, Herbert 'Betinho' de (1995) "A Caminho do Público e da Democracia". *Folha de S. Paulo*, September 12, 1995.

Spink, Mary Jane Paris, ed. (1994) *Cidadania em Construção*. São Paulo: Editora Cortez.

Spink, Peter (1998) *Reforming the Reformers: The Saga of Public Administration Reform in Latin America 1925–1995*. São Paulo: Fundação Getúlio Vargas, Ph.D. dissertation, March 1998.

—— (2001) "Modernización de la Administración Pública en América Latina". *In* Peter Spink et al. (2001) *Nueva Gestión Pública y Regulación en América Latina*. Caracas: CLAD—Centro Latinoamericano de Administración para el Desarrollo: 15–96.

Spink, Peter et al. (2001) *Nueva Gestión Pública y Regulación en América Latina*. Caracas: CLAD—Consejo Latinoamericano de Administración para el Desarrollo.

Stark, David and László Bruszt (1998) *Postsocialist Pathways*. Cambridge: Cambridge University Press.

Stephens, John D. (2002) "European Welfare State Regimes: Configurations, Outcomes, Transformations". *In* Evelyne Huber, ed. (2002: 303–338).

Sternberg, Edward (1993) "Preparing for the Hybrid Economy: The New World of Public Private Partnerships". *Business Horizons*, 3(6): 11–15.

Stiglitz, Joseph E. (1989) "The Economic Role of the State". *In* Arnold Heertje, ed. (1989) *The Economic Role of the State*. Oxford: Basil Blackwell.

   (1993b) "The Role of the State in Financial Markets". *Proceedings of the World Bank Annual Conference on Development Economics, 1993*. Supplement to *The World Bank Economic Review* and to *The World Bank Research Observer*.

—— (1994) *Whither Socialism?* Cambridge, MA: The MIT Press.

Streeck, Wolfang and Philippe Schimitter, eds. (1985) *Private Interest Government: Beyond Market and State*. London: Sage Publications.

Sutcliffe, Bob and Andrew Glyn (1999) "Still Underwhelmed: Indicators of Globalization and Their Misinterpretation". *Review of Radical Political Economics*, 31(1) March 1999: 111–131.

Sutherland, S. L. (1993) "Independent Review Agencies and Accountability: Some Lessons and Conclusions". *Optimum—The Journal of Public Sector Management*. 24(2), Autumn 1993: 23–40.

Swank, Duane (2002) *Global Capital, Political Institutions, and Policy Change in Developed Welfare States*. Cambridge: Cambridge University Press.

Tanzi, Vito and Ludger Schukenecht (2000) *Public Spending in the 20th Century*. Cambridge: Cambridge University Press.

Taylor, Charles (1995) *Philosophical Arguments*. Cambridge: Cambridge University Press.

Thakur, Ramesh and Edward Newman, eds. (2000) *New Millenium, New Perspectives: The United Nations, Security, and Governance*. Tokyo: The United Nations University Press.

Therborn, Goran (1977) "The Rule of Capital and the Rise of Democracy". *New Left Review*, n°.103, May–June: 3–42.

Thoenig, Jean-Claude (2001) "Evaluating Public Sector Reforms: Learning from Practice". *International Journal of Political Studies*, n°.3, September 2001: 193–214.

Tilly, Charles (1992) *Coercion, Capital, and European States.* Cambridge, MA: Blackwell.

—— (1998) "Where Do Rights Come From?". *In* Skocpol, ed. (1998: 55–72).

Tirole, Jean (1994) "The Internal Organization of Government". *Oxford Economic Papers*, n°.46, 1994: 1–19.

Titmuss, R. (1958) *Essays on the Welfare State.* London: Allen & Unwin.

Tomkins, Cyril R. (1978) *Achieving Economy, Efficiency and Effectiveness in the Public Sector.* Edinburgh: The Institute of Chartered Accountants of Scotland.

Touraine, Alain (1992) *Critique de la Modernité.* Paris: Fayard.

—— (1999) *Comment Sortir du Libéralisme?* Paris: Fayard.

Trevelyan, George M. (1942) *English Social History.* London: Longmans, Green and Co.

Trosa, Sylvie (1995) *Moderniser L'Administration.* Paris: Les Éditions d'Organization.

Truman, David B. (1951) *The Governmental Process.* New York: Alfred A. Knopf.

Unger, Roberto Mangabeira (1997) *Politics: The Central Texts.* London: Verso.

Vallemont, Serge (1996) *A Modernização do Estado: as Lições de uma Experiência.* Brasília: Escola Nacional de Administração Pública, Texto para discussão, 12, 1996.

Vassalo, Carlos A. (2000) "Decentralización en Argentina". Paper presented to the Vth International Congress of CLAD, Dominican Republic, October 2000.

Velloso, João Paulo and Roberto Cavalcanti Albuquerque, eds. (1995) *Governabilidade & Reformas.* Rio de Janeiro, VII Fórum Nacional, May 1995. Rio de Janeiro: José Olympio and Fórum Nacional.

Wagner, Adolph (1893) *Grundeglung de Politschen Oekonomie.* Leipsig: C. F. Winter'sche Verlagshandlung (surveyed in Wildavsky, 1985).

Wahrlich, Beatriz Marques de Souza. (1970) "Uma Reforma da Administração de Pessoal Vinculada ao Processo de Desenvolvimento Nacional". *Revista de Administração Pública*, 4(1) January 1970: 7–31.

—— (1983) *A Reforma Administrativa da Era de Vargas.* Rio de Janeiro: Fundação Getúlio Vargas.

—— (1984) "A Reforma Adiministrativa no Brasil: Experiência Anterior, Situação Atual e Perspectivas. Uma Apreciação Geral". *Revista de Administração Pública*, 18 (1), January 1984: 49–87.

Wallerstein, Immanuel (1979) *The Capitalist World Economy.* Cambridge: Cambridge University Press / Paris: Maison des Sciences de l'Homme.

—— (1991) *Geopolitics and Geoculture. The Capitalist World Economy.* Cambridge: Cambridge University Press / Paris: Maison des Sciences de l'Homme.

—— (1995) *After Liberalism.* New York: The New Press.

Walzer, Michael (1983) *Spheres of Justice.* New York: Basic Books.

—— (2001) "Liberalism, Nationalism, Reform". *In* Lilla, Dworkin and Silvers, eds. (2001): 169–76.

Weber, Max (1922) *Economy and Society.* Berkeley: University of California Press, 1978. First German edition, 1922.

Weisbrod, Burton A. (1988) *The Nonprofit Economy.* Cambridge, MA: Harvard University Press.

Whitehead, Laurence (2002) "Stirring Mutual Recognition". In Laurence Whitehead, ed. (2002: 1–15.)

——, ed. (2002) *Emerging Market Democracies: East Asia and Latin America*. Baltimore: The Johns Hopkins University Press.

Wildavsky, Aaron (1985) "The Logic of Public Sector Growth". In Jan-Erik Lane, ed. (1985): 231–70.

Wilheim, Jorge, Lourdes Sola and Luiz Carlos Bresser-Pereira, eds. (1999) *Sociedade e Estado em Transformação*. São Paulo: Editora da UNESP, Brasília: ENAP Brasília. This book is a collection of the works presented during the Seminar "Reform of the State and the Society" in São Paulo, 16–28 March, 1998, organized by the Council of State Reform.

Williamson, Oliver E. (1985) *The Economic Institutions of Capitalism*. New York: The Free Press.

Wilson, Woodrow (1887) "The Study of Administration". In *The Papers of Woodrow Wilson*, volume 5. Princeton: Princeton University Press, 1986. Originally published in 1887.

—— (1889) *The State: Elements of Historical and Practical Politics*. Boston: D.C. Heath.

Wistrich, Enid (1992) "Restructuring Government New Zealand Style", *Public Administration*, 70(1), Spring, 1992: 119–35.

Wollmann, Hellmut (2001) "Public Sector Reforms and Evaluation: Trajectories and Trends. An International Overview". *International Journal of Political Studies*, n°.3, September 2001: 11–37.

Wood, B. Dan (1988) "Principals, Bureaucrats, and Responsiveness in Clear Air Enforcements". *The American Political Science Review*, 82(1), March 1988: 213–34.

World Bank (1997) *World Development Report 1997. The State in a Changing World*. Washington: The World Bank.

Wright, Vincent (1994) "Reshaping the State: The Implications for Public Administration". *Western European Politics*, 17(3) 1994.

Yan, Yunxiang (2002) "Managed Globalization". In Berger and Huntington, eds. (2002): 5–47.

Zapico, Eduardo and John Mayne (1995) "Nuevas Perspectivas para el Control de Gestión y Mediación de Resultados". *GAPP* n°3, May 1995: 43–53.

Zifcak, Spencer (1994) *New Managerialism: Administrative Reform in Whitehall and Canberra*. Buckingham: Open University Press.

INDEX

CPSIA information can be obtained at www.ICGtesting.com
Printed in the USA
LVOW081934141111

254988LV00002B/6/A